Alfred Russel Wallace

Alfred Russel Wallace
A Life

Peter Raby

Princeton University Press
Princeton, New Jersey

Published in the United States and Canada
by Princeton University Press,
41 William Street, Princeton, New Jersey 08540

First published in Great Britain in 2001 by
Chatto & Windus
Random House, 20 Vauxhall Bridge Road,
London SW1V 2SA

Library of Congress Control Number 2001087448

ISBN 0 -691-00695-4

This book has been composed in Goudy

Printed on acid-free paper. ∞

www.pup.princeton.edu

1 3 5 7 9 10 8 6 4 2

Contents

Illustrations

Illustrations in the Text

Maps

Foreword and Acknowledgements

Writing is a solitary occupation, but writing a biography inevitably brings the writer into contact with a great many people, and I have been extremely fortunate in the help that I have been given: Wallace inspires affection and admiration in successive generations. My first, and greatest, thanks is to Wallace's grandsons, John and Richard Wallace, and their families. They have made their family papers and archives available, in a most generous and unpressured way, given me permission to use material, answered my questions patiently, and offered me encouragement and hospitality in large measures.

Wallace's letters, notebooks and specimens are scattered through the world, and it would be a long journey to visit them all. This makes the assistance of librarians and archivists the more vital, and I am grateful for the prompt and helpful way they have responded to my enquiries. My local library, at Cambridge University, has been most frequently in the firing line, not only because of its Wallace holdings, such as his letters to his agent Stevens and to his friends Charles Darwin and Alfred Newton, but because of the siting there of the Darwin project. It is a nice irony that so many of the key holdings of books in the field, including Wallace's autobiography and published letters, as well as those of Bates and Spruce, are on permanent loan to the project, in service as it were to Darwin, and have to be tracked down and consulted in a special area. One can imagine a wry comment on the subject from Wallace to Professor Poulton. There are, of course, benefits to this arrangement, not least the company and help of the Darwin research team.

I should like in particular to thank the Trustees, curators, librarians, archivists and staff of the following institutions for their assistance, and for permission to quote from material in their keeping: the British Library;

Cambridge University Library; City of London Record Office; Hertford County Archives; Imperial College, London; Leicester County Archives; the Linnean Society (and especially Gina Douglas); Natural History Museum, London; Neath Public Library; Oxford Museum of Natural History (and especially Stella Brecknell, of the Hope Entomological Collection); Royal Geographical Society; Royal Botanic Gardens, Kew (and especially Lesley Price); Royal Geographical Society; San Jose Public Library; Surrey History Centre; University College, London; Zoological Society, London.

Many others have given me help, advice, information and encourage-ment, at different stages. I would like to mention specifically George Beccaloni, at the Natural History Museum, who has shared his knowledge and enthusiasm with me; John Beer, for doing some research on my behalf in Boston; Michael Brooke, for ornithological advice; Andrew Carter; John Dickenson, for information on Wallace and Bates and the Royal Geographical Society; Robert Dimsdale, for his knowledge of Hertfordshire, and of vaccination; Robert Francis, who was our guide in Sarawak; David Hanke, for reading and commenting on sections of the text; Walter Henderson; Richard Ironside; Bob Lashmar; Perry O'Donovan, of the Darwin project; Michael Pearson, for drawing several articles to my attention, and for providing me with a typed transcript of Wallace's American journal; Christopher Roper, and Landmark Information Group, Exeter, for making available Ordnance Survey maps and information on Wallace's houses at Gray's, Essex, and Broadstone, Dorset; Sister Rita; Peter Searby; John Webb, of the Thurrock Local History Society; John Wilson, for his generous help; and Christopher Wells, for many conversations and insights. Elizabeth, my wife, as well as organising my trip to Singapore and Sarawak, and acting as photographer on that and many other expeditions, has had to live patiently and, luckily for me, happily with Wallace for a number of years. My editors, Jenny Uglow at Chatto and Windus and Sam Elworthy at Princeton University Press, have been wonderfully supportive, and I would like to thank Jenny Uglow for her suggestions and comments at every stage; these, however painful at the time, invariably led to something better (a true Wallace principle).

Names: I have usually retained the names used by Wallace in his writing, and indicated the modern equivalent in brackets on the first occasion, for example Barra (Manaos), Gilolo (Halmahera). One exception to this practice is the river Vaupés, where Wallace uses 'Uaupes', a form I struggled with. Spelling on the maps also generally follows Wallace's practice.

1   Introduction

Alfred Russel Wallace wrote to his friend Henry Walter Bates in 1847 after spending a week beetle-hunting with him in Wales,

> I begin to feel rather dissatisfied with a mere local collection, little is to be learned by it. I should like to take some one family to study thoroughly, principally with a view to the theory of the origin of species. By that means I am strongly of opinion that some definite results might be arrived at.[1]

He was twenty-four, training himself as a field naturalist, and enjoying a self-administered crash course in scientific theory. Three years earlier, he had been introduced to the wonders of beetles by Bates, and was amazed to discover that there were perhaps a thousand different kinds to be found within ten miles of Leicester. Only one year after writing this letter, in

1848, he and Bates would be plunging through the rain-forest on the banks of the Amazon, catching beetles, spiders, butterflies and birds. A further decade on, and Wallace would mail an elegant, tightly argued essay to England from the Spice Islands, in which he laid out his independent explanation of the way species evolve by natural selection. He sent this with a covering letter to Charles Darwin.

Wallace's achievements are spectacular. He made independent, courageous journeys up the Amazon, and through the length of the Malay Archipelago, and wrote about them vividly. He became an expert field naturalist, collecting countless species and discovering or identifying many for the first time: insects, birds, fish. But he was, too, as that letter to Bates indicates, a theoriser, travelling and observing minutely in order to test a theory, seeking always to understand the world more clearly, to fit each minute piece of knowledge, each fact, within a pattern that was logical and harmonious. He was in love with the natural world: the Alpine flowers, the richness of the forest fauna, rare fish in the black waters of the Rio Negro, the dazzling beauty of a bird of paradise or an elusive butterfly moved him to wonder. Capturing a female of the species *Ornithoptera croesus*, he describes the intense excitement when he first took it from his net: 'My heart began to beat violently, the blood rushed to my head, and I felt much more like fainting than I have done when in apprehension of immediate death.'[2] This was not hyperbole: apprehension of immediate death was something he frequently experienced.

He was equally interested in man. Although he cherished solitude, he responded to the vitality and culture of cities as diverse as Paris, Cairo, Singapore and San Francisco, and he observed and recorded the remote peoples among whom he lived quite as minutely as he described the habits of a bird or insect. He was, in many ways, as much an anthropologist as a field naturalist, recording customs, languages and artefacts, and speculating about the development, and the chances of survival, of particular races. He tested the categories of the 'civilised' and the 'savage', from the point of view of someone who was sharply critical of many aspects of so-called civilisation, and who rated the intellectual and moral dimension more highly than material success. In the second half of his life he wrote as much about society as about the natural world, and took every opportunity to justify his conviction that man's destiny and development lay in co-operation rather than competition.

In an article on 'The Celt in English Art', Grant Allen added Wallace to his long list of imaginative, artistic Celts – William Morris, Edward Burne-Jones, George Bernard Shaw, Oscar Wilde, and social thinkers such as Annie Besant and Henry George – on the grounds that his name meant Welshman and that he was born in Usk, and commented: 'The Celt comes back upon us with all the Celtic gifts and all the Celtic ideals – imagination, fancy, decorative skill, artistic handicraft; free land, free speech, human equality, human brotherhood.'[3] The contrast Allen makes is with Teutonic, or Teutonised, England. Whether or not Allen was strictly correct in claiming Wallace as a Celt, the company with whom he aligns him alerts us to his artistic, aesthetic and sympathetic nature and temperament. Wallace shared many ideals and ideas with Morris and Shaw, and believed with Wilde that Utopia was a country worth visiting. Accompanying the energy and curiosity that led to the diversity of his discoveries is the continuously challenging and probing quality of his thinking. He wanted to know what was there in the forest, but he also wanted to know why, and at the same time longed to understand the facts in as much detail as possible. To help him answer those questions, he constructed his own programme of study, shifting outwards from botany to every area of natural history, moving back in time through a growing understanding of geology, and onwards, towards overarching scientific and philosophical concepts. His was an astonishing intellectual odyssey, fed by the Victorian institutions of self-help, the mechanics' institutes and local lending libraries, popular journals and magazines, but without any systematic discipline, and with limited and erratic access to state-of-the-art scientific thinking.

To this driving intellectual curiosity can be added resilience, persistence, self-reliance, and an incurable optimism, and behind these positive-sounding virtues, the shadow of other, harder-edged traits: obstinacy, ruthlessness, self-absorption, obsessiveness – qualities that drove him forward, brushing aside obstacles, refusing to allow him to be deflected from his goals, ensuring his survival, and his success. He had very few material advantages in life, in terms of wealth, education, or social connections, and had an uncertain feel for those subtle networks that guided the progress of his contemporaries and competitors through the maze of nineteenth-century scientific Britain. Like Willie Loman's Uncle Ben in *Death of a Salesman*, he went out into the jungle, and came back with the diamonds.

There are several paradoxical aspects to Wallace. He was by his own admission extremely shy, and in public appeared reserved, even awkward at times. He had little small talk. He was reticent, especially about his personal life. He positively enjoyed travel, and welcomed solitude, which was just as well. His dream, whenever he was exhausted by illness and the wearing routines of continuous travel, was to marry, build a house, create a garden, and settle down to enjoy and write up his collections, a modest enough ambition. Things did not work out quite so simply. For such a pragmatic and practical man, with twenty-five years or so of independence in four continents behind him, Wallace remained strangely innocent, even naïve, both in his personal affairs and in his public life. Tall, gangly, spectacled, he might have been the model for the scientist in *The Water-Babies*, 'the simplest, pleasantest, honestest, kindliest old Dominie Sampson of a giant that ever turned the world upside down without intending it'.[4] He got into scrapes. He took people to court. He frittered money away in disastrous financial ventures. He became embroiled in public controversies and social issues, some of which – spiritualism, vaccination, land nationalisation – probably harmed him in the eyes of the Victorian great and good, who distributed influence and made recommendations about appointments.

This diversity of interest was a source of strength, and a sign of his integrity. He was very tough, tough on himself, and tough on the people he worked with – his young assistant Charlie Allen had a difficult time in Singapore and Sarawak – and quite tough, as well as very loving, towards his children. He takes himself to task for lack of assertiveness, but a quick glance through his correspondence shows him ready, almost too ready at times, to take up the cudgels, with opponents such as William Carpenter over spiritualism, or George Romanes, but also with friends such as Alfred Newton, over classification of species. He suggests that words did not come easily to him – 'I rarely find the right word of expression to confirm or illustrate my argument'[5] – yet he was ready to enter into public discussions of his own papers, at the meetings of the Anthropological or Geographical Societies, or at the annual gatherings of the British Association. He accuses himself of being lazy: he wrote twenty-two books, and some seven hundred articles, published letters and notes. He gives himself no credit for physical courage, but repeatedly on his journeys faced and overcame severe illness, countless hardships, and extreme dangers.

Underpinning his personality, and his achievements, are his beliefs. He shared the ideals of the Enlightenment. He believed in freedom, in the individual, and in progress. These were not just slogans for him: he campaigned actively for any change in the law that he thought would improve the living conditions of the majority. Like so many of his contemporaries, he wrestled with questions of faith, but in a rather distinctive way. Unlike Matthew Arnold, who heard only the 'melancholy, long, withdrawing roar' of the Sea of Faith's retreat, he developed an unshakeable, if unorthodox, conviction that man was essentially spiritual, and that the material world was shaped by spiritual intelligences.

Suitably for a traveller, Wallace left many traces of himself around the world, most famously in the example of Wallace's Line on the map of the Archipelago, a signal instance of a speculative theory confirmed by bio-geographical fact. He lends his name to bird and insect. The birds and moths and butterflies he collected can be seen at the Natural History Museum in London, at Tring, at Cambridge, and in museums around the world. With *Travels on the Amazon* or *The Malay Archipelago* in hand, you can follow his routes, and verify the accuracy and vividness of his observations. Although there is no single spot in Britain dedicated to his achievements, it may be more appropriate to pursue his slightly restless, elusive, enquiring presence through the scattered towns and landscapes through which he moved: a strong, solid, handsome building in Neath; a plaque on a museum in Leicester; a road in Bournemouth, and a lecture theatre in the University there, and the name of a house he built in Broadstone with its reference to Lewis Carroll and 'Jabberwocky', 'Tulgey Wood'[6] and, apt for a man with a strong sense of place and a sharp distaste for pomp, a bench on the bank of the river Usk, just opposite the cottage where he was born. Sitting there, you can look upstream to the hills in which he made his first explorations of the natural history of the world.

2   The Evolution of a Naturalist

Alfred Russel Wallace was born on 8 January 1823, in a cottage on the banks of the river Usk, half a mile or so from the town of Usk, in Monmouthshire, on a road that led to the village of Llanbadoc. Eleven days later, according to the family prayerbook, he was 'half-baptized', and the full baptism took place at Llanbadoc church on 16 February.[1] He had two older brothers, William and John, and two older sisters, Eliza and Frances, or Fanny. John, four and a half years the elder, was his closest sibling, and after Alfred came the Wallaces' last child, a fourth boy, Herbert Edward. Perhaps the half-baptism was a precaution, because Alfred was a frail baby. Three other girls did not survive childhood, two of them dying at the cottage at Usk.

Alfred's parents, Thomas Vere Wallace and Mary Anne Greenell, illustrate in many respects the changes in British society that followed the Napoleonic wars, as the solid certainties of the eighteenth century began to fade or disintegrate. Their miniature portraits have a Georgian assurance. Thomas's white neck-cloth and frilled shirtfront, his blue coat and slightly ruddy complexion, suggest both elegance and well-being: a pleasant, confident man about to marry a sweet-faced, much younger wife, from a prosperous-enough Hertford family. Before his marriage Thomas Wallace had lived the leisured life of an independent gentleman. Although he was articled to a firm of solicitors, and sworn in as an attorney-at-law in 1792, a private income of £500 had freed him from the need to practise, and instead he enjoyed himself in London or Bath, gently pursuing his literary and artistic interests: 'He appears', wrote his son, 'to have lived quite idly.'[2] When marriage and a growing family started to eat into his income, he put some capital into a new illustrated magazine. It folded almost immediately. This was just the first of a series of financially disastrous decisions, a pattern of ill-advised speculation that continued into the next generation; and there were few other family members to help them out. Wallace's opening comment in his autobiography is: 'Our family had but few relations.'[3] He never saw a grandparent.

The move to Usk from London was made for economy. Later, the family flitted from one house to another, and Thomas Wallace from one ill-paid job to another, in a bewildering and restless succession. But Alfred, resilient and optimistic by nature, remembered with gratitude the many good things in his childhood. However difficult the practical circumstances might have been, he found plenty of affection and security within his immediate family.

One of his earliest memories is of sitting on his mother's lap, or on a footstool, listening to fairy-tales, or being read to from *The History of Sandford and Merton*. Thomas Day's Utopian perspective, with its reflection of Jean Jacques Rousseau and vision of a natural upbringing, burned into his consciousness. John, taking on the role of Sandford, led Alfred and his sisters up the steep bank behind the cottage, where they made a fire, and roasted potatoes on the embers. They played in the garden, or beside the river that flowed in front of the cottage – no flood banks then – where they watched men fishing for salmon and trout from coracles; a little further downstream, where a rock fall provided standing places in the water, they scooped up young lampreys with an old saucepan, which were fried for supper. It was the actual place, and above all the outdoor surroundings, that Wallace would later recall so sharply, whereas his father and mother, even his brothers and sisters, existed in his memory only as blurred images:

7

The form and colour of the house, the road, the river close below it, the bridge with the cottage near its foot, the narrow fields between us and the bridge, the steep wooded bank at the back, the stone quarry and the very shape and position of the flat slabs on which we stood fishing, the cottages a little further on the road, the little church of Llanbadock and the stone stile into the churchyard, the fishermen and their coracles, the ruined castle, its winding stair and the delightful walk round its top – all come before me as I recall these earlier days with a distinctness strangely contrasted with the vague shadowy figures of the human beings who were my constant associates in all these scenes.[4]

Alfred, in recollection at least, spent most of his days out of doors, so that his memories were of the free-flowing river, the fields and woods along its bank, and the view of the Abergavenny mountains to the north-west. To the Welsh-speaking neighbours, he was, with his long, flaxen hair, 'the little Saxon'.

The Welsh idyll ended. Mrs Greenell, Mary Wallace's stepmother, died in 1826, and, with the prospect of a small legacy, the Wallaces decided to move their family to Hertford, Mary's home town.[5] There was the slightly alarming experience of crossing the Severn estuary in a sailing ferry, and a few days in aunt Wilson's impressive house at Dulwich, meeting a large batch of cousins. Then, after a short spell at a little school in Essex, Alfred joined the rest of his family in the first of a succession of homes, in St Andrew Street in the heart of the town.

Hertford, a compact country town, was built in the broad valley of the river Lea. There were six working watermills, including the old town mill which was owned by a cousin of Mary Wallace. There were the more gentle waters of the river Beane, with sandy shallows and deeper holes where you could swim – and where Alfred was rescued from drowning by his brother soon after he arrived. There was an expansive public space called Hartham, and a fir-covered slope called the Warren beside a footpath which led to the village of Bengeo. But for all this appearance of being on the edge of the country, Hertford was also an unpleasantly crowded urban environment. Britain was moving towards the Reform Act, but Hertford was an open borough, and each male householder whose hearth was of the right size had a vote. The great political families who owned most of the property in the town – the Cecils, the Barclays, the Dimsdales – competed fiercely with each other, building small dwellings in the side yards of the larger town houses in order to increase the number of tenants, and so influence the voting for the two Hertford Members of Parliament. The yards were over-crowded, the sanitation inadequate, and disease spread rapidly; typhoid, tuberculosis, scarlet fever were common, cholera a constant threat.[6] Alfred caught scarlet fever, and was 'within a few hours of death', according to his family. (Characteristically, he chose to minimise the fever and the horrid dreams he experienced, and to recount the few weeks of luxury that followed, lying in bed with tea and toast and grapes.) The Wallaces' first houses were not so cramped – later they were to shrink in size with the family's fortunes – though the St Andrew Street one was crowded enough with the half-dozen pupils that his father took in to provide a little income. Among Alfred's early memories was the open-air free dinner in Hertford, to celebrate the passing of the Reform Act of 1832; and Thomas Slingsby Duncombe being chaired through the streets after his election to Parliament.

Besides his father's young scholars there were, for the first time, neighbours to play with. A small boy looked over the garden wall: 'Hallo! Who are you?'[7] It was George Silk, who became a life-long friend. When the Wallaces moved to a house at Old Cross, a few hundred yards away, by which time the four-year gap between Alfred and John seemed less significant, there was a good-sized garden and, best of all, a stable with a loft, which John made their base and playroom. Alfred looked on this as the happiest part of his childhood in Hertford. Even school did not intrude unpleasantly, because John was a pupil there too. Their father seemed content, with an allotment where he grew fruit and vegetables, and a brewhouse where he made wine. In the 'delightful privacy' of the loft, after school, John instructed his younger brother, making elaborate fireworks, or putting together toys and gadgets from *The Boy's Own Book*.

This was a short, intense period of rare content, and the last time Alfred was to experience a settled family life for another thirty years. First, his sister Eliza died in 1832, aged twenty-two, and though he says he was not old enough at nine to feel it very deeply, being closer to John and Fanny, he was aware of the grief his parents suffered. Next, financial problems began to bite. This happened, as often with Wallace family affairs, in an indirect, complex and frustrating way. Mary Wallace – and her children –

9

had inherited some money from her father's family, and the controlling trustee was her sister's husband, Thomas Wilson, a lawyer. He was declared bankrupt in 1834, and the funds of the legacy were somehow dragged into the proceedings. The Wallaces' income was drastically reduced. As the children became old enough, each left home to earn a living. William, the senior, was already a long way into his career. He had been apprenticed to a firm of surveyors when the family was still at Usk, and then, after a spell with a Hertford architect, worked for a large building firm, Martin, on a major construction project at King's College, London. John went to London, too, apprenticed to another master-builder, Webster. Fanny, intelligent and artistic, was dispatched to Lille, to learn French with a view to teaching. When the Wallaces moved temporarily to a much smaller cottage, Alfred went for a while to Hertford Grammar School as a boarder, leaving only the youngest child, Herbert, at home. Mary Wallace wrote anguished letters to her brother-in-law, asking pertinent questions, and urging her children's needs. John's employer Mr Webster was looking for half a year's board that was due. William was afraid to show himself in London – an apothecary had threatened to arrest him for a debt of £20. What about the interest? What about Alfred's £100, which he would not be able to touch until he was twenty-one? She trusted to Wilson's honour.[8] She had no satisfactory reply at the time, though eventually most of the money was disentangled before the Wilsons emigrated to a new life in South Australia. Meanwhile, the Wallaces moved house, and improvised.

In 1831 Alfred had followed John to Hertford School, where the headmaster was a 'rather irascible little man' called Clement Cruttwell – a good master, commented Wallace, 'inasmuch as he kept order in the school, and carried on the work of teaching about eighty boys by four masters, all in one room, with great regularity and with no marked inconvenience'.[9] He makes it quite clear that, for all 'Old Cruttle's' classical scholarship, the system was perfectly hopeless, at least as far as his own learning was concerned. He gained a better idea of Virgil from Cruttwell's readings aloud of a verse translation 'than from the fragmentary translations we scrambled through'. Latin grammar was painfully difficult, and he never even embarked on Greek. Geography, which he would later find so absorbing, was only slightly less agonising, and consisted of memorising the chief towns in each English county. Mathematics, too, was largely an exercise of memory, while history was learning names and dates by rote and reading 'the very baldest account of the doings of kings and queens, of wars, rebellions, and conquests'.[10] A standard English education, in fact, but with very few compensations. He gained more, he claimed, from Shakespeare's plays and Scott's novels.

Wallace learned at an early age to read and write fluently, and the family resources, fragile and erratic in many respects, were comparatively rich in books. First, there were the 'good old standard' works in the house: *Gulliver's Travels*, *Robinson Crusoe*, *The Pilgrim's Progress*, *The Vicar of Wakefield*, which he read again and again. Each year, too, they bought Thomas Hood's *Comic Annual*, and Alfred associated Hood's poem 'Number One' with their first Hertford house, Number One, St Andrew Street, learning it by heart at the age of seven. The puns and conundrums of the *Comic Annual*, and the irreverent wit, pathos and social commentary of Hood's poetry, struck a sympathetic chord with him. Did Hood's 'Ode to Mr Malthus' lodge in his memory, particularly since Malthus himself was a Hertfordshire resident?

> Oh, Mr Malthus, I agree
> In everything I read with thee!
> The world's too full, there is no doubt,
> And wants a deal of thinning out – . . .
> Why should we let precautions so absorb us,
> Or trouble shipping with a quarantine –
> When if I understand the thing you mean,
> We ought to *import* the Cholera Morbus![11]

In 1832, cholera duly broke out in Hertford, a very specific memory for Wallace to salt away in illustration of Malthus's theories about the control of excess populations.

Alfred's father belonged to a book club, and would read aloud in the evenings from Mungo Park's travels, or Defoe's *Journal of the Plague Year*. Later, he took a modest job at the town's proprietary library, and Alfred would join him there for an hour after school on Tuesdays and Thursdays, 'four o'clock days'. He spent every wet Saturday afternoon squatting on the floor in a corner and making his way through the fiction: Fennimore Cooper, Harrison Ainsworth, Captain Marryat, Bulwer Lytton, as well as classics such as *Don Quixote*, *Roderick Random* and *Tom Jones*. These alone

11

would be enough to give him the idea that life was a journey, and a series of adventures. Besides, he read – 'partially or completely' – *The Faerie Queen*, *Paradise Lost*, Dante's *Inferno*, Pope's *Iliad*, and 'a good deal of Byron and Scott': all this before he was fourteen. In fact, he recalled, he read almost any book that he heard spoken of as 'celebrated or interesting'. He never lost his love of romantic fiction, or for poetry: in his library were volumes of Browning, Cowper, Dryden, Thomas Moore, Pope, Shelley and Tennyson.[12]

His religious upbringing was relatively conventional. He described his parents as 'old-fashioned religious people belonging to the Church of England'. This meant normally attending church twice each Sunday, after learning the collect of the day; or, if it was too wet to walk to church, there would be a chapter from the Bible and a sermon from a book instead. For variation, the family might go to the Friends' Meeting House, which Alfred found dull when there was silence, and even duller when someone was moved to speak. At the Dissenters' Chapel, the third possibility, there was more vitality: extempore prayers, fervent preaching, impassioned hymn-singing. This was the only period of his life, he commented later, when he felt 'something of religious fervour'; but, he added, as 'there was no sufficient basis of intelligible fact or connected reasoning to satisfy my intellect, the feeling soon left me, and has never returned'.[13] When he later raised the question of the origin of evil with his father, he 'merely remarked that such problems were mysteries which the wisest cannot understand, and seemed disinclined to any discussion of the subject'. There was no rigidly imposed set of beliefs to rebel against, no deep-rooted investment in orthodox Christianity of the kind that troubled Charles Darwin or tormented Samuel Butler.

Alfred's formal education began to draw to a close as the purse strings became more and more tightly drawn. In his last year, part of his school fees was remitted, and in exchange he took the younger boys for the 'three Rs'. What embarrassed him was not the task itself, but the fact that it made him different from the other boys. There were twenty boys in the school older than he was, and yet they were simply 'scholars'. Even worse was a humiliation inflicted on him by his mother. She made him black calico over-sleeves for his jacket, to protect the cuffs and elbows from being worn bare by leaning on the desks, or ruined by cleaning slates. In spite of his protests, he was ordered to put them on just before he arrived at school. He could not bring himself to do it, brought them home, and dutifully told his mother. Then one morning the 'thunderbolt' fell on him:

On entering school I was called up to the master's desk, he produced the dreaded calico sleeves, and told me that my mother wished me to wear them to save my jacket, and told me to put them on. Of course I had to do so. They fitted very well, and felt quite comfortable, and I dare say did not look so very strange. I have no doubt also that most of the boys had a fellow feeling for me, and thought it a shame to thus make me an exception to all the school. But to me it seemed a cruel disgrace, and I was miserable so long as I wore them. How long that was I cannot remember, but while it lasted it was, perhaps, the severest punishment I ever endured.[14]

Recalling that awful humiliation, years later, Wallace linked it to the idea of 'saving face', and 'the fundamental right of every individual to be treated with personal respect'. His own boyhood embarrassment helped him to appreciate 'the agony of shame endured by the more civilised Eastern peoples, whose feelings are so often outraged by the total absence of all respect shown them by their European masters or conquerors'. Wallace felt intensely about the sanctity of self-respect, calling it 'the deepest of human feelings'. He noted that it was much more apparent in non-European societies, where a man would refuse to enter an empty house in the owner's absence, or hesitate to wake, or even touch, someone who was asleep.[15] Wallace remained acutely sensitive to slights, to invasions of privacy, all his life.

His ordeal as pupil–teacher did not last long. His parents were getting ready to move to a small cottage at Hoddesdon. He was fourteen: time to learn a trade. In Mrs Cruttwell's account book, for 18 March 1837, along with 'Hot × Buns – 2s' and 'Hair cutting (27) – 6(s) 9(d)', is the entry: 'Alfred Wallace left'; and in the shillings column: 10, either his final reward, or a return of fees.[16] Alfred was sent off to London, to lodge with his favourite brother John, now nineteen, at Mr Webster's house in Robert Street, off Hampstead Road, between Regent's Park and the future site of Euston station. It was an area of London he would return to later in his life, with the attraction of the Zoological Society's gardens a short walk away.

These next few months in London were Alfred's first taste of the adult world, and the tougher environment of an expanding city. Without any fixed occupation, he could make himself useful doing odd jobs in the workshop, and listen to the talk and the jokes. There wasn't too much to shock a shy fourteen year old – not nearly as much swearing as he met with later; and when one of the workmen, 'a very loose character', went too far in describing his exploits, the foreman would 'gently call him to order'. (At home, he had never heard 'a rude word or an offensive expression'. There may be a touch of New Lanark idealism in these memories, but Webster's was a well-run business, and John, a skilled carpenter, would later marry a Webster daughter. The building industry was still in the pre-factory era, and almost everything that went into the houses the firm built was made in the yard: floorboards, windows and doors, cupboards and staircases. The carpenters and joiners worked a ten-hour day, six days a week, and earned thirty shillings a week at sixpence an hour. Even a married man with children could save a little, wrote John fifty years later, a little optimistically – so long as he was frugal, and of steady habits, and so long as he kept in good health, and continued to find employment.[17] If your job was on site, as a bricklayer, there was less margin, for there was no payment if bad weather stopped work. The labourers and the hod-carriers received just three shillings a day, and their wives had to work 'out' at washing, or whatever else they could find – so the children might be neglected as a consequence. Alfred watched, and listened, and never forgot the struggle that most people were forced to endure simply to survive, let alone prosper.

In the evenings, John might take his young brother off to look at the West End shops, and admire the window displays. But more often they would go to the 'Hall of Science' a few blocks away, off Tottenham Court Road, a kind of mechanics' club. They read books and magazines, played draughts and dominoes, drank coffee, and attended lectures on the teachings of Robert Owen: secularist, socialist, agnostic, idealist. Alfred read Thomas Paine's *The Age of Reason*: he might have taken Paine's statement, 'It is necessary to the happiness of man that he be mentally faithful to himself', as part of his private gospel. On one memorable occasion he heard Owen himself, with his 'tall spare figure, very lofty head, and highly benevolent countenance and mode of speaking'. As Wallace observed, Owen influenced his character more than he then realised. But his young mind was grappling with issues that some of his contemporaries would engage with only as adults. He struggled with the attempt to reconcile the existence of evil with the concept of a benevolent, omnipotent God; and he was struck, too, by a tract on 'Consistency' by Owen's son, Robert Dale Owen, condemning the 'horrible' doctrine of eternal punishment. He accepted Owen's conclusions, that orthodox religion was degrading, and that 'the only beneficial religion was that which inculcated the service of humanity, and whose only dogma was the brotherhood of man'.[18] The foundations of Wallace's religious scepticism were complete.

In the summer of 1837, Alfred began his apprenticeship as a surveyor, a pupil to his brother William. This phase of his life would last for six and a half years, during which he not only trained in the practical details of his job, but, crucially, began to prepare himself for his future career, a preparation that was at first more instinctive than systematic. Although the survey work was quite demanding, there were also long evenings, and Sundays, to fill. The brothers lived in inns and lodgings, moving from district to district and job to job. There were few distractions, or temptations – and, in any event, no money to spare. Alfred spent long periods on his own.

The first contract was in the parish of Higham Gobion, Bedfordshire. The Tithe Act of 1836 had made it compulsory for all church tithes to be commuted to a cash payment, which meant lots of work for surveyors, mapping and measuring the church parishes of England and Wales. William hired rooms at the Coach and Horses at Barton-in-the-Cley, on the Luton to Bedford coach road, and each day Alfred would set out armed with a bill-hook, chain, flag, rods and pegs, and map out a section of the parish. He learned the basic rules of surveying, mapping and trigonometry. It was enjoyable, open-air work, with lunch of bread and cheese and beer under a hedge. Following William's example, he experimented with smoking a pipe, and had such a violent headache that he never smoked again. He also began to learn a little geology, and became curious about the fossils to be found in the chalk, and in the gravels of the Ouse, much like his famous predecessor as a surveyor-turned-geologist, William Smith.

When this first assignment came to an end, Alfred walked the thirty miles home to Rawdon Cottage, Hoddesdon, and then walked back to Barton in January, and a further twenty miles beyond Bedford to Turvey, for another tithe survey. Each survey led to another, though they were doing little more than paying their way. In all the years he spent with William,

Alfred hardly ever received more than a few shillings for personal expenses. Each year or so, when he went home, he would be bought new clothes if it was absolutely essential, and given ten shillings or a pound to keep him going.

On another job, at Soulbury near Leighton Buzzard, Alfred could see the three great transport systems of the 1830s in action. The mail-coach road to Birmingham and Holyhead ran two miles to the east of the Ouzel. Parallel with the river was the Grand Junction Canal, and half a mile to the west a hive of activity marked the construction of the London and Birmingham railway. On Christmas Eve 1838, Alfred and William travelled from Berkhamsted to London on the first section to be opened – third class, naturally, which meant standing in an open truck, or sitting on the floor when the wind became too cold.

A lull in survey work led to a change of plan. William had become friendly with a surveyor, William Matthews, who also ran a watch- and clock-making business at Leighton Buzzard – in addition, as a young Victorian entrepreneur, he was the engineer in charge of the town gasworks. Alfred, by now sixteen, dutifully adopted his brother's suggestion, and went to live with the Matthews, to learn how to take watches and clocks to pieces, and repair jewellery. He liked the family, but was relieved after nine months when Matthews accepted a job in London, and William arrived to take him west to the Herefordshire/Radnorshire border. There they worked under contract for the firm of surveyors and estate agents at Kington where William had learned his trade, William and Morris Sayce. This move Wallace afterwards considered to be one of several important turning-points in his life, when he was 'insensibly' directed into the course best adapted to develop his 'special mental and physical activities'.[19]

Here was a far more exciting landscape, Alfred wrote to George Silk, 'to be (literally) "cutting" all over the country, following the chain and admiring the beauties of nature, breathing the fresh and pure air on the hills, or in the noonday heat enjoying our luncheon of bread-and-cheese in a pleasant valley'.[20] They lodged with an old gunmaker and his wife, known to the town as Alderman Wright 'on account of the size of his corporation', sharing one bedroom, and one bed. 'If you fancy Mr Pickwick with his nose a little rounder and his corporation a little larger you will have an exact idea of Alderman Wright. Mrs Wright is an old woman something like Mrs Nickleby but very Religious (in talk),' he reported to John – and begged

John to write to him with news of his adventures. Alfred's questions to his friend George Silk sound wistful: even the shared experience of his schooldays now held a certain attraction. 'How does Mr Crutwell alias Crut'll get on – Has he any more "young 'uns" yet. Are FitzJohn, Goodwin & Holdsworth there still? . . . Are there any more pretty girls in the Town now than there used to be. There are a pretty fair lot here. I suppose you will be looking out for a <u>wife</u> soon.'[21]

Alfred observed his Welsh surroundings with an amused and quizzical eye, but he had no intimate friend at hand to share his thoughts. The small securities and pleasures of Hertford were distant, and vanishing. The subscription library was deceased, the books sold. The Hertford Literary Society had been 'sewed up'. He missed his games of chess with George, who was now studying learned legal tomes instead of playing hockey. Alfred hoped he wouldn't be charged 6s 8d for reading the letter. But he never complained. When he found himself on top of a bare hill, with the wind and sleet chilling him to the bone, there would soon follow the compensating pleasure of getting indoors in the evening, and sitting down to a warming, well-cooked dinner, even if it was served to the accompaniment of Mrs Wright's 'pretty considerable tarnation long tongue'.[22] At seventeen, he was tall, thin, unusually long-legged, slightly awkward in his movements, but mentally and physically resilient. He needed to be. One freezing February day, surveying at Rhayader on the upper Wye, he slipped into a boghole, and was trapped in the icy mud before a fellow worker managed to haul him out. His lungs were badly affected, and the local doctor insisted he should go to London, where Dr Ramage diagnosed an extensive abscess of the lungs. Dr Ramage's methods were not wholly orthodox, and included the application of half-a-dozen leeches to Alfred's chest at a spot marked with ink. But the key factor was a small bone breathing tube, which brought immediate relief. Alfred spent two months convalescing at Hoddesdon before he was strong enough to return to the Welsh borders. He suffered from bronchial asthma for the rest of his life.

Two aspects of Wallace's experience in Wales held particular significance for his later development. Much of the surveying work he and his brother were engaged in arose out of the Tithe Act; but one particular survey at Llandrindod Wells was in connection with the General Enclosure Act. The underlying principles – or lack of principles – outraged Wallace. The cottagers who held common rights over the moors and mountain, enabling them to keep a horse, or a cow, or a few sheep, found these stripped from them. Anyone who actually owned land received a miserable compensation; but in the case of tenants or leaseholders, it was a case of 'simple robbery'. 'If this is not obtaining land under false pretences –', Wallace wrote years later, still steaming with indignation, '& legalised robbery of the poor for the aggrandisement of the rich, who were the lawmakers – words have no meaning.'[23] This sense of the injustice visited by the strong on the weak, coupled with a belief that every individual had a fundamental right to a share in the earth's resources, never left him, surfacing specifically in his long campaigns for land nationalisation. At the time, he assumed there must be some 'right and reason' for enclosure, though recognising that the process was unjust, unwise and cruel. Meanwhile, he breathed the pure air of the moorland, read Byron's 'The Age of Bronze' to stoke his indignation, and in the evening settled down to the unforgettable taste of a Welsh leg of mutton.

He also made full use of the educational opportunities that Kington and, later, Neath offered. Throughout Britain, mechanics' institutes were being founded, and the Kington Institute was opened in 1841, with Morris Sayce as Treasurer. Wallace, eighteen now, wrote a five-page article 'on the best method of conducting the Kington Mechanics' Institute'. With an epigraph from Bacon, 'Knowledge is power', Wallace argued for the primary place of science within the institution's organisation. Instead of the *Penny Magazine* and the *Magazine of Science*, he proposed a subscription to the Annual Reports of the British Association; and his suggestions for the library included Charles Lyell's *Principles of Geology*, Roderick Murchison's *Silurian System*, John Lindley's *Natural System of Biology*, and Humboldt's and Bonpland's *Personal Narrative of Travels*.[24] This was a formidable wants list, indicating a systematic programme of study into the history of the Earth and its systems of life. By reading Lyell's *Principles*, Wallace would have access to an interpretation of geology as the first historical science, an account of the development of the Earth that would serve as the foundation for *The Origin of Species*; and, through Humboldt's great South American explorations, an alluring perspective on the natural world outside Europe. It was, Wallace argued, through science that the human race could develop. 'How know we that we have not a Herschell [sic], a Stephenson, a Simpson, or a Watt within this town; who want but the means of acquiring that knowledge which they might give back one hundred fold to the world?'[25]

Very early in his life Wallace expressed confidence in the limitless power of the individual mind, so long as it was fed by favourable opportunities to accumulate knowledge. There is something of the restless, questing, striving spirit of Goethe's Faust in his optimism and intellectual hunger, or, to turn to one of his favourite authors, Byron's Manfred.

The brothers then moved for some months to the Brecon hills – young Herbert received a rhyming letter charting their progress. There Alfred was at the source of the Usk, beside which he had been born, and lodged happily for a while on his own, among Welsh speakers, while he surveyed the valleys and enjoyed long expeditions over the Brecon Beacons. From the Beacons they travelled down the valley to Neath, in the autumn of 1841, to undertake yet another parish survey. For a year or so they stayed at a farm, Bryn-coch, just north of the town – home-baked bread, butter and eggs, fresh milk and cheese – before moving closer to town. Once the first parish survey was complete, William travelled about, trying to drum up business, and Alfred was left to occupy himself. Because he had been trained to use a sextant, he experimented with astronomy, making simple observations and constructing a home-made telescope. But his chief area of study was botany. Starting with a shilling paperback published by the Society for the Diffusion of Useful Knowledge, he graduated to Lindley's *Elements of Botany* (something of a disappointment, as it did not distinguish British plants). But he borrowed a copy of John Claudius Loudon's 1836 *Encyclopaedia of Plants*, and annotated Lindley from it. He bought his copy of Lindley in 1842, and transcribed two passages from Darwin's *Journal of the Voyage of the Beagle* into it, including the following:

> I am strongly induced to believe that as in music, the person who understands every note will if he also possesses a proper taste more thoroughly enjoy the whole so he who examines each part of a fine view may also thoroughly comprehend the full and combined effect. Hence a traveller should be a <u>Botanist</u>, for in all views plants form the chief embellishment.[26]

He began to create his own herbarium, learning how to dry specimens effectively, and spending his evenings identifying the treasures he brought back from his long mountain walks. William did not approve, as Alfred learned in a letter from his mother. But he persisted, slowly building up a picture of species, genera and orders. This focus on species was to be at the centre of his scientific thinking, and although he would later be better known for his work on butterflies and birds, plants were his first love. This time, he afterwards reflected, was 'the turning-point' of his life, 'the tide that carried me on, not to fortune, but to whatever reputation I have acquired, and which has certainly been to me a never-failing source of much health of body and supreme mental enjoyment'.[27] On 30 September 1842, he bought William Swainson's 1835 volume, *A Treatise on the Geography and Classification of Animals* – two of his later preoccupations – and annotated it vigorously. Swainson's attempts to bring zoology and geography into line with the Bible seemed absurd to Wallace: 'To what ridiculous theories will men of science be led by attempting to reconcile science to scripture!'[28]

Thomas Wallace died in May 1843, leaving his wife with very little money, and young Herbert still to educate. In Neath, paid jobs remained scarce. Surveying contracts dried up, and William scratched around for building opportunities. He and Alfred took soundings of the river, and designed and supervised the construction of warehouses. William did secure one major contract, to extend and renovate the town gaol, but there was not really enough income to justify keeping Alfred. Clearly, William failed to appreciate how drying wild flowers was going to lead to success – it must have seemed only too like one of their father's profitless enthusiasms; and Alfred's attempts at journalism – he wrote an article on 'The South Wales Farmer' – did not seem likely to earn any money (though in retrospect this seems evidence of a mind relentlessly enquiring into whatever subject lay to hand – it was his first attempt at anthropology). Alfred would be twenty-one in January 1844, and would come into a small legacy of £100: it was time for him to stand on his own. Their sister Fanny's little school at Hoddesdon was failing, and she began to look for teaching posts abroad. They gathered for a last family Christmas at Hoddesdon. The cottage was given up. Mary Wallace accepted an engagement as a housekeeper, and Alfred went to share John's lodgings in London while he hunted for work. Scouring the agencies, he discovered a teaching vacancy that called for drawing, mapping and surveying skills. He took along a coloured map of Neath and some sketches to the interview, and was offered the job. The headmaster, a young clergyman called Abraham Hill, was friendly, and Wallace was soon on his way to the Collegiate School, Leicester, where he would live in the Hills' house, supervise the boarders' evening preparation, and have a modest salary of £30 or £40 a year. Conscientiously, uncomplainingly, he settled down to yet another possible career.

Wallace never felt at ease as a schoolmaster – he claimed he had no vocation for teaching – but throughout his life he remained interested in the process of education, and his belief in knowledge helped him to overcome his instinctive shyness. Hill, finding Wallace knew a little Latin, gave him the bottom class to take, and offered to help him make progress with mathematics. With Hill's assistance, he worked his way stage by stage through Hind's *Algebra* and *Trigonometry*, but was finally baffled by the 'almost trackless wilderness' of integral calculus. His teaching and supervision duties still left him several hours a day free, and, with a little money to spare for the first time in his life, he paid his subscription to the town library. New horizons opened before him: he read William Prescott's *History of the Conquest of Mexico* and *History of the Conquest of Peru*, and William Robertson's *History of America*, and, at last, Alexander von Humboldt's *Personal Narrative of Travels in South America*, the first book that gave him a desire to visit the tropics. Humboldt was the great inspiration of nineteenth-century travellers. Darwin had read his *Travels* aboard the *Beagle*: 'I formerly admired Humboldt, I now almost adore him.'[29] Humboldt gave such a vivid impression of the tropical forest, and from every page flowed the sense of quest, and discovery. But perhaps the 'most important' book Wallace read at this time, as he suggests in *My Life*, was Thomas Malthus's *Essay on the Principle of Population*, which he admired for its 'masterly summary of facts and logical induction to conclusions': 'It was the first work I had yet read treating of any of the problems of philosophical biology, and twenty years later gave me the long-sought clue to the effective agent in the evolution of organic species.'[30] From Malthus he received that clear exposition of 'the positive checks to increase' of the populations of 'savage races', disease, accidents, war, famine, which both he and Darwin would later transfer to animal populations. That 'twenty years' is a kind of biblical reckoning, an obvious but interesting error, or perhaps an unconscious echo that Darwin too, as Wallace later discovered, had hit on the same Malthusian clue twenty years before the events of 1858, and their joint presentation on natural selection at the Linnean Society.[31] For now, the arguments lodged in Wallace's mind, as he shifted the focus of his self-education from literature to the natural world.

Most significantly for his future career as a naturalist, Wallace met, while at Leicester, Henry Walter Bates. Bates's family was in the hosiery business, and Bates was working out an apprenticeship while pursuing his enthusiasm for entomology. He, too, had embarked on his own rigorous programme of self-education. They met, appropriately, at the library. Bates was two years younger, but had already contributed an article to the *Zoologist*. He showed Wallace his beetle collection, and a set of British butterflies. The beetles, especially, were a revelation. Almost all had been collected around Leicester. There were, perhaps, a thousand species to be found within a ten-mile radius, and some three thousand, Wallace learned, in the British Isles. Soon Wallace had added beetles to botany, bought a collecting bottle, pins and store-box, and got hold of a copy 'at wholesale price' of James Stephens's *Manual of British Coleoptera*. The combination of Malthus and Bates marked Leicester as crucial in Wallace's development. For the first time, too, he was wholly independent, without an older brother looking over his shoulder in disapproval at the way he spent his leisure. He and Bates went collecting together, in Bradgate Park and Charnwood Forest to the north-west, whose owner, Lord Stamford, conveniently did not 'strictly preserve for game'.[32]

One other of Wallace's enthusiasms, or obsessions, began at Leicester. He went with a few of the senior boys to see lectures and demonstrations on Mesmerism by Spencer Hall. Wallace was immediately impressed, especially since Hall's manner was 'serious', not at all that of 'the showman or conjuror'. Back at the Collegiate School the older boys carried out some successful experiments on the younger ones, and invited Wallace to see. He decided to try his own powers, and found he could 'produce catalepsy of any limb or of the whole body, and in this state they could do things which they could not and certainly would not have done in their normal state'.[33] Fortunately, his experiments were relatively low key, and he was acutely aware of the risk of physical injury. 'For example, on the rigid outstretched arm I would hang at the wrist an ordinary bedroom chair, and the boy would hold it there for several minutes, while I sat down and wrote a short letter . . .' No one seems to have considered the psychological danger, and when he informed the headmaster, Hill invited two or three friends along to observe the experiment.

Wallace had already come across the subject of phrenology. William had introduced him to George Combe's writing, and after reading the Scottish lawyer's *The Constitution of Man,* a popular account of natural religion, he explored some of Combe's specialist writing on phrenology. At Hall's lecture he had seen a demonstration 'of exciting the phrenological organs by touching the corresponding parts of the patient's head'. As Wallace did not possess a chart, he now bought a phrenological bust, and continued his investigations. When he touched a particular point on his subject's head, the expression on his face would correspond with the 'natural' expression of the emotion controlled 'by the phrenological organ situated at that part': combativeness, fear, wonder. Wallace's temperament was a mixture of rationality, enthusiasm and naïvety. If he believed something was true, because of the evidence of his own eyes, he would not be easily shaken from the explanation in which he had placed his faith. 'The importance of these experiments to me', he wrote defiantly,

> was that they convinced me, once for all, that the antecedently incredible may nevertheless be true; and, further, that the accusations of imposture by scientific men should have no weight whatever against the detailed observations and statements of other men, presumably as sane and sensible as their opponents, who had witnessed and tested the phenomena, as I had done myself in the case of some of them.[34]

This is the kind of justification that could be applied to a personal religious experience. The independence, obstinacy, persistence, that stood Wallace in such good stead in formulating his theories about species (an area in which, oddly, he *was* prepared to adapt and rethink) would make him in later years impervious to opposing arguments concerning some of his spiritualist and psychological convictions. These Mesmerist experiments, continued in the Amazon, retained their hold in his thinking, and helped to prepare the way for his later interest in spiritualism.

Early in 1845, he learned of his eldest brother's sudden and unexpected death. William perished, an indirect victim of railway mania. He was on his way back to Neath from London, where he had been giving expert evidence as a surveyor before a committee on the South Wales Railway Bill. Travelling at night in an open third-class carriage, he caught a chill which swiftly developed into a fatal attack of pneumonia. Alfred and John went to Neath for the funeral – Fanny was in America, teaching at a college in Macon, Georgia – and discovered that William's business was a little more substantial than they had realised. In one of his sudden entrepreneurial fits, Alfred negotiated to leave the Collegiate School at Easter 1845, and returned to Neath to sort out William's affairs. He and John did the rounds of William's creditors, before John returned to London, leaving Alfred free to botanise, and to pick up any surveying and building work he could find. He seems to have been rather out of touch with William in the months before his death, a little hurt, perhaps, by being cast off so abruptly. He had locked himself into his own affairs at Leicester where he was 'altogether out of the business world', and never even read a newspaper, so knew nothing of the railway boom.[35] He knew now. A civil engineer in Swansea was on the look-out for surveyors: two guineas a day, with all expenses paid, including hotels – real money at last.

A railway line was being proposed, to run from the Vale of Neath to Merthyr Tydfil, and bring coal and iron down to the port of Swansea. Wallace was in his element. He did not know the south-east side of the valley, and the route took him up 'one of the wildest and most picturesque glens': Wallace and his workforce had to clamber over huge rocks, scale cascades, and take levels up steep banks and densely wooded precipices.[36] Far more railway lines were surveyed than were ever completed, but while the speculation lasted there was good money for surveyors and engineers. Wallace worked relentlessly through the summer and autumn, and then found himself temporarily accommodated in a London hotel in the Haymarket – a rare luxury – while the report on the railway proposal was being drafted in November 1845. In his leisure moments, he ploughed on with his reading, bombarding Bates with questions and suggestions.

In Neath, Alfred had secured comfortable and central lodgings with the Sims family, and in January 1846 he persuaded John to join him. Although they had a tough time squeezing money out of William's debtors, they were confident that they could make a living. Eventually, they rented a cottage next to Llantwit church, a mile from town, overlooking the canal and river, complete with a garden, sheds and henhouses. Their mother came now to live with them, and Herbert, who was unhappy in his apprenticeship to a London luggage-maker, found an opening at the Neath Abbey ironworks; John, when business was slack, built a boat, light enough to be carried from canal to river and back again, and spacious enough to ferry the whole family down to Swansea.

Wallace's autobiography gives the impression that his time at Neath was a rather fractured, temporary business, a brief prelude before the main purpose of his life became clear. But he was based there for some six years in all, and for nearer three than two in this second phase.[37] Optimistic as always, resilient in the face of setbacks, he tackled another tithe commutation survey, in conjunction with the agent of the Gnoll Estate. Much to his disgust, he found himself landed with the additional task of extracting payment from the farmers, both difficult and uncomfortable since many were poor, spoke no English, and could not be made to understand what it was all about. Building work was more agreeable, and here John's expertise could be put to good use. The Wallace brothers built a cottage for a client, and failed to get the contract to design a new town hall for Swansea; but they did design and supervise the construction of the new Mechanics' Institute at Neath, which was officially opened in 1848, after Alfred had left for the Amazon.

Wallace took a more active part in the intellectual life of Neath during his second stay, much of it revolving around the Mechanics' Institute, founded by a friend of his brother's, William Jevons. Over the course of two winters, he gave a series of lectures on basic science at the Institute. The town library was pretty good, but frustratingly it would have no works but those of general interest. However, he became Curator of the Neath Philosophical and Literary Institute – it was a 'nice little Museum but they have little to spare for books' – while at the Philosophical Society at Swansea there was a good selection on natural history, though scarcely one on entomology. He was in correspondence with Lewis Weston Dillwyn, of Sketty Hall, one of the leading naturalists of South Wales; but, he complained to Bates, he did not know a single person in Neath who studied any one branch of natural history: 'I am all alone in my glory in this respect.'[38] He wanted to specialise, and achieved his first mention in a scientific journal, in the *Zoologist* of April 1847. 'Capture of *Trichius fasciatus* near Neath – I took a single specimen of this beautiful insect on a blossom of *Carduus heterophyllus* near the falls at the top of the Neath Vale. Alfred R. Wallace, Neath.' This was the fruit of Bates's training, even if the editor's comment was a little dismissive: 'The other insects in my correspondent's list are scarcely worth publishing.'[39]

The beetle was a memorable, and symbolic, capture. In June 1846, Alfred and John had walked up the valley from their Neath lodgings, then followed the western branch to the Rocking Stone, where he discovered

Trichius fasciatus – the only time, Wallace commented, that he ever captured it. They went as far as the Gladys and Einon Gam falls, retraced their route, and walked on to Ystrad-fellte for the night: a leisurely twenty miles or so. Next morning, they climbed up the Beacons, and ate their picnic by a spring on the southern slope, the source of the river Taff; then back again to Ystrad-fellte – but only to eat, not sleep. They headed instead for Porth-yr-Ogof, a limestone cavern where the river Mellte runs underground. According to Wallace, 'We had both of us at this time determined, if possible, to go abroad into more or less wild countries, and we wanted for once to try sleeping out-of-doors, with no shelter or bed but what nature provided.'[40] They had a little food, and they lit a fire, just as they had done in the woods at Usk in early childhood. For a while, they could enjoy the romantic aspects: the flickering flame on the cavern roof, the glimmer of the stars through the trees outside, the gentle murmur of the water. These pleasures soon palled. Wallace confessed that, while in health, he had never passed a more uncomfortable night. But there was a common understanding between the brothers. England and Wales were crowded, competitive: even in Neath, with a population of under six thousand, 'Wallace and Wallace' formed only one entry on a list of eight surveyors. The two men had proven skills, energy, and a sense of adventure. As they lay on the turf their imaginations moved beyond the mountains and valleys to the Bristol Channel, and on to the opportunities offered by Australia, New Zealand, North and South America. Three years later, Alfred would be a thousand miles up the Amazon, and John in the California goldfields.

Crucially, in Bates Wallace had found a fellow enthusiast, someone with whom to exchange monthly lists of captures, to share ideas and reactions to reading. In 1845, Wallace read *Vestiges of the Natural History of Creation*, the popular book that, for all its wild speculations, alerted him to a new perspective on the formulation of species. Bates was more critical; but, Wallace responded,

> I do not consider it as a hasty generalisation, but rather as an ingenious speculation strongly supported by some striking facts and analogies but which remains to be proved by more facts & the additional light which future researches may throw up on the subject – It at all events furnishes a subject for every observer of nature to turn his attention to; every fact he observes must make either for or against it, and it thus

furnishes both an incitement to the collection of facts & an object to which to apply them when collected –

I would observe that many eminent writers give great support to their theory of the progressive development of species in animals & plants.[41]

The anonymous author of *Vestiges*, Robert Chambers, was just the man to strike a resonant chord with Wallace. His work was popular, unstuffy, and uncompromising, with one grand idea, transmutation, at its centre, even if he did not identify the mechanism: 'It being admitted that the system of the Universe is one under the dominion of natural law, it follows that the introduction of species must have been brought about in the manner of law also.'[42] As propounded by *Vestiges*, species changed, developed, progressed. Also, the author was not afraid to discuss man as a species, something that appealed strongly to Wallace. Read Lawrence's *Lectures on Man*, he advised Bates. William Lawrence's lectures, now published 'in a cheap form' – that is, in an unauthorised edition – argued, as did James Prichard, that 'the varieties of the Human race have not proceeded from any external cause but have been produced by the development of certain distinctive peculiarities in some individuals which have become propagated through an entire race'.[43] Wallace, focused on man, concluded that the Negro, the Red Indian and the European were distinct species of the genus *Homo*. Most professional scientists ignored the huge sales and interest, and preferred to jump on the book's numerous errors; its championing of evolution, following Jean Baptiste Lamarck and Erasmus Darwin, was confidently dismissed. The idea of creation, or of a succession of creations, still held.

The exchanges continued: Bates was reading Lyell, perhaps on Wallace's recommendation. Wallace was re-reading Darwin's *Journal*. He could have ordered the revised 1845 edition for the Neath Philosophical & Literary Society. In this edition he might have remarked on Darwin's more expansive comments on the Fuegians; and on the hints about the 'little world within itself' of the Galapagos Islands, where, 'but in space and time, we seem to be brought somewhat near to that great fact – that mystery of mysteries – the first appearance of new beings on this earth'.[44] Of the thirteen species of the 'most singular group of finches', all peculiar to the archipelago, Darwin commented, 'Seeing this gradation and diversity of structure in one small, intimately related group of birds, one might really fancy that, from an original paucity of birds in this archipelago, one species had been taken and modified for different ends.'[45] Such hints were not lost on Wallace, who stored away the Galapagos comment for future reference. By April 1846, Wallace was keeping a natural history journal – 'a sort of day book in which I insert all my captures in every branch of Natural Hist. with the day of the month, locality etc and any remarks I have to make on specific characters, habits, etc'.[46] He accepted Bates's invitation to exchange monthly lists.

Wallace was gearing himself up for his new career. Bates came and stayed with him in Wales, where they hatched their idea of a joint expedition – 'rather a wild scheme'. Bates's apprenticeship had come to an end, and he was working as a clerk for Allsopp's, the brewers, at Burton-on-Trent. In the autumn of 1847 Wallace travelled to London to meet his sister, back from Georgia, and, armed with a letter of introduction from Bates, he spent part of the last week of September looking at the collections in the British Museum. He had bought a small collection of American insects, and spent five hours going through the coleoptera in an attempt to identify and name them. Then he went with French-speaking Fanny to Paris, his first trip abroad. He loved the atmosphere, he reported enthusiastically to Bates, the style, the elegance – and the free access to museums and galleries, libraries, public buildings and churches – 'a great contrast to our own capital where there is little to be seen without favour or payment'. He was impressed, too, by the natural history collections, and spent two whole days at the Jardin des Plantes. Inspired by what he had seen there, he returned to the great issue: 'I begin to feel rather dissatisfied with a mere local collection – little is to be learnt by it. I shd. like to take some one family, to study thoroughly – principally with a view to the theory of the origin of species,' he added, with engaging frankness. 'By that means I am strongly of opinion that some definite results might be arrived at. One family of moderate extent would be quite sufficient – can you assist me in choosing one that it will not be difficult to obtain the greater number of the known species?'[47]

Those two weeks in London and Paris greatly strengthened Wallace's determination to become a professional collector, or, rather, to use the profession of collecting in order to pursue his growing preoccupation with species and their origin. Three years before, he had been a raw amateur. Now he had been cited in the *Zoologist*, and, when the British Association came to Swansea in 1848, Lewis Dillwyn added a generous note to his 'Materials for a Fauna and Flora of Swansea': 'I have been favoured by Mr Alfred Wallace with the following list of Coleoptera which he has added to the catalogue I printed in 1829, and which are placed in the Museum at Neath.' Wallace proudly took Fanny to a conversazione of the Swansea Literary and Scientific Society, held to coincide with the British Association meeting.

Wallace's purchase of American Coleoptera had been made with a view to preparing himself for the next stage. From the Bloomsbury Street natural history agent and dealer, Samuel Stevens, he learnt about the opportunities and the economics of the specimen trade. Edward Doubleday, at the British Museum, showed him the insect collection – a hasty glance at the butterflies intrigued but slightly fazed Wallace: 'The differences between genera appear so slight & arbitrary while the actual number of sp. is so great as to render them quite bewildering.'[48] But beetles had been equally bewildering until he met Bates.

Slowly that winter, as Wallace continued his science lectures – and added another on his week in Paris – his plans began to take shape. His family responsibilities were eased, now that Fanny was back, and living in Neath with their mother, and Herbert. She was, too, forming a promisingly close relationship with Thomas Sims, elder son of the family with whom he had lodged in Neath. John, as restless and enterprising as his brother, was prepared to have one last attempt at a British career, by trying his hand at dairy farming. Wallace and Bates were poised to travel; but to which country? Wallace had £100 saved from his railway surveying fees, enough to pay for passage and equipment, and still leave a little to live on until he could earn some income from collecting. Bates, with a secure family business behind him, had different family pressures to contend with: his father clearly thought the scheme ridiculous, but agreed to advance him the money. Even so, their budget was tight. Sir William Hooker calculated that the total annual cost to Kew of supporting an overseas plant hunter in the field was £600, including a salary of £100. That was the most straightforward method. More independent was the approach of Richard Spruce. When he went to the Amazon in 1849, he, like Wallace and Bates, was unsalaried, but unlike them he had secured commitments from eleven initial subscribers who agreed in advance to pay for sets of botanical specimens; while George Bentham undertook the task of identifying and sorting the consignments, distributing them to museums and private collectors, obtaining payment, and then sending the proceeds off to Spruce in the form of a letter of credit via Messrs Singlehurst, the shipping agents at Liverpool. But Spruce, after a successful expedition to the Pyrenees, was in a different league from Wallace and Bates: he was a proven specialist and collector, with a close network of botanical contacts. The two young men did not yet have the benefit of official or even semi-official support systems. They would be totally dependent on results, and on the market.

A book, naturally, clinched the issue of where to go. William Edwards, an American, published *A Voyage up the Amazon* in 1847. Edwards was engagingly enthusiastic about the freshness and beauty of the Amazon – 'where the mightiest of rivers rolls majestically through primeval forests of boundless extent, concealing, yet bringing forth the most beautiful and varied forms of animal and vegetable existence'.[49] Although Edwards, with only a touch of irony, invoked the full range of traveller's tales – including Amazonian women, cannibal Indians and epicurean anacondas, as well as roguish descriptions of mermaids with long floating hair, darting through the surf like brown sea-nymphs – he was a serious entomologist, and he painted an attractive picture: the people were friendly, the living was cheap, the climate agreeable. According to Bates, the Amazon was Wallace's suggestion. They checked with Doubleday: northern Brazil had wonderful insects, and was relatively uncollected. They re-read the descriptions of Humboldt and Darwin, settled on Pará (modern Belém), at the mouth of the Amazon, as their first destination, and moved to London to make final preparations. There they re-scrutinised the collections of American insects at the British Museum. They met Edwards, who gave them letters of introduction to American traders at Pará. They cross-questioned Thomas Horsfield, an experienced tropical traveller, at the British East India Company's museum. They trekked out to Kew to study tropical vegetation, and secured an interview with Sir William Hooker, who gave them an idea of what would be acceptable for the collection there, and promised to send them a copy of the printed instructions Kew issued to collectors. They wrote courteously, deferentially, to jog his memory, and to obtain something in writing:

We think an official letter from you, referring to what you wish us to obtain for the Kew Museum, and accompanying the printed instructions you were so kind as to offer to send us, would be of great service to us. It would serve to shew that we were the persons we should represent ourselves to be, and might facilitate our progress into the interior.[50]

Sir William obliged, and the innocents duly thanked him – the letter helped them obtain their passports. Wallace had himself vaccinated, and bought spare spectacles. Then they set off north, via Bates's home at Leicester. They spent a week practising shooting and skinning birds, and made a detour to Chatsworth, which gave them another chance to inspect more palm trees and orchids in the hothouses. Wallace was twenty-five, Bates twenty-three, when they left Liverpool on 26 April 1848, the only two paying passengers aboard the sailing barge *Mischief*.

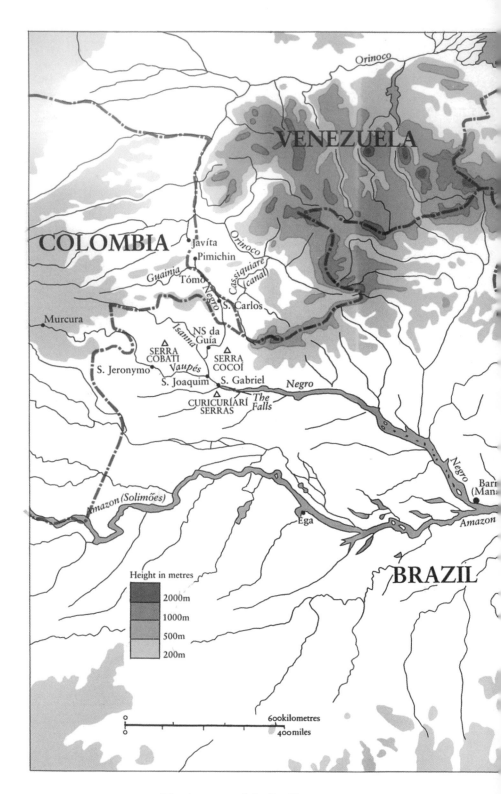

The Amazon and the Rio Negro

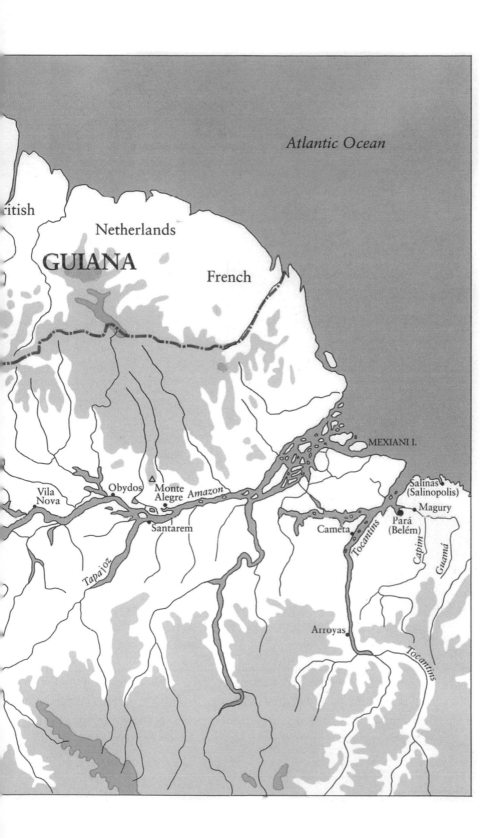

Atlantic Ocean

ritish

Netherlands

GUIANA

French

MEXIANI I.

Vila
Nova

Obydos

Monte
Alegre *Amazon*

Santarem

Tapajóz

Salinas
(Salinopolis)

Magury

Pará
(Belém)

Cameta

Tocantins

Capim

Guamá

Arroyas

Tocantins

Umbrella Bird.

3 Apprenticeship on the Amazon

After an unpleasant passage through the Bay of Biscay, during which Wallace stayed put in his berth, the *Mischief* made good time to reach the Brazilian coast at Salinas on 26 May 1848, thirty days out from Liverpool. Once a pilot had been taken on board, the ship glided up river, and finally anchored two days later: 'and when the sun rose in a cloudless sky, the city of Pará, surrounded by the dense forest, and overtopped by palms and plantains, greeted our sight, appearing doubly beautiful from the presence of those luxuriant tropical productions in a state of nature, which we had so often admired,' Wallace commented with some exaggeration, 'in the conservatories of Kew and Chatsworth'.[1]

The two young naturalists, poised to enter a new world and a new profession, borrowed the captain's telescope; to the east, the country seemed unremarkable, slightly undulating, with bare sand hills and scattered trees; but to the west they could see 'a long line of forest, rising apparently out of the water; a densely packed mass of tall trees, broken into groups, and finally into single trees, as it dwindled away in the distance'. This was the frontier of the great primeval forest, 'which contains so many wonders in its recesses, and clothes the whole surface of the country for two thousand miles from this point to the foot of the Andes'.[2] Here Bates would pass 'eleven of the best years' of his life; Wallace was to spend just over four years, with more mixed reactions.

They saw ships, large and small, canoes moving along the shore, vultures in the sky, white buildings with red-tiled roofs, towers and cupolas of churches and convents sharply defined against the clear blue sky – and then they heard the ringing of bells and firing of rockets which greeted a Roman Catholic festival day. Even within the city – with a population of fifteen thousand, it was the largest city on the Amazon – there was vegetation everywhere, sprouting from ledges and mouldings, growing on the tops of walls and from the window openings of the churches, while the squares and public areas were more like village greens than urban spaces – and everywhere, 'above and below and behind the city', the unbroken forest.[3]

On landing, they went to call on Mr Miller, the *Mischief*'s consignee and also the British Vice-Consul, who invited them to stay until they could find their own accommodation. They soon met the few English and American residents, all traders, and began to familiarise themselves with the city and the immediate surroundings.

After traversing the few streets of tall, gloomy, convent-looking buildings near the port, inhabited chiefly by merchants and shop-keepers; along which idle soldiers, dressed in shabby uniforms, carrying their muskets carelessly over their arms, priests, Negresses with red water-jars on their heads, sad-looking Indian women carrying their naked children astride on their hips, and other samples of the motley life of the place, were seen; we passed down a long narrow street leading to the suburbs. Beyond this, our road lay across a grassy common into a picturesque lane leading to the virgin forest. The long street was inhabited by the poorer class of the population. The houses were of one storey only, and had an irregular and mean appearance. The windows were without glass, having, instead, projecting lattice casements. The street was unpaved, and inches deep in loose sand. Groups of people were cooling themselves outside their doors – people of all shades in colour of skin, European, Negro and Indian, but chiefly an uncertain mixture of the three. Amongst them were several handsome women, dressed in a slovenly manner, barefoot or shod in loose slippers; but wearing richly decorated ear-rings, and around their necks strings of very large gold beads. They had dark expressive eyes, and remarkably rich heads of hair. It was a mere fancy, but I thought the mingled squalor, luxuriance and beauty of these women were pointedly in harmony with the rest of the scene; so striking, in the view, was the mixture of natural riches and human poverty.[4]

It is characteristic for Bates and Wallace to walk immediately away from the 'convent-looking buildings', from the government and commercial areas, towards the virgin forest; and to embrace the human and natural beauty and riches that met them, amidst the dilapidated houses and weed-grown gardens, with hogs and goats and ill-fed poultry wandering in and out through the broken wooden palings. It is more characteristic of Bates to write about the beauty of the women in the city; Wallace tended to be less expansive in such descriptions, except in a strictly anthropological context: 'Every shade of colour is seen here in the people,' he commented, 'from white to yellow, brown and black – Negroes, Indians, Brazilians, and Europeans, with every intermediate mixture.'[5] But each was drawn, as if by a magnet, to the surrounding forest. Amidst all, 'and compensating every defect, rose the overpowering beauty of the vegetation'.[6]

Initially, both Bates and Wallace seem to be writing relatively standard descriptions of their first impressions: 'The massive dark crowns of shady mangoes were seen everywhere amongst the dwellings, amidst fragrant blossoming orange, lemon, and many other tropical fruit trees; some in flower, others in fruit, at varying stages of ripeness.' Yet, as they expand, you realise that even in their notes on Pará each is writing with a professional naturalist's eye:

Here and there, shooting above the more dome-like and sombre trees, were the smooth columnar stems of palms, bearing aloft their magnificent crops of finely cut fronds. Amongst the latter the slim assai-palm was especially noticeable, growing in groups of four and five; its smooth, gently curving stem, twenty to thirty feet high, terminating in a head of feathery foliage, inexpressibly light and elegant in outline. On the boughs of the taller and more ordinary-looking trees sat tufts of curiously leaved parasites. Slender woody lianas hung in festoons from the branches, or were suspended in the form of cords and ribbons; whilst luxuriant creeping plants overran alike tree-trunks, roofs and walls, or toppled over palings in copious profusion of foliage. The superb banana (*Musa paradisiaca*), of which I had always read as forming one of the charms of tropical vegetation, here grew with great luxuriance: its glossy velvety-green leaves, twelve feet in length, curving over the roofs of verandas in the rear of every house. The shape of the leaves, the varying shades of green which they present when lightly moved by the wind, and especially the contrast they afford in colour and form to the more sombre hues and more rounded outline of the other trees, are quite sufficient to account for the charm of this glorious tree. Strange forms of vegetation drew our attention at almost every step.

The luxuriance, the diversity, the anticipated, the unexpected, hit their senses – overwhelmingly attractive to newcomers, as Bates commented, whose last and quite recent country ramble 'was over the bleak moors of Derbyshire on a sleety morning in April'. And when the brief twilight began, there came the whirring of cicadas, the shrill stridulation of a vast variety of field crickets and grasshoppers, the plaintive hooting of tree frogs: 'the audible expression of the teeming profusion of Nature', to be joined, as night came on, by the croaking and drumming of many species of frogs and toads – the 'uproar of life'.[7] This was what they had come to find: the amazing variety of species assaulting their eyes and ears, thrusting towards them as they walked towards the forest; and the climate was beautiful, 75° Fahrenheit before sunrise, 85 to 87 in the afternoon: hot, but by no means oppressive. 'I enjoy it as much as the finest summer weather in England,' Wallace reported to Silk.[8]

The first flush of ecstasy was followed by a slight sense of disappointment, or at least adjustment. Pará itself was not the rain-forest; the birds were less spectacular than either had imagined, the butterflies less numerous. The lamplighter knocked on the door to show them a boa-constrictor he had met making its way down the street, but the only vertebrates in large numbers were lizards, which they found difficult to catch. They set the local boys to go after them with bows and arrows. At least there were plenty of ants, intensely interesting to Bates in particular.

They could not initially find a suitable house, so Miller lent them his *rocinha*, his country house, half a mile from the city. They bought a few essentials, such as a table and chairs and hammocks, hired an old cook, Isidoro, and got down to work, learning Portuguese when they were not 'investigating the natural productions of the country'. After a fortnight, they heard of a *rocinha* available to rent a mile and a half from the city, at Nazaré, and moved in for a stay of several months. (The Portuguese merchants had not fully recovered confidence after a series of revolutions, and many had abandoned their country houses for the greater security of the city.) The house had four good-sized rooms, with a cool veranda all round it under a projecting tiled roof, excellent for sitting and working. On one side lay the small village square, with the shrine of Our Lady of Nazaré, a centre of devotion, opposite their gate; on the other three sides lay the forest, and behind the house ran the main forest road, with paths leading off it into the woods, badly overgrown but quite passable to determined collectors. Not far away was the house where the German naturalists Johann Baptist von Spix and Karl Friedrich von Martius had lived in 1819: to be following the trail of such famous predecessors boosted their self-esteem.[9] They would rise soon after dawn, for coffee, and then spend two hours on ornithology, under a cloudless sky, and in a pleasant temperature.

All nature was fresh, new leaf and flower-buds expanding rapidly. Some mornings a single tree would appear in flower amidst what was the preceding evening a uniform green mass of forest – a dome of blossom suddenly created as if by magic. The birds were all active . . .

Ornithology, of course, meant not primarily observation, but capture. Then they had breakfast, after Isidoro had come back from Pará with fresh provisions for the day, followed by entomology, from ten until two or three in the afternoon, 'the best time for insects in the forest being a little before the greatest heat of the day'. The temperature rose, and when Wallace and Bates returned tired from their 'ramble', they would see their neighbours asleep in hammocks, or resting in the shade. The clouds would build up, the wind would rise, and a late-afternoon rainstorm would deluge down. Then life would revive, and the 'ringing uproar' from bush and tree would resume: 'The following morning the sun again rises in a cloudless sky, and so the cycle is completed; spring, summer, and autumn, as it were, in one tropical day.'[10] They dined at four, took tea at seven, and spent their evenings preserving their collections, and making notes. Occasionally they might walk to Pará, to watch the night life of the city, or spend a few hours with the European or American residents. Their house proved an ideal location. Humming-birds 'vibrated their gilded plumes' at the blossoms on the neighbouring trees. The black-eyed Indian girls came into their garden to gather flowers for their hair. There were three labourers at the house, employed to tend the coffee and fruit trees in the garden. One of them, Vincente, had a high reputation as an insect- and reptile-catcher. He soon presented Bates with a mygale, a huge bird-eating spider half a foot across, and proved an excellent ally; the taciturn Isidoro was more knowledgeable about the names and properties of plants and trees than any man in Pará, and Vincente was a 'glorious fellow to get wasps' nests and to dig out the holes of monstrous spiders'.[11] Wallace was highly impressed by Isidoro's knowledge of the trees, of their uses and properties.

Their collections grew. Bates specialised in insects, especially butterflies, spiders and beetles. Wallace was also looking for plants and trees – Isidoro would instruct his foreign employers by addressing a series of parenthetical remarks on the trees they passed, appearing to speak 'rather to them than to us'.[12] Wallace wanted a specimen of the caripe tree, whose bark was used in pottery manufacture, and Isidoro led them deep into the forest, axe on shoulder. The caripe they eventually found was young, without fruit flowers, so it was spared; but they came upon all kinds of magnificent specimens of palms, especially the paxiuba. There were twenty-three specimens of palms around Pará which had distinct native names, Wallace reported later to Hooker.[13] Wallace, especially, would try his hand at anything. The veranda began to fill up: one morning, they discovered a ten-foot boa outside, tied to a good-sized stick. They had a box fitted with bars, and the boa was installed with some difficulty: its breathing sounded like 'high-pressure steam escaping from a Great Western locomotive'.[14] Antonio, an Indian boy who had joined their hunting parties, brought them a young sloth, which slept peacefully on the back of a chair for three days, but refused food, and died of hunger: another skinning job for Wallace.

In search of new locations they made two visits to the rice and timber mills at Magury. Leavens, the Canadian manager, had invited them, after receiving their letter of introduction from Edwards. The first time they

Wallace's drawing of trees near Pará

walked the twelve miles, a journey that took them six hours because of all the natural diversions on the way, including many plants, and several butterflies they had not seen before – the *Haetera esmeralda,* and gigantic blue morphos that evaded capture. This first meeting led to a longer stay, during which Wallace made his first 'acquaintance' with monkeys. One was finally shot: 'The poor little animal was not quite dead, and its cries, its innocent-looking countenance, and delicate little hands were quite childlike.' Wallace's feelings were laced with pragmatism: 'Having often heard how good monkey was, I took it home, and had it cut up and fried for breakfast' – it tasted a bit like rabbit.[15] He also tried agouti, a kind of guinea-pig – 'rather dry and tasteless'. There were many different varieties of birds, too, to supplement their collection. Leavens was planning a major expedition up the Tocantins river, to search for a supply of cedar, *Cedrela odorata,* much prized for cabinet-making and canoe-building. He invited Wallace and Bates to join him, and, while he was making the arrangements, they went back to Pará to pack up their first consignment for England: 553 species of Lepidoptera – including 400 butterflies – 450 beetles, and 400 of other orders, 1,300 different species in all, with a total of 3,635 specimens, and twelve chests of plants. The bulk of this was sent to their agent, Stevens; but there was also a box of dried specimens, principally palms, for Sir William Hooker at Kew, which Wallace hoped would be worth £10 together with the cost of the freight. Wallace gave Hooker details of his forest trip with Isidoro, but took care to make it clear that, as they were attending almost entirely to insects, and intended to move on to birds, it was quite impossible 'to find time to make any thing of a general collection of Plants'. Wallace, no trained botanist, was not quite sure of his ground with Hooker. He certainly did not wish to put himself under any obligation, though it sounds as if they might have had the £10 up front. 'I send the few dried plants (a few hundred specimens) principally ferns – you can perhaps dispose of them and allow what you consider them to be worth.'[16] Hooker would later be a little dismissive about Wallace's book on palms.

The trip to the Tocantins took Wallace and Bates away from Pará for the first time, and was crucial in providing them with experience in long-distance Amazon travel. Leavens had hired a two-masted vigilinga, equipped with two arched wickerwork awnings thatched with palm, one for the three Europeans, one for the provisions and baggage: the vessel was 27 foot long by 8 foot in the beam, and fitted to withstand heavy seas –

'although our voyage was only a river trip, there were vast sea-like expanses of water to travel'. The mouth of the Tocantins lies some eighty miles south-west of Pará, and the river itself has a course of 1,600 miles. They took guns, boxes to store their collections, and three months' stock of provisions, and they had a crew of four, comprising Isidoro as cook, Antonio, the pilot Domingo and Alexandro, an Indian employed by Leavens, 'an expert sailor and indefatigable hunter', according to Bates: 'To his fidelity we were indebted for being enabled to carry out any of the objects of our voyage'; he was 'a quiet, sensible, manly young fellow'.[17] Another Indian 'deserted' just as they were about to leave – this would become a recurring problem. Even for this limited internal journey, they required a whole series of passports and clearances, which, luckily, Leavens managed.

After a voyage of only one day, they began to find species new to them: two butterflies they had never seen at Pará, a long, slender brown snake like the stem of a climbing plant, and a sloth, which ended up as dinner. They sailed and paddled upstream to the town of Cametá, where Domingo, the pilot, went missing. 'If we had had more experience of the Indian character,' Wallace commented, 'we should have waited patiently till the following morning, when we should, no doubt, have found him.'[18] Man-management on the Amazon was a subtle and essential skill. They would have learned little that was useful from Edwards's book: when one of Edwards's crew showed reluctance to take up a paddle he was thrown overboard; Edwards then expressed surprise when the man vanished during the night.

Up river, they stayed at various houses and plantations where Leavens had acquaintances or introductions. Leavens prospected for cedar and bought rubber. Wallace and Bates collected furiously, amusing themselves 'very well, shooting and entomologising'. Bates saw for the first time the sky-blue chatterer, on the topmost bough of a very lofty tree, safely out of range. Wallace was particularly successful with birds – river birds, and birds in the plantations and forests: waxwings, pigeons, toucans, chatterers, a brown jacamar, a purple-headed parrot. When they spent the night in a village, they would attract an interested audience as they pinned out insects or skinned birds.

The constantly repeated remark, on seeing a bird skinned, was, 'Oh, the patience of the whites!' Then one would whisper to another, 'Does he take all the meat out?' 'Well, I never!' 'Look, he makes eyes of cotton!' And then would come a little conversation as to what they could possibly be wanted for. 'Para mostrar' (to show) was the general solution; but they seemed to think it rather unsatisfactory, and that the English could hardly be such fools as to want to see a few parrot and pigeon skins.

The butterflies seemed far less problematic to the spectators: these would provide new patterns for printed calicoes, while the insects must be for medicine.[19]

They made slow progress, as they had difficulty in keeping a crew together. They would cajole, or borrow, a couple of men, only to find them slipping off at the next village. As Bates commented, 'The people of these parts seemed to be above working for wages. They are naturally indolent, and besides, have all some little business or plantation of their own, which gives them a livelihood with independence.'[20] They also had a natural reluctance to commit themselves to a set of foreigners, suspected of being strange in their habits. Nevertheless, Wallace and Bates reached as far as Aroyas (Bates has 'Arroyos'), 'the last abode of civilised people', and pushed on in a smaller open canoe to see the Guaribas rapids – the Indian crew did the pushing, poling them yard by yard against terrific currents. The main fall was about a quarter of a mile wide, 'bounded by rocks, with a deep and very powerful stream rushing down in an unbroken sweep of dark green waters, and producing eddies and whirlpools below more dangerous to canoes than the Fall itself'.[21] They climbed an elevation to gain a better view of the cataract, and were rewarded by the sight of range after range of wooded hills, 'scores of miles of beautiful wilderness'. In the midst of such solitude, the roar of the cataract 'seemed fitting music', and they were disappointed that they could not explore further.[22] They retraced their route, and their men shouted and sang in the most wild and excited manner as they shot down the smaller rapids.

Wallace was distinctly accident-prone on this trip. Chasing some insects in the forest, he was attacked by a swarm of small but well-armed wasps, and was stung in about fifty places. According to Richard Spruce, he dropped his spectacles in battling with the wasps, 'and never more ventured to the place to seek them'.[23] These were the everyday hazards of the collector: Spruce records being set on similarly by ants, and having to go back to the site to retrieve his collector's vasculum, and a shoe he had left behind in his haste to escape. On another occasion, Wallace was out bird-hunting with Alexandro in a small montaria on a lake crowded with alligators. Alexandro fired at one, which turned over, and lay floating with one leg sticking up. Wallace grabbed at the claw, only to find the alligator very much alive. It dived under the canoe, and all but capsized them.[24] On their return down river, his shooting career almost came to an abrupt conclusion. His gun was lying, fully loaded, in the canoe, with Wallace standing on the landing-place steps. He reached out to take the gun by the muzzle: the hammer, jammed in the boards of the canoe, fired, and the charge clipped his hand near the wrist, passed under his arm, and luckily missed a number of people standing behind him. Wallace bound up his hand with a cotton bandage and set off so as not to miss the tide.[25]

Back in Pará on 30 September after their five-week trip, the naturalists' first task was to prepare their collections for shipment. It took them three weeks, and the combined collections, added to the previous consignment, were sufficiently impressive for Stevens to place an advertisement in the *Annals and Magazine of Natural History*:

SAMUEL STEVENS, NATURAL HISTORY AGENT, NO. 24 BLOOMSBURY STREET, BEDFORD SQUARE, begs to announce that he has recently received from South America *Two* beautiful Consignments of INSECTS of all orders in very fine Condition, collected in the province of Pará, containing numbers of very rare and some new species . . . for Sale by Private Contract.[26]

Stevens also placed extracts of Wallace's letters in the *Annals*, describing him and Bates as 'two enterprising and deserving young men'. Bates's letters would appear later in the *Zoologist*. Stevens's action established a practice that Wallace adopted for the rest of his collecting career, and in his letters to Stevens he would often identify a particular section as suitable for publication.

During the months that followed, Wallace and Bates decided to separate, and to work independently. Their published travels are not at all clear about the reasons for this decision, taken after only five months or so of collaboration. Each of them was distinctly reserved, and courteous by nature; there is no evidence of active disagreement, yet there is a slight evasiveness in their accounts. Wallace's *Travels*, published first, are particularly unclear about the split. One moment he and Bates are writing joint despatches to Stevens, the next Wallace is embarking on a series of short independent trips from Pará – and then the 'we' of Wallace and Bates becomes the 'we' of Alfred and his younger brother, Herbert Edward. Bates's account marks the separation, but gives no reason. Uncertainty and tension were probably rooted, initially, in money difficulties. They had been in Brazil for nine months, and still had no clear idea as to how much cash their collections were fetching, and whether there was any profit. Without additional finance, they could not risk a long trip into the interior. Their experience on the Tocantins had taught them the difficulties of sticking to a strict timetable, and of finding, let alone retaining, a crew. Besides, the nineteenth-century naturalist needed to carry masses of equipment; and the bigger the party, the more difficulty there was in securing an appropriate boat and crew. Temperamentally, too, the differences between the two men grew more significant in the Amazon than they had appeared in Leicester, or Neath. Bates was comparatively at ease in company, more tolerant, readier to absorb the atmosphere and accumulate knowledge gradually; Wallace more driven, impatient, competitive. Meanwhile, his wounded hand became inflamed, and he had to spend a fortnight with his arm in a sling unable to do anything, 'not even pin an insect'. The enforced leisure at least meant that he could spend more time observing the habits of the small birds round the house. There was time, too, for speculation:

> In all works on Natural History, we constantly find details of the marvellous adaptation of animals to their food, their habits, and the localities in which they are found. But naturalists are now beginning to look beyond this, and to see that there must be some other principle regulating the infinitely varied forms of animal life.[27]

As soon as his hand had healed, Wallace made a four-day voyage with an orchid-collector, Yates, to Mexiana, a flat island in the mouth of the Amazon used as a cattle ranch, in search of water-birds. He shot and skinned a great many birds – seventy different species in ten days – and took part in the annual alligator hunt. Then he moved into a small house at Nazaré, close to where he and Bates had first lived, and went on collecting. Bates, although he was present in Pará for some of this time, did not join him: 'I get on very well with the Indians,' Bates commented, 'being far more at home and friendly with them than with the Brazilian and European residents.' Wallace was lucky to recruit Luiz, a Congolese who had originally worked for the Austrian naturalist Dr Natterer in the 1830s, and who proved an excellent hunter. He also made a trip up the Guama river, buying a small canoe, and fitting it up for a small-scale collecting expedition: he was preparing now for greater things, and had written to suggest that his younger brother Herbert might join him. Meanwhile, he explored the west branch of the river, the Capim, as he had a letter of introduction to an estate-owner. Senhor Calistro was extremely hospitable, though Wallace was clearly shocked to discover that such a humane, good-humoured man owned some fifty slaves.

> Can it be right to keep a number of our fellow creatures in a state of adult infancy, – of unthinking childhood? It is the responsibility and self-dependence of manhood that calls forth the highest powers and energies of our race. It is the struggle for existence, the 'battle of life', which exercises the moral faculties and calls forth the latent sparks of genius. The hope of gain, the love of power, the desire of fame and approbation, excite to noble deeds, and call into action all those faculties which are the distinctive attributes of man.[28]

But such views, Wallace comments, are 'too refined for a Brazilian slave-holder'; they are the views of a young man driven, if not by the love of power, at least partly by the love of gain and a desire for fame.

Alfred had been the catalyst drawing John, Fanny, Herbert and his mother to Neath, but the family was beginning to disperse once more. Fanny was married now to Thomas Sims, and the couple moved to Weston-super-Mare to set up a photographic business. Herbert was finding life frustrating. He had tried his hand at teaching French as a possible new direction, without much success. 'Taking every circumstance into consideration,' he wrote to his sister, 'upon receiving Alfred's letters we thought it was best that I should join him in Pará ...' Ironically, just as he was preparing to leave Neath, people started signing up for lessons. 'But I hope this will be a better speculation for me,' he went on, in a vein that becomes increasingly emotional. His outfit was so expensive that he could not afford a visit to say his goodbyes in person.

We are doomed to be a scatter'd family, and if it must be so, if circumstance has so ordered it let us meet it bravely, and with honest hearts go forth, resigned and cheerful under the Dispensations of Providence; Farewell my dear Fanny, perhaps we may in some future time yet meet again . . . Fare thee well and if for ever, now for ever, fare thee well.[29]

So Herbert left the Neath Abbey ironworks, and caught a ship at Swansea for Liverpool; while John, despairing of making a living as a farmer, headed for San Francisco and the California goldfields. Herbert sailed for Pará on 7 June 1849. He found himself in the company of Richard Spruce, the botanist, bound for the Amazon with his own assistant, Robert King.

Herbert joined his brother, and was taken into the forest for his initiation as a collector. To Alfred's pleasure, he soon shot one of the elusive imperial parrots, *Conurus carolineae*. They had to wait a while for a suitable boat to take them up river to Santarem, since the canoe on which Wallace had already laid out £10 proved unsuitable for a five-hundred-mile voyage. Eventually they set off at the beginning of August. They slung their hammocks in the covered area, sharing it with a bundle of hides and a powerful smell of salt fish, and settled down to while away long hours waiting for the tide, or warping laboriously along the shore when the wind failed, happily sustained by a pile of books. It was twelve days before they left the labyrinth of channels and moved finally out on to the broad stream of the Amazon itself:

Our imagination wandered to its sources in the distant Andes, to the Peruvian Incas of old, to the silver mountains of Potosí, and the gold-seeking Spaniards and wild Indians who now inhabit the country about its thousand sources. What a grand idea it was to think that we now saw the accumulated waters of a course of three thousand miles; that all the streams that for a length of twelve hundred miles drained from the snow-clad Andes were here congregated in the wide extent of ochre-coloured water spread out before us! Venezuela, Columbia, Ecuador, Peru, Bolivia, and Brazil – six mighty states, spread over a country far larger than Europe – had each contributed to form the flood which bore us so peacefully on its bosom.[30]

Alfred shared his love of reading with his younger brother. Their minds had always been full of stories, of history and travel: Humboldt's *Narrative*, Prescott's *The Conquest of Peru*. Now they luxuriated in the reality, moving slowly up river towards the heart of the continent. They had taken enough provisions for the whole voyage, but supplemented them by catching fish, or by buying fruit when they went ashore. There was plenty to see: flocks of parrots, and great red and yellow macaws, flying across the pale olive, muddy water morning and evening; herons and rails in the marshy places on the banks; gulls and terns swooping over the sandbanks; divers and darters, porpoises 'constantly blowing in every direction', and the occasional alligator swimming slowly across the stream.

After a month, they arrived at Santarem, situated at the mouth of the clear blue waters (olive green, according to Bates) of the Tapajóz, four hundred miles from the sea. The town, slightly elevated, had a clean, cheerful appearance: whitewashed, red-tiled houses, above a fine sandy beach, with a fresh breeze blowing up river. In fact, the wind was sometimes so strong that it could be difficult to make one's way against it. The population was about 2,500: 'Not quite a modern Babalon [*sic*],' Herbert reported to Fanny, 'about the size of Neath, although the grass growing in the streets might remind you of some deserted city of the ancients.'[31] (Three years later, the American naval officer Herndon reported that Santarem boasted a billiard table.) In Santarem, he teased her, he had made a 'Zoological discovery': at Neath there was a 'Blue Pig' on an inn sign, considered an eccentric whim of the sign-painter: 'Let the people of Neath know that I have seen in Brazil, a living breathing, live Blue Pig.' Wallace had letters of introduction to Captain Hislop, a 'sturdy, rosy Scotsman', who had been trading on the Amazon for forty-five years. He kept files and files of old newspapers, though apart from these he claimed to read only two books: Constantin Volney's *Ruins of Empires*, and the Bible. After a few glasses of port, he liked to talk about Moses, 'a great general, and a great lawgiver, but a great impostor'.[32] Hislop organised a house for them – mud walls and floors, with a high, tiled roof, 'all very dusty and ruinous' – but it would do for a while, and they moved in, accepting the captain's invitation to take dinner with him, in his house overlooking the river. In the evening, the local-government officials and the principal traders would gather in front of Hislop's place, to smoke and take snuff and talk politics. Wallace thought poorly of the prevailing mores: 'There are here, as in Pará, many

Richard Spruce, View of Santarem

persons who live an idle life, entirely supported by the labours of a few slaves which they have inherited.'[33] However, he was glad to be introduced to the commandante militar, the delegado de policia, and the juiz de direito. He had met the judge before, in Pará, who now offered to lend him his canoe – and an Indian – to go to Montealegra, two days downstream on the northern bank. The hills there were nearly a thousand feet high, and might prove better territory for Coleoptera.

Wallace was full of energy and enthusiasm. His initial walks round Santarem suggested that it would prove a good station for butterflies, at least; but suddenly, fired by his conversations with Hislop, the whole continent seemed accessible. What about Matto Grosso in the province of Cuyaba as a locality, he asked Stevens. Was Bolivia at all known? There were only five or six Erycinidae in the British Museum catalogue, so there was plenty of scope. Either of these areas would be as easily reached as the Andes by way of the Amazon. Meanwhile, he was already planning to go up the Rio Negro towards the sources of the Orinoco; and the bathing in the Tapajoz was luxurious, and oranges were fourpence a bushel. 'The more I see of the country, <u>the more I want to</u>; and I can see <u>no end</u> of, the species

49

of butterflies when the whole country is well explored.'[34] It looked wonderfully straightforward on a large-scale map.

Wallace did some exploring, as well as collecting, from Montealegra, though he found it less attractive than he anticipated, as the village was plagued by mosquitoes. He went off to inspect some Indian picture-writings on a mountain a few miles away: his interest in the lives and habits of the local population was beginning to grow, now that he was increasingly removed from European culture. He was, too, beginning to accept, with reluctance, the different customs and priorities of Brazil. There was a festa in Montealegra during their stay, and 'their' Indian was needed to play the violin; he 'did not think it at all necessary to ask us in order to absent himself two days', recalled Wallace, more as a comment than a complaint – he and Herbert simply accepted the situation, and cooked their own meals. Wallace was successful in buying a canoe: it was a bit leaky, and they had to carry out a number of impromptu repairs on subsequent trips, but at least it provided more independence. They sailed it back to Santarem, and now settled down to a pleasant routine. It was the dry season, with very little rain, and a cloudless sky for weeks together, with the heat moderated by the fresh breeze. They rose at six, to sort out their nets and collecting-boxes; breakfast at seven, prepared by an old village woman; off at eight, for a three-mile walk to a good area just below the town; then collecting until two or three, especially butterflies – the beautiful *Callithea sapphira*, and brilliant Erycinidae; a refreshing bathe in the Tapajoz on the way home, with no fear of alligators because of the swiftness of the current, followed by a snack of watermelon; then a change of clothing, dinner, and a session of insect-setting; finally, in the cool of the evening, tea and social calls. Even better, Richard Spruce, with his young assistant Robert King, had arrived in Santarem. This was Wallace's dream: exercise, pure air, good simple living – beef, fish, milk, fresh bread supplied by Louis the French baker; wonderful collecting-grounds within an easy stroll; and congenial company: 'I have never altogether enjoyed myself so much.'[35]

Spruce had been partly encouraged to go to the Amazon from hearing about the collecting success of Wallace and Bates. The son of a Yorkshire schoolmaster, and himself a reluctant teacher for a few years, he had already carried out a year-long expedition in the French Pyrenees. Now, with William Hooker's encouragement and with George Bentham offering to act as his distributor, he committed himself to serious plant-hunting at the age of thirty-two with truly vocational zeal. Wallace was delighted to have again a sympathetic friend, and an intellectual companion whose general approach to life, and collecting, complemented his own. Spruce was philosophical, questioning, agnostic; dedicated, persistent, methodical; unstuffy, and with a minimum of social and racial prejudices. Perhaps, too, because Spruce was principally a botanist, Wallace did not feel that he was in direct competition with him, as he was with Bates. The two men became life-long friends and in those relaxed, balmy days at Santarem Wallace was able to expand on his own theoretical lines of enquiry, especially those concerning the distribution and definition of species, including man. He also began to speculate on species distribution, now that he had collected on both sides of the Amazon, and had begun to suspect that the river itself formed the boundary for some species.

While Wallace and his brother had been at Montealegra, Bates sailed past to Santarem. He paused there for the night, dining, no doubt, with Captain Hislop, meeting, presumably, Richard Spruce, and discovering that Wallace would be returning shortly. His narrative comments: 'From information obtained here, I fixed upon the next town, Obydos, as the best place to stay at a few weeks, in order to investigate the natural productions of the north side of the Lower Amazons.'[36] Later in his travels he would make it his headquarters for three and a half years; for the moment, Santarem may have held too many competing collectors. Bates left for Obydos, fifty miles away, at sunrise the next morning, and would not meet up with Wallace until the end of January 1850. All the same, on this one short stretch of the Amazon were three of the greatest naturalists of their time, members of the new species of freelance, self-financing, collectors. The Reverend Leonard Jenyns, recalling the enthusiasm for natural history in Cambridge in the late 1820s, commented that the entomologists, in particular, were so numerous 'that several persons among the lower classes derived a part of their livelihood during the summer months from collecting insects for sale'.[37] With the Amazon as a glorious substitute for the Cambridgeshire fens, these three men were poised to emerge triumphantly from their relatively lowly status.

Wallace sent three boxes from Santarem to Stevens, mostly Lepidoptera, as the beetles would not make their appearance until the rainy season. One, a rare *Callithea sapphira*, he described as 'the most beautiful thing I have yet taken':

It is very difficult to capture, settling almost invariably high up in trees; two specimens I climbed up after and waited for; I then adopted a long pole which I left at a tree they frequented, and by means of persevering with it every day for near a month have got a good series: the sexes I have no doubt whatever about, though I have not taken them *in copula*; the female flies lower and is easier to take than the male.

He also included a small stuffed alligator, 'a species I think they have not in the Museum; it is the *Jacare tinga*, of which the tail is *eaten* and is very good; they are an immense deal of trouble in skinning'.[38] Another larger alligator, and some extra vertebrae, made up the parcel, with two Indian calabashes as a present for his agent, sent down river with a request for volume IX of Godard's *Encyclopédie Méthodique*. But now the weather was changing; the skies were overcast, and the rain was setting in. The naturalists were on the move. Spruce was offered a passage in a trading vessel. It was time for Wallace to head upstream towards the Rio Negro, but first he had to organise repairs to his own canoe, plugging the cracks with cotton dipped in hot pitch, and collecting a crew.

For the next two months, November and December 1849, the three parties leapfrogged each other up the Amazon. Wallace reached Obydos to find Bates already gone, while Spruce, who had left Santarem a week before him, had arrived only the evening before. At Obydos, there was more canoe-repairing and crew-hunting: the Santarem Indians returned home, and eventually Wallace found two replacements for the next stage. At the next settlement of Villa Nova the same problem occurred. Wallace enjoyed the company of the padre, but a week in the rains translating English conundrums into Portuguese was wearing. Letters requesting help were sent to the commandante, who was at his country house. Eventually, the padre negotiated a complicated deal, by which a trader would 'lend' Wallace three of his Indians, in exchange for the ones the commandante would surely send in the course of time.

One of the Indians, however, did not choose to come, and was driven to the canoe by severe lashes, and at the point of the bayonet. He was very furious and sullen when he came on board, vowing that he would not go with me, and would take vengeance on those who had forced him on board.

Wallace offered him good pay and food, but the man was adamant – and at the same time 'very civil', assuring Wallace that he bore him no ill will personally.[39] At the first stopping place, he politely wished Wallace goodbye, and returned home to his village by way of the forest. A replacement was eventually found, and they slowly moved up river, sailing sometimes but more often rowing, soaked with the almost incessant rain, and tormented by mosquitoes. On 30 December 1849, they reached the junction of the Amazon with the Rio Negro:

> After the muddy, monotonous, mosquito-swarming Amazon, it was with great pleasure we found ourselves in the black waters – black as ink they are, and well deserve their name; the shores are rugged and picturesque – and greatest luxury of all, mosquitoes are unknown except in the islands.[40]

Twelve miles further, on the east bank of the Rio Negro, was the city of Barra (now Manaos), named after the fort that formed the original settlement. They went at once to present their letter of introduction to the leading Italian businessman, Senhor Henrique Antony, the warm-hearted and 'never-failing friend of stray travellers': he immediately offered them two large rooms in a new house he was building, as well as the hospitality of his own.[41]

Senhor Henrique was welcoming, as he had been to Edwards before, and to Bates and Spruce in turn, and he had a pretty, clever and amiable wife in Donna Leocadia. But Barra, although larger than Santarem with a population of five or six thousand, had little to recommend it to Wallace. The more civilised inhabitants had 'literally no amusements whatever', unless you counted drinking and small-scale gambling. Few of them ever opened a book, or had any mental occupation; and the morals were 'perhaps at the lowest ebb possible in any civilised community'.[42] The wet season had set in properly, and a few days in the surrounding area soon proved that Barra was little use for collecting birds, or even insects: it was almost impossible 'to get half a dozen in a day worth bringing home'. Wallace had not clawed his way a thousand miles from Pará to be idle, and each unproductive day was a debit entry on his balance sheet. More Indians were procured. Herbert was dispatched to visit a neighbouring estate, to see what he could do independently. Wallace headed off in his own canoe for some islands three days' voyage up the Rio Negro, where he hoped to find the umbrella chatterers in plumage.

He gained two important benefits from this month up river. First, he learned to rough it. The lodging he was found was a small room in a hut, itself part of a very small settlement in the forest. There were three openings hung with palm-leaf mats, and the floor was at such a steep angle that everything tended to slide off it. Second, he was forced to improve his languages. Only one man in the settlement spoke Portuguese, but the boy sent with him by Henrique could interpret, and Wallace set himself to learn as much of the Lingoa Geral, the common Indian language, as he could. The two other rooms in his hut housed three families, so he was able to observe the Indians' way of life at close quarters, and was astonished to note how hard they all worked, and how little they ate. The four huts were 'imbedded in the forest' – they were less than twenty yards apart, but invisible from each other.[43]

Wallace's hard-working hunter arrived, and immediately set off for the islands, the habitat of the umbrella birds which, Wallace believed, never appeared on the mainland. Over the next weeks he produced twenty-five specimens: not a huge return by Wallace's standards, but quite a challenge, since the whole of the bird's neck was 'covered internally with a thick coat of hard, muscular fat, very difficult to be cleaned away'.[44] The umbrella bird is about as big as a raven (or, according to Bates, a common crow), and much the same colour. It has a thick crest of feathers which, when raised, curve over its head like a fringed sunshade, and another ornamental plume on its breast. Wallace gave the bird's Indian name as 'ueramimbe', 'trumpet bird', Bates as 'uira-mimbeu', 'fife' or 'panpipe bird'. Bates later described a performance he saw: 'It drew itself up on its perch, spread widely the umbrella-formed crest, dilated and waved its glossy breast-lappet, and then, in giving vent to its loud piping note, bowed its head slowly forwards.'[45] On the last day, the hunter presented Wallace with a live male bird, shot but apparently only stunned. Wallace fed it cautiously with bits of banana and fruit, and it survived a fortnight, which gave him the opportunity to observe it closely, and note its method of expanding and closing its beautiful crest and neck plume.

The umbrella birds formed the pick of a consignment of birds and insects Wallace sent to Stevens on 20 March. There were also a little bristle-tailed manikin, and two 'bad' specimens of the 'bell bird' – bad because they needed five or six shots to bring them down from the treetops. But his concentration on the umbrella birds helped to shift Wallace from collector to observer, and formed the subject of his first scientific paper from the Amazon, short enough, but even so something more than a mere catalogue of captures and locations.[46]

By the time Wallace returned to Barra, with his prize umbrella bird, Bates had arrived from Obydos, to be received as part of the extended family by Senhor Henrique. Their two accounts present a sharp contrast. Wallace complained that he now had a 'dull time of it' – by which he meant that the rain, and the humidity, made collecting extremely difficult. Bates's presence was welcome, but Wallace was impatient to be gone. His initial plan, he told Stevens, was to have been up the Rio Negro by March, where he intended to get as many live animals as he could, take them with him to Pará, and be back in England by Christmas. But the weather and lack of funding was keeping him boxed up at Barra. For Bates, on the other hand, these weeks provided an interlude of 'pleasant society'. There were half-a-dozen foreigners, English, American, German, all of them traders, besides Wallace and another naturalist, the bird-collector Hauxwell. After a frustrating voyage from Obydos, sodden by the rain and plagued by mosquitoes and the dreaded 'piums', it was a pleasure to ramble through the neighbouring forest in the dry spells, and especially along a beautiful road that ran to a waterfall:

> The waters of one of the largest rivulets which traverse the gloomy wilderness here fall over a ledge of rock about ten feet high. It is not the cascade itself, but the noiseless solitude, and the marvellous diversity and richness of trees, foliage, and flowers, encircling the water basin, that form the attraction of the place. Families make picnic excursions to the spot; and the gentlemen – it is said the ladies also – spend the sultry hours of midday bathing in the cold and bracing waters.[47]

(Bates had an eye for the ladies, and was prepared to admit it.) The waterfall had been, too, a favourite spot of Spix and Martius in 1820, and so 'classic ground to the naturalist'. Bates was able to relax and make the most of the opportunities offered by the little European community: 'We', he recalled, generously including his former companion, 'passed a delightful time.'

At this point in his long stay Bates was having second thoughts about the Amazon, and was under considerable pressure from his parents to return home. His father and mother had called on Stevens in London, where Mr Bates quizzed Stevens on the financial rewards, and 'stated to him my opinion that your time would be much safer and more profitably employed as a manufacturer than in your present occupation'. The hosiery business was booming; free-trade measures had resulted in a 'splendid' export market – '& that makes the home trade good as well'. Mr Bates senior made his opinion of collecting very clear, informing Stevens 'that the occupation might do very well as a dernier resort to one who had tried other things and they had proved failures & instanced Mr Wallace'.[48]

In Barra, Wallace and Bates discussed their future plans, like politicians parcelling out spheres of influence. 'Mr Wallace chose the Rio Negro for his next trip, and I agreed to take the Solimões' – that is, the upper Amazon.[49] The division seems logical, and amicable. Wallace had been planning the trip for months, ever since he reached Santarem. They had the opportunity, too, to continue their discussions about species. Bates was content, temporarily, to defer to Wallace. He left for Ega, four hundred miles up river, on 26 March. At the end of the year, isolated and a little disheartened, he was ready to cede the whole continent to his competitor. 'Mr Wallace, I suppose, will follow up the profession,' he wrote generously to Stevens, 'and probably will adopt the track I have planned out to Peru; he is now in a glorious country, and you must expect great things from him. In perseverance and real knowledge of the subject, he goes ahead of me, and is worthy of all success.'[50]

Wallace, still waiting for letters and money from England, was not going anywhere much. Unwilling to be unproductive, he spent two months a hundred miles or so up the Amazon – presumably, this minor expedition did not count – staying with Henrique's father-in-law, Senhor Brandão, a well-educated Portuguese settler who appealed to Wallace's views on economy because he was farming in a systematic way. There was something 'racy and refreshing' in his conversation – 'such an absence of information, but such a fertility of ideas'; he had planted fruit trees, stocked his pastures with cattle, sheep, pigs and poultry, and cultivated tobacco.[51] Wallace sent for his hunter, and collected what he could.

Back at Barra, the weeks passed wearily. Herbert had discovered that, like his elder brother, he had the ability to mesmerise people, and he would call little Indian boys from the street, give them a copper 'and by a little gazing and a few passes send them into the trance state'. On another occasion when they were out collecting, Herbert 'quietly began mes-merising a young man nearly his own age. He did not entrance him, but obtained enough influence to render his arm rigid. This he instantly relaxed, and asked the Indian to lie down on the floor, which he did. My brother then made a pass along his body, and said, "Lie there till we return." ' They walked out, assuming that the influence would fade, but two hours later found the man still on the ground. Herbert released him, and they gave him a small present, 'but he did not seem much surprised or disturbed, evidently thinking we were white medicine-men'.[52] This sort of incident helped to convince Wallace about the universality of such phenomena.

Senhor Lima, a Portuguese trader generally considered 'a very good sort of fellow', had promised to take Wallace at least as far as the falls of the Rio Negro, and was persuaded to wait. At last, on the evening of 30 August, Bradley's boat arrived: letters from Pará, letters from his Wilson cousins in Australia and his brother John in California, letters from his family in England, and, crucially, letters of credit from Stevens. Wallace sat up most of the night, answering them, then went out and bought additional essentials for his projected voyage: he was preparing for a seven-hundred-mile trip, and for an absence of twelve months. His brother was to stay at Barra. Herbert had decided that he was not cut out to be a collector, though he wrote cheerfully enough on the subject to Spruce:

> A Lodge is gained at last – here we are in a Barra!! – 'Here we work with Net and Trigger/By the famous river Nigger . . .' – o'er whose midnight waters never is heard the hum of the sanguinary Carapana – where 'sleep which knits up the ravelled sleeve of care' hath no intruder –[53]

All the same, he intended to do enough to pay for his passage home. His elder brother lent him £10, all he could spare from the money Stevens had forwarded – 'and I have given him a receipt to pay him when able', he informed Fanny and his mother in August. 'I am a thousand miles from Pará, and my present plan is as follows; to hire a hunter immediately, and go for a couple of months into the country to make a collection of Birds and Insects which will be sufficient to pay my voyage to England, and I hope leave a few pounds in my pocket besides.' In place of the naturalist's life, his family suggested he try California – but that theme did not appeal. 'I wish I was a little more unpoetical; but as I am what I am, I must try and do the best for myself I can. "Trifles light as air" begone!! I have business before me – and *must look sharp* –' (a favourite phrase, probably, of his sister). 'P.S. You may expect me home at Christmas.'[54]

At two o'clock on a fine bright afternoon, from the relative comfort of a 'tolerably roomy' canoe, Alfred Wallace waved farewell to his brother, and left Barra looking forward 'with hope and expectation to the distant and little-known regions' of the upper Rio Negro. At last he felt wholly independent, heading into the forest on his own.

4　Hunting the White Umbrella Bird

Wallace sailed off for the upper Rio Negro with high hopes of what these little-known regions might offer. Two years in Brazil had given him confidence, and even his enforced stay at Barra had been useful, in that he had been compelled to become more familiar with the trading community, and able to integrate smoothly – if not always comfortably – with their way of life. Senhor João Antonio de Lima was a middle-sized, grizzly man with a face 'something like that of the banished lord in the National Gallery', who graciously placed his boat at Wallace's service.[1] The vessel was crammed with trading goods: bales of brilliantly coloured cloth and calico, cottons and handkerchiefs, axes and cutlasses, knives and fish hooks, gunpowder and shot, beads and mirrors, as well as six months' supplies for Lima's family: rum and wine, tea, coffee, sugar, cooking oil, butter, garlic, pepper. In the evening, Wallace and Lima would stand on a plank at the entrance to the palm-leaved roof of their *tolda*, or shelter, or perch on it to

59

sip their coffee and enjoy the fresh air and the cool, dark waters around them, while the goat-suckers hunted for insects, the tree frogs started up, and the monkeys filled the night with their howlings. Sometimes they might moor, hanging their hammocks from a tree on shore, or Wallace would roll up under the *tolda*, while Lima slept outside. They ate off the land, buying a fowl or eggs, oranges and bananas, from a cottage, or feeding off a turkey-like curassow or a guan shot in the forest, or a twenty-pound pirahiba hooked during the night. Many of the villages they passed were almost deserted, but Lima knew someone in most of the places where they stopped, and Wallace would find himself dining on turtle with silver knives and forks, but sitting cross-legged on a mat spread over the bare earth.

The weather was fine. More often than not, there was a sharp afternoon storm, which passed in an hour or two and left the atmosphere mild and clear; and – a great luxury – there were no mosquitoes. Often two men would be sent off to fish early in the morning, and Wallace began to take a closer interest in what they caught. He made accurate drawings and descriptions, and this became a major source of interest, and a fresh focus for his collecting, during the following year.

A month passed before they could see the opposite side of the river clearly once more and the landscape began to change, with slabs of granite conspicuous, and rocky islands in the river. After three more weeks, Wallace was excited to have a clear view of the Curicuríarí Serras, three thousand feet high, irregular conical masses of granite, jagged and peaked, covered in forest but with bare precipices shining with quartz.

They entered the falls, a new adventure. Their first boat had been exchanged for two smaller canoes because of the increasingly difficult passage, and now they were reduced to one. Sometimes the Indians dragged or pushed it through narrow channels, plunging through the water themselves like fish; sometimes everyone clambered out on to the rocks, and the canoe was hauled a little further round some projecting obstacle with a tow rope; sometimes they paddled furiously, using the shelter of an island, or a rock, to make a few yards' headway, zigzagging from bank to bank. At São Gabriel, the canoe had to be completely unloaded, while Lima and Wallace dressed formally to call on the commandante at the fort. Official permission was needed before anyone could proceed further up river. Wallace brought the customary letter of introduction, and was invited to breakfast the following morning: they spent the evening with an old Portuguese trader Wallace had met at Barra.

Above the rapids, the water was smooth as they approached the Equator, and they passed the mouth of the Vaupés river, three hundred yards wide with a stronger current than the Rio Negro, and also a 'black'-water river. Then on 24 October, nearly eight weeks after setting off from Barra, they reached the small village of Nossa Senhora de Guía, which was Lima's home: fifteen houses with a church, according to Robert Schomburgk in 1839.[2] Wallace recorded a row of thatched mud huts, some of them whitewashed, others the colour of the native earth. He met Lima's children, four daughters, two of them grown up, and a little boy of eight; a good-looking half-Indian woman was introduced by Lima as 'the mother of his younger children'. The mother of the elder girls had been turned out, it transpired, because she was an Indian, and could speak only her own language, and so the children would never learn Portuguese. Wallace noted that the family welcomed the patriarch 'in a very cold and timid way', coming up and asking his blessing 'as if they had parted from him the evening before, instead of three months since'. Wallace found himself in a slightly awkward position: he was wholly reliant on Lima's good will and assistance, yet found it difficult to condone his attitude. He was offered a little house opposite Lima's. He hung up his hammock, arranged his boxes, and set off to explore the immediate neighbourhood. While the village celebrated the return of the crew with drinking and dancing, Wallace had unpacked his gun and was busy shooting chatterers in the fruit trees. There seemed relatively few insects in the forest, but he soon discovered some rare butterflies near the riverbank. A couple of Indian hunters were procured for him by Lima, and they brought him a few birds killed by their blowpipes, but in a rather half-hearted way: they frequently returned without any birds, Wallace complained, 'telling me that they could not find any, when I had very good reason to believe that they had spent the day at some neighbouring *sitio*'.[3] Annoyingly, there were no good paths in the forest, so he could not go far himself. Fishes, however, were much more easily come by, and he was able to add to his notebook of drawings, and even preserve a few of the smaller species in spirits. Clearly Guía was not ideal as a permanent base, and Wallace began to plan a longer expedition, to the granite Serra, just north of Guía, where the gallo de Serra, the 'cock-of-the-rock', was said to breed.

This was more challenging, another step closer to 'unknown territory' –

unknown, that is, to European scientific naturalists and explorers, though wholly familiar to Brazilian and Venezuelan traders and priests. On the upper Rio Negro, Wallace was following a highway travelled by a select band of famous predecessors. In 1800, Humboldt and Bonpland had passed through a hundred miles to the north, exploring the junction between the Rio Negro and the Orinoco. Dr Johann Natterer of Vienna, who collected in Brazil from 1817 to 1835, travelled up the Rio Negro as far as its junction with the Cassiquiare, which linked it to the Orinoco. (At Guía, Wallace encountered a beautiful seventeen-year-old girl, whom he realised must be Natterer's daughter.) Robert Schomburgk had come down river in 1839, on his two-thousand-mile round trip from Guyana.

Now Wallace could begin to explore genuinely. He borrowed a canoe from Lima, and set off with an Indian who was returning to his village, together with his two hunters. They turned into the Isanna, half a mile wide, and from there followed a smaller stream on the south bank. Each night they camped, slinging their hammocks from stakes driven into the ground. On the third day the landscape changed, with moss-covered rocks, and virgin forest sloping up from the riverbanks. Wallace was led to the village, five or six huts embedded in the forest, and offered one for his own use: three doors, no windows. He placed his bird box as a table, slung his hammock, and was ready to explore the forest. Wherever he went, he was followed by the village boys, who either acted as 'spotters' and 'pointers', or supplemented his shooting with their blowpipes.

Learning that there were no gallos in the immediate vicinity, Wallace proposed a trip to the Serra de Cobati, ten or twelve miles away through the forest, and by offering generous payment persuaded the whole male population to go with him. For provisions, they took just flour and salt, intending to live off what they caught. Wallace found his clothes and equipment a nuisance: his gun would catch on overhanging branches, and the hooked spines of the climbing plants caught in his shirt-sleeves, or knocked his cap off. 'The Indians were all naked, or, if they had a shirt or trousers, carried them in a bundle on their heads, and I have no doubt looked upon me as a good illustration of the uselessness and bad conse-quences of wearing clothes upon a forest journey.'[4] After five hours walking at a pace that would have been impressive on level ground, they were enjoying a rest, and a drink from a small stream, when they heard a distant grunt. The Indians prepared their blowpipes, grasped their knives, and

Channel among granite rocks

disappeared, leaving Wallace with the youngest boys. He cocked his gun, heard crashing and gnashing, but no wild pigs appeared. The men returned and directed the boys to lead Wallace to the Serra, while they continued the hunt. They took him to a cave at the foot of the mountain, and soon three men joined them with a hog slung on a pole, which they proceeded to skin, cut up, stew and smoke.

The next morning, the rest of the party turned up with the prime pieces of three more hogs carefully packed in palm leaves. They now split into groups, to tackle the Serra – 'an ascent up rocky gorges, over huge fragments, and through gloomy caverns' – sometimes hauling themselves up precipices by roots and creepers, sometimes crawling over a surface composed of gigantic, serrated blocks of stone. At last, an old Indian took Wallace by the arm and, pointing into a thicket, whispered quietly, 'Gallo!' After looking intently for a while, Wallace 'caught a glimpse of the magnificent bird sitting amidst the gloom, shining out like a mass of brilliant flame'. He shot and missed. The bird flew off, but Wallace soon had another shot at it, and brought it down. When it was given to him, he was 'lost in admiration of the dazzling brilliancy of its soft downy feathers. Not a spot of blood was visible, not a feather was ruffled, and the soft, warm, flexible body set off the fresh swelling plumage, in a manner which no stuffed specimen can approach.'[5] It was a defining moment, described with an intensity that foreshadows his future encounters with the birds of paradise. Time seems to stop in his memory of the event, as he holds the brilliantly plumaged bird, as though it is still alive. But at the end of the day, he skinned it, before night fell. Then the fires were made up, and the joints of pork hung over them to smoke; and around him were thirteen naked Indians, talking in unknown tongues:

> Two only could speak a little Portuguese, and with them I conversed, answering their various questions about where iron came from, and how calico was made, and if paper grew in my country, and if we had much mandiocca and plantains; and they were greatly astonished to hear that all were white men there, and could not imagine how white men could work, or how there could be a country without forest. They would ask strange questions about where the wind came from, and the rain, and how the sun and moon got back to their places after disappearing from us; and when I had tried to satisfy them on these points, they would tell me forest tales of jaguars and pumas, and of the fierce wild hogs, and of the dreadful curupurí, the demon of the woods, and of the wild man with a long tail, found far in the centre of the forest.[6]

Wallace spent nine days on this expedition to the Serra: his twelve hunters produced ten gallos, while he shot two himself. In addition, he captured numerous birds: two trogons, several blue-capped manikins, barbets, and ant-thrushes. Back at the village, where he spent another fortnight, he added to his bird collection, and made more drawings of fish, before making his way up river again to Guía. He was eager now to leave for the upper Rio Negro. The padre, however, Frei José, was in the area, and no one would set off until his visit, for there were baptisms and weddings to be conducted. Frei José dos Santos Innocentos arrived eventually, carried up the hill in a hammock: 'a tall, thin, prematurely old man, thoroughly worn out by every kind of debauchery', according to Wallace, who commented that Don Juan was an innocent by comparison. He had a fund of anecdotes, 'disgustingly coarse', but so cleverly told that they were irresistibly ludicrous. Wallace's Portuguese was improving rapidly, and he could appreciate Frei José's use of idiom. Wallace, sturdily agnostic at this point in his life, noted that the 'seven or eight distinct processes' in the rite of baptism were sufficiently like the complicated operations of the Indians' own ceremonies 'to make them think they had got something very good in return for their shilling'.[7] A few weddings followed the baptisms, and Frei José delivered a practical homily 'which might have done some good, had the parties to whom it was addressed understood it'; but as the homily was given in Portuguese, they did not. The only two white men present, besides Wallace and Frei José, were Lima and the local commandante, who both had large families without benefit of marriage. The padre's response was: 'Never mind what these white people do, they will all go to purgatory, but don't you be such fools as to go too!' Wallace reported that, while the white men roared with laughter, the Indians 'looked much astonished'; he, like Spruce, remained highly sceptical about the imposition of Christian ritual on the local people.

The forest expedition, hunting for gallos, had been important for Wallace. Just by making that twelve-mile trek, he was shifting himself beyond the trading and Christianity culture mapped out by the great river systems, towards a way of life that he was beginning to understand and appreciate on its own terms. The story about his clothes is significant: the Indian ways were more appropriate, and he was able to see himself partly from their perspective. He had stumbled on a far more effective method of hunting, by attaching himself to a hunting party, and taking on a much less directive role. There is, rarely for him, no hint of impatience when the men break off for a pig hunt. He was beginning to adjust to the rhythms of forest life, and to examine the tribes with different eyes.

The post arrived at Guía, bringing letters from home of May and July 1850: it was now 17 January 1851. There was one from Stevens, acknowledging safe receipt of the umbrella birds; three letters from his brother John Wallace, now in California; and a 'most acceptable' packet of the *Illustrated London News*. John had received a tough initiation. He had reached San Francisco at the wrong season to travel to the mines, and had become involved instead in an unsuccessful woodcutting venture: 'His only choice was to work or be idle, and I think he did perfectly right to undertake it,' Alfred, working continuously if not very profitably, pronounced. But if his collections were not yet very successful, he told his brother-in-law

Thomas Sims, he had certainly not been idle, and was forwarding a small box to Stevens, containing the celebrated cocks-of-the-rocks: only a dozen, he complained, instead of the fifty he had been expecting. The magical, idealised atmosphere of the account he afterwards gave in his *Travels* is suppressed in this particular letter, in favour of the hardship and inconveniences he suffered.

Something had happened on this journey that allowed him to see himself as a professional traveller, and potential writer, rather than just a struggling, self-financed collector. Now that he was firmly established on the upper Rio Negro, he had earned the right to become part of a different, more classical tradition. He outlined his plans to Sims: first, the trip up to Venezuela, in which he would be following in the tracks of Humboldt, Natterer and Schomburgk; then a voyage up the 'great river Vaupés', and another up the Isánna:

> . . . not so much for my collections which I do not expect to be very profitable there, but because I am so much interested in the country and the people that I am determined to see and know more of it and them than any other traveller. If I do not get profit I hope at least to get some credit as an industrious and persevering traveller.[8]

On the subject of his writing, he set out his publication plans: it makes an impressive list. Firstly, there would be his journal – Sims had already received the first part, but the extension went on steadily, better written and more interesting. Secondly, a work on fishes, with figures of all the species: 'I am very interested in them and have already made drawings of one hundred different kinds' – almost all since he left Barra. The fish in the black waters were different from those in the Amazon, and those from the temperate regions of the Andes different again. Thirdly, he was making sketches and notes of the palms: he had already drawn thirty, so that should make another volume. Then he was collecting information and thinking about a work on the physical history of the Great Amazon valley – geography, geology, distribution of animals and plants (always a key concept for Wallace), meteorology, and the history and languages of the aboriginal tribes. Fifthly, he thought he might have enough information, 'from personal observation and from the Indians', for a separate little work on the habits and natural history of the animals. Lastly, there would be his collection of butterflies, and all the work involved in describing the numerous new species. This would keep him occupied for two or three years, he estimated optimistically – but he asked Sims not to make his plans public, as he knew he might not accomplish half his programme. If Sims assumed, wrote Wallace, by his blithe talk of journeys to the Andes that he did not wish to return home, he was greatly mistaken: 'Not a day or a night passes that I do not think of you all.' But it was only because he was determined to return with satisfaction and credit both to himself and them that he was resolved 'on thoroughly investigating this wonderful country, not merely seeing and doing what others have done before me, but adding something to the stores of science, and giving some information to the world that I alone shall be able to do – It is this that impels me.'[9] Wallace was transferring himself in his imagination from collector to scientific traveller: he was buoyed up by his vision of the opportunities before him, and fired by the will to succeed.

Once Frei José had left the village, Wallace could gather together his group for the journey north, not exactly into the unknown, but to locations that held significance for European readers. In a borrowed, rather leaky, canoe, with four Indians, only one of whom had a smattering of Portuguese, Wallace was able to travel lightly – lightly, that is, for a Victorian naturalist. He lists his essential equipment: watch, sextant and compass, insect and bird boxes, gun and ammunition, salt, beads, fish hooks, calico and cotton cloth. But the basket of salt weighed a hundred pounds, and there were four baskets of farinha, a jar of oil, a demi-john of molasses: at Javíta, all this would translate into at least a dozen loads for the porters. The Indians, he noted, had a more refined baggage: *gravatánas* (blowpipes) and poisoned arrows, shirt and trousers, paddle, knife, tinderbox and *rédé* (hammock).

After five days they reached the Serra of Cocoí, which marked the boundary between Brazil and Venezuela. The piums were out in force, but the weather was fine, and Wallace identified his 'old friend, the pole star' on the clear horizon up river. On 4 February, they arrived at São Carlos, the most southerly point on Humboldt's journey fifty years earlier: sacred ground to Wallace, who had read Humboldt's journey ten years or so before. Wallace did his best to add some Spanish vocabulary to his Portuguese. They paddled on, passing the mouth of the Cassiquiare, the link between the river systems, and found that they had at least progressed beyond the pium sector. The weather was hot, the river low, and sometimes they had to drag the boat over the rocks. At Tómo, Wallace met Antonio Dias, a boat-builder, of whom he had heard a good deal, a man 'rather notorious, even in this country of loose morals, for his patriarchal propensities'.[10] Tómo was a boat-building centre: boats of up to 200 tons were built in the region. They would go downstream, laden with bulky produce – farinha, piassaba, pitch – in the high water, descend the falls, and there be sold for the Rio Negro and Amazon trade. Wallace's canoe was too large to proceed further. Dias organised a replacement for him, an *oba*, made from a single piece of timber, and in this he reached Pimichin, a 'village' of only two houses. Taking possession of an old shed – the 'travellers' house' – Wallace set out on foot to explore the forest road, which here ran for ten miles through the forest to Javíta, a village on a river which formed part of the Orinoco system. He was, in fact, at the watershed. Walking in the evening with his gun, he strolled along the road a little way into the forest, at this place he had so long looked forward to reaching – 'and was rewarded by falling in with one of the lords of the soil, which I had long wished to encounter':

> As I was walking quietly along I saw a large jet-black animal come out of the forest about twenty yards before me, which took me so much by surprise that I did not at first imagine what it was. As it moved slowly on, and its whole body and long curving tail came into full view in the middle of the road, I saw that it was a fine black jaguar. I involuntarily raised my gun to my shoulder, but remembering that both barrels were loaded with small shot, and that to fire would exasperate without killing him, I stood silently gazing. In the middle of the road he turned his head, and for an instant paused and gazed at me, but having, I suppose, other business of his own to attend to, walked steadily on, and disappeared in the thicket. As he advanced, I heard the scampering of small animals, and the whizzing flight of ground birds, clearing the path for their dreaded enemy.
>
> This encounter pleased me much. I was too much surprised, and occupied too much with admiration, to feel fear. I had at length had a full view, in his native wilds, of the rarest variety of the most powerful and dangerous animal inhabiting the American continent.[11]

Dazzled by this epiphany from the forests of the night, Wallace returned to his shed. The next day he walked the length of the Estrada de Javíta, until he met an Indian planting cassava, who turned out to be the village capitaão. Wallace, in his imperfect Spanish, convinced the man that he was a harmless 'naturalista', and arranged for porters to transfer his luggage. The porters duly turned up: one man, and ten women and girls. But Wallace's Indians could not keep up with the pace, and there was a confusion of loads being hastily dumped in the forest, and gropings around in the dark – visions of a jaguar's glaring eyes, or the deadly fangs of a jararáca in his leg – before Wallace was finally installed in the old priest's house. Javíta promised well, with the convenient road offering easy access to the forest: an ideal spot for a collector.

One factor told against him. The rains set in the very night he stumbled into Javíta. The seasons were different from the Rio Negro, and he had arrived on the last day of summer. This was a blow, but not a disastrous one. Insects – collectable insects – were less numerous, and the processes of drying and preserving made difficult. But he still found forty species of butterflies that were new to him, and the great blue butterflies, such as *Morpho menelaus* and *Morpho hellenor*, were prolific, sitting in dozens on twigs by the roadside. During his forest excursions, he saw wild pigs, agoutis, coatis, monkeys, many beautiful trogons, and numerous snakes; and he was brought a curious little alligator, *Caiman gibbus*, which he skinned and stuffed to the amusement of the spectators. He also continued to add to his collection of fish, preserving the smaller kinds in spirits, and drawing any specimens in the late afternoon after his return from the forest. At this hour he was set on by sandflies, till his hands were as swollen, rough and red as a pair of boiled lobsters, and he was forced to soak them in water to bring down the swelling. Even so, their bites were more tolerable than those of the pium or the mosquito.

Rain and sandflies apart, Wallace enjoyed his time at Javíta, living in a village of some two hundred inhabitants, all of them, so far as he could tell, Indians of 'pure blood'. Their industry, and sense of community, appealed to his work ethic. They had two main sources of income: cutting piassaba in the forest, which was either exported raw, or turned into cables and cordage; and portering goods from one river system to the other along the Estrada – although traffic was intermittent, and had not recovered from the civil unrest, the trade route was well established. Every week, the whole village would be hoed and weeded, and each morning and evening the girls and boys met at the church for a hymn or a psalm. It was a kind of Owenite Utopia, all the more appealing for its rain-forest setting. Wallace observed, and admired, but beyond attending one or two festas, he spent the long evenings on his own, without company or even books. His Spanish was limited, and the Indians' language new to him. In a state of 'excited indignation against civilised life', he wrote a blank-verse description of the village. The perhaps unconscious model was William Cowper's 1785 poem *The Task*, well known to the Wallace family, and quoted by Herbert in his letters. Book Two begins:

> Oh for a lodge in some vast wilderness,
> Some boundless contiguity of shade,
> Where rumour of oppression and deceit
> Of unsuccessful or successful war,
> Might never reach me more!

Where Cowper imagines the 'gentle' – and noble – savage Omai back in the South Seas after his trip to Europe, straying along the beach and wondering whether the waves at his feet have ever washed England's distant shore, Wallace draws a direct comparison between the constrictions of England and the freedom of the Indian girls, sporting like mermaids in the sparkling wave, or the boys, whose every motion is full of grace and health:

> And as they run, and race, and shout, and leap,
> Or swim and dive beneath the rapid stream,
> Or, all bareheaded in the noonday sun,
> Creep stealthily, with blowpipe or with bow,
> To shoot small birds or swiftly gliding fish,
> I pity English boys; their active limbs
> Cramp'd and confined in tightly fitting clothes;
> Their toes distorted by the shoemaker,
> Their foreheads aching under heavy hats,
> And all their frame by luxury enervate.
> But how much more I pity English maids,
> Their waist, and chest, and bosom all confined
> By that vile torturing instrument called stays!

It is not, he argues, that he places the 'civilised' below the 'savage man':

> The thousand curses that gold brings upon us,
> The long death-struggle for the means to live . . .

The savage man is spared these competitive pressures.

> But then the joys, the pleasures and delights,
> That the well-cultivated mind enjoys;
> The appreciation of the beautiful
> In nature and in art; the boundless range
> Of pleasure and of knowledge books afford;
> The constant change of incident and scene
> That makes us live a life in every year; –
> All these the savage knows not and enjoys not.[12]

Yet these pleasures, reasons the embryonic socialist, are bought at a terrible cost: millions suffer while only a few enjoy the fruit. Millions of Europeans live a 'lower' life – lower in physical and moral health – than the Red Indian. Where Cowper saw the city, and London, as the symbol of all that was wrong in society, Wallace more simplistically – and slightly illogically, considering that he was busy trying to convert *Morpho ulysses* into money – ascribes the failure of 'civilised' man to the joy of getting gold. The wonders of nature, philosophy, poetry, history, immortal deeds, noble sacrifices, all the things that Wallace himself cherished, were relegated in favour of wealth and property: profit, rather than credit. He turned his back – in his verses – on materialism, and committed himself to the simple life:

> Rather than live a man like one of these,
> I'd be an Indian here, and live content
> To fish, and hunt, and paddle my canoe,
> And see my children grow, like young wild fawns,
> In health of body and in peace of mind,
> Rich without wealth, and happy without gold!

Wallace was fully aware of the skewed perspective encouraged by this temporary idyll. He confessed that the sentiments in the poem did not entirely match his sober and matter-of-fact judgement when he sat down to write *Travels on the Amazon* in 1853, in a London whose streets were swept with piassaba brushes. But Javíta provided him with one striking model of ideal community life, in which the Indians seemed to him largely self-governing, yet able to benefit from their favourable location by trading with the rest of the world without apparently being exploited. It was a model to which he would return again and again in his later writing, in which he remained convinced that it was possible to re-create a version of Rousseau's Social Contract based on the example of natural, forest life. Spruce, writing to Sir William Hooker two years later, saw the country through less rose-tinted lenses:

> A country without priests, lawyers, doctors, police, and soldiers, is not quite so happy as Rousseau dreamt it ought to be; and this, in which I now am, has been in a state of gradual decadence ever since the separation from Spain, at which period (or shortly after) the inhabitants rid themselves of these functionaries in the most unscrupulous manner. San Carlos seems to have fallen off much since Humboldt visited it.[13]

Spruce, although quite as skilled as Wallace in maintaining good relations with the peoples he moved among, escaped with his life only after great difficulty in this very same area.

Wallace's idyll ended abruptly. One morning, he woke to find his comforting routine at an end: there was no fire on his veranda, and no sign of his Indians. They had been growing progressively uneasy, living among a different people, and had been eating up the supplies of farinha at a great rate, Wallace thought, hoping to precipitate a move. Now that he had just bought another basketful to block that excuse, they had obviously decided to take independent action. Wallace, unfazed, set off as usual with his insect net. The Javíta Indians who called round that evening were slightly surprised to find the 'rationale' preparing his own dinner. He tried, unsuccessfully and to his obvious disappointment, to persuade one of the 'brown damsels of the village' to take over these duties – in other villages of the Rio Negro, he complained, 'I might at any moment have had my claim of half a dozen' – and went on doing his own housekeeping for a fortnight, living luxuriously on Venezuelan dried beef and cheese, roasted plantains and cassava bread.[14] Then his coffee supplies ran out. This was more serious, so he went and begged an old Indian 'por amor de Dios' to spare him some from his little plantation. When Wallace returned from the forest six hours later, the beans had been picked, washed, dried, husked, roasted, and pounded in a mortar, and he was able to enjoy one of the most delicious cups of coffee he had ever tasted.

Now the rains set in properly, whole days and nights of rain, and breaks of even a few hours' sunshine grew rarer. Drying specimens became almost impossible – most annoying, because Wallace had recently initiated the village boys into beetle-catching, rewarding them with a fish hook per specimen. It was time to move. He had already planned an expedition up the Vaupes with Lima; and even his loose talk would be a welcome contrast.

Wallace was away from his main base at Guía for about three months on this occasion. In spite of the enforced solitude, and the lack of 'civilised' conversation, he left Javíta with much regret. He had done well in terms of collecting, though, as always, he was acutely conscious that he might have achieved more; and he had felt at ease with the Indian community, able at least to imagine what it would be like to be a more integrated part of it.

There were the usual annoying delays at Guía, but on 3 June they started for São Joaquim, at the mouth of the Vaupés. They made slow progress against the current, and because the waters were so high had difficulty in finding suitable stopping places to make a fire, and cook food, though Wallace was initiated into roast anaconda one evening – excessively tough and glutinous. After four days, however, they reached a *malocca*, a hundred feet long, by forty wide and thirty high, with a broad aisle, and, projecting inwards from the walls on each side, palm-thatch partitions 'exactly similar in arrangement to the boxes in a London eating-house, or those of a theatre': each the private apartment of a separate family. On entering, Wallace was delighted to find himself 'at length in the presence of the true denizens of the forest'. They were so different from the 'half-civilised races' among whom he had been living that it was as if he had been suddenly transported to another quarter of the globe. Two days later, they arrived at a village where a dance was taking place, and entered the *malocca*:

Some two hundred men, women, and children were scattered about the house, lying in the maqueiras, squatting on the ground, or sitting on the small painted stools, which are made only by the inhabitants of

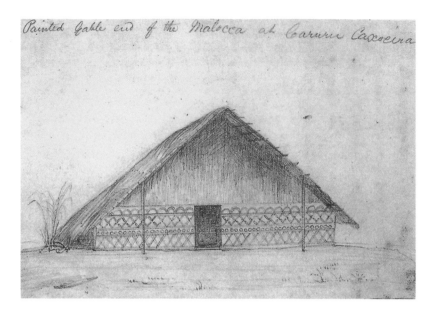

Painted Gable end of the Malocca at Carura Caxoeira

A malocca

this river. Almost all were naked and painted, and wearing their various feathers and other ornaments. Some were walking or conversing, and others were dancing, or playing small fifes and whistles. The regular festa had been broken up that morning: the chiefs and principal men had put off their feather head-dresses, but as caxirí still remained, the young men and women continued dancing . . . The men and boys appropriated all the ornaments, thus reversing the custom of civilised countries and imitating nature, who invariably decorates the male sex with the most brilliant colours and most remarkable ornaments . . . The wild and strange appearance of these handsome, naked, painted Indians, with their curious ornaments and weapons, the stamp and song and rattle which accompanies the dance, the hum of conversation in a strange language, the music of fifes and flutes and other instruments of reed, bone, and turtles' shells, the large calabashes of caxiri constantly carried about, and the great smoke-blackened gloomy house, produced an effect to which no description can do justice, and of which the sight of half-a-dozen Indians going through their dances for show, gives but a very faint idea.[15]

Wallace was entranced, and intrigued, and found himself equally a great object of admiration, principally on account of his spectacles, 'which they saw for the first time and could not at all understand'. This was precisely the kind of experience he had been longing for, and when he and Lima reached Jauarité, just below a great rapid which barred further easy progress, they settled down for a week, Lima to buy farinha and sarsaparilla, Wallace to naturalise. The Indians bred birds and animals of many kinds, and he conceived a plan of making a live collection in the area. By now he seemed thoroughly acclimatised to a largely fish diet. There were yams, sweet potatoes, delicious drinks from the fruits of different palms; and, for once, Wallace comments on the attractiveness of the women – though some were too fat, 'most of them had splendid figures, and many of them were very pretty'.[16] At Lima's suggestion, the head man organised a festa, and Wallace was privileged to observe, and record, the elaborate dances. Most of the women wore the *tanga*, or small apron of beads, but some were perfectly naked. 'Several wore large cylindrical copper ear-rings, so polished as to appear like gold. These and the garters formed their only ornaments, – necklaces, bracelets, and feathers being entirely monopolised by the men. The paint with which they decorate their whole bodies has a very neat effect, and gives them almost the appearance of being dressed . . .' There was far more immodesty, he comments, 'in the transparent and flesh-coloured garments of our stage dancers, than in the perfect nudity of these daughters of the forest'.[17] Then there was a 'snake' dance, with two groups of young men and boys carrying forty-foot long artificial snakes of twigs and bushes, advancing and retreating and having a kind of fight inside the great house; and later fires were lit outside, and the young men jumped through and over them. After three hours, Wallace retired to his own house, he is careful to record. He let Lima smoke the ceremonial cigar on his behalf, but did manage to empty a calabash of caxirí, and pronounced it exceedingly good (even though the mandiocca cake of which it was made had been chewed 'by a parcel of old women'). He passed up the chance to try the powerful narcotic caapí, unlike Richard Spruce on another occasion.

Pausing at São Jeronymo, as they headed down river towards Guía, Wallace revised his strategy. As well as the attraction of the Indians' way of life, and the chance of penetrating further up river than any European traveller, other objectives beckoned. A mile from the village he came on an abundance of orchids – thirty different species in an hour's ramble: a complete natural orchid-house; and more fish. Then there was the variety of live specimens, monkeys, parrots and other birds, which could be bought for a few cheap goods. His notes record: 'Heard much about the upp part of the river – painted turtles – White umbrella bird etc Determine to go to Barra and return to spend the dry season in this River & give up for the present any journey to Peru.'[18] A white umbrella bird would be a real prize. The need to go to Barra, a round trip of fifteen hundred miles, was frustrating, but essential. To spend four months, as he planned, on the Vaupes, at the low-water period, would require fresh supplies, and goods for barter. As rapidly as he could, Wallace returned to Barra, collecting commissions from every village he stopped at on the way, and arrived on 15 September. The whitewashed houses and open situation seemed strangely attractive after the forest-buried huts of the Rio Negro; and his friend Richard Spruce was there, living in Dr Natterer's former residence. He also found some bad news: a letter from the Vice-Consul at Pará, Miller, telling him that Herbert was dangerously ill with yellow fever. The letter was three months old.

Wallace was left, as he afterwards put it, 'in a state of the greatest suspense'.[19] If Herbert had recovered, he would surely have written before sailing to England. If he had died, surely some other resident at Pará would have sent word. (What Wallace could not know was the severity of the epidemic: Bradley and Berchenbrinck, two young traders, were also dead; Bates himself had been seriously ill.) To go down to Pará might take three weeks; to return again as many months. Besides, there was no guarantee that the journey would do any good. He decided to remain in Barra, preparing for his return to the Vaupés.

Herbert Edward Wallace had died on 8 June 1851. Bates, who nursed him for four nights before falling ill with the same symptoms, broke the news to Mrs Wallace 'as the only person here nearly connected to your sons'.[20] Herbert had reached Pará in May, taken lodgings in the house he once shared with Alfred, and booked his passage to Liverpool. In his last moments he told Miller that 'it was very sad to die so young', but he did not mention his brother, or any of his friends, or express any particular wish before he died. He was twenty-two. Bates, writing again to the family that October, still did not know whether Alfred had been informed of what had happened. 'I think no one knew where he was residing & many months have passed since he wrote to Pará. I have just heard however that he is expected daily at the Barra of the Rio Negro with a very rich collection &

I intend to write him by the first canoe that leaves for that place.'[21]

But Wallace was off again before any letter could reach him, after a fortnight's frenzied activity: buying and selling, arranging his collections, constructing his own insect boxes and packing cases in the absence of the only carpenter, and, in his rare spare moments, luxuriating in the pleasure of 'rational conversation' with Spruce. Spruce, himself impatient to head up the Rio Negro, was waiting for a crew. He accompanied Wallace for a day paddling alongside him in a *montaria*, a small canoe, before returning to Barra. Wallace made his way up river but suffered all kinds of delays and difficulties. He had a bout of fever, and found himself 'quite knocked up, with headache, pains in the back and limbs, and violent fever'. He took a purgative, and began a regime of quinine and cream-of-tartar water: the Indians paddled on, and for days and nights he hardly cared if 'we sank or swam', half thinking, half dreaming, of all his past life and future hopes, perhaps all doomed to end on the Rio Negro; and he thought of the 'dark uncertainty' of his brother's fate.[22] But, he comments, with returning health these gloomy thoughts passed away, and he consoled himself by rejoicing that this was his last voyage. At São Joaquim, however, he relapsed, with violent and recurring fever. Lima, fortunately, was there: but for days Wallace lay, unable to turn over in his hammock, unable to write, even to speak intelligibly. Spruce, who had now made his own base at São Gabriel, wrote to Kew at the end of December with bleak news of his friend:

> He writes me by another hand that he is almost at the point of death from a malignant fever, which has reduced him to such a state of weakness that he cannot rise from his hammock or even feed himself. The person who brought me the letter told me that he had taken no nourishment for some days except the juice of oranges and cashews . . . The Rio Negro might be called the Dead River – I never saw such a deserted region . . .[23]

The simple business of procuring enough nourishment took precious time and energy. Spruce found that the mechanical labour of drying plants was so great that he had little time for anything else, such as making geographical observations. The naturalist's life was arduous, dangerous, and wearing.

Spruce went to see his friend; and, as soon as Wallace was strong enough to walk with a stick to the riverside, he was canoed down to visit his fellow naturalist at São Gabriel. Spruce was not exactly comfortable there: instead of the snug cabin in his canoe, he had to contend with an old hut whose thatch was stocked with rats, scorpions, cockroaches and vampire bats, and an earth floor undermined by sauba ants, who attacked his dried plants. The vampire bats were especially active: when Spruce first entered the house, he noted the large patches of dried blood on the floor. But he wore stockings, wrapped himself in a blanket, covered his face with a handkerchief, and kept a lamp burning all night. He and Wallace had much to talk about. Spruce, for a start, had to break the news of Herbert's death, which had reached him at Barra in the month after Wallace's departure. The three men had got on very well together. For Wallace, there must have been a touch of guilt to add to his grief, for it was his example and suggestion that encouraged Herbert to try his hand at the collecting trade. All those glowing reports of healthy living on the Amazon seemed to belong to another era.

The two men talked at length, too, on the question of species. Years later, after the publication of Darwin's *The Origin of Species*, Spruce reminded Wallace of these discussions: 'If you recollect our conversations at São Gabriel, you will understand that I have never believed in the existence of any permanent limits – generic or specific – in the groups of organic beings.'[24] Later and more expansively, Spruce wrote a 'Note on the Theory of Evolution', placing his conclusions on the subject to 'about 1852':

Whilst travelling in S. America (long before I heard of Mr Darwin & his speculation) I thought much of this subject, and I came to the conclusion that surely the same laws & the same forces are in existence now as have been from all eternity, and will continue to be, *in saecula saeculorum*. Also that The Evolution of Organic Forms is continuous, without any break. It follows that the incessant variation of living beings is a movement of progression – not merely an oscillation around fixed points which we choose to call species; so that if we could have before our eyes all the individuals now existing, & that have ever existed, of any (so-called) species or genus, we should find it impossible to draw any lines of separation – or to include any central (specific) points – distinguishing our species & genera.[25]

Wallace, his mind as sharpened by the effects of fever as his body was dull, would have found confirmation in the views he and Bates had already explored together. He would have sympathised, too, with Spruce's thoughts on progression and development:

The one thing certain (for me) is that this universe is regulated by immutable laws; that to find out those laws – physical, moral etc – is to bring ourselves into closer relation with the Supreme Intelligence from whom they emanate, & who must be far greater than all the gods mythologists (or theologists, for there is no difference) have ever invented. In fact those very gods, and the religions founded upon them, do but endure until Natural Selection shall substitute for them something more in accord with man's increasing needs and intelligence.[26]

This statement of Spruce comes from 1870, long after his return to England. But his letter to Wallace about their conversations at São Gabriel implies that his views on the transmutation of species, at least, were already formed. All these ideas Wallace stored away for future reference.

Heartened by his days with Spruce, Wallace bought a little wine and some biscuits from the commandante, and, reasoning that he might just as well recuperate in a canoe as in his hammock, set off once again to ascend the Vaupés. This was to be, positively, his last Amazon trip: his objectives were the white umbrella chatterer, the painted turtle, and as many live birds and animals as he could acquire.

The journey did not have quite the excitement of his first ascent. Without Lima, the Indians proved less reliable, slipping away after taking him one or two stages, or providing less-experienced substitutes, and once breaking open the sealed flask of spirits, which he had with him solely for preserving purposes. Wallace's patience was beginning to fray, and his fever returned. Nevertheless, with extraordinary persistence, he pushed up river, an enterprise that involved negotiating some fifty falls. Sometimes the canoe could be pushed up by the crew. Once, he had to summon reinforcements from a neighbouring village, and it required the combined strength of twenty-five men, pushing, and pulling on ropes, to manoeuvre the unloaded boat over the bare rocks. The water level was falling, and he waited five days to have a smaller canoe built. On 13 March, he reached

Mucura, his farthest point: the next falls were a week away, and Wallace decided to call a halt, satisfied that he was now in a part of the country never before visited by a European traveller. He did his best to map the place, although his boiling-point thermometers were lost or broken, and he had only a pocket surveying sextant. He sent his men out to buy supplies, and any birds and animals they could find. He collected what he could in his fortnight's stay, but blamed the months he had lain half dead at São Joaquim for the shortage of birds, fish and insects: the fruit season was over, the fish were less numerous, even the painted turtle which was reportedly waiting for him secured in a trap disappeared; and no white umbrella chatterers were to be found. Wallace now doubted their very existence, and the relentless fatigue of the isolated and precarious existence was sapping his spirit, as it did with Spruce and Bates. What he could acquire easily, though, were Indian artefacts. He bought weapons, implements, ornaments and dresses, and recorded the local vocabulary. Now it was time to go home. England beckoned, a distant paradise of green fields, flowery paths and neat gardens, and visions of the fireside tea table, with familiar faces round it, and the luxury of bread and butter.[27]

He retraced his route, stopping, once he reached the Rio Negro, to say goodbye to Senhor Lima at São Joaquim, and to make some cages for his birds, and also to pay a farewell visit to Richard Spruce at São Gabriel. He left São Joaquim with fifty-two live animals. The numbers fluctuated. Some escaped, and a monkey ate two of the birds; more were purchased, parrots especially. At Barra, he picked up four large cases of specimens which should have been shipped to England the previous year, but which had been held up by customs regulations. By the time he left for Pará, the hundred or so creatures he had acquired had dwindled to thirty-four: five monkeys, two macaws, twenty parrots or paroquets, a white-crested pheasant, some small birds, and his favourite, a fully grown and very tame toucan. Later, down river, he was given a forest wild dog to add to the collection. The night before he sailed, the toucan flew overboard, and was drowned. It was a bad omen. On the voyage down the Amazon, he stopped at Santarem to visit his friends. Captain Hislop was there, but Bates had left a week before, on a trip up the Tapajóz. Wallace continued to suffer from recurrent bouts of fever, and when they arrived in Pará he did little beyond booking his passage on the brig *Helen*. Yellow fever was still claiming victims. Wallace carried out one last sad duty, and visited the cemetery to see Herbert's grave. It was crowded with crosses: every dwelling in the city was 'a house of mourning'. He wrote to Spruce, and on 12 July embarked with his cargo and the remains of his menagerie.

Two days out, he had another attack of fever, sharp enough to make him wonder whether he had contracted yellow fever. Some calomel set him right, but he remained weak, and mostly stayed in his cabin reading. One morning three weeks out, Captain Turner came in after breakfast with the alarming words: 'I'm afraid the ship's on fire. Come and see what you think of it.' Dense smoke was pouring from the forecastle – 'more like the steam from heating vegetable matter than the smoke from a fire': the cargo was largely indiarubber, with cocoa, balsam and piassaba.[28] The crew attempted to break into the hold, to find the source, but were beaten back by the smoke. The ship's boats were launched. Wallace went to his cabin, found a small tin box with a couple of shirts, and put in his drawings of fishes and palms, and a few valuables such as his watch. In the suffocating smoke it was impossible to search further: his clothes, his journals, and a large portfolio of drawings were left behind: 'I did not care to venture down again, and in fact felt a kind of apathy about saving anything, that I can now hardly account for.' They took to the boats. The balsam was bubbling, the fire rushed up the sails, the decks were fiercely alight. Some of the parrots and monkeys retreated to the bowsprit, and as it caught fire, they ran back, and disappeared in the flames. Only one parrot, clinging to a rope, fell in the water, and was picked up. The *Helen* burned all night, and the next morning the boats' sails were set, and they made for Bermuda, seven hundred miles distant.

Wallace had plenty of time to contemplate his losses, as he later wrote to Spruce. Why had he bothered to save his watch, and a few sovereigns? Hat, shoes, coat and trousers would have been much more useful. But there was never any hope of saving his collections, which he estimated to be worth £500. Even worse, his private collection of insects and birds, which he had kept with him from the beginning, was lost, 'hundreds of new and beautiful species, which would have rendered (I had fondly hoped) my cabinet, as far as regards American species, one of the finest in Europe'; and the sketches, drawings, notes, and three of the most interesting years of his journal: 'You will see that I have some need of philosophic resignation to bear my fate with patience and equanimity.'[29]

Even when they were picked up by the *Jordeson*, two hundred miles short of Bermuda, their anxieties were not over. The *Jordeson* was old, slow, cumbersome and leaky; Wallace was not reassured when the captain one night slept with an axe close at hand – 'to cut away the masts in case we capsize'; and with all the extra men aboard, provisions ran short. There was no spare water for washing, and Wallace's shirts were in a state 'of most uncomfortable dirtiness'. They caught a few dolphins, which were not bad eating, but one by one the staples were exhausted – first the cheese and ham, then the peas, the butter, and finally the pork, to leave them on a diet of biscuit and water. Almost the worst experience was a violent gale in the Channel on 29 September. Wallace was sitting on the poop with Captain Turner at the height of the storm, and as they rolled with a bigger wave than usual the captain said quietly, 'If we are pooped by one of those waves we shall go to the bottom', adding that he would rather be back in the two small ship's boats 'than in this rotten old tub'.[30]

However, they survived the fearful storm, which left them with four feet of water in the hold, and 1 October was a glorious day, eighty days out from Pará, on shore at last in a Deal inn: a glorious warm bath, and 'Such a dinner, with our two captains! Oh, beef-steaks and damson tart, a paradise for hungry sinners.' But even as the solid comforts of England wrapped him round, he was beginning to envy Spruce, still in 'that glorious country where "the sun shines for ever unchangeably bright", where farinha abounds, and of bananas and plantains there is no lack!'[31] This was not quite the triumphant homecoming Wallace had dreamed of in the upper reaches of the Vaupés.

RARE FERNS ON MOUNT OPHIR.

5   Planning the Next Expedition

Wallace, shivering in his calico suit and weak in the legs after the eighty-day voyage, was welcomed by his agent. Stevens took him to a ready-made clothes shop for his immediate needs, had him measured for a new suit by his tailor, and invited him to his own home in Norwood, where Mrs Stevens senior fussed over him, and in a week fed him back to his 'usual health and vigour'.[1] Stevens had also saved his client from complete financial disaster by insuring the cargo for £200. (The true loss of the collections was probably more intellectual than financial: Bates calculated his own overall profit for one 20-month period at £26 19s.) Wallace was alive, and well, and ready to plan his next trip. During the gloomy days and nights in the *Helen*'s long boat, and the damp, cramped misery on board the *Jordeson*, he had vowed never to trust himself to the ocean again. But good resolutions soon fade: would it be a second westward journey up the Amazon to the Andes, or east to the Philippines? Meanwhile, he would

83

need to be a fixture in London for at least six months and was determined to make up for lost time by enjoying himself as much as possible for a while, he informed Spruce. He brought him up to date with the latest news. Wellington, the Iron Duke, was dead, and the Crystal Palace was being pulled down and rebuilt: the Hackney nurserymen Loddiges' collection of plants had been bought to stock it, and thanks to Sir Joseph Paxton's ingenious heating plan the whole world's plants, temperate and tropical, could be displayed in one undivided building.[2] A thriving exhibition and museum industry was vital for the collecting profession.

On 4 October, Wallace attended the Entomological Society's meeting as a visitor. By this time, his name, if not his face, was well known in London scientific circles. Stevens had already published extracts of his letters in the *Annals and Magazine of Natural History*, just as he published those of Bates in the columns of the *Zoologist*. At the Entomological Society's meetings, he would regularly show some of the new species he received from Wallace and Bates; for example, on 7 April 1851, 'Mr Stevens exhibited, from a collection just received from Mr Wallace, *Papilio columbus*'; on 5 May, there were Lepidoptera and Coleoptera from Mr Bates in Ega, 'now on his way home'; and again, on 4 August, more specimens from Bates in Ega and from Wallace in Guía. Significantly, on 1 September 1851, at a Special General Meeting, a revision of the by-laws created a new class of members, Associates, 'to admit working entomologists to the advantage offered by the Society's meetings, Library, and Collection'. Samuel Stevens became a member of the Council in 1851, and Treasurer the following year. It was natural for him to take Wallace along, a living specimen of a working entomologist, and his plight was fully recorded in the Society's minutes – both the fact that he had lost 'the whole' of his valuable collections, and, in rather more graphic terms than Wallace himself used, that he had 'narrowly escaped death in an open boat, from which, after long privation and suspense, and while yet in the midst of the Atlantic Ocean, he and others were taken up by a vessel bound for London'.[3] Bates, hearing of Wallace's loss, expressed heart-felt sympathy: 'Had it been my case I think I should have gone desperate, because, so far as regards the unique specimens, the journal &c., such a loss is irreparable.'[4]

In the course of the following year, 1853, Wallace read two papers to the Society. It was an excellent base, both for meeting naturalists, and for getting his name known through the journal. Darwin was a member, though he seldom attended meetings; so were Thomas Bell, the President of the Linnean Society; George Waterhouse and J. E. Gray, both on the staff of the British Museum; Richard Owen, at that time Hunterian Professor at the Royal College of Surgeons; Darwin's neighbour the anthropologist John Lubbock; the insect and shell specialist Thomas Wollaston; ornithologist and taxidermist to the Zoological Society John Gould; entomologist and artist John Curtis; and the natural-history writer and enthusiast Edward Newman. Working entomologists such as Wallace, however, were not accepted without a slight struggle. Newman, in his presidential address of January 1854, had to underline the value of the 'actual collector', as opposed to the professional experts in the museums of London, and the connoisseurs of the rectories and country houses:

> The monographer cannot say to the collector, he specified, I have no need of you; the very admission of such a thought is a stumbling-block . . . I wish to be understood as applying this last observation especially and emphatically to the case of the actual collector; to the man who, in whatever station of life, devotes his time, by night and by day; at all seasons, in all weathers; at home and abroad, to the positive capture and preservation of those specimens which serve as the objects for all our observations: he is the real labourer in the field, and if we would keep the lamp of our science constantly burning, it is to him alone that we can look for fuel to feed its flame.

Newman had in mind professional collectors based in Britain, such as Bouchard and Foxcroft, and those working abroad, such as Wallace and Bates, both of whom he alludes to at length.

> Such men do great, permanent and continual good: they render our science an unquestionable service, and their motives are no more to be called in question than those of the artist or the author, who receives the just reward for his well-directed labours.

But to work abroad entailed substantial costs. Newman outlined these, and reminded his audience that both Bates and Wallace were more than simple collectors, contributing 'observation as well as manual industry', never failing to make the needful commentary on the habits and manners, food and metamorphoses of the specimens.[5] That Newman found it necessary to make his appeal is a sign of the lingering prejudice against the working collector. But a breach had been made in the closed circle, and Stevens led Wallace through it. In 1854, both Wallace and Bates were elected corresponding members of the society.

Meanwhile, Wallace had to rebuild his personal life. His only surviving brother John had come back to England in the winter of 1850–51, married Mary Webster, the daughter of the master-builder to whom he had been apprenticed, and returned to California. With John abroad indefinitely, and Fanny married to a not very successful photographer, Wallace saw himself as the head of the family. He could not afford to go far from London, so he invited his mother, and Fanny and Thomas Sims, to join him there. He took a house at 44 Upper Albany Street, close to Regent's Park, and by Christmas they were all installed. There was the opportunity now to read over Herbert's Amazon letters to Fanny, and to his mother, as well as Bates's poignant description of his final illness.

Of the three brothers who had emigrated, Alfred had come close enough to success to be convinced that the instincts that first prompted his visit to the Amazon were sound. He had been given a ticket for the Zoological Gardens – Stevens was a fellow of that society too – and was invited to attend the Zoological's scientific meetings: in December, he gave a paper 'On the Monkeys of the Amazon', and heard T. H. Huxley lecture on 'The Anatomy and Development of Echinococci in the Liver of a Zebra'.[6] He was so impressed by Huxley's fluent, confident style that he assumed he must be a much older man than himself – in fact, Huxley was two years younger. At the meeting on 8 February 1853, G. W. Earl gave notes on the zoology of the Malay Peninsula; Wallace said that he attended these meetings very regularly, so there is every chance he was present on this occasion. The Royal Geographical Society, too, opened its doors to him. His notes and readings on the Upper Rio Negro and the Vaupés, however imperfect, had been preserved, and he duly presented them: they offered clear proof of his credentials as an explorer.

Wallace's reputation as a traveller and a naturalist had risen as a result of his American expedition. He obtained an introduction to the philologist, Robert Latham, and consulted him about the South American Indian vocabularies he had collected. Latham was also in charge of the Ethnological Department at the Crystal Palace, and Wallace went there to advise on the life-size clay models of Indians. The head modellers were Italians, and tended to give the figures the attitudes and expressions of Roman statuary. Wallace was able to nudge them in the direction of realism.[7] This was all interesting enough, but there were few material rewards, and Wallace's transference from field collector to recognised writer and naturalist was tentative and precarious. Of all that heady list of projects conceived on the river Vaupés, only two materialised. *Palms of the Amazon and Rio Negro*, a small, popular volume, in the author's self-disparaging words, was published at his own expense, much of which was taken up with commissioning illustrations from Walter Fitch.[8] The print run was limited to 250 copies, and Wallace just about covered his costs. *Travels on the Amazon and Rio Negro*, 'that absurd book' as he later described it to George Silk, was put together with the help of letters and scraps of notes after the loss of two years' journals in the ship's fire, and he arranged for its publication on a shared-profit basis. It was nine years before there was anything to share. Clearly, he needed to make another major expedition.

Wallace called his eight years of wandering through the Malay Archipelago 'the central and controlling incident' of his life, and in his autobiographical account he gives the impression that the choice of destination came about through a logical and systematic process of elimination. He had listened attentively at meetings of the learned societies, he had studied the collections at the British Museum. Most expeditiously, he made the acquaintance of Rajah Brooke, the first white rajah of Sarawak, a contact that promised safe access to part of Borneo: Brooke, on the point of leaving England, wrote in April 1853 to assure Wallace that he would be very glad to see him at Sarawak.[9] The Archipelago was relatively unexplored by naturalists, while the Dutch administration that controlled much of it would provide a logistical safety net. There were always, of course, the rich natural resources of South America, but across the Atlantic Bates, having finally decided to remain in Brazil, was firmly established in the insect line, and there was already a successful bird-collector, Hauxwell, on the upper Amazon. Everything pointed him towards the East. Wallace began to make notes and sketches of the rarer – and more valuable – species of birds, butterflies and beetles.

For all his apparent naïvety, Wallace was never reluctant to ask for assistance, especially when he believed that he had earned the right to it. He had met Sir Roderick Murchison when he made his presentation on the

Rio Negro to the Royal Geographical Society. In June 1853, he put together an extremely impressive proposal about his plans, and asked for the Society's services in obtaining a free passage.

> He proposes leaving England in the Autumn or Winter of the present year, and, making Singapore his headquarters, to visit in succession Borneo, the Philippines, Celebes, Timor, the Moluccas and New Guinea, or such of them as may prove most accessible, remaining one or more years in each as circumstances may determine.
>
> His chief object is the investigation of the Natural History of the Eastern Archipelago in a more complete manner than has hitherto been attempted; but he will also pay much attention to Geography, & hopes to add considerably to our knowledge of such of the islands as he may visit.[10]

He emphasised that he intended to carry out a substantial amount of geographical readings and measurement – in fact, he implied that he could not afford the instruments as well as the fare, and ended his appeal by reminding the Council that he had lost an extensive and valuable collection as well as his books and instruments in the mid-Atlantic fire. On 22 July, Wallace's application was read before the Committee on Expeditions, in the Society's premises in Waterloo Place. Wallace joined the meeting, and after some discussion it was resolved

> that in order to enable Mr Wallace to prosecute with success the scientific objects of his voyage, Sir Roderick Murchison be requested to apply to HM's Government to grant Mr Wallace a free passage to Singapore and to procure letters of introduction for him from the Governments of Spain and Holland to their East India Colonies.[11]

Wallace, having set the wheels in motion, delivered the manuscript of *Travels on the Amazon* to his publisher and went off to France and Switzerland for a holiday with George Silk. He failed to estimate the speed at which Sir Roderick Murchison could work. A passage to Trincomalee was offered, and Wallace found himself in the embarrassing position of turning it down, when the letter from the Geographical eventually reached him in France. 'The journey from Trincomalee to Singapore & from

Singapore to Borneo would entail considerable expense & loss of time,' he explained unconvincingly to Norton Shaw, the secretary of the RGS, on 27 August. But, in the same breath, conscious that he might have sounded ungracious, he floated an alternative plan, 'to attempt the exploration of the snowy mountains in Eastern Africa, instead of going to Borneo'. This was the suggestion of August Petermann, and he was 'quite ready to give it up or go with it as the Geographical Society may think best'; he left it to Shaw and the Society to decide 'which journey they would find most interest in'. He would be back in a fortnight; meanwhile, Shaw could reach him at Chamonix.[12] Wallace was in no mood to break off his excursion. He and Silk travelled on to Geneva, gazed at Mont Blanc, and then explored the Alps from Chamonix, Le Montenvert and Flegère. From there they walked over the Tête Noir pass and down to Martigny, took a chaise along the Rhône valley to Leuk, trekked up to Leukerbad (having hired a porter to carry their luggage), stayed at the inn at the top of the Gemmi pass, and strolled down to Thun. This was Wallace's first of many visits to Switzerland, and it sharpened the appetite for geology as well as for mountain botanising he had acquired in Wales.

Sugar palm

The autumn passed. Loss of time no longer seemed an issue. The two Amazon books were published to modest interest. *The Annals and Magazine of Natural History* praised them both – the book on palms was 'a highly valuable companion to the great work on Palms by Martius'. Sir William Hooker was magisterial, sarcastic, and caustic, leaping on errors and questioning the identification of the piassaba palm, where the author had the temerity to disagree with the great von Martius:

> We do not in the least call in question the accuracy of Mr Wallace's statement that his is the tree which now furnishes, on so large a scale, the brooms and brushes of modern days; nor are we able to deny its being a Palm hitherto unknown to Botanists; but we do complain that a Naturalist who is able 'to make out its geographical range so exactly, from having resided more than two years among people whose principal occupation consisted in obtaining the fibrous covering of this tree, and from whom no locality of it can have remained undiscovered', should never have been at the pains to procure flowers and fruit for the illustration of so interesting a plant.

'We trust,' Hooker added, twisting the knife dextrously, that 'Mr Spruce, now in that country, will make up for this deficiency.'[13] As a final thrust, he concluded that the work was 'certainly more suited to the drawing-room table than to the library of the botanist'. This was brutal treatment from the man whose letter of recommendation Wallace and Bates had flourished on their arrival in Pará, and a useful warning for Wallace on the need for accuracy – he had certainly not spent two continuous years in piassaba country.

Fortunately for Wallace's confidence, this particular review did not appear until he was out of the country. The lithographic plates were not as accurate as Wallace's original pencil sketches, and Wallace was not so expert in plants as in other fields; even so, five species of Amazonian palms are still known by the scientific names Wallace gave them,[14] and the book's main focus is on the economic uses that the Indians made of different kinds and parts of palm, for their houses, weapons and food. Hooker, fierce but fair, partly made up for things later by publishing a letter suggesting that there were *two* commercially exploited piassabas, the *Attalea funifera* of von Martius, and the *Leopoldinia piassaba* of Wallace. At the same time, he revealed something of the palm project's genesis, by printing a letter from Spruce, who had been sent a copy of the book by the author:

> When Mr Wallace came down the Rio Negro, in September, 1851, he showed me a few figures of Palms. I pointed out to him which seemed to be new, and encouraged him to go on. I also proposed that we should work them up together, I taking the literary part and he the pictorial, which he declined.

By printing that comment, Hooker is clearly implying that Wallace would have done much better for the cause of science to have collaborated with a specialist. More unkindly, he also published Spruce's unofficial 'review': 'The descriptions are worse than nothing – in many cases not a single circumstance that a botanist would care to know; but the accounts of the uses are good.'[15] People were more forgiving about the travel book, conscious of the losses Wallace had sustained. There are wonderful sequences within it, but Wallace could not decide whether he should concentrate on a personal narrative of his travels, or attempt a work of systematic and scientific observation. In attempting to do both, he ended up with a hybrid, and the sections of minute detail, for instance in his final chapter 'On the Aborigines of the Amazon', draw attention to the earlier gaps and absences, no doubt caused by the loss of some of his journals. It is still a remarkable book, suffering only in comparison with his later writing, or with Bates's *The Naturalist on the River Amazons*.

Meanwhile, Wallace bought Lucien Bonaparte's 1850 study *Conspectus Generum Avium*, and copied additional notes on Malaysian species on its wide margins, so providing himself with the nearest thing to a field guide. He also acquired J. A. Boisduval's 1836 volume *Diurnes: Papilionidae, Pierides*, to assist with identification of the butterflies. He read books of more general interest, including one that would leave a powerful impact on him, Herbert Spencer's *Social Statics*, especially the chapter on 'The Right to Use the Earth'. The broad evolutionary flow of Spencer's arguments, and their application to social issues, seeped into Wallace's thinking to take an influential place beside the ideas of Robert Chambers's *Vestiges*. He spent long hours in the insect room of the British Museum. There, one day, he was introduced to another visitor, Charles Darwin, or so he recollected. The meeting, if it took place, made little impression on either.

A second application was made to the Lords of the Admiralty. Dr Shaw was empowered to apply to the Peninsular and Oriental Steam Navigation Company to grant Wallace a free passage. Meanwhile Wallace kicked his heels in Upper Albany Street, and wrote a reference for a friend of his brother John, James Wilson, who volunteered to join an expedition to Northern Australia sponsored by the Royal Geographical – 'a good bushman', he commented on Wilson – and it even crossed his mind to try Australia himself. But at last the Admiralty connection came good. Wallace dispatched his heavy equipment to Singapore, including most of his books, by the cheaper Cape route, and went down to Portsmouth in January 1854 to take up his quarters on HMS *Frolic*. The *Frolic* was bound for Sydney, from where Wallace would make his way to the Eastern Archipelago. Newman, in his presidential address to the Entomological on 23 January, quoted at length from *Travels on the Amazon*, and wished Wallace better fortune and God speed on behalf of the Society.[16]

Wallace settled himself in on board. He was given a friendly welcome by Captain Nolloth, invited to sling his cot in a corner of his cabin, and provided with a small table to write and read at. He began to look forward to a voyage in the congenial company of a remarkably pleasant set of officers, and amused himself by matching individuals to the types he had met in Captain Marryat's seafaring novels. For a while, he must have imagined himself almost in the position of Darwin on the *Beagle*. Days and weeks passed on board, and then the ship's sailing orders were cancelled. The *Frolic* was to be diverted to the Crimea. Wallace wrote off to the Admiralty, lugged all his chattels grumpily to the Keppels Head at Portsea, and prepared to face the less attractive alternative of heading for Australia by a 'circuitous' route in HMS *Juno* under Captain Freemantle, who, Wallace informed Shaw, was 'not spoken well of'. He was doing his best to exercise patience 'as much as on the Amazon', but would be glad of any certainty instead of the 'disagreeable suspense I have been & am in'.[17] The flow of brisk requests continued. He already had a general letter of recommendation to Her Majesty's Consuls. He now sought a letter from the Admiralty for commanders of ships on the Australia and East India stations to offer him facilities for exploring any little-known islands they might touch at. He wrote accepting the offer on the *Juno*, but soon changed his mind. A few days later he was back in London knocking on Sir Roderick Murchison's door, and received, for his persistence, a first-class ticket to

Singapore on the next P. & O. steamer, the *Euxine*.

This was an unexpected bonus, allowing him the comparative luxury of taking an assistant, Charles Allen, as apprentice collector, something that could not have been accommodated on a naval ship. Charlie was an undersized sixteen-year-old, who looked more like thirteen or fourteen, the son of a carpenter who had done some work for Wallace's sister. It must have been a sudden decision on the part of both parties, and one that both would have cause, at times, to regret.

The *Euxine* sailed in March for Gibraltar, Malta and Egypt, taking Wallace away from the frustrations of his English interlude. Whisked from the quay to his Alexandria hotel by omnibus, he decided to go for a quiet stroll with Charlie, and found himself catapulted into the noise and bustle of an eastern city:

> Now, then, behold your long-legged friend mounted upon a jackass in the streets of Alexandria; a boy behind, holding by his tail and whipping him up; Charles, who had been lost sight of in the crowd, upon another; and my guide upon a third; and off we go among a crowd of Jews and Greeks, Turks and Arabs, and veiled women and yelling donkey-boys, to see the city. We saw the bazaars, and the slave-market (where I was again nearly pulled to pieces for 'backsheesh'), the mosques with their graceful minarets, and then the pasha's new palace, the interior of which is most gorgeous. We passed lots of Turkish soldiers, walking in comfortable irregularity; and after the consciousness of being dreadful guys for two crowded hours, returned to the hotel, whence we are to start for the canal boats.

One of Wallace's strengths as a traveller was a strong sense of his own absurdity, and his ability to see himself through the eyes of others, whether Indians from the Vaupés, islanders from Aru, or the donkey-drivers of Alexandria. Another was his inexhaustible enthusiasm for other ways of life, and for seeing at first hand the scenes he knew only from literature. Read Thackeray's 'First Day in the East' again, he advised George Silk – 'and you will understand just how I think and feel'. Everything was of interest – taken up the Nile on barges, 'with a panorama of mud villages, palm trees, camels, and irrigating wheels turned by buffaloes, – a perfectly flat country, beautifully green with crops of corn and lentils; endless boats with immense triangular sails'.[18] Then the Pyramids, and Cairo – Grand Cairo! the city of romance – and a walk in the city, very picturesque and very dirty; and brown bread and fresh butter in a quiet English hotel; and then on to Suez the next morning, in a small four-horsed two-wheeled omnibus, with a meal every three hours, and the skeletons of hundreds of camels lining the road – 'endless trains of camels' passed along the route, bearing the Indian and Australian mails, and all the parcels and goods of the passengers. At the eating places, he picked a few of the desert plants, and pocketed a few land shells. They reached Suez at midnight, and the following day were relieved to be on board the *Bengal*, with large, comfortable cabins, very superior to the *Euxine*. They stayed a day at desolate, volcanic Aden, and sailed to Galle in Ceylon, present-day Sri Lanka. There they changed ship for the third time, and proceeded on the *Pottinger* to Penang, with its picturesque mountain, spice trees and waterfall, and from there south through the Straits of Malacca to Singapore.

Wallace arrived in Singapore on 20 April 1854, and spent the first three months of his 'eight years wandering' in the Malay Archipelago there, learning about the East, and exploiting the island's rich resources as a location for beetles and butterflies. Singapore, governed by the English, energised by the Chinese, offered a cross-section of the Archipelago's populations: to the native Malays were added Portuguese from Malacca, Klings from western India, Bengalis, Parsees, Javanese sailors, and traders from all the islands to the south and east. Wallace loved the bustle and industry of the city, especially the entrepreneurial activities of the Chinese: in the island's interior, the Chinese were cutting down the forest trees for timber, and growing vegetables and pepper in the clearings. Wallace befriended the French Jesuit missionaries at Bukit-tima, in the centre of the island, and profited by the woodcutters' tracks, and by the piles of dead and decaying leaves and bark and sawdust, wonderful nourishment for insects and their larvae. He set to work within the same kind of regime that he had established in Pará:

> Get up at half-past five, bath, and coffee. Sit down to arrange and put away my insects of the day before, and set them in a safe place to dry. Charles mends our insect nets, fills our pin-cushions, and gets ready for the day. Breakfast at eight; out to the jungle at nine. We have to walk about a quarter mile up a steep hill to reach it, and arrive dripping with

perspiration. Then we wander about in the delightful shade along paths made by the Chinese woodcutters till two or three in the afternoon, generally returning with fifty or sixty beetles, some very rare or beautiful, and perhaps a few butterflies. Change clothes to sit down to kill and pin insects, Charles doing the flies, wasps and bugs; I do not trust him yet with beetles. Dinner at four, then at work again till six. Then read or talk, or, if insects very numerous, work again till eight or nine. Then to bed.[19]

This might have been routine for Wallace – but it was a rugged initiation for a London boy of sixteen.

That patch of jungle, not much more than a square mile, provided a fair collection of butterflies and other orders of insects, and an exceptional range of beetles – no fewer than 700 species, many of them 'new', including 130 'distinct kinds of the elegant longicorns (Cerambycidae) so much esteemed by collectors'.[20] This was an excellent start, both commercially and in terms of knowledge. But birds and animals were scarce, apart from the tigers (Wallace reckoned that these killed on average a Chinese every day, principally in the plantations, and their occasional roarings made it rather nervous work hunting for insects among the old sawpits). He decided to try his luck at Malacca, and moved there for two months. He engaged two Portuguese, one to cook and one to shoot and skin birds, and set off inland, where he began to obtain good specimens of birds: eastern trogons, green barbets, a green gaper which was like a small cock-of-the-rock, kingfishers, cuckoos, doves and honeysuckers, all of which kept him 'in a state of pleasurable excitement'. Back in Malacca, he suffered an unpleasant attack of fever, but on the government doctor's advice took much larger doses of quinine than he had ever done in the Amazon. He went to stay inland at the government bungalow at Ayer-panas, and in a fortnight recovered enough energy to plan an expedition to climb Mount Ophir, thirty miles to the east. He found a local man interested in natural history, engaged six Malays to carry the baggage, and set off on his first major trek.

The walk there was hard going, along paths often knee deep in mud, 'swarming with leeches' which crawled all over them, and 'sucked when and where they pleased'. But they made a camp at the foot of the mountain in a little hut built by his men near a rocky stream, caught some fine new butterflies, and climbed the mountain. There were wonderful ferns – groves of *Dipteris horsfieldii* and *Matonia pectinata* – and pitcher plants. Water was short, so Wallace sampled the half-pint or so contained in each pitcher, which was full of insects and looked uninviting, but turned out to be quite palatable, though rather warm. Refreshed, he went on to the summit, four thousand feet above sea level, as he confirmed when making his coffee by checking with a boiling-point thermometer, cross-checking his readings with a sympiesometer (he was doing his stuff for the Geographical). The top was 'a rocky platform covered with rhododendrons and other shrubs. The afternoon was clear, and the view fine in its way – ranges of hill and valley everywhere covered with interminable forest, with glistening rivers winding among them.' From the scenic point of view, he preferred Switzerland, even Snowdon. But there were other headier excitements: the cry of the great Argus pheasant, elephant dung, rhinoceros tracks. They kept up a fire 'in case any of these creatures should visit us, and two of our men declared that they did one day see a rhinoceros'. Mount Ophir had 'quite a reputation for fever', and when they returned to Malacca everyone was astonished at their recklessness in staying so long.[21]

Wallace's narrative in *The Malay Archipelago* strives to create excitement and danger out of a relatively routine expedition, and he excuses its 'meagreness and brevity' by lamenting lost letters and notebook, and a paper sent to the Royal Geographical Society 'which was neither read nor printed, owing to press of matter at the end of a session, and the MSS. of which can not now be found'.[22] (In fact, it was judged too short to be printed, and remains in the RGS archives.) But Sir William Hooker printed a long descriptive letter about the trip to Mount Ophir in his *Journal of Botany*. This piece may be something Wallace chose to forget, as it contains some of his less thoughtful and objective writing. For example, writing about the Malays:

> They are of short stature, well made, but certainly not good-looking; and, taking the women and girls I have occasionally seen as a fair sample, there is very little necessity for their hiding themselves or covering their faces, unless indeed they are ashamed of them.[23]

This is a rare example of Wallace writing as the wrong sort of Englishman abroad, with one eye on his public, as though from the balcony of a club in

Singapore. Borneo would change him. All the same, this expedition proved a useful first foray, and he never forgot his first introduction to mountain scenery in the eastern tropics.

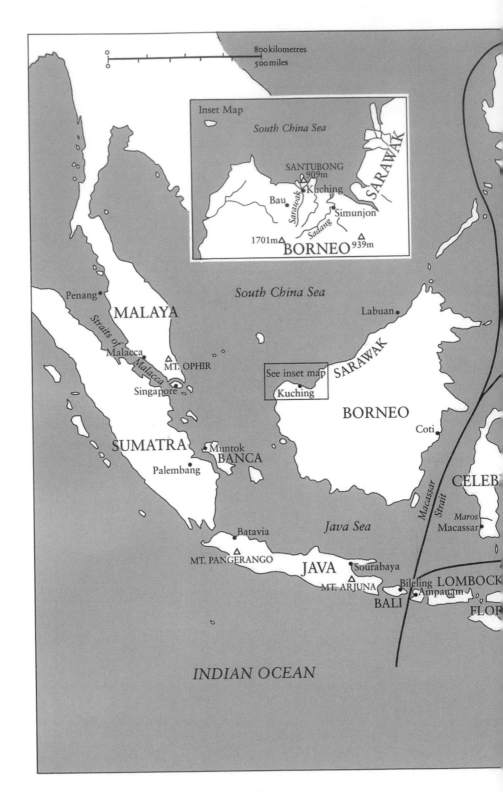

The Indonesian Archipelago

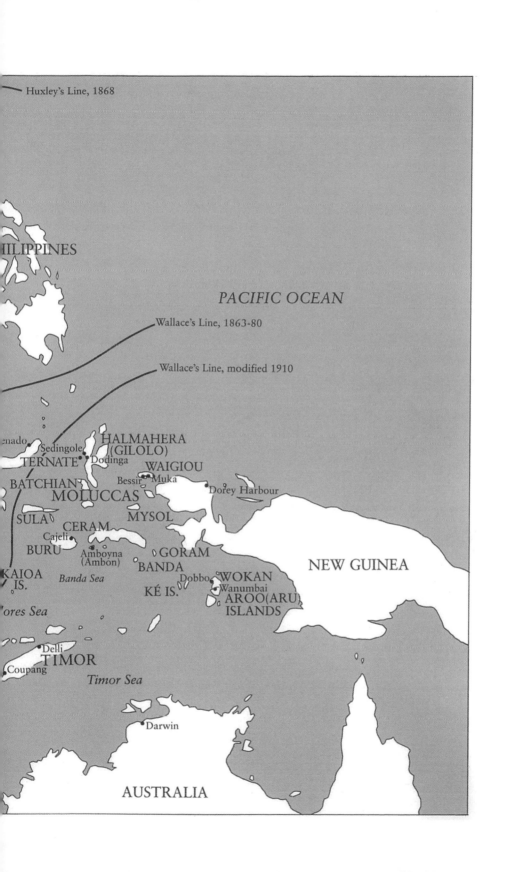

Huxley's Line, 1868

ILIPPINES

PACIFIC OCEAN

Wallace's Line, 1863-80

Wallace's Line, modified 1910

HALMAHERA
(GILOLO)
Sedingole • Dodinga
TERNATE •
WAIGIOU
BATCHIAN
Bessir • Muka
Dorey Harbour
MOLUCCAS

MYSOL
SULA
CERAM
Cajeli •
BURU
Amboyna
(Ambon)
GORAM
BANDA
KAIOA
IS.
Banda Sea
Dobbo • WOKAN
Wanumbai
KÉ IS.
AROO(ARU)
ISLANDS

NEW GUINEA

ores Sea

• Delli
TIMOR
Coupang •

Timor Sea

• Darwin

AUSTRALIA

6 The Land of the Orang-utan

Returning to his Singapore base in September 1854, Wallace busied himself in dispatching consignments to Stevens, in visiting his old friends, and in making final preparations for a major expedition. His books and instruments had arrived from England, via the Cape, so he was fully equipped at last. He took the opportunity of having lots of jackets and trousers made for him by a Chinese tailor, at two shillings a pair. Rajah Brooke was in Singapore, reluctantly preparing to give evidence to the special commission set up to investigate his controversial anti-piracy activities. Brooke's hospitality and influence would be crucial for Wallace's success. Wallace met up with him in September, and, as Brooke most kindly offered him 'every assistance in exploring the territories under his rule', he decided to make Borneo his next destination, rather than to go to Cambodia with his French Jesuit friend from Bukit-tima.[1] Wallace arrived off the coast of Borneo on 1 November 1854. He was to spend longer continuous time there – almost fifteen months – than in any other location on his eastern travels, write his most significant scientific paper to date, and encounter, in its natural habitat, the orang-utan, the great man-like ape of Borneo. As his ship approached the coast, the impressive mass of Santubong mountain appeared, 'like a great fortress commanding the entrance to the Sarawak river' in the words of the Italian naturalist, Odoardo Beccari.[2] Santubong, a limestone mountain, rises sharply from the surrounding flats, its apparently sheer sides densely covered with forest; the shoreline, scattered with small islands, is fringed with sandy beaches or mangroves, or places where the forest falls right to the sea's edge. On the riverbanks grow nipa and nibong palms. Wallace was now on the edge of his first great collecting ground in the East, a region as rich, and as comparatively untouched by the naturalist, as the Amazons. 'I am much pleased with the appearance of the country,' he wrote to Dr Shaw, '(though I am only three days here) there being many more hills than I expected offering facilities for <u>mapping</u>, which I trust to make good use of.' Remembering the support he had received from the Society, he emphasised the geographical aspects of his enterprise, and enclosed a brief description of Mount Ophir, as further evidence of his industry.[3]

For the first two months, Wallace used the Sarawak and the Santubong rivers as his means of transport – there were no alternatives – collecting from the river mouths up to Sarawak city – modern Kuching – and then up river as far as the Chinese gold workings at Bau. It was the rainy season, and collections were, by Wallace's exacting standards, poor. He spent Christmas as a guest of Brooke in Sarawak, and enjoyed the company of the handful of Europeans who formed the compact administration of the rajah, and the contrasting group who were the nucleus of the Anglican mission. Then he moved down river, and in a little house by the mouth of the Sarawak river at the foot of Santubong mountain – directly opposite the present site of Bako National Park – he sat out the rains with his books, his notebooks, and his thoughts, with just a Malay boy to cook for him; Charles Allen he left at the mission. During his evenings in Singapore, he had begun to make notes which eventually developed into a plan for a book, provisionally entitled 'The Organic Law of Change'. Now, insulated from company, he took advantage of the enforced break from collecting to set out the first stage of the theory, in a paper he entitled: 'On the Law Which Has Regulated the Introduction of New Species'.[4]

Brooke's bungalow on the Sarawak river

The immediate impetus for the paper was the 'polarity theory' of Edward Forbes, which was distinctly creationist, and argued for a 'Divine scheme of organized nature', an 'ideal absurdity' as Wallace described it later to Bates.[5] Forbes first put forward this theory as part of his presidential address to the Geological Society on 17 February 1854, just before Wallace set off for the East, but Wallace is more likely to have come across it in journals sent out to Singapore by Stevens. Other influences include Charles Lyell's *Principles of Geology*, François Jules Pictet's *Traité de Paléontologie*, the evolutionist theories of Jean Baptiste Lamarck and Robert Chambers's *Vestiges*. In his lucid essay, Wallace set out his simple law: 'Every species has come into existence coincident both in time and space with a pre-existing closely allied species.'[6] The key idea that emerges is that of evolution by means of gradual change, so that his law explains 'the natural system of arrangement of organic beings, their geographical distribution, their geological sequence, the phenomena of representative and substituted groups in all their modifications, and the most singular peculiarities of anatomical structure' (by these 'peculiarities' Wallace was referring to what he described as 'rudimentary organs', such as 'the antitypal sketch of a wing adapted for flight in the scaly flapper of the penguin', not realising at the

102

time that the majority of such instances were 'vestigial' features). Although Wallace was presenting a powerful synthesis of existing knowledge and theory, summarising widely accepted propositions about organic geography and geology, the argument he puts forward is based strongly on his own observations. By travelling and noting so minutely the patterns of distribution of particular classes, orders, families, genera and species, he was able to verify that his broad statements fitted the facts. For example, he used his knowledge of birds he had actually collected to demonstrate one major geographical proposition: 'When a group is confined to one district, and is rich in species, it is almost invariably the case that the most closely allied species are found in the same locality or in closely adjoining localities, and that therefore the natural sequence of the species by affinity is also geographical' – a proposition that helps to answer the questions: 'Why are the closely allied species of brown-backed trogons all found in the east, and the green-backed in the west? Why are the macaws and the cockatoos similarly restricted?'

One striking section of argument derives directly from Darwin's *Voyage of the Beagle*:

> The Galapagos are a volcanic group of high antiquity, and have probably never been more closely connected with the continent than they are at present. They must have been first peopled, like other newly formed islands, by the action of winds and currents, and at a period sufficiently remote to have had the original species die out, and the modified prototypes only remain. In the same way we can account for the separate islands having each their peculiar species, either on the supposition that the same original emigration peopled the whole of the islands with the same species from which differently modified prototypes were created, or that the islands were successively peopled from each other, but that new species have been created in each on the plan of the pre-existing ones.

(Wallace was clearly using the word 'create' in the sense of 'evolve'.) He also illustrated the relationship between past and existing species through the metaphors of a tree – a gnarled oak – or the vascular system of the human body:

Again, if we consider that we have only fragments of this vast system, the stem and main branches being represented by extinct species of which we have no knowledge, while a vast mass of limbs and boughs and minute twigs and scattered leaves is what we have to place in order, so as to determine the true position which each originally occupied with regard to the others, the whole difficulty of the true Natural System of classification becomes apparent to us.

Wallace claimed for his law

a superiority over previous hypotheses, on the ground that it not merely explains, but necessitates what exists. Granted the law, and many of the most important facts in Nature could not have been otherwise, but are almost as necessary deductions from it as are the elliptic orbits of the planets from the law of gravitation.

The theory was clearly stated, but Wallace did not enter into the question of the mechanism, the how. This was certainly no surreptitious, cautious testing of the water, but a public challenge: Forbes had just been elected to a chair at Edinburgh, and, because of the openness and generosity of his nature, was thought highly of even by those who disagreed with his views. He was likely to respond. Wallace clearly wished for a debate, even at long distance, and was not to know, as he wrote out his argument while the rain thundered down on Santubong, that Forbes had died in November at the age of thirty-nine. He sealed up the essay, and sent it to Stevens for forwarding to the editor of the *Annals and Magazine of Natural History*. Then he went on with his reading, transferring key passages to his Species Notebook, and developing his ideas for the full-scale treatment he was planning, until the rainy season was past. In noting Lyell's views on the 'balance of species', he commented, 'To human apprehension this is no balance but a struggle in which one often exterminates the other.' A little later, he comments, 'Introduce this and disprove all Lyell's arguments first at the commencement of my last chapter.'[7] His mind was humming.

His collecting so far had been sporadic, and certainly not spectacular. He needed to make his way, if not into the heart of Borneo, then at least to new territory away from the Sarawak and Santubong rivers, and back in Sarawak he asked for advice. To the east, a coal works was being opened on the

Simunjon river, a small branch of the Sadong river, at the foot of an isolated hill, and Ludwig Helmes suggested Wallace should try his luck there. So Wallace transferred his base, living at first with Coulson, the Yorkshire engineer in charge. He found it such a productive locality that he had a small, two-roomed house built for himself and Charlie Allen, and installed his considerable baggage, everything from camp-bed to teacups and teaspoons. Then there were his scientific instruments, compasses, thermometers, barometers, sympiesometer, and his books, and medicines, and a strong-box for his money and valuables. But it was the collecting gear that took up most space: collecting-nets and boxes, bottles of chemicals and spirits for preserving, and more boards and boxes and jars and casks for the specimens he captured.

Simunjon became his home for the next nine months. In the eyes of an entomologist, it was an ideal location. For hundreds of miles in every direction 'a magnificent forest extended over plain and mountain, rock and morass'; the rains were receding, the daily sunshine increasing; and, just where he was situated, Chinese and Dyak labourers were felling the virgin forest to clear the ground for mining, and cutting a two-mile swathe for a railtrack to the Sadong river. There were sawpits in the jungle for beams and planks. Everywhere timber was lying on the ground, bark and leaves drying and decaying, rich ground for beetles and insects; and in the sunny clearings and pathways butterflies and wasps abounded.

> March 12th. The day was a fine one; – flies, hymenoptera, & wasps were abundant & among them a few longicorn beetles occasionally appeared, sometimes too a bright green buprestis would whiz by & then settle on some trunk or log exposed to the hottest sun, starting off again however on the slightest attempt to approach him.[8]

Wallace paid the labourers a cent for each insect they brought him. In the previous four months he had collected 320 different kinds of beetles: now in only two weeks he matched that total, an average of 24 separate species a day, and on one memorable day, 76, of which 34 were new to him. His total – and Wallace always kept his eye on the total, as it represented his future bank balance – for Borneo was a round two thousand, and of these all but a hundred were collected at Simunjon, on scarcely more than a square mile of ground. He was delighted now that he had had nothing to do with the Australian expedition. Borneo was the best possible location, and he had even spoken to the rajah about a possible opening for George Silk.

Encouraged by this brilliant start, Wallace settled down for a long stay. He acquired fowls and pigs, planted pumpkins and onions – 'or we should have nothing to eat'.[9] Shoes were a problem – he was busy dissecting and patching, and had become quite an expert in the internal machinery. The other irritation was Charles Allen. Sister Fanny was threatening to send him another assistant: what were his qualities? Did they include neatness and perseverance? 'Do not tell me that he is "a very nice young man". Of course he is. So is Charles a very nice boy, but I could not be troubled with another like him for any consideration whatever.' Charles – the son of a carpenter – was hopeless at carpentry, setting butterflies or putting up a bird – and this 'after twelve months' constant practice and constant teaching!'[10] Yet out of doors Charles did very well, was an effective collector, an increasingly accurate shot, and good at skinning. But to keep the specimen production line moving, an insect and bird setter was vital, or Wallace would never be able to move from his table.

It was not just beetles that he was acquiring. The butterflies, not so abundant, were spectacular, none more so than a beautiful creature with very long and pointed wings, 'deep velvety black, with a curved band of spots of a brilliant metallic-green colour extending across the wings from tip to tip, each spot being shaped exactly like a small triangular feather' – he named it *Ornithoptera brookeana*, (now *Trogonoptera brookiana*), after the rajah.[11] There was a large tree frog brought to him by one of the Chinese, a 'flying frog' that Wallace sketched, a new species, he decided, of the genus *Rhacophorus*. Sometimes the sky was dark with immense flights of fruit-eating bats. Not having a dedicated professional hunter at this point, the birds, including the hornbills, escaped comparatively lightly as Wallace was so busy with insects, but he nevertheless acquired five squirrels, two tiger-cats, the *Gymnurus rafflesii* – 'a cross between a pig and a polecat' – and the rare otter-like *Cynogale bennetti*. His notes were not restricted to an animal's habits: 'Cuscus – eats fruit and leaves – flesh tender and well-flavoured'; 'mouse deer – admirable eating – jugged'.[12] But these were incidental treasures. Simunjon, his informants had told him, was an excellent locality for orang-utans. A week after his arrival, and only a quarter of a mile from his house, he was out collecting insects when he heard a rustling in a nearby tree: he looked up, and saw his first 'mias', moving slowly from branch to branch. He followed it through the jungle until the ground became too swampy. He recorded it in his notebook: 'Monday March 19th. This was a white day for me. I saw for the first time the Orang Utan or "Mias" of the Dyaks in its native forests.' On a tree near by, he found 'its nest or seat formed of sticks & boughs supported in a forked branch'.[13]

Wallace's objectives were to see the orang-utan, or mias, in 'his native haunts', to study his habits, and to obtain a range of good specimens. Being a mid-nineteenth-century naturalist, he saw nothing contradictory about doing these things simultaneously. The orangs appeared to be abundant; and they ate a lot of fruit, especially durian, so the Dyaks looked on their destroyer as a benefactor. Wallace entered each specimen in the sequence in his notebook, and later added the eventual purchaser – the British Museum, the Derby Museum – and the price. Over the next six months he shot fifteen. Charles Allen and a Chinese boy were kept busy skinning the animals. The skulls and skeletons were dried, the skins preserved in medicated arrack. The bones were boiled in a great iron pan, covered over at night with boards and heavy stones; even so, the Dyak dogs managed to carry off the greater part of one orang, as well as chewing the leather off Wallace's boots, and a chunk of his mosquito-net.[14] He pursued orangs relentlessly, once wading waist deep to get a good shot at an old male, towing the body down stream behind the boat, and then, unable to spot a convenient place on the bank, hauling him into a clump of trees for the skinning and measuring. The often lengthy stalkings and pursuits gave him a chance to observe both the animal's feeding habits and the different ways a mias would move through the forest, and this first-hand information was supplemented by what he learned from the Dyaks, especially Kesim, the local head man.

At the same time, he had the rare chance to nurture a baby mias. He shot the mother – no. 7 – on 16 May. No. 8 was lying face down in a bog. He cleaned it up, and carried it home, while it clung on tightly to his beard.[15] It was four weeks old. There was no milk to be had, so he fed it rice water from a bottle with a quill in the cork, occasionally adding sugar and coconut milk. He fitted up a little box for a cradle, duly recorded when it cut its first teeth, and soon began to feed it from a spoon. He also found a companion for it, a young hare-lip monkey whom he called Toby, after Uncle Toby in *Tristram Shandy*. In *The Malay Archipelago* he puts down all these details with affection, but with a certain objectivity. In a letter to his sister, however – and in an article he sent to *Chambers' Journal* – he writes in human terms about 'an orphan baby' whose mother was a wild 'woman of the woods': 'I am afraid you would call it an ugly baby, for it has a dark brown skin and red hair, a very large mouth, but very pretty little hands and feet . . .'[16] But his hopes of one day introducing the little girl to fashionable society at the Zoological Gardens were dashed. The baby mias failed to thrive, and, he noted on 16 July, 'after this very ill from dropsy'. In *The Malay Archipelago* he recorded its death, and his deep regret at the loss of his little pet. The Notebook reveals that he put her out of her misery – 'killed'; 'skin in arrack with bones of limbs'; 'BM £6'.[17]

For the months of July and August, Wallace was immobilised with an ulcerated ankle, which gave him the leisure to write his various accounts of the orang, including a scientific paper for *The Annals and Magazine of Natural History*. He was also able to expand the notes for his projected book. Mail reached him even at Simunjon, with a box containing a welcome pair of shoes, and a piece of bacon. 'The bacon I fear is not eatable,' Wallace reported to his sister. What did she expect? It had not been scientifically packed and sealed. Next time he would send to Fortnum and Mason direct. After breakfast, he added a softer postscript: 'The bacon is eatable, just! but very high & very rich of a dark brown colour.'[18] There was also family news, and as usual he had a lot of advice to dispense. Fanny and Tom Sims had taken premises for their photography business in Conduit Street – he advised them to put up a handsome plate advertising their 'palace of photography' on the corner of Regent Street. Mother ought to go and live in a little cottage somewhere near London, a much better plan than lodging or boarding with them. His brother John and his wife Mary were settled in California; Wallace planned at this stage to return home to England by continuing his journey eastwards, and perhaps doing a little surveying work in America if it promised to pay well.

As the year drew on, and the wet season approached, Wallace began to plan his next stage. He needed fresh funds before he could undertake another major expedition, and that meant a return to Singapore. First, he decided to explore further inland, so he sent Charles back from Simunjon to Sarawak by river with the collections and the bulk of the luggage, and set off with a Dyak-speaking Malay boy up the Sadong river. He stayed at Dyak longhouses, and it was on this trip that he was able to observe and admire the Dyaks' way of life, and to note the wonderful use they made of the plants and trees around them, especially the bamboo: 'one of the most wonderful and most beautiful productions of the tropics, and one of nature's most valuable gifts to uncivilized man'.[19] He saw, too, pitcher plants and orchids, and collected fifty species of ferns without devoting much time to the search. He was puzzled by one thing: why were the Dyak villages so small and so widely scattered, when all the conditions most favourable to a rapid increase of population were apparently present – abundance of food, a healthy climate, early marriages? Only one Malthusian check was apparently present – the infertility, as Wallace supposed, of the women, for which he supplied the reason: their incessant hard labour and the heavy weights they had to carry. But he did not stay long enough to absorb the complexity of their society and culture – he gave a very unflattering account of the dancing – though noting their friendliness and curiosity; many of the women and children had never seen a European before, and he obliged by rolling up his trouser leg to reveal his white skin. He slept at night on the longhouse verandas, often with half-a-dozen smoke-dried human skulls suspended above him, and marvelled at the sense of security, and honesty, that prevailed. He reached the hills, and the watershed between the Sadong and Sarawak rivers, and then made his way down river to rejoin the rajah, and recuperate in his bungalow.

It was early in December 1855, and there was no boat leaving for Singapore before the end of January. So he accepted an invitation to spend some time with Brooke and his secretary, Spencer St John, at Brooke's mountain retreat, a cottage built for him twenty miles up the Sarawak perched just below the summit of a steep thousand-foot hill. The way up was by a succession of ladders, bamboo bridges and slippery paths. Durians and coconut palms grew all around, though not so thickly as to block out the view stretching in one direction up the Sarawak valley to the mountains, and in the other across the green carpet of vegetation to the sea, and the distinctive outline of the Santubong mountain. Swifts darted overhead, and a few steps below the cottage was a cool spring emerging from a cave, for refreshing baths and drinking water, while the local Dyaks brought daily supplies of delicious fruits such as mangosteens and lansats. This was both luxury and stimulus for Wallace. He found Brooke, a fellow chess-player, good company, and, without the restraint of anyone from the mission, the talk ranged freely. Brooke was a firm creationist, but he loved speculation and debate. According to St John, Wallace was even then 'elaborating in his mind the theory which was simultaneously worked out by Darwin – the theory of the origin of species; and if he could not convince us that our ugly neighbours, the orang-outangs, were our ancestors, he pleased, delighted and instructed us by his clever and inexhaustible flow of talk – really good talk'.[20] (Brooke's own observations on the orangs had been published in the *Proceedings of the Zoological Society*, 1841.) Then it was back to Sarawak for Christmas, before Wallace returned to the cottage with Charles and Ali, a Malay boy, for three weeks' intensive collecting: ferns, orchids (*Vanda lowii* was particularly abundant), land-shells, butterflies and, supremely, moths: one dark rainy night he captured 260, and he was kept catching and pinning until past midnight. He stayed as long as he could, allowing himself only a week to sort out his collections before the short voyage to Singapore.

When he sailed on 25 January 1856, he left Charles Allen behind. Bishop McDougall was short of teachers for the mission, and offered to educate and train the young man, who was 'of a religious turn'. Charles had proved a frustrating apprentice, and although Wallace offered to take him with him on different and more generous terms, paying him piecemeal as a collector, he preferred to stay in Sarawak. Wallace hardly knew whether to be glad or sorry: 'It saves me a great deal of trouble and annoyance, and I feel it quite a relief to be without him,' he admitted to Fanny. 'On the other hand, it is a considerable loss to me, as he had just begun to be valuable in collecting.'[21] He felt Charles would be secure enough, with the McDougalls and Brooke as his mentors. In Charles's place went the fifteen-year-old Ali, a promising shot and a more tractable apprentice. It was also much cheaper and simpler to travel without having to worry about food and bedding for a second European.

For almost four months, Wallace found himself pinned down in Singapore, waiting for funds, waiting for a ship. After the excitements of Borneo, it was particularly irksome to be wholly dependent on the mail from England, especially when the burden of Stevens's next letter was a complaint that the recent consignment was 'a very poor lot for Borneo'. Wallace leaped to his own defence. They were all collected in the wet season – before the Simunjon idyll – and he had characterised them himself as 'a very miserable collection' apart from the moths. He despaired of specimen-fanciers who despised small insects and who assumed, quite wrongly, that tropical insects were in general large and brightly coloured.

The constant cry before he left London was 'Do not neglect the small things'; 'The small things are what we want because they have never been collected in the Tropics.'[22]

Meanwhile, he desperately needed money for the next expedition. Insects that he had caught at Simunjon during his first months in Borneo had left Singapore on the *Cornubia* in August 1855, sailing via the Cape. Stevens acknowledged their arrival in a letter of 6 January 1856, to which Wallace responded on 10 March. Until the collections had been placed and sold, no money would be forwarded to Singapore – and that could be another three months: it was a slow and uncertain process. Stevens had, in fact, been as active as he could on Wallace's behalf. The *Ornithoptera brookeana* was described to the Entomological Society on 2 April 1855, and a 'splendid specimen' was exhibited on 4 June; another box of Coleoptera from Borneo was shown on 5 November, and a box containing three fine species of *Lucanidae*, including a remarkable variety of *L. brookiana*, on 7 January 1856, one day after their arrival in London.[23] Wallace's name, extracts from his letters, his latest specimens, were a constant theme at the Society's transactions, but that did not necessarily translate into profit. Wallace smarted at the implied rebuke, 'a very poor lot for Borneo'; Stevens also informed him that several naturalists expressed regret that he was 'theorizing', when what was needed were more facts. In other words, he should stop writing speculative papers, and concentrate on his collecting.

The Sarawak paper was published in September 1855. Wallace waited in vain for reaction, either hostile or complimentary. None came, apart from Stevens's annoying message. Darwin read the paper, and made some annotations in the margin of his copy: 'Nothing very new' – 'Uses my simile of the tree' – 'It seems all creation with him'.[24] Darwin cannot have read the paper very carefully, and was perhaps misled by Wallace's use of the word 'create' in connection with the Galapagos species, or by his unusual use of the word 'antitype', when 'prototype' might have made the meaning clearer. He might, too, have already discounted Wallace as a potential theoriser of any weight, judging him by his inconsistent and comparatively amateurish book on the Amazon. But others had absorbed the implications, and alerted Darwin. Edward Blyth, whose own writings had been noted carefully by Wallace, wrote from Calcutta, 'Good! Upon the whole!'; friend Wallace had 'put the matter well'. 'Has it at all unsettled your ideas regarding the persistence of species,' Blyth asked directly, unaware of the private direction of Darwin's thoughts, 'not perhaps so much from novelty of argument, as by the lucid collation of facts and phenomena?' Charles Lyell's own monumental works on the geological record provided the underpinning for Darwin, as indeed they did for Wallace, and perhaps not surprisingly Lyell sensed the significance of the Sarawak paper. He began a new notebook on species, and started to contemplate the worrying possibility of transmutation. On a visit to Down, Darwin's Kent home, Lyell was initiated into Darwin's theory of natural selection.[25] In return, he urged Darwin to accelerate, and to publish, in case he should be forestalled.

Oblivious of any such impact on the world of scientific thinking, Wallace plunged back momentarily into the economics and practicalities of collecting. The Borneo Company's vessel the *Water Lily* sailed on 5 March with a batch of orang skins and skeletons, and five thousand insects for sale, including fifteen hundred moths, which he worked very hard to get: he claimed, not entirely accurately, that he had stayed 'alone up on the top of the mountain for a month or more'.[26] There was also a human skull for Dr Joseph Davis, provenance unknown.

Wallace did not let time pass unprofitably, while he kicked his heels in Singapore, staying with his French missionary friends, and fasting with them each Friday on omelettes and vegetables, 'a most wholesome custom'. Stevens had sent him a box of books, and he could therefore press on with his researches, annotating and transcribing into the Species Notebook – and Singapore offered a library, and journals. He could, too, practise his Malay with Ali, and asked Stevens to buy Crawfurd's *Malay Dictionary*, and send him the second volume by post; he would manage without the grammar. He also continued to collect on Singapore island, training Ali as he did so. In Singapore, too, he could be in touch with other naturalists: by letter with John Bowring, collecting in Java, and in person with the plant-collector Thomas Lobb, who had been in Moulmein and was setting off to Labuan, in Borneo, plant-hunting for Veitch's the nurserymen. He also wrote a letter at Stevens's prompting to Bates, although with no mention of his Sarawak paper. Now, on 12 May, his vessel was almost ready to sail for Macassar, calling for a few days first at Bali, a voyage of some forty-five days against the monsoon. It had been extremely frustrating, he told Stevens, '6 months utterly lost and at great expense. Such things people never reckon when estimating the profits of collectors.' But prospects now were good, he assured his agent: 'I have made preparations for collecting extensively by engaging a good man [not Ali, a Portuguese called Fernandez] to shoot and skin birds and animals, which I think in the countries I am going to will pay me very well.'[27] It was crucial for continued success that Stevens should instruct Hamilton Gray & Co. to forward money to him. They were allowing him to draw only up to £100, and his living expenses and stores for the trip had made a great hole in that already. What animals did people want? Lories, and cockatoos, he assumed, 'and if I can reach the bird of Paradise country (the Arroo Isles) I shall be able to prepare good specimens of those gorgeous birds, one of the greatest treats I can look forward to'. By moving backwards and forwards through the islands for the next two years, he planned to escape the wet season.

In the event, the voyage to Bali was swift: twenty days from Singapore, in the *Kembang Djepoon* ('Rose of Japan'), a schooner owned by a Chinese merchant, with a Javanese crew and an English captain, before they anchored at Bileling, on the north side of the island. They were there for just two days, time enough for Wallace to be astonished and delighted by the intensity of cultivation, and for him to secure a few birds and butterflies. (He looked back with regret at a lost opportunity, not realising at the time how significant a location he was in.) Then they sailed on to Ampanam, in Lombock, where he planned to await a passage to Macassar. He and his boxes passed safely through the heavy surf, and he took up quarters with an English trader, an ex-sea captain called Carter.

Lombock, like Bali, was wonderfully and intensely cultivated: rice, tobacco, coffee, cotton and hides were exported in abundance. 'Our manufacturers and capitalists are on the look out for a new cotton producing district,' Wallace informed the world. 'Here is one to their hands.'[28] The level of cultivation meant that the territory was disproportionately the poorer for collecting; but by travelling to the south part of the island Wallace was able to overcome this drawback. To his great excitement, he discovered that the bird population was entirely unexpected, and threw 'great light on the laws of Geographical distribution of Animals in the East'.[29] The islands of Bali and Lombock were of nearly the same size, the same soil, aspect, elevation and climate; and they were within sight of each other – the Lombock strait is no more than twenty-eight kilometres at its widest point. Yet the fauna of each was distinct; in fact, Wallace stated, they 'belong to two quite distinct Zoological provinces, of which they form the extreme limits'. As an instance he cited the cockatoos,

> . . . a group of birds confined to Australia and the Moluccas, but quite unknown in Java, Borneo, Sumatra and Malacca. One species however (*Plyctolophus sulphurens*) is abundant in Lombock but unknown in Bali, the island of Lombock forming the extreme western limit of its range and that of the whole family. Many other species illustrate the same fact and I am preparing a short account of them for publication.[30]

Wallace had, fortuitously, come across the dividing line between the Asian and the Australian biological regions, a major discovery in his thinking about species, and about their distribution and evolution.

Buoyed by this breakthrough, Wallace enjoyed himself in Lombock. He employed an additional bird-skinner, a Portuguese from Malacca called Manuel, hired a small boat, and tracked along the coast to a wilder spot, where he made a good collection of birds: cockatoos, honeysuckers and mound-makers, large green pigeons which were also excellent eating, an Australian bee-eater, the beautiful ground-thrush *Pitta concinna*, little crimson and black flower-peckers, large black cuckoos, metallic king-crows, golden orioles, eight species of kingfisher, and the fine jungle-cocks – 'the origin of all our domestic breeds of poultry'.[31] But while the spoils were rich, collecting operations were carried out under more than usual difficulties. He had just one small room for eating, sleeping and working, for store-house and dissecting room: no shelves, cupboards, chairs or table, and everything shared not only with his host but with swarms of ants and any dog, cat or fowl that happened to wander in. The box on which he skinned the birds, and an old bench whose four legs were placed in water-filled coconut shells to thwart the ants, were the only safe places for his two insect boxes and the hundred or so bird skins that might be drying at any one time. As he explained, all animal substances require some time to dry thoroughly, and 'emit a very disagreeable odour while doing so'.[32] Nevertheless, he shipped off a case to Stevens via Singapore, which included about three hundred birds for sale. 'The domestic duck is for Mr Darwin and he would perhaps also like to take the jungle-cock, which is often domesticated here and is doubtless one of the originals for the domestic breed of poultry.'[33] Wallace had been pressed into Darwin's network of collectors – these already included Rajah Brooke – who were sending him specimens of pigeon and poultry skins from all round the world as part of his study of domestic and wild varieties of fowl. Darwin wrote to Wallace for the first time in December 1855, with a wants list, opening the way for a more regular correspondence.

Lombock was not quite so peaceful as Sarawak had seemed. A Balinese woman living with an Englishman was ordered to be 'krissed' – a kris is the sharp Malay dagger – by the rajah, because she had accepted a flower from another man. (For a more serious infidelity, a woman and her lover would be tied back to back and thrown into the sea, to be eaten by crocodiles.) Wallace went for a long walk into the country, to avoid being a witness. Then the raja, it was reported, had ordered heads to be cut off to secure a good crop of rice: Manuel would not go out shooting alone, and Ali refused to fetch water unless he was armed with a spear. Wallace made light of these rumours, but Fernandez had had enough, and took the next ship back to Singapore and safety. A few days later, a small schooner arrived, and Wallace was able to secure his passage on the short voyage northwards to Macassar in the south-west corner of Celebes (Sulawesi), arriving there on 2 September.

This was the first of four visits Wallace made to various parts of Celebes, and his initial reaction was one of disappointment. After three weeks he had done little except spy out the nakedness of the land – 'and it is indeed naked', he complained to Stevens: 'I have never seen a more uninviting country than the neighbourhood of Macassar.'[34] There were no insects, no beetles, very few butterflies; birds were slightly more promising, especially the raptors. He hoped to find a house inland, in more promising territory, but that meant negotiations with the rajah. Then Ali had been ill with malaria, and as soon as Wallace had nursed him back to health he fell sick himself, which took a week's regime of quinine to cure, after which he had to do the same once more for Ali – though he was well enough in the morning to cope with the cooking. Reinforcements were clearly needed, so Wallace added another boy who could cook and shoot, named Baderoon, to the party, and a 'little impudent rascal of twelve or fourteen', Baso, to carry the gun or the insect net.[35] Thus equipped, and with the loan of a pack-horse from a Dutch friend, Wallace shifted his scene of operations to a more promising stretch of forest, and began to realise that the island's species had 'a surprising amount of individuality'. 'While it is poor in the actual number of its species, it is yet wonderfully rich in peculiar forms; many of which are singular or beautiful, and are in some cases absolutely unique upon the globe.' These forms would continue to puzzle him for many years. Meanwhile, he needed to move on. The rains were coming, and both he and Ali had been unwell again – he suspected a polluted water supply. Back in Macassar, there was mail to answer. Sir James Brooke wrote to bring him up to date. Brooke had been summoned before a commission of enquiry in Singapore, set up by the British Parliament, alarmed by reports of his high-handed ways at putting down insurrections. He could report now that the storm that had been raging on his head had 'at length blown over', but the British government was still not prepared to recognise him as 'an independent sovereign' in Sarawak.[36] The news about Wallace's protégé, Charles Allen, was not very encouraging: 'They say he is not clever at books.' Brooke had read Wallace's 'little brochure' – the Sarawak paper on species – with satisfaction, 'but I am somewhat misty on these subjects': at least *someone* had read it. Wallace had had no reaction so far from England, but he wrote his first letter to Darwin, using the topic of domestic and wild varieties as an entrée. A letter from a proud Mrs Wallace told him that his brother John had had a son. Now that Wallace was an uncle, he had another reason to return home via America: 'The far East is to me what the far West is to the Americans. They both meet in California where I hope to arrive some day.'[37] Wallace was about to make his most adventurous voyage to date, and was in mischievous mood: 'Has Eliza Roberts got rid of her moustache yet?' he asked his sister. 'Tell her in private to use tweezers. A hair a day would exterminate it in a year or two without anyone's perceiving.' He was setting off for his 'Ultima Thule', committing himself to a thousand miles' voyage in a native boat, to a place from where the two kinds of birds of paradise known to Linnaeus, the King Bird of Paradise, *Paradisea regia*, and the Great Paradise bird, *Paradisea apoda*, were first brought to Europe. Even by the Macassar people themselves, commented Wallace, usually rather sardonic about standard travellers' tales, the voyage to the Aru Islands 'is looked upon as a rather wild and romantic expedition, full of novel sights and strange adventures'.[38]

7   Heading East

Neither a false start, nor four days confined to his cabin in Macassar harbour because of incessant rain, could puncture Wallace's enthusiasm. The boat was a prau, shaped something like a Chinese junk and about seventy tons with great mat-sails. There was a thatched cabin on deck, and he secured a section of this to himself – four feet high, six and a half feet long, five and a half feet wide – 'the snuggest and most comfortable little place I ever enjoyed at sea'. The cabin had a split bamboo floor, covered with fine cane mats; gun-case, insect boxes, bags of shot and powder, clothes and books against the far wall, mattress in the middle, canteen, lamp and little store of luxuries, tobacco and beads for trading, while guns, revolver and hunting knife hung conveniently from the roof. (The little store of luxuries, and necessities, was quite extensive. Besides an eight-month supply of sugar, coffee and tea, he had a keg of butter, sixteen flasks of oil, and a quantity of bread cut thin, and dried, and slightly toasted, plus a dozen bottles of

Madeira and some beer. There was also common starch, 'good to clean feathers of birds'.) On board, everything smelt so sweetly. There was no paint, tar, new rope, grease, oil, or varnish, but just bamboo and rattan, coir rope and palm thatch, 'pure vegetable fibres, which smell pleasantly if they smell at all, and recall quiet scenes in the green and shady forest'.[1] The captain, Herr Warzbergen, was half Javanese, the crew of thirty mostly from Macassar; there were other traders, and Wallace's three servants, Ali, Baderoon and Baso, who had now been taught to cook tolerably. Baderoon was in disgrace. He had persuaded Wallace to advance him four months' wages, claiming he was buying a house; then he had gambled the lot away, and came on board without any spare clothes or provisions. Once under way, Wallace settled down to one of the pleasantest and most peaceful voyages he ever experienced: a calm and efficient captain, a civil good-tempered crew, complete freedom about meals and dress – luxuries far surpassing those 'of the most magnificent screw-steamer, that highest result of our civilisation'. He tried a little fried shark, celebrated Christmas Day with an extra glass of wine to accompany the usual rice and curry, saw his first active volcano as they passed the Banda group, and admired flying fish rising and falling like swallows. As the year ended they approached the Ke Islands. The water was as transparent as crystal, with colours varying from emerald to lapis lazuli:

> The sea was calm as a lake, and the glorious sun of the tropics threw a flood of golden light over all. The scene was to me inexpressibly delightful. I was in a new world, and could dream of the wonderful productions hid in those rocky forests, and in those azure abysses. But few European feet had ever trodden the shores I gazed upon; its plants, and animals, and men were alike almost unknown, and I could not help speculating on what my wanderings there for a few days might bring to light.[2]

It was the men who first struck Wallace. He had an immediate opportunity of comparing 'two of the most distinct and strongly marked races that the earth contains', as he stood among the quiet, unimpulsive Malay crew and watched the Ke men singing and shouting as they paddled up in long canoes decorated with shells and waving plumes of cassowaries' hair, and scrambled aboard, swarming all over the vessel with exuberant enjoyment; and the physical contrast was as remarkable as their 'moral features', equally pointing to 'absolute diversity'. It was a busy few days, as the captain supervised the building of two small praus – the Ke Islanders were superb boat-builders – while the crew traded and bartered; and Wallace, naturally, did a little business of his own, once he had convinced everyone that he was willing to exchange fragrant tobacco for black and green beetles. Offerings were brought to him contained in lengths of bamboo, and frequently the inhabitants had eaten each other into fragments after a day's confinement. But he was pleased with one particularly grand – and quite 'new' – beetle, glittering with ruby and emerald tints: a Bupestrid, *Cyphogastra calepyga*, first spotted decorating a tobacco pouch. There was a lack of convenient paths, and the terrain was rugged, but even so he captured 35 species of butterfly, many of them unknown in European collections, 13 species of birds, and 194 species of insects, in the four days. He also encountered an old man in the forest, who watched quietly and politely while Wallace caught an insect, pinned it and put it away in his collecting-box until he could contain himself no longer, 'but bent almost double, and enjoyed a hearty roar of laughter'.[3] Wallace, reflecting on the diversity of man, and now even more conscious of the European constructions of the civilised, and of the savage or barbarous, made the thirty-hour passage to Dobbo, and the flat, forest-covered Aru Islands.

Dobbo was the trading settlement for the Bugis and Chinese, three rows of houses – large thatched sheds really – stretched out on a sand spit, with good anchorage on either side. As it was the very beginning of the trading season, the place was almost deserted, so Wallace took possession of a house near Warzbergen's, installed a cane chair and a bamboo bench for bed and sofa, rigged up boards for a table and shelves, had a window cut in the palm-leaf wall, and pronounced himself quite content. After an early breakfast, and with Baderoon to cut a path with his chopper if necessary, he set off with a guide to investigate the virgin forests. They did not manage more than a mile before the path disappeared altogether, forcing them to turn back. But the expedition lasted long enough for Wallace to take thirty species of butterfly – more than he had captured in one day since the riches of the Amazon; and three days later he had the good fortune to sight 'one of the most magnificent insects the world contains', the great bird-winged butterfly *Ornithoptera poseidon*:

I trembled with excitement as I saw it coming majestically toward me, and could hardly believe I had really succeeded in my stroke till I had taken it out of the net and was gazing, lost in admiration, at the velvet black and brilliant green of its wings, seven inches across, its golden body, and crimson breast. It is true I had seen similar insects in cabinets, at home, but it is quite another thing to capture such one's self – to feel it struggling between one's fingers, and to gaze upon its fresh and living beauty, a bright gem shining out amid the silent gloom of a dark and tangled forest.[4]

The village of Dobbo held that evening at least one contented man.

In spite of such excitements, his collections came on slowly. The weather was poor – only four good collecting days out of the first sixteen – but the quality was excellent, most of the birds being either known but rare New Guinea species, or completely new. There were spiders, lizards and crabs in abundance, and after a windy night the beach was strewn with wonderful shells, fragments of coral, and strange sponges. He paid one brief visit to the larger island of Wokan, where he delighted in the palms and tree ferns, but could not move his base for a while because of the very real threat of pirates. Finally, his boat was ready, and he and his men sailed across and trekked inland for two hours, till they reached a house – 'or rather a small shed, of the most miserable description' – where, the steersman assured him, he could get every kind of bird and beast to be found in Aru.[5] Wallace negotiated a week's rent – the price was one sheath knife, or parang – for a five-foot section of the hut, and got ready for work with keen expectation.

After two or three wet days he was beginning to despair when Baderoon returned with a small bird, slightly smaller than a thrush:

The greater part of its plumage was of an intense cinnabar red, with a gloss as of spun glass. On the head the feathers became short and velvety, and shaded into rich orange. Beneath, from the breast downward, was pure white, with the softness and gloss of silk, and across the breast a band of deep metallic green separated this colour from the red of the throat. Above each eye was a round spot of the same metallic green; the bill was yellow, and the feet and legs were of a fine cobalt blue, strikingly contrasting with all the other parts of the body. Merely in arrangement of colours and texture of plumage this

The village of Dobbo

little bird was a gem of the first water, yet these comprised only half its strange beauty. Springing from each side of the breast, and ordinarily lying concealed under the wings, were little tufts of greyish feathers about two inches long, and each terminated by a broad band of intense emerald green. These plumes can be raised at the will of the bird, and spread out into a pair of elegant fans when the wings are elevated. But this is not the only ornament. The two middle feathers of the tail are in the form of slender wires about five inches long, and which diverge in a beautiful double curve. About half an inch of the end of this wire is webbed on the outer side only, and coloured of a fine metallic green, and being curled spirally inward, form a pair of elegant glittering buttons, hanging five inches below the body, and the same distance apart. These two ornaments, the breast-fans and the spiral-tipped tail-wires, are altogether unique, not occurring on any other species of the eight thousand different birds that are known to exist upon the earth; and, combined with the most exquisite beauty of plumage, render this one of the most perfectly lovely of the many lovely productions of nature.[6]

Wallace had obtained a specimen of the King Bird of Paradise.

> I knew how few Europeans had ever beheld the perfect little organism I now gazed upon, and how very imperfectly it was still known in Europe . . . I thought of the long ages of the past, during which the successive generations of this little creature had run their course – year by year being born, and living and dying amid these dark and gloomy woods, with no intelligent eye to gaze upon their loveliness – to all appearances such a wanton waste of beauty. Such ideas excite a feeling of melancholy. It seems sad that on the one hand such exquisite creatures should live out their lives and exhibit their charms only in these wild inhospitable regions, doomed for ages yet to come to hopeless barbarism; while on the other hand, should civilised man ever reach these distant lands, and bring moral, intellectual, and physical light into the recesses of these virgin forests, we may be sure that he will so disturb the nicely balanced relations of organic and inorganic nature as to cause the disappearance, and finally the extinction, of these very beings whose wonderful structure and beauty he alone is fitted to appreciate and enjoy. This consideration must surely tell us that all living things were *not* made for man.[7]

The bird aroused such complex, contradictory and prescient thoughts in Wallace's mind that for a moment, especially in his appreciation of the fragility of organic and inorganic nature, he sounds like a twenty-first-century ecologist. The Victorian naturalist soon asserted himself, and he acquired another, equally perfect, and a young specimen of the Great Paradise bird. Lying in his hut before dawn, he awoke to their cries as they went to seek their breakfast. These birds were not yet in full plumage, but he was able to stay in Aru until they were, shifting his base yet once more, further away from Dobbo. He remained long enough to acquire knowledge of their habits, partly from his own observation, but mostly from his hunters, and from talking to the Aru people. For Wallace was largely hut-bound for much of the time. The mosquitoes and sandflies had attacked his feet, and after a month's punishment they broke out in ulcers which were so painful that he could not walk. He would crawl down to the river to bathe, only to be taunted by the sight of the blue-winged *Papilio ulysses*, and then have to drag himself reluctantly back to the bird-skinning table.

Baderoon and Ali kept him well supplied.

As always, enforced leisure, personally frustrating from the naturalist's point of view, was highly productive in terms of reflection. As he had done in the Amazon, Wallace observed the human inhabitants of the forest, noting and analysing the diet and the way of life of the Aru Islanders. The first group among whom he lived ate relatively little meat, and, growing no rice, depended on the sago palm: he thought this diet responsible for the high incidence of skin disease. But in his second location, there was much more hunting. The men and boys were expert archers and shot birds, pigs and kangaroos, so they had a tolerably good supply of meat to go with their vegetables. The result of this was superior health, well-made bodies, and generally clear skins. He spent long evenings in conversation with them, and carefully recorded the details of their ornaments and utensils – the pandanus sleeping mat, 'clothing, house, bedding, and furniture, all in one'; palm-leaf boxes, lined with pandanus leaves or plaited grass, the joints and angles covered with strips of split rattan, the lid covered with the watertight spathe of the areca palm. As among the Dyaks of Borneo and the Indians of the Amazon, he was

> delighted with the beauty of the human form, a beauty of which stay-at-home civilised people can never have any conception. What are the finest Grecian statues to the living moving breathing forms which everywhere surround me. The unrestrained grace of the native savage as he moves about his daily occupations or lounges at his ease must be seen to be understood. A young savage handling his bow is the perfection of physical beauty. Few persons feel more acutely than myself any offence against modesty among civilised folk, but here no such ideas have a moment's place; the free development of every limb seems wholly admirable, and made to be admired.[8]

As with the Dyaks, Wallace commented, perhaps with an eye on his readership, the women were not so pleasant to look at, except in extreme youth: early marriages and hard work soon took their toll of their grace and beauty. But, all in all, here was a people superbly adapted to the particular environment. He gave them presents when he left, and believed that on the whole his stay 'among these simple and good-natured people was productive of pleasure and profit to both parties'. Had he known that he was to be prevented from returning, he would have felt 'some sorrow in leaving a place where I had first seen so many rare and beautiful living things'.[9]

Back in Dobbo, he found the town so full that he had to move into the court-house. For six weeks he was confined indoors, but he had plenty of work, writing up his notes and arranging his collections. Ali was sent off solo to Wanumbai, to buy paradise birds and prepare the skins: he came back with sixteen glorious specimens, and would have done even better had he not been ill for some of the time. Baderoon, however, reprimanded for laziness (very high on Wallace's list of faults), took his wages and resigned. He soon lost the lot, borrowed some more money, lost that, and ended up as a 'slave' to his creditor. Now, at the end of June, the monsoon was approaching, and the merchant praus were being loaded. Wallace stowed his treasures on board: nine thousand specimens, of about sixteen hundred distinct species.

> I had made the acquaintance of a strange and little-known race of men; I had become familiar with the traders of the far East; I had revelled in the delights of exploring a new flora and fauna, one of the most remarkable and most beautiful and least known in the world; and I had succeeded in the main object for which I had undertaken the journey – namely, to obtain fine specimens of the magnificent birds of paradise, and to be enabled to observe them in their native forests.[10]

Flushed with this success, some travellers might have contemplated sailing home. But, as the prau surged back before a favourable wind to Macassar, covering the thousand miles in less than ten days, Wallace resolved to continue his travels. He felt full of confidence about the value of his collections, and his mind was richly stocked.

In Macassar, he spent the rest of July preparing the Aru collection for shipment to London: if it left Singapore by the *Mavor* early in September, it ought to arrive during January 1858. 'Should fetch near £500,' he guessed. For once, he underestimated hugely: the collection was sold for a thousand pounds. His agent was finding a good market for Wallace's treasures: between March 1855 and June 1863, the British Museum bought 20 per cent of his shipments, 2,707 specimens. There was a box waiting for him from Stevens: the double-barrelled shotgun he had ordered the year before, and a new stock of pins, arsenic and other collecting essentials. He kept in touch with the Geographical: 'I went principally to shoot Birds of Paradise,' he informed Shaw about the trip to Aru, and, he added nonchalantly as though he had been on a grouse moor, 'had capital sport.'[11] There were papers to send: 'On the Great Bird of Paradise' and 'On the Natural History of the Aru Islands', both for the *Annals*, and a great batch of letters to reply to: from his cousin Wilson in Australia, his brother John in California, from Spruce, from Bates, a lot of Stevensian dispatches, and one from Darwin. But he did not answer any of them for a while. He felt eager to get back to work. Leaving Ali in hospital, Wallace hired a boat and set off thirty miles or so to the north, where Jacob Mesman, the brother of his Dutch friend in Macassar, had offered to look after him. In a little valley surrounded by mountains, he found a delightfully tranquil spot. Mesman quickly had a bamboo house built for him, and he settled down for a relaxing stay, with constant supplies of pork, fowls and eggs, and a daily delivery of buffalo milk in a bamboo. There were enough birds and beetles to keep him occupied, but his chief excitements were the butterflies: so active and shy that they were difficult to capture, but always worth the effort – the blue-banded *Papilios, miletus* and *telephus*, the superb gold-green *Papilio macedon*, and the rare little swallow-tail *Papilio rhesus*. He also made a memorable trip to the falls of the Maros river, where he was lucky to obtain six specimens of the large swallow-tailed *Papilio androcles*. The geological structure of this part of Celebes intrigued him, limestone mountains apparently resting on a bed of basalt. He returned to his hut as the rains began, an encouragement for insect-collecting, but bringing with it other hazards: fever, dysentery, swollen feet. Snakes became more evident, sometimes turning up in his collecting-net when he dragged it through piles of leaves in search for insects. He went back to Macassar, to await the Dutch mail steamer.

By this time, he had digested and had time to compose a reply to the letter that had arrived from Darwin. Wallace's first letter from Celebes, to which this was a reply, has been lost, though some of its contents are clear enough from Darwin's responses.

> I am much obliged for your letter of Oct. 10th, from Celebes, received a few days ago: in a laborious undertaking sympathy is a valuable & real encouragement. By your letter & even still more by your paper in Annals, a year or more ago, I can plainly see that we have thought (very) much alike & to a certain extent have come to similar

conclusions. In regard to the Paper in Annals, I agree to the truth of almost every word of your paper; & I daresay that you will agree with me that it is very rare to find oneself agreeing pretty closely with any theoretical paper, for it is lamentable how each man draws his own different conclusions from the same fact.[12]

Darwin, shaken by Lyell and Blyth, had by now reassessed the Sarawak paper on species. He proceeded, in the words of Adrian Desmond and James Moore, to give Wallace 'the nicest kind of trespass notice':[13]

This summer will make the 20th year (!) since I opened my first note-book, on the question how & in what way do species & varieties differ from each other. – I am now preparing my work for publication, but I find the subject so very large, that though I have written many chapters, I do not suppose I shall go to press for two years. – I have never heard how long you intend staying in the Malay Archipelago; I wish I might profit by the publication of your Travels there before my work appears, for no doubt you will reap a large harvest of facts. –

The collection of facts, he seems to imply, is to be Wallace's province, rather than more theory:

It is really *impossible* to explain my views in the compass of a letter on the causes & means of variation in a state of nature; but I have slowly adopted a distinct & tangible idea, – Whether true or false others must judge; for the firmest conviction of the truth of a doctrine by its author, seems, alas, not to be slightest guarantee of truth. –

He also discussed domestic and wild varieties of duck – the specimen Wallace had dispatched to him via Stevens had arrived – and closed with another significant enquiry:

One of the subjects on which I have been experimentising, & which cost me much trouble, is the means of distribution of all organic beings found on oceanic islands – & any facts on this subject would be received most gratefully: Land-Molluscs are a great perplexity to me.

To Wallace, the letter must have seemed like an open invitation to continue the exchanges, from a man who was thinking along the same lines. He did not have many scientific correspondents – Bates, of course, but that was necessarily a slow-moving and uncertain business. He neatly returned the ball, expressing satisfaction that his 'views on the order of succession of species' were in accordance with Darwin's:

The mere statement & illustration of the theory in that paper is of course but preliminary to an attempt at a detailed proof of it, the plan of which I have arranged, & in part written, but which of course requires much [research in English] libraries & collections, a labour which I look –[14]

The fragment ends, but Darwin must have been reassured that Wallace did not intend to write a proper book until he had returned from his travels: no competition, apparently, from that quarter.

On the other side of the world, on the Amazon, Bates had now read Wallace's Sarawak paper. 'I was startled at first to see you already ripe for the enunciation of the theory,' he commented. 'You can imagine with what interest I read and studied it, and I must say that it is perfectly well done. The idea is like truth itself, so simple and obvious that those who read and understand it will be struck by its simplicity; and yet it is perfectly original.' Then he added, 'The theory I quite assent to, and, you know, was conceived by me also, but I profess that I could not have propounded it with so much force and completeness.'[15] Was there a mild rebuke in that 'was conceived by me also'? Wallace had made no acknowledgement to Bates, on a line of enquiry which for him had its origins in 1845 during his various discussions with Bates and, almost certainly, with Spruce on the Amazon. Like Wallace, Bates was turning over the question of species and varieties, and the effect of a particular locality:

What a noble subject would be that of a monograph of a group of beings peculiar to one region but offering different species in each province of it – tracing the laws which connect together the modifications of forms and colour with the *local* circumstances of a province or station – tracing as far as possible the actual *affiliation* of the species.

Tracing the actual affiliation – Bates was closing on the key issue of 'how'.

Life aboard the Dutch mail boat that took Wallace from Macassar to Banda and Amboyna was comparatively luxurious. In spite of his previous praise of the simple life, he put up with the succession of meals, coffee, gin and bitters, claret and beer that punctuated European shipboard routine. They called briefly at Timor, and at Banda, before reaching Amboyna (Ambon), the capital of the Moluccas. He had, as usual, letters of introduction, and found two local naturalists, both doctors: Dr Mohnike specialised in beetles – his collection included magnificent Japanese specimens – and Dr Doleschall in flies and spiders, but with some spectacular local butterflies. He lodged with Mohnike, and enjoyed long conversations with the young Hungarian, Doleschall, blundering along gloriously in fluent though fearfully ungrammatical French. Following his established pattern, he sought out a more remote locality, and hired a boat to transport him to the north of the island – 'with difficulty', he grumbled, 'for the Amboynese are dreadfully lazy'.[16] He noted the wonderfully clear water in the harbour, and the richness of the marine life. In collecting terms, his great treasure here was the racquet-tailed kingfisher. He also found himself sharing his hut one day with a twelve-foot python, which had climbed up one of the posts and installed itself under the thatch within a yard of his head. His own boys would have nothing to do with ejecting it, but a local snake expert volunteered, and 'proceeded to work in a business-like manner', with a long pole and a strong noose of rattan.[17] The incident made a good illustration for *The Malay Archipelago*.

The month drew to an end, and as he packed his boxes and waited for the steamer, he began another letter to Bates:

> To persons who have not thought much on the subject I fear my Paper 'On the Succession of Species' will not appear so clear as it does to you. That paper is of course merely the announcement of the theory, not its development. I have prepared the plans & written portions of an extensive work embracing the subject in all its bearings & endeavouring to prove what in the paper I have only indicated.

Then, responding to Bates's surprise that he had published so soon, he explained: 'It was the promulgation of "Forbes' theory" which led me to write & publish for I was annoyed to see such an ideal absurdity put forth when such a simple hypothesis will explain <u>all the facts</u>.' He told Bates about the letter from Darwin, and his agreement with '<u>almost every word</u>' of the paper; Darwin's 'Species and Varieties' might save Wallace the trouble of writing the second part of his hypothesis, 'by proving that there is no difference in nature between the origin of species & varieties, or he may give me trouble by arriving at another conclusion, but at all events his facts will be given for me to work upon.' Tactfully, perhaps recalling Bates's shared views, he added, 'Your collections & my own will furnish most valuable materials to illustrate & prove the universal applicability of the hypothesis.'[18] He did not complete this letter to Bates for another three weeks.

On 8 January 1858, Wallace arrived at Ternate, a small island off the west coast of the large island of Gilolo (Halmahera). Through the influence of a wealthy Dutchman, Duivenboden – who owned half the town, a great many ships, and more than a hundred slaves – Wallace rented a spacious house. This had four rooms, a large hall, two verandas, a deep well, and a garden well planted with fruit trees. It was only five minutes from the beach and the market, and beyond in the other direction lay the slopes of the mountain, whose summit, four thousand or so feet, was perpetually wreathed with smoke – a still active volcano. Here Wallace could make a semi-permanent base, and he used this house as his principal residence for the next three years. Duivenboden traded in wild nutmeg from New Guinea, and Wallace booked his passage there on one of his schooners, which was due to sail in March. Meanwhile, the neighbouring island of Gilolo beckoned, 'the most perfect Entomological "terra incognita" now to be found', he told Bates in an addition to his letter. 'In about a week I go for a month's collecting there.' He was also intrigued to meet the human inhabitants. R. C. Latham, in *The Natural History of the Varieties of Man*, had written about the possible origin of the Papuan race:

> The probable source, however, of the Papuan population must be sought for in the parts about Gilolo. Here the distinction between these islands which constitute the more eastern and northern portions of the Moluccas, and those which are considered to belong to New Guinea, must be drawn.

Wallace was as interested in human races and varieties as he was in trogons and Heliconidae. Having secured his base in Ternate, he set off for Sedingole on Gilolo with two of Duivenboden's sons, the brother of his Ternate landlord, a young Chinaman, and a Papuan crew. Sedingole, their destination, proved unsatisfactory for collecting, so Wallace hired a small boat, which deposited him, his two men and baggage at Dodinga, at the head of a deep bay opposite Ternate on the narrow central isthmus of the island. He persuaded its owner to vacate a small hut for a month's rent of five guilders, installed himself and Ali, and on his very first walk obtained a few insects that were quite new to him. Things were looking good, when he fell ill with malaria.

He remained at Dodinga for just over a month. His field journal for the period is sparse, with only three entries covering nine pages, describing his accommodation, the location of Dodinga, and the inhabitants:

> The natives of this large and almost unknown island were examined by me with much interest, as they would help to determine whether, independent of mixed races, there is any transition from the malay to the papuan type. I was soon satisfied by the first half-dozen I saw that they were of genuine papuan race, lighter in colour indeed than usual but still presenting the marked characters of the type in features and stature. . . . The stature alone marks them as distinct being decidedly above the average malay height, while the features are as palpably *unmalay* as those of the Europeans or the negro.[19]

Weakened by malaria, Wallace turned his attention to the one species he could observe without moving far from his hut, man.

As often during times of enforced leisure, Wallace's mind went into overdrive. His letters to Bates and Darwin show the general direction of his speculations. His Sarawak paper stated his clear understanding that species changed by natural succession and descent, one species 'becoming changed either slowly or rapidly into another'. But the exact process of the change and the causes which led to it were unknown.

> The great difficulty was to understand how, if one species was gradually changed into another, there continued to be so many quite distinct species, so many which differed from their nearest allies by slight yet perfectly definite and constant characters.[20]

This was the question that he turned over and over in his thoughts, as he lay down recovering from the succession of hot and cold fits, shivering and wrapped in blankets even though the thermometer was 88°; and on one of these days, the answer presented itself.

One day something brought to my recollection Malthus's 'Principles of Population', which I had read about twelve years before. I thought of his clear exposition of 'the positive checks to increase' – disease, accidents, war, and famine – which keep down the population of savage races to so much lower an average than that of more civilised peoples. It then occurred to me that these causes or their equivalents are continually acting in the case of animals also; and as animals usually breed much more rapidly than does mankind, the destruction every year from these causes must be enormous in order to keep down the numbers of each species, since they evidently do not increase regularly from year to year, as otherwise the world would long ago have been densely crowded with those that breed most quickly. Vaguely thinking over the enormous and constant destruction which this implied, it occurred to me to ask the question, Why do some die and some live? And the answer was clearly, that on the whole the best fitted live. From the effects of disease the most healthy escaped; from enemies, the strongest, the swiftest, or the most cunning; from famine, the best hunters or those with the best digestion; and so on. Then it suddenly flashed upon me that this self-acting process would necessarily *improve the race*, because in every generation the inferior would inevitably be killed off and the superior would remain – that is, *the fittest would survive*. Then at once I seemed to see the whole effect of this, that when changes of land and sea, or of climate, or of food supply, or of enemies occurred – and we know that such changes have always been taking place – in conjunction with the amount of individual variation that my experience as a collector had shown me to exist, then all the changes necessary for the adaptation of the species to the changing conditions would be brought about; and as great changes in the environment are always slow, there would be ample time for the change to be effected by the survival of the best fitted in every generation. In this way each part of an animal's organisation could be modified exactly as required, and in the very process of this modification the unmodified would die out, and thus the *definite* characters and the clear *isolation* of each new species would be explained. The more I thought over it the more I became convinced that I had at length found the long-sought-for law of nature that solved the problem of the origin of species. For the next hour I thought over the deficiencies in the theories of Lamarck and of the author of the 'Vestiges', and I saw that my new theory supplemented these views and obviated every important difficulty.[21]

Wallace wrote several accounts of this great moment of illumination, all of them retrospective. There is no reference to the event in his field journal, and in *The Malay Archipelago* he is silent about it, as he is about the Sarawak paper. In his version for the Darwin–Wallace Celebration in 1908, he expands the narrative: 'Then there flashed upon me, as it had done twenty years before upon Darwin, the *certainty* . . .'[22] By that time, he had been able to read the parallel episode in Darwin's autobiography:

In October 1838, that is, fifteen months after I had begun my systematic enquiry [on how species become modified] I happened to read for amusement Malthus on Population, and being well prepared to appreciate the struggle for existence which everywhere goes on from long-continued observation of the habits of animals and plants, it at once struck me that under these circumstances favourable variations would tend to be preserved, and unfavourable ones to be destroyed. The result of this would be the formation of new species. Here then I had got at last a theory by which to work; but I was so anxious to avoid prejudice, that I determined not for some time to write even the briefest sketch of it. In June 1842 I first allowed myself the satisfaction of writing a very brief abstract of my theory in pencil in 35 pages; and this was enlarged during the summer of 1844 into one of 230 pages, which I had fairly copied out and still possess.[23]

If the moment of inspiration, the flash of insight, was similar, the two men's subsequent actions could not have been more contrasted. Wallace waited only for his malarial fit to subside to begin making notes for a paper. 'The same evening I did this pretty fully, and on the two succeeding evenings wrote it out carefully in order to send it to Darwin by the next post, which would leave in a day or two.'[24]

Alfred Russel Wallace,
aged 24

Thomas Vere Wallace

Mary Anne Wallace

Wallace's birthplace, near Usk

The house in Hertford

Hertford Grammar School

Wallace's sketch
of Derbyshire

Neath Mechanics
Institute

Lantwit Cottage,
by William
Weston Young

Wallace's drawing, Mandobé,
Upper Rio Negro

Butterflies from the Amazon,
collected by Wallace

H.W. Bates,
'Night adventure with alligator'

Fowls on the 50~ cost an average 6-8
books a ½d each — a few things I find
a half a dozen per apples cost the
same — Canas a yams, sweet
potatoes, bananas, cassava bread all
— the same proportion —
Umbypuara — above falls — River now
risen — walked thigh the foot to the
village — Canoe came in the afternoon
nearly lost very dangerous — wet
weather — Stay at St Jeronymo
falls — the first — abundance of
Orchids — new fish — Heard much
about the upper part of the River —
painted turtles, beautiful birds —
White Umbrella bird &c Determine
to go to Barra & return & spend the
dry season in these rivers & give up
for the present my journey to Peru
Reasons which render this advisable

Indian distrust of Spaniards — Swe of the —
dogs eaten dried — Piritintiris why poison
Jungu monkey but eat —
Death of a boy in the village — crying
burying neighbors &c —

Wallace's Amazon diary

Wallace, a Sarawak tree

Acorns

Flying Frog,
Borneo

Honeysuckle

Santubong Mountain

The Three Wise Men: Darwin, Hooker and Lyell

Ali, 1862

Wallace in the wild

Wallace and Geach in Singapore, 1862

Orang attacked by Dayaks

Treeps, Hurstpierpoint

Annie Mitten

Wallace with his son Bertie

Architectural drawing of The Dell, Grays

The Dell

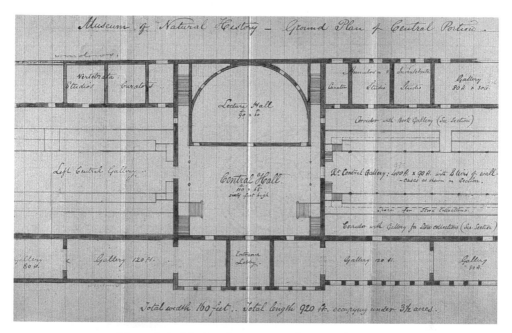

Plan of the National Museum of Natural History

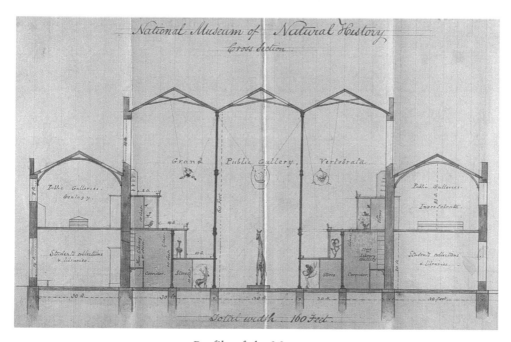

Profile of the Museum

(*Facing page*) Tree kangaroo and New Guinea birds

Corfe view

Old Orchard,
Broadstone

Family picnic at
Badbury Rings

Wallace,
by William Rothenstein

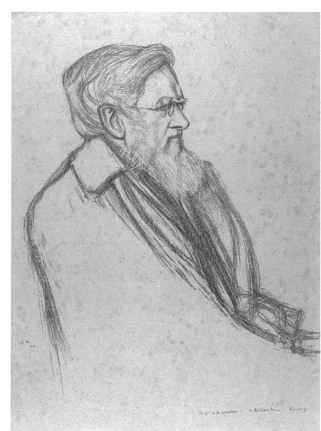

Wallace's funeral

Alfred Russel Wallace, by Roger Remington, 1998

According to his field journal, he returned to Ternate on 1 March, although his paper, entitled 'On the Tendency of Varieties to Depart Indefinitely from the Original Type', is headed 'Ternate, February, 1858'. The probable explanation for this inconsistency is that Wallace simply gave his main residence, and postal base, on his letters, rather than pedantically, or romantically, heading them 'temporary hut near beach on almost unknown island'. The next mail boat was due on 9 March, so he had a few days to prepare his correspondence. He enclosed his letter to Bates with another to Bates's brother Frederick: curiously, in view of the comments he had already written, he made no mention to Bates of the fact that he had by this time actually tackled the 'development of the theory'. Instead, he wrote a letter to Darwin 'in which I said that I hoped the idea would be as new to him as it was to me, and that it would supply the missing factor to explain the origin of species. I asked him, if he thought it sufficiently important, to show it to Sir Charles Lyell, who had thought so highly of my former paper', the Sarawak one.[25]

How did Wallace know about Lyell's opinion? It can have been only from Darwin, who wrote about it to him on 22 December 1857, in a letter that must have arrived in Ternate while Wallace was marooned with fever at Dodinga, unless it came on the very same inter-island mail boat from Batavia that carried Wallace's manuscript on the first leg of its journey to England. Darwin wrote:

> I am extremely glad to hear that you are attending to distribution in accordance with theoretical ideas. I am a firm believer, that without speculation there is no good & original observation. Few travellers have [at]tended to such points as you are now at work on; & indeed the whole subject of distribution of animals is dreadfully behind that of Plants.

(Wallace had been telling Darwin about his ideas on the geographical distribution of animals, and indicating that he planned to spend another three or four years in the East.)

> You say that you have been somewhat surprised at no notice having been taken of your paper in the *Annals*: I cannot say that I am, for so very few naturalists care for anything beyond the mere description of

species. But you must not suppose that your paper has not been attended to: two very good men, Sir C. Lyell, & Mr E. Blyth at Calcutta specially called my attention to it. Though agreeing with you on your conclusion[s] in that paper, I believe I go much further than you; but it is too long a subject to enter on my speculative notions. –

Instead, he proceeds to discuss Wallace's 'doctrine of subsidence', in regard to the former connection of islands with continents, and to answer his questions about the introduction of land-shells on oceanic islands by man's agency. Then he responds to a more leading question:

You ask whether I shall discuss 'man'; I think I shall avoid the whole subject, as so surrounded with prejudices, though I fully admit that it is the highest & most interesting problem for the naturalist. – My work, on which I have now been at work more or less for 20 years, will not fix or settle anything; but I hope it will aid by giving a large collection of facts with one definite end: I get on very slowly, partly from ill-health, partly from being a very slow worker. – I have got about half written; but I do not suppose I shall publish under a couple of years. I have now been three whole months on one chapter on Hybridism![26]

Much as Darwin had done with his first reading of the Sarawak paper, Wallace interpreted Darwin's letter selectively, taking literally the sentence that the work he was engaged on would not 'fix or settle anything', and totally ignoring the implications of 'I believe I go much further than you; but it is too long a subject to enter on my speculative notions'. Wallace, 'the young man in a hurry' as he later described himself, sealed up the fair copy of his new theory, and sent it to England for Darwin's opinion.

Wallace was eagerly preparing for his next expedition, bound for the mainland of New Guinea in Duivenboden's schooner. He had high hopes of repeating his Aru success. He now had four servants to cater for, including Ali as head man, and he wasted valuable time searching out provisions and equipment. After his brilliant burst of theorising, it was back to the daily trials and frustrations of the European collector. He scoured the Ternate stores for beeswax, metal spoons, a penknife, wide-mouthed phials, even for a staple such as flour.

8   In Search of Paradise Birds

Wallace and his men sailed slowly east to New Guinea, at first almost
becalmed, and in the later stages tacking against the wind. With every trip
he made he was better prepared, and more self-sufficient: this time he took
with him eighty pandanus-leaf mats, to protect his baggage and help roof
his house when he arrived. New Guinea lay on the extreme edge of Dutch
influence, *terra incognita*. As they neared the coast, Wallace gazed with
intense interest on the rugged mountains, 'retreating ridge behind ridge
into the interior, where the foot of civilised man had never trod' – the
country of the cassowary and the tree kangaroo, 'in whose dark forests lived
the most extraordinary and the most beautiful of the feathered inhabitants
of the earth', the many different species of birds of paradise.[1] Wallace
waited impatiently for the wind to change and allow the *Hester Helena* to
enter Dorey harbour, so that he might at last follow in the footsteps of the
great French naturalist René Lesson, who had described birds of paradise on

135

New Guinea in his *Zoologie du voyage autour du monde* in 1829, a voyage accomplished on board the corvette *La Coquille*.

From the start, nothing quite fulfilled his expectations. He was welcomed by two German missionaries, whom he compared unfavourably to the French Jesuits he had known in Singapore: 'Trading missionaries, teaching what Jesus said, but not doing as He did, can scarcely be expected to do more than give them [savage tribes] a very little of the superficial varnish of religion.'[2] They received him hospitably enough, and one of them, who spoke the language, made arrangements to lend him some men to cut wood, rattan and bamboo. The houses were wretched and dilapidated, built out over the water, and the large council-house was supported on posts grossly carved to represent a naked male or female figure, with other carvings 'still more revolting' placed on the platform before the entrance. Wallace, normally tolerant, found little to please him in these early encounters, and the local workforce proved apathetic and inefficient. Nevertheless, after three days he had a wooden house twenty feet by fifteen, with a bamboo floor, a thatch door, and a large window overlooking the sea: New Guinea palm-leaf mats formed the walls, and his imported mats were used on the roof, as planned. The Papuans were paid with knives and choppers, the schooner sailed east, and Wallace congratulated himself on being the only European inhabitant on the New Guinea mainland (the missionaries lived on a nearby island). For a few nights, the strangers set a watch and slept with loaded guns to hand, before deciding that the people were, despite popular rumour, well disposed.

The collecting business looked promising to begin with, lories and parroquets, a grackle, a king-hunter, a racquet-tailed kingfisher. But it was hard work: the wet season had left the countryside saturated and muddy. For a naked Papuan, this was not a problem – he would wade through it, and the next water-course would clean him up. For Wallace, in boots and trousers, it was extremely disagreeable. But far less bearable than the mud was the absence of birds of paradise. Dorey, apparently, was not a good centre for them, and they had to be sought for much further away. The natives, he decided, were poor creatures – they scarcely shot a thing, or if they did, they did not bring it to him. Insects, as always, cheered Wallace up: he obtained four distinct species of a new genus of horned flies, later named by William Saunders as *Elaphomia*, or deerflies, including *Elaphomia wallacei*. But then his old foot trouble returned – an ankle wound, suffered as he clambered about among fallen tree trunks, turned septic, and kept him indoors for several weeks, especially tantalising when he could see troops of grand butterflies whizzing past the door. He read every line of the *Family Herald*, and consoled himself with Dumas's novels, notably *La Reine Margot*, but his impatience grew. Even more infuriating was the arrival of the Dutch warship *Etna*, with the Prince of Tidore and the Resident of Banda on board, providing blatant competition. They sent men round in every direction, and were known to be in the market for birds of paradise, while anything less exotic that the local people had for sale was taken straight on board. Wallace was forced to change his tactics, and quietly arranged for Ali to slip away by boat for a month, with instructions to buy all the birds of paradise he could find.

On 18 June 1858, Wallace's letter reached Darwin at Downe, with its enclosure; and Darwin's reaction was a mixture of amazement and despair. In Wallace's later words, the effect of his paper on Darwin 'was at first almost paralysing'.[3] It was as if Darwin were reading his own theory, or an abstract of the 'big' book he was working on, *Natural Selection*. Painfully he composed a letter to Lyell.

> Some year or so ago, you recommended me to read a paper by Wallace in the *Annals*, which had interested you & as I was writing to him, I knew this would please him much, so I told him. He has to day sent me the enclosed & asked me to forward it to you. It seems to me well worth reading. Your words have come true with a vengeance that I shd. be forestalled.

Darwin had never seen a more striking coincidence (understandably, at first he noticed the similarities rather than the differences of emphasis). Any idea of his own priority vanished: his originality was smashed.

> I never saw a more striking coincidence, if Wallace had my M.S. sketch written out in 1842 he could not have made a better short abstract! Even his terms now stand as Heads of my Chapters. Please return me the M.S. which he does not say he wishes me to publish; but I shall of course at once write & offer to send to any Journal . . . I hope you will approve of Wallace's sketch, that I may tell him what you say.[4]

Lyell duly read Wallace's paper, and replied to Downe with an alternative proposal, a compromise whereby Darwin and Wallace would announce their discoveries jointly. Darwin was distraught. His baby son Charles was seriously ill with scarlet fever, and died on 28 June. He forced himself to try to concentrate on the moral dilemma of priority.

> There is nothing in Wallace's sketch which is not written out much fuller in my sketch copied in 1844, & read by Hooker some dozen years ago. About a year ago I sent a short sketch of which I have copy of my views (owing to correspondence on several points) to Asa Gray, so that I could most truly say & prove that I take nothing from Wallace. I shd. be <u>extremely</u> glad <u>now</u> to publish a sketch of my general views in about a dozen pages or so. But I cannot persuade myself that I can do so honourably. Wallace says nothing about publication, & I enclose his letter. – But as I had not intended to publish any sketch, can I do so honourably because Wallace has sent me an outline of his doctrine? – I would far rather burn my whole book, than that he or any other man shd. think that I had behaved in such a paltry spirit. Do you not think that his having sent me this sketch ties my hands?[5]

Whatever Darwin may have been hoping for, in terms of a response, he was certainly laying out a strong case against himself: 'I could send Wallace a copy of my letter to Asa Gray to show him that I had not stolen his doctrine' . . . 'base & paltry' . . . 'This is a trumpery affair' . . . 'This is a trumpery letter influenced by trumpery feelings'. All the same, would Lyell forward the trumpery letter, and his reply, to Hooker, so that he could have the opinion of his two best and kindest friends? He added a postscript to make the case against himself as strong as possible, and concluded that 'First impressions are generally right & I at first thought it would be dishonourable in me now to publish.' Letters passed to and fro, between Lyell, Hooker and Darwin. Darwin, grieving over Charles and thoroughly demoralised, distanced himself from the decisions. Lyell and Hooker conferred. They agreed, on the basis of their knowledge of Darwin's hitherto unpublished work, and work in progress, that it would be fair to both parties to arrange a joint publication, and chose a meeting of the Linnean Society on 1 July 1858 as the occasion. The timing was fortuitous: this was an extra meeting arranged after the previous one had been cancelled following the death on 10 June of the great botanist Robert Brown, a former President of the Society. Hooker and Lyell were present, and introduced the papers: extracts from Darwin's unpublished 1844 essay, which Hooker (but not Lyell) had indeed read; a section of a letter to the American naturalist Asa Gray written by Darwin in September 1857, which contained a sketch of his views, including the part played by the principle of divergence; and thirdly Wallace's Ternate paper, 'On the Tendency of Varieties to Depart Indefinitely from the Original Type', in that order – the strict chronological order.[6] In one important respect, Darwin's misgivings had been met. He was not asked to prepare a new sketch of his theory, but was represented by documents, extracts of documents, intended for other purposes, whereas Wallace's paper was polished and fluent (even if he had, of course, no chance to correct it). On the other hand, by presenting the papers in the order of writing, Hooker was ensuring greater prominence, and effective priority, for the much better-known Darwin.

There was no discussion, but the theory was out in the open. Hooker commented that

> . . . the interest excited was intense, but the subject was too novel and too ominous for the old school to enter the lists, before armouring. After the meeting it was talked over with bated breath: Lyell's approval, and perhaps in a small way mine, as his lieutenant in the affair, rather overawed the Fellows, who would otherwise have flown out against the doctrine. We had, too, the vantage ground of being familiar with the authors and their theme.[7]

(They were familiar with Darwin, and the theme, but not with Wallace.) Darwin was not present to read his contributions; his little boy was buried on the very same day as the meeting. Wallace had not been consulted. His agreement might have taken six months to obtain, and in any case, since Lyell had helped to orchestrate the decision, in one sense his wishes were being fully met. All the same, some rather carefully composed letters would need to be written. Darwin, once he had recovered his composure, settled down to work on a 'short' version of his book, the text that was published as *Origin of Species*, urged on by Lyell, Hooker and Huxley.

Wallace was not, in fact, totally ignored in the immediate aftermath of the Linnean presentation. When Alfred Newton received the published papers, he sat up late to read them.

> Never shall I forget the impression it made upon me. Herein was contained a perfectly simple solution of all the difficulties which had been troubling me for months past. I hardly know whether I at first felt more vexed at the solution not having occurred to me, than pleased that it had been found at all . . . All personal feeling apart, it came to me like the direct revelation of a higher power; and I awoke the next morning with the consciousness that there was an end of all the mystery in the simple phrase, 'Natural Selection'.[8]

In September that year, Richard Owen, later a fierce opponent, gave cautious recognition to both men in his presidential address to the British Association at Leeds.

In New Guinea, Wallace may have been wondering about Lyell's reception of his theory, but he had many other practical problems to contend with. Disappointments and setbacks continued. Ali came back from his bird-of-paradise sortie empty-handed. Wallace visited a German naturalist, Rosenberg, draughtsman to the *Etna*'s survey staff, and admired, longingly, some rare skins of paradise birds. He began to realise that most species came from deep in the interior, passing from village to village by barter till they reached the coast, where they would be sold to Bugis or Ternate traders. To interrupt this chain of supply would be difficult and dangerous. Then Wallace went down with a sharp bout of malaria, and two of his men fell ill in turn, with dysentery and fever. He used his depleted stock of medicine, but the quiet eighteen-year-old lad, Jumaat, died. Wallace provided some new cotton cloth for a shroud, and the other men, fellow Muslims, performed the burial rites. The days dragged on, and Wallace's persistence was repaid with a good haul of insects, especially beetles. But at the end of July, when the *Hester Helena* arrived, they said farewell to Dorey without much regret. Continual rain, continual sickness, one death, little wholesome food and finally a plague of ants and blowflies dampened even Wallace's ardour. The ants swarmed over his work table, carrying off his precious insects under his very nose, even tearing them from the cards on which they were gummed; and the flies settled in swarms on his bird skins, filling their plumage with masses of eggs which turned into maggots the next day. It was a great relief to return to Ternate, and to be able to enjoy milk with his tea and coffee, fresh bread and butter, and fowl and fish daily for dinner. Recalling the episode in *The Malay Archipelago*, he wrote in a comparatively rare first-person plural that 'This New Guinea voyage had used us all up'; just as rare was the feeling of comparative failure.[9]

As soon as he had recovered his energy, he made a short side trip to Gilolo, perhaps with one eye on the next mail boat. When it arrived, it brought a letter from Darwin, and another from Hooker, with news that his paper had been read at the 1 July meeting of the Linnean Society. 'I have received letters from Mr Darwin and Dr Hooker,' he reported to his mother,

> two of the most eminent naturalists in England, which have highly gratified me. I sent Mr Darwin an essay on a subject upon which he is now writing a great work. He showed it to Dr Hooker and Sir Charles Lyell, who thought so highly of it that they had it read before the Linnean Society. This insures me the acquaintance of these eminent men on my return home.[10]

In this contemporary reaction, there is a clear note of deference. His comments in *My Life* are more rounded:

> Both Darwin and Dr Hooker wrote to me in the most kind and courteous manner, informing me of what had been done, of which they hoped I would approve. Of course I not only approved, but felt that they had given me more honour and credit than I deserved, by putting my sudden intuition – hastily written and immediately sent off for the opinion of Darwin and Lyell – on the same level with the prolonged labours of Darwin, who had reached the same point twenty years before me, and had worked continuously during that long period in order that he might be able to present the theory to the world with such a body of systematised facts and arguments as would almost compel conviction.
>
> In a later letter, Darwin wrote that he owed much to me and his two friends, adding: 'I almost think that Lyell would have proved right, and that I should never have completed my larger work.' I think, therefore, that I may have the satisfaction of knowing that by writing my article

and sending it to Darwin, I was the unconscious means of leading him to concentrate himself on the task of drawing up what he termed an 'abstract' of the great work he had in preparation, but which was really a large and carefully written volume – the celebrated 'Origin of Species', published in November, 1859.[11]

Knowing how carefully Wallace used words, it is possible to infer a slight but significant distinction between the two paragraphs, between his approval in 1858, and the later recognition that, but for Wallace's paper, Darwin might never have been pushed into writing *The Origin of Species* in the particular form he gave it. At the time Wallace seems to have been genuinely delighted; and his other contemporary comments, to George Sims, to Bates, to Stevens, are entirely consistent. He instructed Stevens to obtain copies of the proceedings. 'Send one to Bates, Spencer and any other of my friends who may be interested in the matter and who do not attend the Linnean,' he wrote, much as he might have done with a paper on the Aru Islanders or the orang-utan – and this was request number three in his letter, following a complaint about the length of the no. 14 pins Stevens had shipped out: 'perfectly useless'.[12] Darwin had approved of the paper, and had forwarded it, as asked, to Lyell. Hooker and Lyell had, effectively, refereed it and presented it to the scientific world, alongside papers from Darwin. How could Wallace, locked into his slow island-hopping rhythm, not be pleased? In addition, the Aru collection had been a huge success – £1000 worth actually sold already. Another year or two, and he might realise enough to live on, and carry out 'long-cherished plans of a country life in Old England'.[13] He made calculations on the cost of annuities. The idea of going back to England via California was fading. Once his explorations were complete, he would be glad to return home as quickly and cheaply as possible. As for his own big book, he seems to have had no urgent plans to push ahead with it, even after receiving the good news of the Ternate paper's reception; besides, while it might be planned, it could scarcely be written during his travels.

The financial success of the Aru collection spurred him on. For his next trip, he became even more independent, hiring a boat and a pilot, who together with his four assistants – Ali included – made up the entire complement. A twelve-day voyage via the Kaioa Islands brought them to Batchian (Bacan). The morning after he had set up his establishment, he wandered off alone to investigate likely collecting grounds, having first sent his boys off to shoot. Ali came back with several birds hanging from his belt, and held up one for Wallace's inspection: 'Look here, sir, what a curious bird!'

> I saw a bird with a mass of splendid green feathers on its breast, elongated into two glittering tufts; but what I could not understand was a pair of long white feathers, which stuck straight out from each shoulder. Ali assured me that the bird stuck them out this way itself when fluttering its wings, and that they had remained so without his touching them. I now saw that I had got a great prize, no less than a completely new form of the bird of paradise, differing most remarkably from every other known bird.[14]

To Stevens, he could not conceal his joy: it was

> ... the finest and most wonderful bird in the whole island: a new Bird of Paradise! of a new genus!! quite unlike anything yet known, very curious and very handsome!!! When I can get a couple of pairs I will send them overland to see what a new Bird of Paradise will really fetch. I expect £25 each! ... I consider it the greatest discovery I have yet made ...[15]

George Gray, the Ornithological Curator at the British Museum, named it after its collector, *Semioptera wallacei*, or Wallace's standard-wing. This was the kind of boost Wallace needed to drive him forward. From now on, birds of paradise remained at the forefront of his plans: he might discover more species in Gilolo or Ceram. To set against the honour and acclaim of the theoretical paper on how species evolved, Wallace could happily weigh the beauty of some new and perfect organism that he had chanced on, in the remote solitude of the islands. Returning to Ternate on a government boat – he had sent his own back some while before – he had one unnerving encounter. On retiring for the night, he put out his candle, as there was still an oil lamp burning, and stretched out a hand to pick up his handkerchief, which he thought he saw on a box beside his bed. He felt instead something cool and very smooth, which moved as he touched it: another aspect of paradise, a highly poisonous snake that must have come on board in a bunch of plantains. It was swiftly dispatched, in a joint effort between Wallace and Ali.

> Thinking it very unlikely that two snakes had got on board at the same time, I turned in and went to sleep; but having all the time a vague dreamy feeling that I might put my hand on another one, I lay wonderfully still, not turning over once all night, quite the reverse of my usual habits.[16]

By April 1859, Wallace had been away from England for five years, and he was coming under pressure from his family to return home: the success of his collecting, his assured scientific reputation, his bouts of illness, were all put forward as good reasons, especially by his brother-in-law Thomas Sims, perhaps acting as family spokesman. These were ingenious arguments, Wallace admitted, but they left him quite unmoved. 'I have much to do yet before I can return with satisfaction of mind; – were I to leave now I should be ever regretful & unhappy . . . I feel my work is here as well as my pleasure & why should I not follow out my vocation.' He agreed that he already had enough materials for a 'life's study' of entomology as far as 'the forms & structure & affinities' of insects were concerned.

> But I am engaged here in a wider & more general study – that of the relations of animals to time & space, or in other words their Geographical & Geological distribution & its causes. I have set myself to work out this problem in the Indo-Australian Archipelago & I must visit & explore the largest number of islands possible & collect animals from the greatest number of localities in order to arrive at any definite results. As to health & life, what are they compared with peace & happiness.[17]

This was the master plan underpinning his relentless quartering of the Archipelago, and it may be significant that this expansive study – 'of the relations of animals to time & space' – pre-dated his reading of *The Origin of Species*. He continued to work at the problem. Celebes, in particular, puzzled him, and he stayed at or near Menado, on the end of the north-eastern peninsular, between June and September 1859. From the social perspective, he found the island, under the Dutch system, a model of what he thought colonial government should be: paternal despotism, acceptable because it led to moral and physical improvement.

> If we are satisfied that we are right in assuming the government over a savage race and occupying their country; and if we further consider it our duty to do what we can to improve our rude subjects and raise them up toward our own level, we must not be too much afraid of the cry of 'despotism' and 'slavery', but must use the authority we possess to induce them to do work which they may not altogether like, but which we know to be an indispensable step in their moral and physical advancement.[18]

By the time he wrote the concluding sections of *The Malay Archipelago*, Wallace was giving greater emphasis to that 'if'. But he remained convinced that the Dutch system was, at the very least, superior to the English, because it was allied to the grand law of continuity and gradual development: it was evolutionary, leading the people on – and, of course, upwards – by gradual steps towards a 'higher' state of civilisation. The British attempted to force *their* 'civilisation' on a subject people at once: 'We demoralise and we extirpate, but we never really civilise.'[19] Certainly, the Dutch system made this part of the island a very convenient and comfortable place to collect in. The local people were the most industrious, peaceable and civilised in the whole Archipelago; luggage was delivered as promised, houses prepared, boats or guides were available for hire, and Wallace found a particularly helpful ally in the eldest son of the governor of the Moluccas, who organised a large hunting party for him.

The island's geology and its fauna intrigued him. While he was there he experienced an earthquake, serious enough to make him appreciate the vast forces at work: 'We feel ourselves in the grasp of a power to which the wildest fury of the winds and waves are as nothing.'[20] Near by there were hot springs and craters, spurting jets of steam and boiling mud. These phenomena made him especially conscious of the geological changes that must have taken place in remote epochs. The species he collected were of extraordinary individuality: eighty species of birds peculiar to Celebes; eleven out of fourteen species of terrestrial mammals, including the sapiutan, or wild cow, and the babirusa, or pig-deer (both captured in the hunt); of the swallow-tailed butterflies, the Papilionidae, there were twenty-four species, of which eighteen are not found on any other island. Another feature was the complete absence of several groups found in the Moluccas as well as in Borneo and Java, but not here. All this, to Wallace, pointed to an origin for Celebes of the remotest antiquity. He continued to think over the problem for the rest of his life.

Leaving Celebes for the third and final time, he decided to make Amboyna his base temporarily, while he filled in the gaps in his knowledge of the Archipelago, and in particular Ceram, and the adjacent islands. A preliminary reconnaissance on Ceram, involving long wet treks through the forest, yielded magnificent butterflies, but left Wallace in a very poor state of health. He had been bitten all over – 'covered head to foot with inflamed lumps' – and he was laid up for two months, confined to his house.

He had plenty of reading matter. Darwin sent him, naturally, a copy of *The Origin of Species* (he may have sent him the proofs), and Wallace responded with a typically generous but objective appraisal. 'I most completely agree with you', replied Darwin, 'on the parts which are strongest & which are weakest.' Darwin reached out over the oceans to include Wallace in the campaign to promote natural selection: 'I can very plainly see, as I lately told Hooker, that my Book would have been & be a mere flash in the pan, were it not for you, Hooker & a few others.'[21] As well as these pleasant thoughts of his place in the scientific community, Wallace now had a European companion to talk to. Charles Allen had withdrawn from the mission in Sarawak, and, with Brooke's help, found temporary employment with the Borneo Company. Wallace persuaded him to take up his former occupation, this time as a freelance collector paid largely by results. He found Allen two assistants, Cornelius, a lad from Menado – 'very quiet and industrious' – and a local man, Theodorus Matakena, whom he had trained to skin birds. Four more years in the east had matured Allen, and Wallace was able to enjoy his company for a while, and to plan the next phase. Allen was dispatched to the north coast of Ceram, and from there to the 'unexplored' island of Mysol; Wallace headed east, along the southern coast of Ceram, with his final destination Waigiou: he was off again in search of paradise birds.

But first he made a detour down the chain of coral islands that stretched towards Ke and Aru. This satisfied his curiosity, but did not bring many rewards in terms of collecting. There were, too, several unnerving episodes: one small hired prau was borne on strong currents, and only a timely issue of spirits put enough vigour into the rowers' arms to pull them to safety. A second, equally miserable vessel took him further east, but the currents and winds proved too much for his crew. The alternatives seemed to include a week at sea in a small, open and heavily laden boat, or the risk of being driven ashore on the coast of New Guinea, where they might all be murdered, the recent fate of the crews of two local trading praus. Reluctantly, Wallace ordered a return to Goram. Here he bought a small prau for £9, and decided to convert it to his own specifications. He got out his saw and chisels, and set to work, to general astonishment. He arranged for a Ke boat-builder to fit new ribs, and, in the absence of augers, had to bore all the holes with hot irons. But even when leading by example, he could not instil a satisfactory work ethic into his labourers, whom he had hired to complete the prau and then crew her to Mysol, Waigiou and Ternate. Perhaps it was fortunate that when they reached Ceram, the entire crew decamped overnight. Wallace seemed inclined to put all this fecklessness down to the local diet of sago, which was far too readily available. He calculated the economics: in ten days a man could produce enough food for a whole year, a cost, in money terms, of twelve shillings. There was no proper incentive to progress. He managed to scrabble together a crew to take him to Wahai, where he was hospitably received by the Dutch commandant and by his old New Guinea acquaintance, Rosenberg. Rosenberg lent him some money to pay off his men and hire a fresh crew. He also found a *cri de coeur* from Charles Allen, who was running out of supplies on Mysol – rice and, crucially and less easily solved, insect pins.[22]

The first leg of the voyage was about sixty miles of open sea. The wind and the current carried them vigorously past Mysol, and poor Allen was left to fend for himself. Wallace then steered for a group of small islands, and after four days of being tossed about in the open boat they managed to find an anchorage. Two of the men were put on shore to cut jungle rope, and make the prau secure. Suddenly, the anchor slipped, and the boat drifted slowly but inexorably away on the current, which was too strong to row against. There was a lot of frantic shouting and gesticulating, and the two men disappeared from sight into the forest. Wallace presumed they were going to build a raft. However, he soon saw smoke rising: they had decided to build a fire to cook shellfish. Wallace was now anxious about his own predicament, and he and his crew just managed to reach the safety of a small island two miles off. They rested there, and the next day scoured the island for water, eventually finding some in a sheltered rock-hole. There was no sign of the two marooned men, but Wallace was not so worried about them. They had choppers, and could cut down a tree to make sago. They could dig for water, and harvest for shellfish. On the third day he sailed on to Waigiou. Once established there, he hired a boat to go and rescue his abandoned crew, who eventually turned up 'in tolerable health, though thin and weak', after surviving for a month on roots, shellfish and turtles' eggs. Conscious that his actions might seem a little ruthless, he gave an extensive commentary:

> Having swum to the island, they had only a pair of trowsers and a shirt between them, but had made a hut of palm leaves, and had altogether got on very well. They saw that I waited for them three days at the opposite island, but had been afraid to cross, lest the current should have carried them out to sea, when they would have been inevitably lost. They had felt sure I would send for them on the first opportunity, and appeared more grateful than natives usually are for my having done so; while I felt much relieved that my voyage, though sufficiently unfortunate, had not involved loss of life.[23]

Wallace could now turn his attention to the natural history of the island.

As there were no suitable houses available in the scattered village of Muka, Wallace had one built on the edge of the forest, siting it near the path and the stream, and close to a fine fig tree. It was a kind of lean-to shed, with walls of thatch, supplemented by the prau's sails, and with palm-leaf mats for the roof. After some adjustments, the roof was made relatively watertight, and he could concentrate on birds of paradise. The villagers maintained that none were to be found in the immediate vicinity, but Wallace could actually hear them, and the very first day he went into the forest he saw one, the rare red species *Paradisea rubra*, found only on Waigiou. His hunter brought him a female, and there was a good deal of shooting and missing. Then the figs began to ripen, and the birds came to feed. The birds moved so quickly, and the foliage of the surrounding trees was so dense, that there was as much watching as shooting of a bird in many respects more remarkable and beautiful than the two large species he had already obtained:

The Red Bird of Paradise

The head, back, and shoulders are clothed with a richer yellow, the deep metallic green colour of the throat extends farther over the head, and the feathers are elongated on the forehead into two little erectile crests. The side-plumes are shorter, but are of a rich red colour, terminating in delicate white points, and the middle tail feathers are represented by two long rigid glossy ribbands [sic], which are black, thin, and semi-cylindrical, and droop gracefully in a spiral curve.

He had managed to shoot only two males on 'his' tree, 'when they ceased visiting it, either owing to the fruit becoming scarce, or that they were wise enough to know there was danger'. They had to be hunted in the forest.[24]

Muka was not a comfortable base: there was very little fresh food to buy, apart from the occasional fish. As in Ceram, the people were dependent on the abundant sago palm, so did not grow vegetables or fruit: in Wallace's view, this kept them in poverty, and poor health, and as the majority seemed to have a Papuan slave to do all the labour, they lived in almost absolute idleness. They appeared to be a mixed race, part Malay and Alfuro from Gilolo, part Papuan from New Guinea; Wallace saw this as more evidence of the distinctness between the two races of the Malay Archipelago, which had intermingled in unoccupied territory 'at a very recent epoch in the history of man', rather than being a modification of one and the same race.[25]

Since birds of paradise remained his principal goal, Wallace eventually took the locals' advice, and made for Bessir, where the specialist hunters operated. He left his helmsman behind with the prau, hired an outrigger, and spent a disagreeable day being tossed about on his way to what was in fact a separate island of raised coral. There was a little hut just above a white sandy beach, which the chief offered to him – a dwarf's house, eight feet square, with the ridge over the raised level only five feet from the floor, and the space below offering scarcely four and a half feet clearance. Wallace fixed up a small table and shelves in this cramped space, and would crawl inside to work, or to have his meals; at night, he slept above, while his men spread their sleeping mats on the ground. This was his home for six weeks.

It was a good opportunity to re-read *The Origin of Species*, and to write to George Silk about it. Wallace was still largely unaware of the public's response to Darwin's book. But he had read it through, now, five or six times, each with increasing admiration – it would live as long as Newton's

Principia:

> The cycles of astronomy or even the periods of geology will alone
> enable us to appreciate the vast depths of time we have to contemplate
> in the endeavour to understand the slow growth of life upon the earth
> . . . Mr Darwin has given the world a *new science*, and his name should,
> in my opinion, stand above that of every philosopher of ancient or
> modern times. The force of admiration can no further go!!![26]

Years later, Wallace confided to his doctor that, when he received the
proofs of *The Origin*, he put aside his own projected book of theory, a
decision that he seems to have kept extremely private.[27] Certainly, he did
not mention to Silk that Darwin's book had effectively blocked his own.
The copious notes on Lyell, all the extracts and references in his notebooks,
would have to serve another purpose.

The hunters arrived, and Wallace paid for his birds up front, with
hatchets, beads, knives and handkerchiefs. Only one hunter was confident
enough to take goods to the value of two birds: the others bided their time.
Three days later, bird one arrived, still alive, but tied up in a small bag and
so with damaged feathers. Wallace explained that he wanted as perfect
specimens as possible: if the birds were to be kept alive, they should be
secured on a perch with a string round one leg. The other hunters now
decided to join in, and compounded for anything from one to six birds.
Even so, many birds arrived in poor condition, but those that had been
caught the same day were put in a bamboo cage, with troughs for food and
water, and Wallace did his best to nurture them, feeding them on fruit and
live grasshoppers. His efforts all failed, but he stayed on for as long as
possible to add to his collection. His own and his men's diet was meagre.
Tough pigeons and cockatoos supplemented the rice and sago, but there
was scarcely enough fruit such as plantains, or vegetables, for the local
inhabitants. He became thin and weak, and suffered from intense head-
aches; and an attack of malaria left him so apathetic that he could not face
the sago diet, and had to fall back for nourishment on his emergency
rations, two tins of soup. It was time to go. The hunters brought their last
birds, and one returned the axe he had received in advance. The man who
had bargained for six came running up just as the boat was being loaded,
and handed over the last bird, saying 'Now I owe you nothing' –

'unexpected instances of honesty' that made a deep impression on Wallace.[28] He took away twenty-four fine specimens of *Paradisea rubra*, as well as several other entirely new or extremely rare species of birds – the New Guinea kite, a new goat-sucker – and wonderful butterflies, with a superb green *Ornithoptera*, 'one of the glories of my cabinet'.

The voyage from Waigiou to Ternate provided a catalogue of obstacles. Rats had gnawed through the sails in twenty places which meant buying new matting. Head winds and contrary tides and currents hindered their progress west, and when they finally arrived at Gilolo, they were forced to the north coast, and even then had to claw their way along by rowing. Wallace listed a set of Pauline disasters: ten times aground on coral reefs, four anchors and a small boat lost, no oil for the compass lamp, shortages of food and water, and *'not one single day of fair wind!'* When they were successively nearly swamped by a tidal wave, and then overtaken by a hurricane, the old steersman was convinced that theirs was an unlucky boat, and that they were paying the penalty for having neglected the Bugis holy oil ceremony when the prau was first refitted. After a total of thirty-eight days, instead of the estimated twelve, they finally reached Ternate, where Charles Allen was waiting. Wallace had received a note from him on the way back, via the captain of a passing trading prau, which had cheered his spirits. Allen had been understandably apprehensive, especially after having been left to his own devices on Mysol. He had done reasonably well there, though he had only collected a few paradise birds. Wallace was impressed by his independence, and courage, and persuaded him to undertake several more dangerous, solo expeditions, to New Guinea, to the Sula Islands, to Flores, and to Coti, on the east coast of Borneo.

This was to be Wallace's last stay at Ternate. He needed, first, to recuperate, and he was pleased to have Allen to help him prepare his collections for shipment to England. He had a great mountain of mail to read and answer, a nine-month accumulation of letters, accounts, papers, magazines and books. He could, too, begin to make definite plans for his return to England, now that Allen was available to map certain key areas of the Archipelago for him, and so fill in the few remaining gaps. He planned a less arduous route for himself, to Timor first, followed by the much more accessible and civilised islands of Java and Sumatra. He also intended to keep his eyes and ears open for any live specimens of paradise birds. Stevens had passed on his terms for live birds to various potential outlets, including the Zoological Society: with any luck they could pay for his passage home.

Among his letters was one from Darwin, acknowledging Wallace's appreciation of *The Origin*. Darwin was equally warm: 'You must let me say how I admire the generous manner in which you speak of my Book: most persons would in your position have felt some envy or jealousy.' Wallace spoke 'far too modestly' of himself: 'You would, if you had had my leisure done the work just as well, perhaps better, than I have done it.'[29] In fact, Wallace seemed genuinely relieved that he had not been compelled to write such a book: certainly, the massed detail that underpinned the argument of *The Origin* would not have been congenial work. As he confided to Bates,

I know not how, or to whom, to express fully my admiration of Darwin's book. To *him* it would seem flattery, to others self-praise; but I do honestly believe that with however much patience I had worked and experimented on the subject, I could *never have approached* the completeness of his book, its vast accumulation of evidence, its overwhelming argument, and its admirable tone and spirit. I really feel thankful that it has not been left to me to give the theory to the world. Mr Darwin has created a new science and a new philosophy; and I believe that never has such a complete illustration of a new branch of human knowledge been due to the labours and researches of a single man.[30]

Publicly, he never wavered in his admiration for *The Origin*, whatever minor reservations he might later have acquired about the Linnean proceedings. Meanwhile Darwin filled him in on the scientific reactions to the subject. There were more converts among the geologists than in any other branch of science, and certainly more than among naturalists, perhaps because they were more accustomed to reasoning. But there was much opposition – an envious and spiteful notice by Richard Owen in the *Edinburgh Review*, savage attacks by Adam Sedgwick and J.W. Clark at Cambridge, hostile reviews by Sir William Jardine and Thomas Wollaston, and '*many others*'. Lyell kept 'firm as a tower', and would declare his conversion in the autumn. He also informed Wallace about Patrick Matthew, who wrote to the *Gardeners' Chronicle* drawing attention to a section of his 1830 work *Naval Timber & Arboriculture*, which contained a statement about natural selection. 'My Brother,' commented Darwin, 'who is a very sagacious man, always said you will find that some one will have been before you.' Matthew could claim priority over them both.[31] Wallace replied with his latest puzzle, 'the repetition of the forms & colours of animals in distinct groups, but the two always occurring in the same country & generally on the <u>very same spot</u>'. This kind of mimicry was a phenomenon he could not at present reconcile with Natural Selection: it was a topic he would continue to work on, and would be illuminated the following year by Bates.[32]

Wallace left Ternate on New Year's Day 1861, for Timor, which formed one of the major gaps in his collections. He had previously stayed briefly at Coupang, in the western part of the island administered by the Dutch. He now based himself near Delli (Dili), in east Timor, governed by the Portuguese. Wallace had not been particularly enamoured of the Portuguese whom he had met on the Amazon. He took a dim view of their mismanagement in Timor: no decent buildings, no roads into the interior to encourage agriculture and trade, a miserable mud fort, and a disproportionate number of officers strutting about in gorgeous uniforms. Added to this, the town was surrounded by swamps and mudflats, and distinctly unhealthy: 'A single night often gives a fever to new-comers which not unfrequently proves fatal.'[33] Wallace did not attempt the experiment. His immediate contact, Captain Hart, an English trader and coffee-grower, always slept at his plantation on higher ground two miles from the town, where Frederick Geach, a mining engineer, also had a house. Geach invited Wallace to join him, and he rode up there in the evening, and settled in.

For several weeks, Wallace did not move far from the house. Seven years in the tropics had left their mark, and his recent long voyage from Waigiou to Ternate especially had knocked the stuffing out of him. He was prepared at last to admit as much in letters home. 'My health, too, gives way,' he confessed to Sims, 'and I cannot now put up so well with fatigue and privations as at first.'[34] He even asked for a plan of his mother's small cottage in Hammersmith, so that he could work out whether there might be room for him there as well. Meanwhile, there was a little valley with a stream nearby, with the water shaded by fine trees, and he rambled about, collecting a few birds and several remarkable and rare butterflies, such as the swallowtails *Papilio aenomaus* and *Papilio liris*. He had just Ali now as his hunter and assistant, and was not collecting with the same intensity as before, though it was as important as ever to him to make systematic notes, vital evidence for his study of distribution. He and Geach, with whom he struck up an immediate rapport, then made a short trip into the mountains, staying at a 'village' – three houses – two thousand feet up: there was a mist or cloud for much of the day, so it was not much good for insects, but Wallace enjoyed eating mutton on evenings cool enough to make a fire an additional pleasure. Geach told him about the absurdity of the Portuguese, who had hired him from England to open up a copper mine without conducting a proper mineral survey. Wallace speculated on what might be done to make the country properly productive: sheep, wheat, rice, potatoes, coffee could all be made to thrive, and pay.

Geach left for Singapore, and Wallace spent his evenings instead with Hart, who borrowed *The Origin of Species* and discussed the issues at length. Wallace continued to collect. The Timor bee-hunters intrigued him – beeswax was an important export. He watched a group at work in his valley: a man would climb a smooth-barked tree with a bush rope, to one end of which a wood torch was attached; seventy or eighty feet up, he would transfer himself to the branch from which the huge honeycombs were suspended, smoke out the bees, slice the comb free with his knife, and then lower it to the ground by a thin cord. Even down on the ground, the disturbed bees became rather numerous, and Wallace had to run for it, beating the bees away with his net but at the same time capturing some (*Apis dorsata*) for specimens. He also acquired one of the honeycombs, which he later presented to Darwin.[35]

Timor was especially significant to Wallace, as it forms, with Lombock and Flores, the third of the group of major islands possessing a distinctive fauna, lying between Java and Australia. When, later, he had the evidence of Charles Allen's collections from Flores to work on in addition, he was able to suggest the intermediate nature of the islands' fauna, and to argue that they were properly oceanic islands, populated by a 'chapter of accidents' from the neighbouring larger land-masses, and never – in terms of recent geological epochs – part of either Java or Australia.

From Timor, he moved to Bouru, west of Ceram, filling yet another gap, a location with attractive potential as it was practically unknown to naturalists. It was on the monthly Dutch mail-steamer route, and he and his men and baggage went ashore on the small boat that came out to receive the post-packet. Wallace took some time before he found a promising collecting-ground, sending Ali off in one direction while he explored inland. Everywhere they encountered mud, high coarse grass, or cajuputi trees – districts 'absolutely destitute of interest for the zoologist'. After further enquiries, some proper forest was located on the south coast, and Wallace set off, initially by boat and then by trekking along the beach, as the coastal waters were too dangerous for praus.

In Bouru, Wallace's years of experience soon transformed the little hut he borrowed: he had learned to travel more lightly. He fixed up a mosquito-net, partly enclosed with a large Scotch plaid, to form a sleeping apartment. He had a rough table made, with its legs buried in the earth floor to form a flat and stable surface, at which he could sit in his portable rattan chair, with his books, penknives, scissors, pliers, pins and specimen labels arranged before him. A line was hung across one corner, to dry his cotton underwear, washed each day. A bamboo shelf held crockery, and other hanging shelves kept the collections out of the ants' path while they were drying. Then out of the boxes which were ranged around the thatch walls would come his few luxuries, coffee or tea, and sugar and biscuits, to the surprise of the local people. Like the Aru Islanders, they could not understand what Europeans could possibly do with the birds and insects that were being so carefully preserved. The conditions on Bouru were tough. Wallace had left his spare boots on board the steamer, and, since his others were dropping to pieces, he had to move about barefoot, risking a wound that might lay him up as in Borneo and Aru. Ali trod on an enormous snake in the long grass, a twenty-footer at least, 'like a tree being dragged along through the grass'. Ali was becoming almost as obsessive a collector as Wallace. He had seen a beautiful small bird of the genus *Pitta*, and he was so intent on securing it that on their last night he went off to sleep at a little hut in the forest, in order to have a last try for it at daybreak: he came back in triumph with two specimens, one with its head blown completely off, but the other in 'very good order', a new species 'very like the *Pitta celebensis*, but ornamented with a square patch of bright red on the nape of the neck'.[36] They returned to Cajeli, packed up the collections, and were ferried out to the steamer, *en route* to Ternate. Everything was transferred on board, and Wallace did the rounds of his friends to say his goodbyes. The steamer headed first west towards Menado, and then south for Macassar and Java.[37] So Wallace finally left the Moluccas, 'among whose luxuriant and beautiful islands' he had wandered for more than three years, and where he had formulated his theory of natural selection.

He landed at Sourabaya, on the north east of Java, and spent a fortnight packing up his recent collections, and writing letters. After all these years of roughing it, he was staying in a hotel – but a noisy one, he hastily added. 'Of course, my dear mother, I shd. not think of living anywhere but with you, after such a long absence, – if you feel yourself equal to housekeeping for us both.' He would need only, besides a small bedroom, one large room 'or a small one if there is besides a kind of lumber room where I could keep my cases & do rough & dirty work'.[38] He was beginning to tune in to events in England once more, asking Silk for news, tracing the current scientific debates in the pages of the *Athenaeum*. But he still had to investigate Java, and Sumatra. He set off towards Mount Arjuna, this time in a carriage, paying, to his disgust, the equivalent of half a crown a mile for post-horses. The expense soon cut down any ambition to make a longer journey. He found a good spot for birds – ninety-eight species in a month – and had time to admire the architectural remains, and, rarely for him, to enjoy local music – the 'gamelang'. He even acquired a two-foot-high bas-relief carving of the Hindu goddess Durga, to be shipped home with the peacocks and hornbills.

He took the opportunity to study in more detail the Dutch system of managing a colony, which he had approved in Celebes. He makes some interesting observations on what occurs when, in his Darwinian terms, men of a 'superior' race trade freely with men of a 'lower' race. Apart from the specific temptations of spirits and opium there is the temptation of obtaining goods on credit, to be paid for by some crop perhaps not yet planted, 'or some product yet in the forest':

> He has not sufficient forethought to take only a moderate quantity, and not enough energy to work early and late in order to get out of debt; and the consequence is that he accumulates debt upon debt, and often remains for years or for life as a debtor, and almost a slave.[39]

Wallace knew all about debt. By instinct he was uncomfortable with the concept of colonisation, but regarded it as inevitable. If it had to be done, then it was better conducted by the Dutch, who, in theory at least, worked in co-operation with the chiefs, on a stake-holder principle which provided

157

a fixed wage, and a share of any surplus profit: a system that should operate to everyone's advantage, and progress, in the most fertile and productive island in the world.

Having exhausted the locality, he decided to try his luck in the west of the island. He moved to Batavia, and stayed a week at the Hotel des Indes – real luxury, with a sitting room and bedroom opening on to a veranda. From there, he took a coach to the Botanical Gardens at Buitenzorg, forty miles inland, rode on another twenty miles into the mountains, and hired a road-keeper's hut for a fortnight. This was a more fruitful collecting-ground, both for birds and butterflies:

> On the very first day, my hunters obtained for me the elegant yellow and green trogon (*Harpactes reinwardti*), the gorgeous little minivet fly-catcher (*Pericrocotus miniatus*), which looks like a flame of fire as it flutters among the bushes, and the rare and curious black and crimson oriole (*Analcipus sanguinolentus*), all of them species which are found only in Java, and even seem to be confined to its western portion.[40]

He was also offered a rare and curious butterfly, *Charaxes kadenii*, 'remarkable for having on each hind wing two curved tails like a pair of callipers'.

The highlight of his visit was a long slow climb to the summit of Pangerango, ten thousand feet. This was his only experience of climbing to such a height near the Equator, and so being able to observe stage by stage as the tropical flora and vegetation gave way to the temperate, and finally to the alpine. At nine thousand feet he found the royal cowslip, *Primula imperialis*. The existence of modified forms of European genera on the mountains of the Himalayas, for example, was a puzzle for naturalists: the distances were too great to be explained by the agency of the wind, or birds. Wallace, who had digested chapter two of *The Origin of Species*, followed Darwin's hypothesis 'for the present' that, during the glacial epoch, temperate forms of plants extended to the tropics, and even, by the most elevated routes, had crossed the Equator and reached the Antarctic regions.[41] Wallace, plotting the fauna of the Archipelago, was confident that Java had formerly been connected to Asia. Here, as he botanised on the rim of the crater, was abundant plant evidence to support the simple hypothesis of modification by natural selection. The European forms – violets, St John's wort, guelder-rose – brought English landscapes to his mind. He was longing for a field of buttercups, he confessed to Fanny: 'A hill of gorse, or of heath, a bank of foxgloves & a hedge of wild roses & purple vetches surpass in <u>beauty</u> anything I have ever seen in the tropics.'[42]

The weather was beginning to break, and, though he tried to find another location, insects and birds were scarce. So he returned to Batavia, packed up his collections, and took the Singapore mail boat as far as Muntok, on the island of Banca. From there he found a passage across the straits to Sumatra, and hired a rowing boat to take him a hundred miles up river to Palembang. As in Java, there was too much cultivation for fruitful collecting. He enquired about forest, and had to kick his heels for a week before he could make arrangements to strike inland, by the military road. He came across an isolated guard-house at Lobo Raman, and settled down to do what collecting he could during the monsoon. If he could not add much in terms of quantity – the shortage of beetles disgusted him, he complained to Bates – there were special features that intrigued him: especially butterflies that seemed to mimic another species.[43] There were rhinoceros in the forest: he once disturbed one feeding; and a curious flying lemur; and a most unusual ape, the siamang. As he had done in the Amazon, Wallace was planning to take some live animals home, and he bought a small siamang. He fixed up two poles underneath his veranda, and tried feeding it by hand in an attempt to tame it, because it had taken an apparent dislike to him. One day, it bit him so sharply while he was giving it food that he lost patience and beat it – 'which I regretted afterward, as from that time it disliked me more than ever'.[44] But it seemed to like his Malay assistants, and kept them all amused for hours as it swung from pole to pole.

Bates had forwarded to him a copy of his 1861 paper on the insect fauna of the Amazon valley, and Wallace urged him to send one to Darwin: it would 'establish your fame and at the same time demonstrate the simplicity & beauty of the Darwinian philosophy'.[45] (Bates had indeed done so; he was already in regular correspondence with Darwin, who on 21 November had heard Bates's second paper on the topic at the Linnean.) Wallace also wrote to Darwin, wanting to know more of what was going on among naturalists. Huxley and Owen seemed to be at open war – 'but I cannot glean that any one has ventured to attack you fairly on the whole question, or ventured to answer the whole of your argument'.[46] From Silk he begged for items of real interest – 'But please! no party politics'. European culture was beckoning to him. Had Silk read *Great Expectations*, or *Essays and Reviews*? What about the Gorilla War, raging around the head of the explorer Paul du Chaillu? Had he been to see Charles Blondin, wire-walking at the Crystal Palace for £100 a performance? Wallace was in the last stages of his travels – 'Then ho! for England!'[47] This time, however, he did not intend to return home empty-handed.

The birds of paradise formed, by his own admission, a chief objective of Wallace's voyages. This was partly because of their strange beauty, a beauty that had already made them objects of value in the Archipelago, as well as in Europe, and partly because they seemed to inhabit the most remote and inaccessible places – Waigiou, the Aru Islands, and the mainland of New Guinea. It was a challenge, first, to purchase them in any shape or form at all, let alone see them in the wild; and the greatest challenge would be to bring one back alive to England. In a letter to Stevens he set out his terms, brisk, businesslike, and somewhat peremptory – he wanted a *definite arrangement* with the Crystal Palace Company, including a free *first-class* passage for himself from Singapore: if he brought back one bird alive, the rate would be £100, £50 for the second, and £25 a head for any more up to ten: 'If they won't give this price I will not trouble myself even if I can get them for nothing.'[48] (Stevens passed these terms on to Philip Sclater, Secretary at the Zoological Society, who eventually agreed them.) 'In my next voyage to New Guinea,' Wallace informed Stevens, 'I think it probable that I may get some live *Paradiseas*.'[49] On Waigiou – July to September 1860 – Wallace was attempting to collect and keep alive the red bird of paradise.

As Wallace's travels extended through 1861, the idea of bringing live birds of paradise back to England assumed greater significance. His motives were partly personal, a stubborn attempt to erase the memory of the live collection from the Amazon that had disappeared overboard or perished by fire, and partly economic. He never lost sight of the fact that this arduous eight-year expedition should provide, in addition to intellectual capital, financial security for the rest of his life. But the birds of paradise meant much more to him than that. They were the vital, stunning proof of the beauty of the natural world, dazzling examples of geographical biodiversity and of the wonders produced by natural selection, his own corollary, perhaps, to Darwin's Galapagos finches. They became a kind of validation for his work, both as a collector, an observing naturalist, and a theorist.

Wallace reached Sumatra in November 1861, on the final phase of his collecting, when he learned shortly before Christmas that there were two lesser birds of paradise for sale in Singapore. His narrative in *My Life* makes no mention of any commission or financial arrangement, but rather gives the impression that the business was almost coincidental: 'While waiting at Singapore for the steamer to take me home I purchased two living specimens of the smaller bird of paradise.'[50] In fact, the prospect of a free passage home was quite enough to persuade him to cut short his stay in Sumatra, where the rainy season was hampering his activities, and begin negotiations. His siamang attracted a great deal of attention in Singapore, where nobody had apparently ever seen one alive before. It was duly dispatched via the Cape, but failed to survive the long voyage. (Curiously, Wallace comments in *The Malay Archipelago* that 'it died just before he started'.)

The two birds of paradise, though, fared better, and Wallace went to enormous trouble to ensure their survival. He bought them on 6 February 1862, for $400 (£92), beating the agent down from the asking price of $500 for the pair, and two weeks later set off via Galle for Bombay, where a stopover allowed him time to lay in a stock of fruit, principally bananas, for the birds. They ate a great many cockroaches, and from Bombay to the Red Sea he swept up a fresh daily supply into a biscuit tin in the ship's store-room.[51] A further stop at Malta was an opportunity to buy melons, and he also found an 'unlimited' cockroach source in a baker's. At each stopover he fired off letters and telegrams. He was particularly anxious about the cold weather, and wanted to hand the birds over as soon as possible: could a keeper come out to meet him at Marseilles, or even Avignon, he enquired of Stevens. From Malta he cabled Sclater: 'The two garadise bards [*sic*] have arrived here in perfect health. I wait your instruction.'[52] No instruction came. Wallace took the next boat to Marseilles, and sent another telegram. This, too, was ignored, and he set off for Paris, with the birds travelling as baggage. A night in Paris followed, and finally Wallace was back in England, almost eight years since his departure. He wrote at once to Sclater from the Pavilion Hotel, Folkestone, expanding on the trouble – and expense – he had taken to preserve the birds – he had accompanied them all night in the baggage train across the desert to Cairo, and he had had trouble to get them well cleaned – 'they make an immense deal of dirt'. He advised Sclater to organise a supply of cockroaches, and stated firmly that he expected to be met at London Bridge the following noon – 1 April – with a keeper and a van. (He was.) Their side plumes, he concluded, were about half grown – hardly visible when he left Singapore, they grew rapidly as far as Suez, when the cold seemed to check them. 'Another year with a genial temperature, flying room, foliage, & abundance of food, I hope they will be glorious.'[53]

Sclater absorbed all these demands graciously. The Maltese arrival was heralded in *The Times*:

> The Zoological Society of London are daily expecting a new and brilliant addition to their collection . . . But one previous instance is known of a Paradise Bird having been brought alive to Europe. This individual was the property of the late Princess Augusta, and died at Windsor about forty years ago.[54]

Meanwhile the Council approved a sum of £20 for 'the reception of these birds', and the society's smith, painter and carpenter were set to work to adapt a large galvanised-iron-wire cage in the former small animal room, whose temperature was now recorded daily. The pair formed an expensive acquisition. Wallace received in all £307 9s: £150 for the birds – making £58 profit on the deal; his fare – £137 3s; and £20 6s for 'sundry expenses', such as the cost of making cages for the different stages of the journey. After a few months, the two young male birds were transferred to a 'more airy situation' in the new aviary, where they occupied the compartment nearest to the main entrance gate, and so formed most visitors' introduction to the zoo's treasures. Accompanied by a text beginning 'Mr A. R. Wallace, the well-known traveller and naturalist', the *Illustrated London News* featured them prominently on 12 April.[55] Wallace was home at last in triumph, accompanied by two living, glorious symbols to mark the 'central and controlling incident' of his life.

9   The Return of the Wanderer

Wallace inevitably speculated about his reception in London scientific circles. The first mark of recognition was his election as a Fellow of the Zoological Society, a resolution passed on 19 March 1862 when Sclater reported to the Council that the birds of paradise had reached Malta. Equally gratifying was the news that, 'in consequence of the eminent services rendered to zoological science', his 'admission fee and composition' would be remitted.[1] Wallace duly wrote a formal acknowledgement to the Council, and began to attend the fortnightly scientific meetings on a regular basis. This was a significant step upwards, and outwards, from the more specialised interests of the Entomological Society, the beetle- and butterfly-fanciers who, at their worst, might be ranked (according to Bates) with collectors of postage stamps and crockery.[2] Thanks to Sclater, Wallace had already been elected a Member of the British Ornithologists Union. He was, naturally, welcome as a visitor at the Linnean. Now, at the Zoological, where the birds of paradise were soon attracting distinguished visitors such as the Duke of Argyll, his circle widened. Regulars at the meetings included John Gray, from the British Museum, and John Gould, taxidermist and illustrator, who had jointly made the proposal about remission of fees; Sclater, as Secretary; Samuel Stevens, his agent; T. H. Huxley; Alfred Newton, from Cambridge; St George Mivart; the ornithologist the Reverend H. B. Tristram; William Henry Flower; George Busk; and his old Amazon companion Bates, finally returned from South America. On 13 May, Wallace attended his first meeting as a fellow. On 27 May, with Huxley in the chair, he gave an account of his expeditions in search of paradise birds. On 10 and 24 June he exhibited 'rare and new birds'.[3]

He was, though, far from well in these first weeks, a legacy of his debilitating travels, and he spent long periods resting in his room. With great regret, he had to decline, for the present, Darwin's immediate invitation to visit him at Downe, because he was being 'doctored a little'. In mid-May, he was cooped up for ten days with a disagreeable 'though far from dangerous' crop of boils. (Darwin's invitation arrived on 7 April and Wallace, in declining, sent Darwin a wild honeycomb from Timor, still full of honey.) At least the enforced leisure gave him plenty of thinking and reading time. He had a great deal to catch up on. There were new publications, such as a presentation copy of Darwin's book on orchids; and he wished to familiarise himself with the full range of reactions to the *Origin*: 'It seems to me that you have assisted those who want to criticise you,' he pointed out to Darwin, 'by your *overstating* the difficulties & objections – Several of them quote your *own words* as the strongest arguments against you.'[4] Was it credible that Richard Owen had written the anonymous article in the *Quarterly*, which spoke so much of Owen as a *great authority* and a *profound philosopher*? (The writer was, in fact, Samuel Wilberforce, though Owen was perfectly capable of favourable self-reference: Wallace was a novice in the finer points of intellectual controversy.) Darwin was understandably interested to know what Wallace planned to write: 'How puzzled you must be to know what to begin at,' he enquired politely.[5]

Wallace suffered an inevitable sense of anti-climax and frustration as he resumed his share of family responsibilities, far easier to exercise in the form of well-meant advice delivered at a safe distance. The years of independence and self-sufficiency were over. However exhausting and time-consuming his life might have been at times in the Archipelago, at least it was largely under his control. Now he moved in to his sister's and brother-in-law's house in Westbourne Grove Terrace, Paddington, where Sims had set up his photographic business in partnership with his brother Edward in 1860, after moving from St Mark's Terrace, Regent's Park. There, in a large empty room at the top of the house, Wallace began to unpack the boxes and cases that Stevens had held in store for him, the rich residue of his eight years' collecting which he had reserved for his own study and delight. Three thousand bird skins, he estimated, covering about a thousand species, and perhaps twenty thousand beetles and butterflies of seven thousand species, together with land-shells, and a miscellaneous selection of mammals. As a personal living memento of the East, he had brought with him a small lory which had survived the journey, unlike the siamang, and showed great affection for Thomas Sims. Wallace concentrated, first, on arranging and annotating these collections, and on formulating papers drawn from them for the Zoological and Linnean Societies. He also began to focus his mind on anthropological subjects, and on applications of the theory of natural selection. He was certainly busy. But he did not tackle either of the major writing projects that might have seemed more immediately pressing now that he had comparative leisure and access to libraries: his own 'big book' of theory – bio-geographical distribution, rather than his original project, which had been trumped by Darwin – or a book about his travels in the Archipelago, the most obvious way to capitalise on his journey and secure his popular reputation. As early as 1859, Darwin had been encouraging Wallace along such lines, asking when he would be returning with his 'magnificent collection & still grander mental materials' – something Darwin could be quite relaxed about, with his own book printed and on the verge of publication – a 'small volume of about 500 pages or so', as he described it ingenuously to Wallace in an earlier letter. If the prospect of matching such an output might have appeared daunting to Wallace far away in the Moluccas, Darwin also added practical advice: 'You will be puzzled how to publish. The Royal Soc. fund will be worth your consideration.'[6]

Wallace claimed later that he deliberately put off writing up his Malaysian travels, until he could 'embody in it all the more generally interesting results derived from the detailed study of certain portions of my collections'.[7] But this idealised image of the dedicated scientific traveller, able to concentrate at last on the fruits of his labours, ignores the amount of time he had to spend both on his own business affairs and, more demandingly, on those of Thomas, Fanny and his mother. The family's luck with money had not improved, and Wallace was the only one with capital, which Stevens had invested for him in railway stocks. Wallace estimated his own annual living expenses at £200, of which he might hope to meet perhaps half from his existing investments. The cheque from the Zoological Society boosted his current balance. But the business side of his travels was far from complete. He had to negotiate the sale, sometimes through Stevens and occasionally freelance, of his most recent collections, which were still arriving by the slow Cape route, along with Charles Allen's consignments, a process that continued for several years. (On 4 June 1864, for example, he sold some 1,500 specimens of butterflies to William Hewitson for £150.) Wallace had also financed, with his Singapore mining friend Geach, a small collecting expedition to Penang, and proposed investing another £300 in a similar venture to New Guinea, to be undertaken by his Australian cousins.[8] All this took time, and energy.

Wallace might have been well on his way to financial independence, had he not agreed to subsidise his brother-in-law's photographic business – worse, to take an active part in its expansion and promotion, treating it as part of his investment programme. In 1864 he spent over £500 on the business, with items ranging from postage stamps for circulars and brass ornamental moulding for frames, to cheques for £50 either for Fanny or for the firm.[9] (He later confessed to his brother John that he had lost £700 in the business.) He was paying the Sims' rent, settling debts, and lending money to his mother. It was not the idyllic homecoming he had outlined in his letters to Silk, where he conjured up his 'hopes for a happy future in Old England, where I may live in solitude and seclusion except from a few close friends'. 'You cannot perhaps imagine how I have come to love solitude,' he had added then. 'I seldom have a visitor but what I wish him away in an hour.'[10] Now, back in the crowded muddle of London, he renewed old acquaintances, and began to extend his scientific friendships and contacts.

His oldest friend, George Silk, lived in Kensington. Wallace saw him frequently, and was introduced to several of Silk's circle, such as Archdeacon Sinclair, the Vicar of St Mary Abbott's, Kensington. He eagerly took up chess again, and, through Silk, was invited to take part in the chess club organised by Lewis Leslie, an auctioneer who lived in

Campden Hill, Kensington. But it was an entirely new network of scientific friends that added a fresh dimension to Wallace's life. Although he never wholly overcame his shyness, and had little to offer in the way of small talk, his achievements, and the recognition of men such as Darwin, Hooker, Lyell and Huxley, gave him confidence. Huxley was among the first to invite him home, and the friendliness of the children, and Mrs Huxley's welcome, the 'whole domestic tone of the house', put him at his ease – although Wallace admitted that he never got over 'a feeling of awe and inferiority' when discussing with Huxley 'any problem in evolution or allied subjects', in spite of being two years older.[11] He attributed this sense of inferiority to Huxley's complete mastery of anatomy and physiology, areas where he himself had to rely on second-hand facts and arguments. He felt, curiously, rather more comfortable with the patrician Sir Charles Lyell, although Lady Lyell, as he learned later from Lyell's secretary, Arabella Buckley, thought poorly of his social gaucheness on first acquaintance.[12] Lyell, too, though undoubtedly gracious and well disposed, could be distinctly patronising. Bates remembered being accosted by Lyell one afternoon near the seal pond in the Zoological Gardens. 'He was wriggling about in his usual way, with spy-glass raised by fits and starts to the eye, and began: "Mr Wallace, I believe – ah—" "My name's Bates." "Oh, I beg pardon, I always confound you two."' As Bates commented dryly, 'His memory must be very bad, for we have often met, and I was once his guest at the Geological Club dinner . . .'[13] There was little physical resemblance between the two collectors, but Lyell might well have thought of them both as belonging to a different variety, if not species, of scientist.

Bates was an old friend, with whom Wallace had shared those early months in the Amazon before they went their separate ways, and with whom he had maintained a regular, if long-distance, correspondence. Bates's field was narrower than that of Wallace, but his mastery self-evident. His brilliant paper on mimicry was read before the Linnean Society in November 1861. Wallace and Bates resumed their friendship, and their discussions, going together to call on Herbert Spencer.[14] 'Our thoughts were full of the great unsolved problem of the origin of life,' Wallace recalled, adding, enthusiastically if rather optimistically, 'and we looked to Spencer as the one man living who could give us some clue to it.' They went, too, to Oxford together, to visit John Westwood and George Rolleston. Westwood, a former President of the Entomological Society, was

167

now Hope Professor of Zoology and Rolleston, Huxley's protégé, Linacre Professor of Anatomy.[15] Walking round the Natural History Museum with Westwood, he could view the site of the 1860 arguments between Owen and Huxley, and the spat between Huxley and Bishop Wilberforce.

By the time Wallace returned from the East, Bates had already made a highly favourable impression on Darwin, both by his powers of detailed observation and argument, and as a man; and Darwin may have imagined Wallace to be somewhat similar. Bates, he informed Asa Gray in commending the paper on mimicry, 'is a man of lowly origin, of great force of character, & wonderfully self-educated . . .'[16] 'What a pity that this man shd. have to work for his daily bread & have only 1 or 2 hours for science,' he exclaimed to Hooker.[17] At last, Darwin had met someone who knew Wallace intimately. Bates spoke 'with admiration' of Wallace's talents, energy and knowledge, he reported. Bates even forwarded one of Wallace's 1861 letters to Darwin. 'He rates me much too highly & himself much too lowly,' commented Darwin in reply. 'But what strikes me most about Mr Wallace is the absence of jealousy towards me: he must have a really good honest & noble disposition. A far higher merit than mere intellect.'[18]

Later in the summer of 1862, the mystery was solved, when Wallace stayed at Downe. If there was any hint of strain in Darwin's attitude, it completely passed Wallace by. This was the kind of visit Wallace especially enjoyed, where he was able to relax, in a family rather than a society context, and talk at leisure, pacing slowly down the sand walk with his benevolent host. The image of the great naturalist and scientific thinker cocooned in his comfortable house and grounds made a vivid impression. This was a model for the kind of life he would ideally like to construct for himself. The two men competed happily in exchanging enquiries about each other's health for the rest of the year, always safe ground with Darwin. Could Darwin send him a copy of the third edition of *Origin*, Wallace enquired from Devon, where he had gone in August in an attempt to shake off a bad cough, and where he hoped to 'lay in a stock of health' to enable him to stick at work on his collections during the winter, which he dreaded.[19] He was staying with his old Neath friend, the Quaker bookseller Charles Hayward, who had bought a farm there. (Another Devon bolt-hole for a few years was Burrator, Rajah Brooke's austere cottage near Plymouth.) The *Origin* was waiting for him when he returned to London in September, and for the first time he was able to read Darwin's introductory historical sketch, which had now been added to the English edition. Darwin in this refers to Wallace more frequently and expansively than in the Introduction itself, though the overall impact of the sketch serves to deflect attention from any question of priority.

Wallace had much to learn, much to catch up on, after his years of isolation; but he did not confine himself to theorists with whom he was in broad agreement and sympathy. He was in no sense exclusive in his friendships, for example dining regularly with St George Mivart, a severely anti-Darwinian evolutionist. In spite of his air of mildness and diffidence, he was never afraid of disagreement, and would always stand his ground in argument. He had a first taste of the battles that had been raging when he visited Cambridge in October 1862 for the British Association meeting. He went there as the guest of Alfred Newton, and stayed with him in Magdalene College.

Wallace had met Newton at the Zoological Society. Newton, six years younger than Wallace, held the Drury Travelling Fellowship at Magdalene. Three years later he would become the first Professor of Zoology and Comparative Anatomy at Cambridge, but at this moment he was best known for his work on birds, and especially for his research on extinct and endangered species – he had travelled to Iceland in 1858 to visit the last nesting-place of the great auk. Interestingly, he was the first person to comment in writing on the significance of the joint Linnean papers of July 1858, advising his correspondent Henry Tristram the following month, 'But for your paper you must consult Darwin and Wallace.'[20] Throughout his career he continued to link Wallace's name with that of Darwin, referring in his address to the Biological Section of the British Association in 1876 to the 'promulgation of a reasonable Theory of Evolution by Mr Darwin and Mr Wallace', and describing their former labours as 'united yet distinct'.[21] Newton, who made light of a congenital hip condition, could talk birds all night in his rooms in the Old Lodge, and was just the right person to ease Wallace through the slightly daunting atmosphere, for a newcomer, of the British Association for the Advancement of Science.

Wallace enjoyed the experience. Newton had invited other ornithologists to join them at Magdalene, and the company was both knowledgeable and congenial. Wallace spent a pleasant evening at Charles Kingsley's house – Kingsley, still working on his manuscript of *The Water Babies* for Macmillan, would have found in Wallace a mirror image of his scientific backwards-running giant, with a great pair of spectacles on his nose, and a butterfly-net in one hand, and a geological hammer in the other. Wallace's simplicity of manner, and openness, made him welcome at the social gatherings. Sclater and Newton planned to hold a strictly ornithological 'Ibis' dinner, but so many others wished to dine that the occasion was turned into a 'Club for Promoting Common Honesty' – in Huxley's words, a 'Society for the propagation', not of Christian Knowledge, but of 'common honesty in all parts of the world'. The participants enjoyed a grand 'feed' at the Red Lion in Petty Cury, with Huxley as President and Kingsley as Vice. The Club had, initially, one rule – anyone drinking Sclater's health was to be expelled (on Sclater's stipulation). As soon as Sclater left, Newton proposed his health, 'and every one drank it; whereby it is difficult to say whether the association did not thereupon dissolve itself!'[22]

In the scientific sessions, there was one issue that gave Wallace pause for thought. He had, of course, missed the vehement argument between Huxley and the creationist Richard Owen at Oxford in 1860, which hinged on the structure of an ape's brain, and the subsequent annihilation of Wilberforce, who made the mistake of asking Huxley whether he was descended from an ape on his grandfather's or grandmother's side of the family (or words to that effect). Huxley, with his book *Evidence as to Man's Place in Nature* completed but not published, decided that the Cambridge meeting was the occasion to demolish Owen. William Flower, the newly appointed Conservator at the Royal College of Surgeons, acted as Huxley's demonstrator, and dissected an ape brain to disprove Owen's theory about the hippocampus. Huxley, by now the Hunterian Professor at the Royal College of Surgeons, presided over the session as Chairman of the Zoology Section. On 3 October, Owen read a paper 'On the characters of the Aye-aye, as a test of the Lamarckian and Darwinian hypotheses of the transmutation and origin of species'. Owen argued that the adaptation of parts of the aye-aye could not be explained either by natural selection or by Lamarckian theory, but was the result of a guiding intelligence. Huxley reported to Darwin that those who could judge saw that Owen was 'lying & shuffling', while the other half regarded him as 'an innocent old sheep, being worried by three particularly active young wolves' – Huxley, Flower and George Rolleston.[23] In Wallace's later description, there was 'a slight recrudescence of the evolution controversy in the rather painful dispute between Professor Richard Owen and Huxley, supported by Flower, on certain alleged differences between the brains of man and apes'.[24] Wallace had had ample time to think about these questions, as he pickled orang-utans in spirits or fed and tended the baby mias in Sarawak. Wallace's own 'special heresy', within the Darwinian creed, was yet to be publicly formulated. But the treatment handed out to Owen left him in no doubt about the way scientific debate was being conducted in Britain. It was a relief to get back to the ornithologists, and to speculation about the dodo and the great auk.

In January 1863, Wallace reached the milestone of his fortieth birthday. Each time he visited his new acquaintances – Darwin, Huxley, Kingsley – he remarked on the happiness of their domestic life. To his intimate friends, such as George Silk or Richard Spruce, he had sometimes discussed the prospect of marriage in a guarded way, writing from his celibate isolation in the Archipelago. 'I am very sorry,' he commented to Silk, 'that you have not been fortunate in your "affaires du coeur". All I can say is "try again". Marriage has a wonderful effect of brightening the intellect' – it had even made his own brother John witty.[25] On his return to London he wrote to Spruce to find out when he planned to return, enquiring as to whether some 'moça of the mountains' was holding him captive there.[26] (Ten years before, a letter from Spruce suggested that he was not living an entirely 'bachelor existence' on the Rio Negro.) Wallace, both shy and modest, though certainly with an eye for beauty, gives no hint that he had ever formed such a liaison himself, but confessed his present ambitions. 'By the bye,' Spruce replied, 'have you, acting on the principle of <u>Natural Selection</u>, yet taken unto yourself "a Signorina, to take care of the tea, shirt-buttons etc", as you once hinted to me you proposed doing? Recollect "There is a tide in the affairs etc" and though yours cannot now be "taken at the full", it may still be taken ere it ebbs out completely.'[27] His other Amazon fellow traveller Bates, as Wallace must have known, was already the father of a baby daughter, Alice, and married her mother, Sarah Ann Mason, on 15 January 1863. It was now or never. He was feeling more himself again, and sent his brother John a new photograph to prove it, taken when the Christmas beef and pudding and a little champagne 'had somehow restored that ancient jollity'.

In his autobiography, Wallace spends several pages narrating his courtship of 'Miss L——' – far more, in fact, than he devotes to the account of his eventual marriage.[28] His chess-playing friend, Lewis Leslie, was a widower with a son and two daughters, and Wallace had the opportunity to spend a little time with them before or after his regular games. The elder, Marion, twenty-seven or twenty-eight years old, was 'very agreeable, though quiet, pleasant-looking, well educated, and fond of art and literature'. Wallace began to feel 'an affection' for her, and to hope that she would become his wife. Some time during 1863, thinking he was 'sufficiently known', he wrote to her describing his feelings, being too shy to make a spoken proposal, and asking whether she could in any way respond to his affection. Her reply let him down gently – clearly she was taken by surprise; but she begged him not to break off his visits to her father because of her refusal. Wallace interpreted this request as tacit encouragement. A year passed. He thought he detected signs of a positive change in her attitude to him. This time he wrote formally to her father. He was interrogated about his means, informed that Marion had a small income, and asked to settle an equal amount on her. Agreement was reached, engagement followed. Wallace, confident about his status with the family, wrote to Newton, introducing Lewis Leslie junior, who was going up to Queens' – 'a pleasant young fellow, but I am sorry to say utterly unconscious of natural history'.[29] Marion called on Fanny Sims and on Mrs Wallace. Wallace visited the Leslies two or three times a week. His life in England was beginning to take shape.

While Wallace was conducting his gentle courtship of Miss Leslie, he occupied himself with the methodical organisation of his collections and the writing of scientific papers. Hooker and Darwin, however, could not quite make up their minds about his intellectual stamina. Hooker commended Wallace's interventions at a Linnean Society meeting, where he 'made a very few remarks worth all the paper', but still found cause to wonder why Wallace did not 'fructify as Bates does'.[30] Bates fructified with a vengeance that summer through the publication of *The Naturalist on the River Amazons*. Darwin acted as godfather to the book, encouraging Bates into action, reading the first chapters, recommending the book to John Murray, the publisher of both *Origin* and of Lyell's *Antiquity of Man*. Darwin's criticisms, he assured Bates, could be condensed into a single sentence: 'It is the best book of Natural History Travels ever published in England' – praise he repeated to Hooker, Lyell and Asa Gray.[31] What was more, Bates had spoken out boldly on species. Darwin drew Hooker's notice

172

to the 'd . . .d' *Athenaeum*, which coolly drew attention to a key issue in a review of Bates's book.[32] In his preface, Bates described a principal object of the journey he and Wallace had embarked on as gathering facts 'towards solving the problem of the origin of species'; and the *Athenaeum* commented, 'He thinks he has found such a solution in adopting Mr Darwin's theory and making many of his facts bend to it.'

This public suggestion that Bates had somehow contrived to write Darwinist natural selection into his narrative retrospectively was intriguing to Darwin and Hooker: the ghost of priority flickered briefly between the lines of their correspondence. Hooker admitted that the book was charming, but yet – it was evident that Bates's 'Darwinistic explanation of what he sees etc are after-thoughts – It is too bad to say that his facts are therefore twisted – but he says here & there, or leaves the impression of saying, in 1849, "We did so & so which is of such importance 'au point de vue' of N. Selection or of Variation & N & S." whereas he never knew aught of these till 1859 –'[33] (Hooker, of course, had no knowledge of any discussions, or correspondence, between Bates and Wallace.) Darwin took up Hooker's cue in his reply: 'With respect to Bates & Wallace having distinct views on species during their Journey; what does astonish me is the extreme poverty of observation on this head in Wallace's book; with one discussion on very dissimilar Birds feeding alike showing, as it seemed to me, complete misunderstanding of the economy of nature.'[34] Darwin was here, perhaps, revealing the reason why he had originally discounted Wallace as a first-class theorist.

Darwin now classed Wallace and Bates in the ranks of the 'half-a-dozen real downright believers in modification of species in all England' who dared – and this was the crux – speak out boldly, along with himself, Hooker, Huxley and Lubbock.[35] Wallace was welcomed as an ally, and reaffirmed by Darwin as a co-owner of the theory of natural selection in a letter to the *Athenaeum*, 9 May 1863:

Whether the naturalist believes in the views given by Lamarck, by Geoffroy St-Hilaire, by the author of the *Vestiges*, by Mr Wallace and myself, or in any other such view, signifies extremely little in comparison with the admission that species have descended from other species and have not been created immutable . . .[36]

Wallace rose to the role of champion. In October, for example, he shredded Samuel Haughton's paper, 'On the form of the cells made by various wasps and by the honey bee; with an appendix on the origin of species' in the *Annals and Magazine of Natural History*[37] – successfully enough for Asa Gray to tell Darwin that he had read Wallace's exposé 'with gusto'. Gray drew Darwin's attention to some choice anti-Darwinian writing by Louis Agassiz: 'Pray set Wallace upon these articles.'[38] Wallace was slowly taking up his rightful place in scientific circles, and offered a paper on one of his special topics, 'On the Geographical Distribution of Animal Life', at the British Association meeting in Newcastle that autumn. He was in the ascendant.

In the first months of 1864, Wallace made the most controversial statement of his views since his return. Everyone else had written their big books: Huxley had published *Evidence as to Man's Place in Nature*, Lyell his *Antiquity of Man*, Herbert Spencer *First Principles*, all in 1863. The time was ripe for him to speak out, not just on birds and butterflies, but on the subject that remained central to him, man. He was still single, had no immediate dependants: he had recovered his health, and his intellectual energy. He was more than holding his own at the learned societies, and Huxley, as swift to praise as he was willing to condemn, had given Wallace the most generous of public tributes in *Man's Place*:

> Once in a generation a Wallace may be found physically, mentally and morally qualified to wander unscathed through the tropical wilds of America and of Asia; to form magnificent collections as he wanders; and withal to think out sagaciously the conclusions suggested by his collections.[39]

Wallace was ready to deliver. The first half of 1864 produced a spate of papers and articles: one on Malay butterflies for the Linnean; another on parrots of the Malayan region for the Zoological; notes and articles for Newton's *Ibis*; 'On some Anomalies of Zoological and Botanical Geography' – a reprint of his Newcastle paper – for Huxley's *Natural History Review*. He was even ready to tackle his travels. 'I am at last making the beginning of a small book on my Eastern journey,' he confided to Darwin on 2 January 1864, a ringing New Year resolution.[40]

Wallace saw his 'Eastern journey' as a whole, an integrated set of experiences that provided him with material from which the major scientific and philosophical questions could be answered, or on the basis of which informed theories might be constructed. Quite consciously and systematically, he had studied the varieties and races of man during his travels as closely as he had charted the geographical distribution of species. 'You ask whether I shall discuss "man",' Darwin had written to him in 1857, guarding his position, 'I think I shall avoid whole subject . . .'[41] Wallace had no such inhibitions. 'Let Ethnology be your hobby,' he advised George Silk in November 1858, in the euphoria of his Linnean publication. He was already preparing to take issue with the established experts such as Robert Latham, who were laying down ethnological grids for the whole world:

> If I live I shall come out strong on Malay and Papuan races, & astonish Latham, Davis etc. etc. . . . I am convinced no man can be a good ethnologist who does not travel, & not travel merely but reside as I do months & years with each race, becoming well acquainted with their average physiognomy & moral character, so as to be able to detect crossbreeds which totally mislead the hasty traveller, who thinks they are transitions!! Latham I am sure is quite wrong on many points.[42]

Wallace was poised now to spell out the implications of natural selection for man, basing his argument on all the facts he had noted during his extended fieldwork. Lyell was asking him for references on his observations in the Malay Archipelago, so that he could incorporate a few sentences into his presidential address for the British Association later that year,[43] and Wallace was suggesting that an expedition should be raised to explore the caves of Borneo 'for fossil anthropomorphs & the missing link'.[44] For Wallace, the laws of varieties and species were quite as applicable to man as they were to the rest of the animal world, as he had suggested as early as December 1845, in a letter to Bates. He outlined his current thinking in two successive papers, 'Varieties of Man in the Malay Archipelago', read to the Ethnological Society in January 1864, and, on 1 March, a more radical and wide-sweeping argument, 'The Origin of Human Races from the Theory of Natural Selection', which he read to the Anthropological Society.

His choice of platform was itself controversial. The Anthropological Society was controlled by white supremacists, led by James Hunt and Charles Carter Blake, who took a fervently pro-South and pro-slavery stance over the American Civil War, as opposed to the stoutly abolitionist position of the longer-established Ethnological Society. The men who controlled the Anthropological held that white and other races had descended from different stocks; the Ethnological that all men derived from one common ancestral stock or form. Huxley wrote to Wallace explaining that his objections to the 'Anthropological people' would not allow him to attend the meeting.[45] (Huxley had resigned his honorary fellowship after the *Anthropological Review* had attacked *Man's Place in Nature* in highly offensive terms.) As to Huxley's opinion of Hunt, Wallace pretty well agreed – 'I do not think he is fit to be President' – but he thought the few meetings he had attended 'quite equal to that of the rival Society'. However, he refused to accept Huxley's opinion that 'there was not the slightest reason' for the Anthropological's existence. It was a necessary protest against the Ethnological being made a *ladies'* society, as the Geographical had also been: 'Consequently many important & interesting subjects cannot possibly be discussed there.'[46] (For 'important and interesting', Wallace presumably meant topics such as sexual behaviour.) Besides, the Ethnological met on the same evenings as the Zoological, 'which I always like to attend', and so having given his first paper to the Ethnological, 'I give the next to the Anthrop'. Wallace was, as often, quite unrepentant in the face of criticism or opposition.

In fact, in his paper Wallace articulated an argument that sought a synthesis of the two opposing theories. To the question, did man develop from unity or from diversity, he argued for the former; but pushed that development so far back in time as to allow for a differentiated impact of natural selection between, broadly, the races of man in the northern and the southern hemispheres. In the north, for example, 'the harsher discipline of a more sterile soil' led to the progressive improvement of the European races, especially in intellectual and moral terms. Wallace presumably believed that he did not have to argue this point, which would have been common ground for his audience, and simply stated it:

The intellectual and moral, as well as the physical, qualities of the European are superior; the same powers and capacities which have made him rise in a few centuries from the condition of the wandering savage, with a scanty and stationary population, to his present state of culture and advancement, with a greater average longevity, a greater average strength, and a capacity of more rapid increase, – enable him when in contact with the savage man to conquer in the struggle for existence, and to increase at his expense, just as the better adapted [more favourable] increase at the expense of the less adapted [less favourable] varieties in the animal and vegetable kingdoms – just as the weeds of Europe overrun North America and Australia, extinguishing native productions by the inherent vigour of their organisation, and by their greater capacity for existence and multiplication.[47]

But Wallace went on to argue that natural selection worked on man in a different way from on other animals; mental development deriving 'from some unknown cause' – ensured that man was able largely to overcome the process of natural selection in so far as it affected the body. (He even speculated about a future when, in terms of the food supply, 'man's selection shall have supplanted natural selection'.) Inevitably, 'the higher – the more intellectual and moral – must displace the lower and more degraded races; and the power of "natural selection", still acting on his mental organisation, must ever lead to the more perfect adaptation of man's higher faculties to the conditions of surrounding nature, and to the exigencies of the social state.' The world would once again be inhabited 'by a single nearly homogeneous race, no individual of which will be inferior to the noblest specimens of existing humanity'. Wallace, having first argued for a unified primitive stock in antiquity, predicted progress towards a unified, and perfected, final state. For a moment, it seemed that he was embracing the most hard-edged doctrine of the survival of the fittest, a process of inter-racial competition in which the 'civilised' would sweep away the 'savage'. But Wallace had not finished. In the Amazon forests, or on the Aru Islands, he had contemplated the nature of the savage and compared it to the civilised, and he did not accept that European society, as it currently functioned, was in fact the superior. He does not make it clear precisely when the European Golden Age occurred, but there was now a clear and indisputable mismatch between moral potential and reality. In the West, the 'marvellous developments and vast practical results of science' had been given to societies 'too low morally and intellectually to know how to make the best use of them'; certainly on the surface, in terms of worldly success and increase in numbers, natural selection seemed to be advancing the mediocre, if not the low. But, being an incurable optimist and a believer in perfectibility, Wallace stated his belief in an intellectual and moral advance, although without reference to any basis for that belief. In his Utopian vision,

> the passions and propensities will be restrained within those limits which most conduce to happiness; and mankind will have at length discovered that it was only required of them to develop the capacities of their higher nature, in order to convert this earth, which had so long been the theatre of their unbridled passions, and the scene of unimaginable misery, into as bright a paradise as ever haunted the dreams of seer or poet.

This was a bold gauntlet to toss at the feet of the Anthropologicals, and a long and heated discussion followed, with Wallace returning point for point.[48]

When the paper was published, Wallace sent copies to Spencer, Lyell, Hooker and Darwin. Spencer approved; Lyell applauded – though correcting him about his comments on the mound-builders of the Mississippi valley, and questioning whether Wallace quite appreciated the length of time available for the development of man. Lyell also commented, 'The manner in which you have given Darwin the whole credit of the theory of Natural Selection is very handsome, but if anyone else had done it without allusion to your papers [sic] it would have been wrong.'[49] A comment by Wallace about Owen sounded alarm signals for Hooker. Wallace had written, 'We can thus understand how it is that, judging from the head and brain, Professor Owen places man in a distinct sub-class of mammalia . . .' Was Wallace deserting the Darwin–Huxley camp, was he about to commit apostasy and return to Owen's creationist views? Wallace wrote to put Hooker right; he had rather mistaken his meaning 'as to the systematic classification of man': Wallace did not agree at all with Owen's system, but there was some reason to class man apart from the rest of organic nature, on account of man's reason and moral faculties as opposed to the 'mental faculties' of the whole of the animal world. Man, he argued, does not differ as much from the chimpanzees as the chimpanzee does from the aye-aye or the lemurs, so, zoologically, Wallace would class man as forming a distinct *family* of the same *order* which contains them all. Then, as if he had disposed of this slight misinterpretation, he changed the subject; seizing advantage of Hooker's position at Kew, he asked if his brother-in-law Thomas Sims could have permission to take photographs there – was there a back entrance that a cab could come in by with the apparatus?[50]

Wallace remained something of an enigma to Hooker. 'I am struck with his negation of all credit or share in the Natural Selection theory,' Hooker commented to Darwin after reading the paper in the *Anthropological Review*, which referred exclusively to 'Mr Darwin's celebrated theory', 'which makes me think him a very high-minded man.' Wallace had, apparently, no difficulty with the idea that man had transmuted from the apes, nor with all the theological implications that followed, and could not comprehend why 'scientific men' – such as Hooker and Darwin – remained so reticent on the subject. 'It is all very well for Wallace to wonder at scientific men being afraid of saying what they think,' Hooker complained to Darwin.

He has all 'the freedom of motion *in vacuo*' in one sense. Had he as many kind and good relations as I have, who would be grieved and pained to hear me say what I think, and had he children who would be placed in predicaments most detrimental to children's minds by such avowals on my part, he would not wonder so much.[51]

Darwin was enthusiastic about Wallace's 'great leading idea' on the distinction between man's body and his mind, or brain; it was 'grand and most eloquently done'. Darwin always praised Wallace's style, even when he had misgivings about his argument. Darwin had his own theory as to the agent of change in man, and offered his view that 'a sort of sexual selection has been the most powerful means of changing the races of man'.[52] He even offered to show Wallace his notes on man, a generous suggestion that Wallace declined.

In the spring of 1864, Wallace considered applying for the Assistant Secretaryship of the Royal Geographical Society, and found he was in competition with Bates. Bates, married and with a child, had already been passed over for a post in the British Museum in April 1862, the Trustees deciding to appoint Albert Gunther, who had the voice of the Superintendent, Richard Owen. Another opening at the Museum came up the following year, and again Bates was bypassed, in favour of the eighteen-year-old poet Arthur O'Shaughnessy. Men like Bates and Wallace, with years of highly successful experience in fieldwork, might have been thought ideal candidate material, to be welcomed with open arms by the scientific establishment. On the contrary, 'It is extremely difficult to establish a footing in London scientific society,' Hooker advised Bates. 'It is all along of the law of the struggle for life!' Besides, he added, 'remember that entomologists are a poor set!'[53] This time, Bates could look for the active support of Darwin, who had not only been impressed by Bates's paper on mimicry, but had recommended Bates's *Amazons* book to John Murray, the publisher. Darwin had gathered all the facts about Bates's finances – £100 a year from his brothers, in exchange for his share of the hosiery business; £23 a year from investments; and anything he could make from his writing – Murray had sent him an advance of £250, but the book had taken him two years to write. Darwin wrote to Murray, and Murray pushed hard for Bates. Among Bates's other assets were his knowledge of German, and his early experience of business and administration. Bates's appointment was unanimous. Wallace must have decided against a formal application; his name does not appear in the list of candidates.[54] What he omits to mention in his autobiography is that he was actually interviewed for the job in June 1863, when Bates was not a candidate, and failed to win the appointment: when the position became vacant again unexpectedly, there was a second round of interviews. Whatever his private disappointment, Wallace expressed no resentment, acknowledging Bates's stronger claims; but this was only the first of several such posts that he investigated, and failed to obtain.

Apart from this setback, life was full of promise. Wallace attended the British Association at Bath, where he heard Lyell's gratifying reference to his concept of the 'two provinces of animal life' in the Archipelago, the concept enshrined in Wallace's line. He also read a paper 'On the Progress of Civilisation in Northern Celebes'. His understanding with Marion Leslie became a formal engagement. Dresses were ordered, the wedding programme settled, and invitations sent out. Richard Spruce, Wallace's old scientific friend, returned from Peru in time for the great day. Suddenly, and without, according to Wallace, the slightest warning, 'the whole affair was broken off'. Wallace called one afternoon as usual at Rothsay Villa, to be told by the servant that Miss Leslie was not at home. She had gone away that morning, and would write. The next day, a letter from Mr Leslie arrived, saying that his daughter wished to break off the engagement. 'The blow was very severe,' Wallace wrote some forty years later, 'and I have never in my life experienced such intensely painful emotion.'[55] He wrote to Marion, strongly, 'perhaps bitterly', trying to express his feelings, assuring her that he had never had a moment's thought of anyone else. He had no reply, and never saw her or any of the family again.

The only explanations he ever received were that he was 'silent' about himself and his family, that he seemed to have something to conceal, and that he had told Marion nothing about a 'widow lady', a friend of his mother's, that he had, it was claimed, almost been engaged to – for Wallace, she was someone as utterly remote 'from all ideas of marriage as would have been an aunt or grandmother'. The information, or misinformation, about the 'widow' can have come only from his mother or sister, or less probably from George Silk. The charge that he was largely 'silent' about himself was, Wallace admitted, true. There may, too, have been other, unstated, reasons for Marion Leslie's change of heart, or mind. The Leslies lived in Kensington, the Wallaces in Notting Hill. Leslie was an auctioneer, but with offices in Mayfair. Wallace, for all his scientific reputation, was far from affluent, and still had no obvious prospects, even two years after his return from the East; he lived above an unsuccessful photographer's shop. The Leslies' neighbours in Campden Hill included the Duke of Argyll, the Earl of Antrim, and the artists Holman Hunt and Augustus Egg. Were Wallace's social credentials a little too fragile? Or was his lack of an official job seen as a disadvantage? Apart from his investments, he had no regular income beyond the bits and pieces he could pick up in journalism, such as writing for the newly established organ of the radical scientists, the *Reader*.

Conceivably, some aspect of Wallace's controversial, or at least unorthodox, views may have reached the Leslie family. Whatever the reasons, the bitter blow of the broken engagement fell on Wallace in the autumn of 1864, soon after he returned from Bath. His confidence was shattered, and his intellectual energies temporarily crushed. He had met with, he confided later to Newton, 'that "tide" Shakespeare speaks of, which I had thought to have taken at the flood & been carried on, not to fortune but to happiness' – to descend from metaphor he had been 'considerably cut up', to such an extent that he had done nothing – scientifically speaking – for the last six months. Work on his eastern journey was suspended: his theory of man put on ice. But, he promised in February 1865, the first time he worked at birds again it would be with the

'Ibis' in his eye. 'I am now working a little at insects, & am also preparing for moving, as I leave here in March & do not yet know where I am going.'[56] Westbourne Grove was too close to the scene of his disappointment. He leased a house just north of Regent's Park in St Mark's Crescent – only a few minutes' walk from the Zoological Gardens – and moved there with his mother in April 1865.

One major comfort was the return of Richard Spruce. Spruce was Wallace's closest friend, the ideal companion who had sustained him in his Amazon sickness, a man whose cast of mind and temperament he shared, and whose dry sense of humour and irony he appreciated; he was, too, bound to him emotionally through the loss of his brother Herbert, and the happy times they shared at Santarem and Barra. Besides, because Spruce specialised in plants, and above all mosses, there was no danger of direct competition, as there was from time to time with Bates. Spruce had been marooned in Peru, a prisoner to a complete breakdown in physical health – sitting at a table was so painful that he spent most of the day in his hammock – and, mentally, he was depressed and slightly bitter. Particularly hurtful, he had confided to Wallace, was a letter from Sir William Hooker 'filled with ungenerous taunts and insults': 'I only regret that he did not write me that letter several years earlier – my fate would assuredly have been different – and I might not have had (as I have now) to pass my last days in poverty, sickness and neglect.'[57] Clearly, he held Hooker responsible for involving him in an arduous expedition to obtain chinchona plants and seeds for the Indian government, for the absence of proper financial reward, and for the subsequent events that led to his extended stay in Peru. But Wallace's letter of 1862, announcing his safe return to England, had helped to shift his despondency. When it reached him, Spruce was 'expecting to start soon for "that undiscovered country, from whose bourne etc"', a journey for which he was preparing by packing up his collections and gathering together his manuscripts.[58] A year later, in November 1863, he signalled that he might have the strength and will to head for England the following spring: 'I can hardly hope to live to publish a connected account of my own wanderings, but I hope,' he hinted, 'to leave my Mss in such a state that someone else may do it.'

In the early autumn of 1864, Spruce was back in England at last, moving between London and the Sussex village of Hurstpierpoint. This was the home of William Mitten, pharmacist and bryologist, who had undertaken to classify Spruce's vast collection of mosses and lichens. (He was taking his time about it, too, much to Spruce's irritation.) Wallace visited Spruce at Hurstpierpoint, where he met the Mittens, and their four daughters, Annie, Rose, Flora and Bessie. Wallace's 'affaires du coeur' were apparently public knowledge. In October 1864, Mitten was enquiring where Spruce proposed to 'hybernate', and confessed to him that 'we are occasionally haunted by our curiosity as to Mr Wallace's matrimonial prospects which we hope are brighter'.[59] In the spring of 1865, emerging from his winter of gloom, Wallace renewed his visits to Spruce. The Mitten family shared a love of wild flowers. Wallace was amazed to see in their house a vase full of orchids – the butterfly and fly orchids – and delighted to be taken to the woods at the foot of the Sussex downs to observe them in the wild, together with bee orchids, giant cowslips, dyer's broom, and a host of other interesting plants. The Mittens' house, Treeps, stands on a ridge on the south side of the village street, and the land falls away sharply into steep meadows, so that the view from the garden looks over a lush green valley to the line of the south downs. The hurts of Kensington were healed in the fields of Hurstpierpoint, as Wallace botanised with the Mittens, and especially with the eldest daughter, Annie.

10 Wallace Transformed

At about the same time that Annie Mitten came into his life, Wallace plunged into another transforming experience. His sustained interest in spiritualism in the years to come is a major factor, affecting not only his inner happiness and his personal relationships, but his public and professional standing, even, arguably, the course of his scientific thinking. After his intense burst of writing in the first six months of 1864, with its focus on man, the emotional turmoil of his engagement and subsequent rejection left him so flat that he produced, for him, very little scientific or literary work in 1865: a list of land-shells, and a description of twenty-one new Malayan birds for the Zoological Society; 'Pigeons of the Malay Archipelago' for the *Ibis*, in October; 'Progress of Civilisation in Northern Celebes' for the Ethnological; and, in June, 'How to Civilise Savages' at Spencer's request for the *Reader* – all spun out of existing material – although he strengthened his language on the subject of the civilised and the savage: 'The white men in our colonies are too frequently the true savages, and require to be taught and Christianised quite as much as the natives.'[1] That summer, however, he embarked on a new voyage into unknown territory, as he began to attend seances.

His enthusiasm had all the intensity of a conversion. He moved, apparently, from a position of general interest – and Wallace was always open to new ideas, and beliefs – to fervent advocacy in a matter of months. Undoubtedly, he was prepared by his earlier contact with Mesmerism and phrenology. His successful experiments with his pupils at Leicester, and with the Indians of the Amazon, and his faith in phrenological 'readings' of his own personality, predisposed him to think that there was a spiritual dimension to existence that could be scientifically analysed, even measured. An initial session on 22 July 1865 in a friend's house – 'with none but members of his own family present' – produced the standard menu of rappings and table shifting.[2] He was confident that these signs had not been produced by the physical action of anyone present, and similar happenings were subsequently reproduced in his own home, 'scores of times'. He moved on to seances with well-known mediums such as Mrs Marshall. What it all might mean was for a future stage of enquiry. But once he had experienced for himself the physical manifestations of tappings and rappings, table tiltings and levitations, names written on blank bits of paper, musical instruments spontaneously producing sounds, and, most wonderful of all, the production of fruit and bunches of flowers, he was convinced that there must be an unseen cause, a force that could not be explained away in conventional physical terms. He was aware that some mediums might be fraudulent; he understood the need for careful, systematic checks. Characteristically, he was inclined to give great credence to events that happened in his own home. In November 1866, Fanny discovered that Miss Nichol, who was lodging with the Sims, seemed to have special gifts. Here Wallace could apply his own tests, secretly stretching thin tissue paper between the table legs, and later constructing a cylinder of hoops and laths, covered with canvas, to protect the table from intruding feet or ladies' dresses. These conditions quite satisfied him, at any rate, that there could be no human physical interference, and still the table rose. As a scientific enquirer, he assumed that everyone else would agree with him that such phenomena demanded serious investigation.

There was a strongly personal dimension to this supposedly objective curiosity. First, he was more readily inclined to be a believer because his sister Fanny was an active spiritualist. Wallace trusted in the innate ability of individual men and women to work things out by the power of their own unprejudiced intellects – and if these individuals were 'ordinary', rather than extraordinary, men and women, so much the better. Throughout his long experience of seances, Wallace's conviction threshold was lowered whenever he came across some apparent fact or reference involving a member of his family. At one early and significant session with Mrs Marshall, a sequence occurred in which letters of the alphabet, identified by rapping, spelled out first the place of death, Pará, and then the name of his brother Herbert, and finally, at Wallace's request, the name of the friend who last saw him, Henry Walter Bates. This was the first of a series of what he interpreted as verifying personal communications which, cumulatively, cemented his belief in the essential truth of spiritualism.[3] For Fanny and Alfred, the certainty that they were in touch with their dead brothers and sisters formed the bedrock of their spiritualist convictions.

Unlike many scientists who became more or less intrigued by the phenomena, Wallace was wholly transparent in his attitude. He had been present when inexplicable things took place. Other men of integrity, many of them initially doubtful, had testified to similar experiences. They were entitled to be believed. If he, Wallace, was satisfied that a table had moved without human agency, or a bunch of flowers had been inexplicably introduced into a room – '15 chrysanthemums, 6 variegated anemones, 4 tulips, 5 orange berried solariums, 6 ferns, of two sorts, 1 auricula sinensis, with 9 flowers – 37 stalks in all', fresh, cold, dewy – others should accept at least the possibility. Naturally, there might be frauds and conjuring tricks, but enquirers should be open-minded; not everything need be a fraud. There had already been many well-publicised attempts to examine the phenomena scientifically: Michael Faraday, for example, had investigated table-turning, and Wallace was likely to have read his account in the *Athenaeum* in 1853; William Carpenter, the same year, had provided a rational explanation of 'intelligent raps'. But once Wallace was on the track of a new idea, he was not going to be put off by received opinion, or hide behind an assumed scepticism. So much new knowledge and understanding was flooding into the world, it seemed entirely logical to him that fresh insights into the nature of reality should become available, even if they might at times manifest themselves in slightly bizarre forms. Through the autumn and winter of 1865, he pursued his researches. On 8 December 1865, he was invited to an evening at the house of John Marshman, the Provincial Emigration Agent for Canterbury, New Zealand. Joining Wallace were Dr William Carpenter, Registrar of the University of London, and former Professor of Forensic Medicine at University College, and Samuel Butler, recently returned from New Zealand: a formidable clutch of spectators. Carpenter, a Unitarian who firmly rejected the idea of miracles, was a close friend and colleague of Huxley; Butler, a professional scoffer, had lost his orthodox Christian faith and was, temporarily, under the influence of Darwin. Butler's note of the occasion was tart and dismissive: 'Transparent humbug. A. R. Wallace and Dr Carpenter both there: the former swallowing everything, the latter contemptuous as well he might be.'[4] This was years before Butler had taken up the cudgels with Darwin and, by association, Wallace, on what he came to see as their mistaken theory of natural selection, so he had no particular axe to grind; though his general attitude may be gathered from a much later letter, which mischievously refers to Wallace's career as a hunter–naturalist: 'If ever a spirit-form takes to coming near me, I shall not be content with trying to grasp it, but, in the interests of science, *I will shoot it.*'[5] Wallace, if not swallowing everything, was prepared to taste again and again. He settled down to research a very different kind of article, 'The Scientific Aspect of the Supernatural'.

In the New Year of 1866, Wallace was visiting Richard Spruce once more, and spending as much time as possible with Annie Mitten, the eldest of the four daughters. The Mittens were a much easier family for Wallace to get on terms with than the Leslies, and the relationship was considerably helped by the mutual friendship of Spruce. As William Mitten was a pharmacist, his business kept him tied to his home village, until his second daughter, Flora, the first woman in Britain to qualify as a pharmacist, was able to relieve him. He was only four years older than Wallace, and the shared pleasures of walking and botanising in the country helped to make Wallace feel part of the family. As he described the affair in his autobiography, rather in the terms of an eighteenth-century novelist, 'This similarity of taste led to a close intimacy, and in the spring of the following year I was married to Mr Mitten's eldest daughter, then about eighteen years old.'[6] She was, in fact, twenty. After their wedding in April 1866, they spent the honeymoon at Windsor, and then returned for a little to St Mark's Crescent, where Wallace's ailing mother also lived.

In June, though, they were back at Hurstpierpoint. 'I am here to eat fruit and gather orchids for another two or three weeks,' Wallace confided to Newton, explaining why he would be unable to contribute to the *Ibis* before October. 'I am at present in a very transitional state of existence, and cannot yet determine whether I shall finally pitch my tent in London or the Country.'[7] Finding a solution to that problem would become a major theme in Wallace's life: since his early childhood at Usk, he had seldom stayed a year at any one address, and longed to put down roots. Meanwhile, he celebrated with one more lotus-eating excursion, spending a month in north Wales at Llanberis and Dolgellau. Wallace loved Wales, and now, with Andrew Ramsay's *The Old Glaciers of Switzerland and North Wales* in hand, he and Annie traced 'the fine examples of ice-groovings and striations, smoothed rock-surfaces, roches moutonnes, moraines, perched blocks, and rock-basins' in the valleys around Snowdon.[8] Not so adventurous in his mountain-climbing as Huxley and John Tyndall, Wallace was an energetic 'high walker', and would happily pursue his twin enthusiasms of alpine plants and Ice Age traces in Wales, the Lake District, and Switzerland.

After attending the British Association meeting in Nottingham, where he chaired the anthropological section, Wallace settled down in London for the winter. He was soon absorbed within his former network, and rejoined the cycle of scientific meetings at his favourite societies. He had sent some eggs of two species of leaf insects, and a walking-stick insect from Java, to Kew, and Hooker was rearing them in the hothouses; he would be over to see them as early as he could.[9] In January, he took the chair at a meeting of the Zoological. But he was most active in pursuing his enquiries into spiritualism. He had his pamphlet, 'The Scientific Aspect of the Supernatural', printed for private circulation and sent off copies to friends and to scientific colleagues, including Darwin: spiritualism, he argued, was a new branch of anthropology. He also bombarded them with invitations to attend seances with Miss Nichol, and was extremely disappointed by their refusal even to come and observe. 'Before finally deciding that we are all mad,' he begged Huxley, but without much confidence,

I hope you will come and see some very curious phenomena which we can show you, <u>among friends only</u>. We meet every Friday evening, &

hope you will come sometimes, as we wish for the fullest investigation, and shall be only too grateful to you or any one else who will show us how and where we are deceived.[10]

This was Wallace's habitual line, though in practice he liked to lay down the ground rules, and robustly resisted all suggestions as to how he might be misled. Huxley was not to be inveigled, having made his own position crystal clear in 1853, when he lambasted the whole 'Witch *Sabbat* of mesmerists, clairvoyants, electro-biologists, rappers, table-turners, and evil-worshippers in general'.[11] To his friend he was more courteous. Although his refusal was absolute, he was 'neither shocked nor disposed to issue a commission of lunacy' against Wallace, but he really could not get up any interest in the subject: 'I never cared for gossip in my life; and disembodied gossip such as these worthy ghosts supply their friends with, is not more interesting to me than any other.' He had half-a-dozen investigations of infinitely greater interest, and any spare time would be devoted to them. 'I give it up,' he concluded, softening his refusal, 'for the same reason I abstain from chess – it's too amusing to be fair work and too hard work to be amusing.'[12] His message was clear: Wallace was wasting his time, when there were far more urgent and significant matters to be dealt with.

Edward Tylor, the anthropologist, was equally curt in his response, while the physicist John Tyndall dismissed the material in Wallace's book as second hand, and poured scorn on the quality of the spiritualist practitioners: 'It is not lack of logic that I see in your book, but a willingness that I deplore to accept data which are unworthy of your attention. This is frank – is it not?'[13] Carpenter did attend once, experienced nothing more than a few raps, and did not bother about a repeat performance. Tyndall, too, turned up, refused to remain passive as requested, but sat some distance away from the table and joked. Again, there was just some desultory rapping, and that was the end of Tyndall's participation. G. H. Lewes declined outright. Wallace persisted with Huxley, hurt by the reference to 'gossip'; he could not let such apparent flippancy pass, arguing, ingenuously, that he too had no interest in 'gossip', but he was intensely interested in 'the exhibition of <u>force</u> where force has been declared <u>impossible</u>, and of <u>intelligence</u> from a source the very mention of which has been deemed an <u>absurdity</u>'.[14] This was proper scientific work. Huxley remained unmoved.

Wallace was by no means an isolated figure among the Victorian

189

intelligentsia, let alone among scientific thinkers, in his fascination with the paranormal. William Crookes conducted a lengthy investigation in the 1870s, and convinced Francis Galton that there was matter 'well worth going into'; Darwin's cousin Hensleigh Wedgwood was an ardent spiritualist, and Wallace attended seances with him in London. Darwin himself was present at one later seance attended by, among others, Hensleigh Wedgwood, G. H. Lewes, George Eliot and Galton, though he left before the furniture began to move around, commenting later, 'The Lord have mercy on us all, if we have to believe such rubbish.'[15] Huxley attended another seance with the same medium, Williams, and was able to reassure Darwin that he was an impostor. Other scientists, George Romanes among them, were more intrigued than they publicly admitted. An amused interest in spiritualism was acceptable, even attendance at a series of enquiries if pursued with sufficient scepticism and scientific objectivity; but Wallace, though professing an open mind, certainly behaved like an ardent believer from a very early stage.

His argument went something like this: a number of intelligent, truthful people have experienced phenomena which, they believe, cannot be explained either by orthodox causes or by coincidence; some of these effects may undoubtedly have been obtained by trickery, but a proportion remain unaccounted for. For the most part those involved are people of good faith. If they think there must be another explanation, it is reasonable to suppose there is one. We do not understand how it all works, but one logical explanation is that there is another – and 'higher' – order of beings, of existence, in the universe. Certain people are able to put us in touch with that higher order. Wallace, a spiritually minded man who had long ago abandoned orthodox religious belief, was not to be easily deterred from seeking proof that man was inherently different from the rest of the animals, even if it led him into strange company.

The little book he had written became itself a site of validation. Inside the cover of Fanny's own copy, she records the following:

This book was written by my brother Alfred and with 24 others was laying on my table they had been there 4 days and I had not made time to give them away. – one morning, I had been sitting at my table writing, and left the room for a few minutes when I returned the paper parcel was opened and the books laying on chairs & tables in every

direction – I immediately called my friend the medium and told her of it, we then said do write out what is the meaning of this, though I can guess, they are to be distributed & not lay here idle, Yes Yes 3 knocks, then was rapped out, this sentence, 'One for my sister Frances, I have marked it' upon this I opened one of the books & looked through the leaves & soon found marks with red crayon which I had on my table. I then said if you could do this while the book was shut you could write my name on this book while it lays under my hand, in a few minutes I opened the book & found <u>Frances Wallace</u> written. I said now dear spirit write my marriage name, I shut the book & in 2 minutes opened it again & the second name was written Frances Sims.
Decr 1866 fS[16]

The passage marked with red crayon is:

There is only to some minds a high improbability, arising from the supposed absence of all proof that there are such beings. Let direct proof be forthcoming, and there seems no reason why the most sceptical philosopher should refuse to accept it. It would be simply a matter to be investigated and tested like any other question of science.

Wallace maintained consistently that the truth would be revealed by observation and experiment.

If he needed the supporting testimony of a powerful thinker, he could find one in his hero Robert Owen, who had been converted to spiritualism in 1853, and believed that the revelations were harbingers of 'a great moral revolution . . . about to be effected for the human race'.[17] Wallace, following Owen, believed fervently in ethical progress, in perfectibility, in the inherent potential for good in humanity: spiritualism, and spiritual manifestations, were the faint but palpable signs that there *was* purpose in the world.

The other persuasive advocate, from Wallace's perspective, was Robert Chambers, author of *Vestiges*, whose letter reached out to include Wallace as a man of science who admitted 'the verity of the phenomena of spiritualism', and congratulated him on having 'leapt the ditch':

I have for many years <u>known</u> that these phenomena are real, as distinguished from impostures; and it is not of yesterday that I concluded they were calculated to explain much that has been doubtful in the past, and when fully accepted, revolutionise the whole frame of human opinion on many important matters.

After regretting Huxley's impatience with the subject, Chambers concluded: 'My idea is that the term "supernatural" is a gross mistake. We have only to enlarge our conceptions of the natural, and all will be right.'[18] This was the quality of affirmation that Wallace sought. He would have been much happier if he could have persuaded some of the scientific hierarchy to join him; and Cambridge seemed a potential source of support: 'Do you know anything about the "Cambridge Ghost Club",' he enquired of Newton, '& can you ascertain if C. Kingsley is a member?'[19]

The regular Friday evenings at Westbourne Grove continued, in addition to other seance-tastings. Spruce, safe in Sussex, quizzed Fanny Sims: 'I presume you continue to deal in the spirit line – a branch of business unknown here.' He reported that one evening, feeling 'unusually light', he

> . . . set to and danced several steps of a hornpipe, by the space of 10 minutes, to the great astonishment of my 'nuss'! . . . I have since in vain attempted to repeat this saltatorian experiment & at the present moment I might as well try to fly as to dance. Now, if you could connect this singular phenomenon with any incantations of your magic circle, it wd. go far to convince me that one living body may act on another at a distance beyond the limit of possible perception by the senses.

Spruce could tease Fanny, and assume that she would pass the letter on to her brother, along with best regards to the 'famille Wallace'.[20] It was not easy to challenge Wallace directly on this sensitive subject.

Inevitably, the spiritualists attracted controversy. One of Fanny Sims's neighbours was an extremely wealthy widow, Mrs Jane Lyon, who lived in Westbourne Place in rooms above a stationer's shop. She took a portrait of her late husband to the Sims' shop, because she wanted it photographed. Her late husband had, she told Fanny, predicted that they would be reunited in seven years; the time was up, and she believed that 1866 would therefore see her death. Fanny Sims assured her that this need not be so; if she were a spiritualist, her husband might be able to come to her 'while she was yet on earth'. So she packed Mrs Lyon off to Camberwell, to a psychic bookshop, whose owners put her in contact with the 'spiritual Athenaeum', where Daniel Home – Mr Sludge the Medium, in Browning's version – operated. Mrs Lyon was so impressed with Home – and his wealthy social connections – that she offered to adopt him, and decided to give him £24,000. A few weeks later she changed her mind, and eventually sued for the return of the money. A lengthy and widely reported court case was finally decided in Mrs Lyon's favour; but no one came well out of the affair, and Fanny Sims was mentioned in evidence. Wallace himself would later become a regular witness in the law courts, testifying on behalf of a series of spiritualists.[21]

All this was wonderfully stimulating, but it did not pay any bills – rather the reverse – and finance began to be a slight concern. Annie was pregnant, and Wallace needed to provide for a family. Stevens had prudently and systematically invested the proceeds from the Archipelago collections in Indian Railway stock, and Wallace's annual income from investments was as high as £300 at one point. But money leaked away in the direction of the Sims family, and his mother; and although he was paid for a few pieces of scientific journalism – 'The Philosophy of Birds Nests' for the *Intellectual Observer*, 'Disguises of Insects' for *Science Gossip* – these were only odd guineas to throw into the equation. He now committed the classic mistake of accepting financial advice from his friends. In the manuscript notes for his autobiography for 1865, he underlined the ominous words 'Began speculation': he did not blame, or name, the first two influences. One was a fellow investigator into spiritualism, Ridsdale, who 'held a good appointment under Government'.[22] Ridsdale played the stock market himself, and thought it absurd that Wallace should have several thousand pounds lying idle. Then George Silk – old childhood friend, 'reader' to Archdeacon Sinclair, involved with the London Diocesan Board of Finance, pillar of the Establishment – became secretary to a group of private investors with offices in Pall Mall, who were buying up slate quarries, and forming companies to exploit them. Wallace was persuaded to buy shares, and even to be a director, on the basis of his practical knowledge as a surveyor. Finally, his friend Geach returned from the East, and encouraged Wallace to invest in lead mines. The worst losses he suffered did not occur for some years, but all these speculative investments began to dilute his capital, and cut back his regular income.

With his wife's encouragement, he began once more to work on his eastern travels, the one major writing project that might help him financially. Newton had invited him to write the volume on Lepidoptera for a series Macmillan was planning – Bates was doing the beetles; he declined: 'Half the time & labour it would take would write my travels, & I think pay me better & get me more credit.' But he asked Newton to remember him if he should hear of 'any vacant good Curatorship or Nat. Hist. Secretaryship': 'If sufficiently good & permanent I would give all my private collections to a local museum.'[23] He also arranged an exhibition of his bird and butterfly collections in the Westbourne Grove photographic gallery, and began to offload some of them to private buyers.

One small indication of his growing insecurity about money occurs in his dealings with the British Museum over a sum of £5 owed to him, which he now called in. He was asked to send a stamped receipt in advance – but when the money came on 25 June 1867, by postal order, the office had deducted the cost of the order (sixpence) and sent him £4 19s 6d. Wallace, outraged, decided against either a County Court summons, or a protracted correspondence, but preserved the 'incriminating documents' for his later public revenge over what he described as both official meanness and 'petty larceny'. He was not always so restrained when it came to going to court.[24]

But he had much more important things on his mind in June 1867: on the 22nd Annie gave birth to Bertie, christened Herbert Spencer – Herbert in memory of his younger brother, Spencer in honour of the social scientist. Within a few weeks, the Wallaces had left London, letting the house near Regent's Park and moving to Hurstpierpoint, where Annie's mother and sisters could help her with the baby, and where Wallace could work on his book. Wallace locked himself away for three months in quiet concentration, with Richard Spruce, still lodging in the village, for additional company.

He allowed himself a pleasant break in the autumn. First he went to Wales, with his father-in-law, botanising; next he attended the British Association meeting in Dundee, revelling in a geological excursion with Sir Archibald Geikie, and calling on Chambers at St Andrews, where the two men shared their spiritualist certainties. Spruce moved to Welburn in Yorkshire that October, and Wallace visited him there after going to

Newcastle to give a public lecture (another indication of his strained finances, as lecturing was not a comfortable process for him, however well he knew his subject). Then he returned to Hurstpierpoint, where he continued to organise his eastern material, and to enjoy being a father. Here at last was the kind of quiet, contented life he had dreamed about.

Through the rest of the winter of 1867, and the following spring, he was hard at work, reshaping the materials of his journey in the Archipelago. From the very start, in January 1864, he had felt overwhelmed by the prospect, confessing to Darwin that he was 'a very bad hand at writing anything like narrative', and regretting dreadfully his lack of 'copious notes on common everyday objects, sights and sounds and incidents', which he imagined he could never forget, but now found it impossible to recall with any accuracy.[25] He was also highly conscious of Bates's brilliant success. In February 1868 he could report to Darwin – who never failed to mention the subject in his letters – that he had been for some time 'hammering away' at his travels, but still feared he would 'make a mess of it'.[26] This was not just conventional modesty on his part: he genuinely mistrusted his narrative and descriptive powers, as opposed to his ability to argue logically and clearly, however strange that might seem to most readers. He scanned all the secondary material he could lay his hands on, drawing on the accounts of the early European travellers as well as more recent books such as Sir Thomas Raffles's *The History of Java* and John Crawfurd's *History of the Indian Archipelago*, together with two recent publications, J. W. B. Money's *Java: or, How to Manage a Colony*, and Eduard Dekker's novel *Max Havelaar*. For primary material, he had his notebooks and four field journals, which he could refine and expand on, supplemented by his letters home and the regular accounts to Stevens, sections of which had already appeared in print. He had, too, by this time published some thirty papers on aspects of his collections, mostly for the Linnean, Zoological and Entomological Societies. His main problem was not material – in contrast to the Amazon experience, there was almost too much – but structure. A strictly chronological account might be puzzling – the pattern of his fourteen-thousand-mile journey was dictated by weather and transport; besides, a chronological sequence would not enable him to address one of his main themes, the geographical distribution and peculiarities of the islands' animals and of their human inhabitants. So he adopted 'a geographical, zoological and ethnological arrangement', taking the reader from one island group to another. (This is, coincidentally, the broad scheme adopted by Bates, who describes the Amazon locality by locality.) By adopting this structure Wallace, characteristically, places the Archipelago in the foreground, while his own activities often assume second place to the orangutan, the Dyak, and the bird of paradise. All traces of his role in the theory of natural selection are omitted: it is the journey, not the scientific papers from Sarawak and Ternate, that he puts forward as the central and controlling incident of his life.

Revisiting the journals and notebooks activated Wallace's thinking on a whole range of issues, especially on the agency of organic life, and on the development of the human races. The year or so that he spent largely at Hurstpierpoint saw an astonishing burst of productivity, when one remembers that he was simultaneously drafting his *Travels*, investigating mediums, and enjoying his first years of marriage and being a father. He published 'Mimicry, and other Productive Resemblances among Animals', in the *Westminster Review* of July 1867: a lengthy survey of facts and arguments about colour, which came down firmly on the law of utility, though with a glance towards the emphasis Darwin placed on sexual selection. He ended the article with a summary that disposed of either mere chance or 'the direct volition of the Creator' as satisfactory explanations of so many much neglected details, indicating that all the instances he cited were part of the subjection of the phenomena of life to the *Reign of Law*. He meant by this term, obviously, natural selection; but it was also a reference to the title of the Duke of Argyll's response to *The Origin of Species*, a work that appealed strongly to the creationists. Wallace disposed of Argyll in a lengthy, closely argued but courteous demolition job published in the *Quarterly Journal of Science*.[27]

Darwin's new book excited Wallace. *The Variation of Animals and Plants under Domestication* appeared in January 1868. The first volume was especially heavy with details, he commented to Newton, though there were hosts of valuable and interesting facts; but the second volume was much more interesting and novel, and the hypothesis of 'Pangenesis' grand and suggestive, and to him 'extremely satisfying'. 'Darwin has gone a step beyond Spencer, & has offered a practical working solution of a problem infinitely more difficult & unintelligible than the mere "origin of species"' – it explained 'such a vast mass of the most curious and extraordinary phenomena of reproduction'. This was the kind of rational speculation

Wallace warmed to: something that offered a key to the issues of generation and reproduction. As for 'the miserable, weak, ignorant, & sneering article' in the *Athenaeum* – who could have the impudence to be the writer? '"Specific characters never vary"!!!' The *Athenaeum* ought to be cut by every naturalist for admitting such an article.[28] To Lyell, Wallace wrote with equal enthusiasm about pangenesis, Darwin's solution to the heredity of acquired characters:

> The hypothesis is *sublime* in its simplicity and the wonderful manner in which it explains the most mysterious of the phenomena of life. To me it is satisfying in the extreme. I feel I can never give it up, unless it be positively disproved, which is impossible, or replaced by one which better explains the facts, which is highly improbable.[29]

Wallace looked for certainties; once convinced of a position, it took a great deal to dislodge him – in this particular instance, Galton's later experiments on blood transfusion with rabbits, and, eventually, August Weismann's theories. Meanwhile, no one championed natural selection, and Darwin, more bravely and vigorously than Wallace. Darwin was much in Wallace's mind this year, as he relived, and continued to develop, his own intellectual odyssey. At the British Association meeting that August, with Hooker as President, Darwin and Darwinism were at the forefront of the agenda. Carl Vogt from Geneva told Wallace that the Germans were being converted by Darwin's *Variation*. Wallace went to stay with Darwin at Down, coinciding on this occasion with Edward Blyth, back from Calcutta, one of the few readers who had been alert to the implications of Wallace's Sarawak paper.

Wallace still had the time and energy to pursue his interests in spiritualism. His sense of justice, and personal pride, was roused by a correspondence in the *Pall Mall Gazette* in May. Tyndall wrote about the medium Home, claiming that he had never been properly investigated by scientists; and G. H. Lewes joined in, suggesting a method of objective investigation. Wallace was indignant. He had invited both Tyndall and Lewes to seances, with a view to just such an investigation. Tyndall had come once, Lewes never. Besides, Home had been investigated by a scientist, Cromwell Varley, who pronounced himself satisfied that nothing fraudulent was involved. Wallace put together a six-page letter, in response to Lewes, and was furious when the editor, who had had enough of spiritualism, refused to publish it. Wallace then accused Lewes of deliberately carrying on a controversy in a journal that gave no right of reply. After this parting shot, he set off for the Continent for a long holiday with Annie, leaving the baby to be cared for by the Mitten family at Hurstpierpoint.

'Wallace minor runs everywhere,' his grandfather reported to Spruce, 'and in the pursuit of his investigations has discovered that strawberries and green gooseberries are used as food, as well as earth, stones, sand, leaves, coals, and cockchafers with which he varies his diet.'[30] The Wallace parents were at Chambéry; 'they have taken papers and boards to express the juices of all the rare alpine plants', and boxes and pins for the butterflies. They were practically the only visitors in a huge new hotel, and walked out each day to look for flowers. Then they crossed over the St Bernard, and walked down to Aosta, from where they ascended the Becca de Nona, a long day's excursion by mule; Wallace climbed the last thousand feet alone, finding two species of androsaces near the summit before moving on to Interlaken and Grindelwald. They returned at the end of June with lots of plants, including saxifrages, primulas, aquiligia, and four species of gentian. 'Wallace couldn't dry the plants as well as he hoped & Annie got nausea when she went up high,' reported Mitten.[31] His daughter was in the early stages of her second pregnancy.

Back in England, Wallace continued to work on his book. It cried out for illustration, and Wallace liaised with artists such as J. G. Keulemans (the birds of paradise); Joseph Wolf (the frontispiece of the orang-utan attacked by Dyaks); Thomas Baines, the African traveller, and Walter Fitch from Kew, who had illustrated his book on Amazonian palms. Some of the illustrations were based on photographs, and some on Wallace's original sketches. Then there was the question of the dedication. 'It will give me very great pleasure if you will allow me to dedicate my little book of Malayan Travels to you,' he wrote to Darwin in January, 'although it will be far too small and unpretending a work to be worthy of that honour.'[32] Darwin accepted graciously.

Wallace's stock was high. In November, he had been awarded the Royal Medal by the Royal Society, perhaps the most public acknowledgement so far of his scientific contribution. But his financial worries weighed heavily on him, as Annie's pregnancy advanced. Soon there would be two children to care for, and educate. He could not go on living indefinitely in his parents-in-law's house, now that his book was finished; and, with the death of his mother on 15 November, he was that much freer to move out of London at last. He needed to find a place to settle, and put down roots. More importantly, with no certainty that *The Malay Archipelago* would sell any better than *Travels on the Amazon*, he badly needed a job. There were plans to reorganise the national collections of the British Museum, spinning off the natural history sections to a new location. Wallace, full of ideas about proper arrangement and display since he first visited the collections of London and Paris, put together a number of schemes, including full-scale drawings, and wrote a long article for *Macmillan's Magazine*, 'Museums for the People'. He circulated a memorial, and wrote to thank Hooker for signing; Wallace hoped it would not be forgotten 'when the British Museum comes to be moved and reconstituted'.[33] With the backing of Hooker, and Darwin and Lyell, together with the publicity over his new book, he was confident of securing some official salaried post. On 27 January 1869, his daughter Violet was born; and on 9 March, only a week after the final agreement with Macmillan was signed, the two volumes of *The Malay Archipelago* were published, in an edition of 1,500 copies. He received an advance of £100, and a royalty of 7s 6d a copy after the first 1000: a second edition of 750 copies was printed in October. The reviews were as positive as the sales.

11   Man and Mind

Darwin purred with pleasure at Wallace's dedication in *The Malay Archipelago* – 'To Charles Darwin, author of *The Origin of Species*, I dedicate this book, not only as a token of personal esteem and friendship, but also to express my deep admiration for his genius and his works' – and wrote to congratulate the author both on the dedication, and the whole appearance of the book – quite beautiful: he had received one of twenty-five copies which Macmillan had had specially cut and gilded. 'As for the dedication, putting quite aside how far I deserve what you say, it seems to me decidedly the best expressed dedication which I have ever met.'[1] By 22 March, he had finished reading it: excellent, and most pleasant to read. 'That you have returned alive is wonderful after all your risks from illness and sea voyages, especially that most interesting one to Waigiou and back. Of all the impressions which I have received from your book, the strongest is that your perseverance in the cause of science was heroic.'[2] But even as he praised the account of the journey out of which those two crucial papers on species had emerged, Darwin knew that Wallace was preparing an unwelcome addendum, as part of his forthcoming review of the tenth edition of Lyell's *Principles*. Darwin was 'intensely curious' to read what Wallace had to say. 'I hope you have not murdered too completely your own and my child.'

Wallace was moving on to the subject of man – as indeed was Darwin, now deep into the writing of *The Descent of Man*. The closing paragraphs of *The Malay Archipelago* had sounded the trumpet call, echoing the perfectionist notes of the 1864 paper on 'The Development of Human Races under the Law of Natural Selection':

We most of us believe that we, the higher races, have progressed and are progressing. If so, there must be some state of perfection, some ultimate goal, which we may never reach, but to which all true progress must bring us nearer. What is this ideally perfect social state toward which mankind ever has been, and still is tending?

Wallace answered the question by reference to what the 'best thinkers' maintain: 'a state of individual freedom and self-government, rendered possible by the equal development and just balance of the intellectual, moral, and physical, parts of our nature . . .'; and then he went on more radically to testify that he had himself experienced an approach to such a perfect social state 'among people in a very low stage of civilisation', both in South America and the East. In contrast, the mental and moral status of European people had regressed. 'Compared with our wondrous progress in physical science and its practical applications, our system of government, of administering justice, of national education, and our whole social and moral organisation, remains in a state of barbarism.' (The word 'barbarism' is asterisked, and receives a whole page of justification.) European civilisation, in short, was a failure, and would always be so, mainly from 'our neglect to train and develop more thoroughly the sympathetic feelings and moral faculties of our nature'. This, concluded Wallace, 'is the lesson I have been taught by my observations of uncivilised man. I now bid my readers – Farewell!'[3]

This resounding conclusion might be read as starry-eyed Utopianism, or incipient socialism. But it stemmed from two major thrusts of Wallace's observations and instincts: firstly, the surprisingly advanced nature of so-called 'savage' man and 'savage' societies; secondly, his separation of the intellectual and, especially, the moral attributes of man from the physical. He is careful not to use the word 'spiritual' at this stage, although his language indicates unease about the results of the 'struggle for life' as practised by the colonialists:

> If the tide of colonisation should be turned to New Guinea, there can be little doubt of the early extinction of the Papuan race. A warlike and energetic people, who will not submit to national slavery or to domestic servitude, must disappear before the white man as surely as do the wolf and the tiger.[4]

Having rejected orthodox Christian doctrines and values, he needed a substitute to defend his shift of position: needed, at least, a logical grounding to challenge or modify the scientific determinism that he had embraced with such enthusiasm.

Wallace's first extensive account of his new theory was published in the *Quarterly Review*, at the close of an evaluation of new editions of Lyell's *Principles of Geology* and *Elements of Geology*. He argued that, first, neither natural selection nor the more general theory of evolution could explain the origin of sensational or conscious life:

> They may teach us how, by chemical, electrical, or higher natural laws, the organised body can be built up, can grow, can reproduce its like; but those laws and that growth cannot even be conceived as endowing the newly arranged atoms with consciousness. But the moral and higher intellectual nature of man is as unique a phenomenon as was conscious life on its first appearance in the world, and the one is almost as difficult to conceive as originating by any law of evolution as the other.[5]

He went even further, and suggested that there were certain physical characteristics of the human race that were not explicable by the theory of variation and the survival of the fittest: the brain, the organs of speech, the hand, and the external form of man. The brain, particularly, exercised Wallace: a 'savage' possessed a brain apparently far too highly developed for his immediate needs, but essential for advanced civilisation; immediate utility was thereby called into question. Then, in his closing paragraphs, came the crunch: the same great laws that had developed all other organised beings were indeed active in the development of man, but there seemed to be evidence of 'a Power which has guided the action of those laws in definite directions and for special ends'. Just as man had intervened to develop the Guernsey milch-cow or the London dray-horse, so there must be a possibility that 'in the development of the human race, a Higher Intelligence has guided the same laws for nobler ends'. This was the direction to pursue, wrote Wallace, in order to find the true reconciliation of science with theology.

> Let us fearlessly admit that the mind of man (itself the living proof of a supreme mind) is able to trace, and to a considerable extent has traced, the laws by means of which the organic no less than the inorganic world has been developed. But let us not shut our eyes to the evidence that an Overruling Intelligence has watched over the action of those laws, so directing their variations and so determining their accumulation, as finally to produce an organisation sufficiently perfect to admit of, and even to aid in, the indefinite advancement of our mental and moral nature.[6]

It was out: Wallace's apostasy from his own doctrine of natural selection, a variation so radical that he later described it to Darwin as his 'little heresy'. Darwin wrote 'No' against the offending passage on his copy of the *Quarterly*, and underlined it three times. 'I differ grievously from you,' he wrote to Wallace, 'and I am very sorry for it.' If he had not known better, he would have sworn that the brain passages had been inserted by some other hand. 'I can see no necessity for calling in an additional and proximate cause in regard to Man.'[7] He wrote, too, to Lyell, bewailing Wallace's apparent volte-face; but Lyell, though not convinced by Wallace's reasoning, was sympathetic to the concept; 'I rather hail Wallace's suggestion,' he replied to Darwin, 'that there may be a Supreme Will and Power which may not abdicate its function of interference but may guide the forces and laws of Nature.'[8] Wallace was careful not to use the word 'God' in his argument, either in this first exposition or in his later refinements and extensions, but talked rather of powers, intelligences, forces, influences – a distinction totally lost on most of his critics. For Darwin, it must have seemed as if

Wallace had reverted to orthodox, eighteenth-century theology, in an adaptation of the argument from design. For Wallace, the theory was corroborated by his experience of the spiritual world. Those phenomena demonstrated, to his satisfaction, the existence of forces and influences 'not yet recognised by science' – evidence that a higher order of intelligences was at work in the world. As for himself, he scarcely budged from this new position, except to refine it in a long essay published in 1870, and he defended himself vigorously against criticism. With this one massive exception, he had not relinquished his basic adherence to the mechanism of natural selection, and he continued to argue, write and lecture on all other aspects of Darwinian theory.

Now that *The Malay Archipelago* was in the bookshops, and selling steadily, Wallace was free to enjoy the summer. First, a walking tour with his father-in-law, and Geach, his Archipelago friend, in Wales: climbing Snowdon, and botanising furiously – Mitten called out 'I've got another species' so often that Wallace thought the little valley below Beddgelert was inexhaustible.[9] Next, the meeting of the British Association at Exeter, where Wallace's shift of position was reported. Wallace, versatile as ever, presented a paper on 'The Measurement of Geological Time' in Section C, Geology, then turned up in Section D, Biology, to contribute to the discussions, for example following Lubbock's paper 'On the Primitive Condition of Man'. He was invited to join the fraternity of the Red Lions, the dining club he attended at the Cambridge meeting of 1862, was entertained at a country house with 'a large party of scientific men', and thoroughly relished the genial, slightly irreverent atmosphere: there seemed to be no signs that he had damaged his reputation by his heretical amendment.[10] He relished, too, the magazine that appeared in parody of the British Association, 'Exeter Change for The British Lion', edited by Snug the Joiner. After twitting Darwin, the author of 'The Development Hypothesis', 'General Fitz-Muddler', went on to tease Wallace:

> After every so-called discovery, some second claimant for the honour is sure to arise, announcing that he had arrived at precisely the same conclusions from widely different evidence; and in this case a Mr Wallace appears on the scene as Mr Darwin's alter ego. Like all the rest of them he has travelled everywhere – restlessness of body, as of mind, being a characteristic of the school. We leave his arguments about

birds of paradise and butterflies and 'simulation' for those who can follow them, alluding only to one of his statements. He says that, somewhere or other in the Eastern Archipelago, there are islands only a few miles apart in which the animals are quite different. Here is a discovery worth going half round the globe for! What would be thought of a gamekeeper that wanted three miles to keep the partridges out of the pheasant preserves. In Regent's Park he would find a very different fauna on either side of a six-foot paling.[11]

The writer then moves on to fresh targets, first, Huxley, and finally Hooker, who as Director of the Royal Gardens, a public officer, 'has so far forgotten what is due to his position' as to have become associated with 'the great heresy' of the nineteenth century. 'Are the conservatories at Kew to be made hot beds of insidious doctrine? and have the Commissioners of Woods and Forests no power in their own borders? Under a more enlightened Ministry these things would see an early doom.' Of the four named natural selectionists in this good-humoured lampoon, Darwin had no need of a salary, and Hooker and Huxley were already secure. The jobless Wallace ran a double risk. He remained distinctly suspect to anyone belonging to the traditional school of Owen, but also, because of his theory of Higher Intelligences, he might no longer be regarded as 'safe' by the champions of the new orthodoxy.

After Exeter, Wallace took the opportunity of travelling further west, to stay with his publisher, Macmillan, at Torquay, where he enjoyed meeting the geologist William Pengelly, before returning to London for the next intellectual season. Pengelly, largely self-educated like Wallace, was particularly interested in the antiquity of man, and carried out systematic excavations at Bovey Tracey, Brixham Cave, and Kent's Hole at Torquay: this was all fascinating and thought-provoking material for Wallace, who was editing a collection of his own essays and articles for Macmillan, including the Sarawak and Ternate papers, a revised version of 'The Development of Human Races under the Law of Selection', and a fresh assault on the problems of consciousness and moral development, 'The Limits of Natural Selection as Applied to Man'. He sent the proofs to Darwin in January. Darwin was horrified: the Lyell review was not an isolated aberration; Wallace was extending and solidifying his line of argument. Much of the book he could assent to – 'But I groan over Man –

you write like a metamorphosed (in retrograde direction) naturalist, and you the author of the best paper that ever appeared in the *Anthropological Review*! Eheu! Eheu! Eheu!'[12] He signed himself 'your miserable friend', and followed this up by a further letter; he had just re-read the *Anthropological* paper (slightly amended by Wallace, incidentally, for its republication) 'and I *defy* you to upset your own doctrine'.[13] Wallace was unmoved. In fact, he seems to have been able to continue his friendships and social life quite untouched, at least from his own perspective, by controversies and differences of opinion: his brush with Huxley over seances did not interrupt their social meetings, and with other scientists, such as Lyell or Mivart, his new position aroused interest rather than lamentation. It was a busy winter: there were meetings of the Entomological Society – he was elected President in 1870 – and the Linnean; and he was also now appearing regularly in *Nature*, for which he was an active reviewer and correspondent from its foundation in November 1869.

Domestically, he wanted to find a home outside London. Bertie, especially, did not seem to thrive in the city, and was often taken down to Hurstpierpoint to be 'put to rights' by his grandmother; and the addition of Violet made a more rural setting increasingly important. Yet London might provide the job he increasingly needed. While the outcome of the desirable museum post at Bethnal Green remained unclear, the Wallaces took a cottage temporarily at Barking, east of London: a 'miserable village', surrounded by marshes and factories, but with pleasant walks beside the Thames, and a convenient railway service that brought both Bethnal Green, and the evening meetings of the societies, within range. They moved there on 25 March 1870, just as *Contributions to the Theory of Natural Selection* came out.

This was the first time Wallace had brought together his theoretical papers, allowing his readers to trace the development of his thought from the Sarawak statement on the introduction of new species, through to his concept of man. The essays represent him at his most impressive, moving from the lucidity of his early theory to the grand philosophical vision of his latest doctrine. But during the first months of 1870 he demonstrated a surprising lack of judgement by becoming embroiled in a ridiculous wager, something that he lived to regret. In the journal *Scientific Opinion*, which Wallace wrote for occasionally, John Hampden issued a challenge to 'scientific men' to prove the convexity of the surface of any inland water, and staked £500 on the outcome, stating that he would acknowledge that he had forfeited the deposit 'if his opponent can exhibit, to the satisfaction of any intelligent referee, a convex railway, river, canal, or lake'. Wallace rose to the bait, having first asked Lyell's opinion. According to Wallace, Lyell actively encouraged him to accept: 'It may stop these foolish people to have it plainly shown them.'[14] Perhaps the £500 was too tempting; perhaps Wallace saw himself undertaking a task of public education for the common good. A six-mile stretch of the old Bedford River was chosen, between Welney and the old Bedford bridge; referees were selected, and the editor of the *Field*, J. H. Walsh, was appointed umpire. It was rather like a duel, fought with poles and discs and calico flags, with spirit-levels and telescopes. Walsh decided unequivocally in Wallace's favour, publishing the diagrams in the *Field*. Hampden refused to accept the verdict, and demanded his money back. Bitter dispute followed: two lawsuits, and three prosecutions of Hampden by Wallace for libel, and one by Walsh; two prison sentences for Hampden; tracts and pamphlets, accusations and defences, were fired off in every direction during the next twenty years. Hampden wrote to every learned society Wallace belonged to, and later distributed a thousand leaflets to most of the residents and tradesmen of Godalming, including 'the professors and tutors of the Charter House', calling him cheat, coward, swindler and impostor, and accusing him of falsehood, embezzlement and theft. What particularly stirred Wallace was a letter to his wife:

Madam – If your infernal thief of a husband is brought home some day on a hurdle, with every bone in his head smashed to pulp, you will know the reason. Do you tell him from me he is a lying infernal thief, and as sure as his name is Wallace he never dies in his bed.

You must be a miserable wretch to be obliged to live with a convicted felon. Do not think or let him think I have done with him.[15]

Wallace should have realised that Hampden was seriously unbalanced, and quietly let the matter drop. Although the courts usually found in his favour, the legal costs mounted, and he ended up as the financial loser. But the rather ludicrous set of proceedings did his reputation no good, besides the harassment and personal abuse he suffered – 'a tolerably severe punishment for what I did not at the time recognize as an ethical lapse', as he comments with characteristic honesty.

At Holly House, Barking, Wallace decided on the subject of his next book: the geographical distribution of animals. This was something he had been intrigued by ever since his collecting in the Amazon, and which became one of his keys to understanding the principles of natural selection as he sifted through the distribution patterns of insects, birds and animals in the Archipelago. 'I have thought of such a book this two years,' he confessed to Newton, but stopped when he found it would be the work of years to do it all thoroughly. 'I had just thought of a comparatively short manual such as you suggest, but Darwin was horrified at my thinking of writing a <u>small</u> book on such a vast subject, – & that put me off.'[16] However, he promised to think of it again. Sclater, too, was urging him in the same direction. It took Wallace the best part of five years, and in the end it was sufficiently substantial to satisfy even Darwin's appetite for thoroughness.

Anchored again by a major project, Wallace threw himself into his usual, and slightly frenetic, range of pursuits, while he waited to hear what might happen about the Bethnal Green Museum. He wrote letters replying to the notices of Natural Selection, and pieces for Nature – reviews of Francis Galton's influential study Hereditary Genius and Edward Tylor's Early History of Mankind. The British Association meeting in September drew him to Liverpool – Sclater was talking about the principles to be observed in establishing a National Museum of Natural History, a topic close to his heart. The Entomological Society's meetings were not to be missed lightly, now that he was President, in succession to Bates. Spiritualism continued to absorb a great deal of his intellectual energy, and his time. He wrote a substantial paper for a spiritualist soirée, 'An Answer to the Arguments of Hume, Lecky, and Others, against Miracles'.

To take on John Hume as a prelude to establishing the credentials of modern spiritualism was an act of some courage, if not folly, but Wallace had boundless confidence in his own power of reasoning, and believed he showed Hume's arguments to be full of 'unwarranted assumptions, fallacies, and contradictions'. His confidence was bolstered by fresh and first-hand experience. William Crookes was actively and 'scientifically' investigating Daniel Home's powers as a medium, and Wallace eagerly became one of the circle. Home was one of the most convincing contemporary practitioners, and Wallace was satisfied that the table lifted without any interference, and that an accordion played several bars of 'Home Sweet Home' – at his own mischievous request – apparently by itself, or by means of a 'shadowy yet defined hand' at the bottom end (one of Home's hands was resting on top of the accordion, the other in full view on the table).[17] Wallace was also an early believer in the 'materialisations' that some mediums, including Mrs Guppy – the former Miss Nichol – seemed able to call into view: confining themselves to a small cabinet, in order to concentrate the energy, shadowy figures would emerge, to touch or to communicate with the observers. The sceptical claimed fraud, or commercial conjuring; the sympathetic, including Wallace, were inclined to accept the validity of at least some of these figures.

In March, his review of Darwin's *The Descent of Man* appeared in the *Academy*. Darwin had continued to keep Wallace abreast of the book's progress; he knew that it was bound to give offence, now that he was unequivocally addressing man – it was half killing him with fatigue and, he confessed, 'I much fear will quite kill me in your estimation.'[18] That was not true; but Wallace refused to accept that man's brain could develop simply by the laws of natural selection alone. It was not the descent from the ape that bothered him, but the mechanism by which this had occurred. Man's

> absolute erectness of posture, the completeness of his nudity, the harmonious perfection of his hands, the almost infinite capacities of his brain, constitute a series of correlated advances too great to be accounted for by the struggle for existence of an isolated group of apes in a limited area.[19]

Wallace expressed his disagreements firmly, but politely. In fact, the tone of Darwin's argument was not all that different from Wallace's approach, humanitarian, even perfectionist in places. Wallace, though, by this time convinced that a spiritual dimension existed outside human consciousness, remained unwavering in his belief that man's moral dimension was imparted from without.

Wallace continued to look for a suitable home, and trusting in his own business sense as well as his practical experience as a surveyor and builder, he decided to start from scratch. He found a four-acre site on the edge of the village of Grays, twenty miles east of London on the north bank of the Thames, and bought a ninety-nine-year lease. The site comprised a disused chalkpit, an acre on the plateau above it, and another acre or so of sloping but cultivatable ground. There were splendid views looking eastward down the Thames, and south across the river to the Kent hills, and with sand and gravel above the chalk there was good drainage. He commissioned an architect and, to take advantage of the gravel and a local cement works, decided to have the house built largely of concrete. He also organised his own water supply, sinking a well a hundred feet into the chalk and installing a small iron windmill to pump the water up. Wallace and his engineering friend Geach did most of this work themselves, and soon an ample – and free – supply of water was obtained for the house and garden. Wallace made frequent visits to inspect the progress of the building, and to check that the gravel was being thoroughly washed. In September, he was already busy stocking the garden. He wrote to Hooker, asking if he could collect a few seeds of hardy plants from Kew, and Hooker responded with a collection of herbaceous seeds, roots of perennials, and shrubs. Halfway through the contract, the builder failed to appear one morning, leaving his men's wages unpaid. The architect sacked the builder, and Wallace took on the job of supervising the completion. He also found himself in receipt of a stream of bills for materials that the builder had ducked. In Holly House, Annie gave birth to William, on 30 December 1871: 'Bertie has got a brother,' Wallace reported to Fanny. 'Annie is pretty well. The baby weighs more than Bertie did, & seems to be about an inch taller, and decidedly better looking than Bertie was at the same age. I am now more busy than ever at the house as we are just doing the waterworks & internal fittings.'[20] The house was finally ready for the family to move into on 25 March 1872, a few weeks after he was elected a Fellow of the Linnean Society.

For someone whose finances were slightly precarious, the Dell was an extremely ambitious project. Wallace was a little better off as a result of his mother's death; he also sold the bulk of his entomological collections, the butterflies going to William Hewitson, and accepted a rather badly paid commission from Lyell, checking the manuscript and proofs for a new edition of *The Antiquity of Man*. But the house was built on a grand scale, and even had a four-roomed entrance lodge for the gardener. There was a hall, drawing room, dining room, library and conservatory on the ground floor, four principal bedrooms, dressing room and bathroom on the first floor, and four more bedrooms, or nurseries above – plenty of room for children, and servants. The rooms were spacious, high ceilinged, full of light; the style plain, but with well-chosen decorations, such as the tiles and coloured glass in the hall. Outside, the grounds were beautifully laid out, both in terms of economy – walled gardens, greenhouses, a fowl house – and pleasure: walks and terraces, ponds, a fountain, a croquet lawn, and, eventually, a rich variety of flowers and shrubs and trees. Wallace had visited Darwin in his secluded and spacious country retreat at Downe. The Dell was to be his personal paradise, a haven for the scientific naturalist, and a secure, healthy environment for his wife and children. A horned toad that John had sent him from California roamed happily in his study. The limited railway service made attending evening meetings in London difficult – but that was a small price to pay.[21]

The months passed peacefully, with research on geographical distribution punctuated by delightful plantings and plannings outdoors. Even a letter from Cole at South Kensington, saying that there was not enough money to pay a separate director of the Bethnal Green Museum, did not alarm him unduly, though it led to his accepting a number of examining jobs, and prompted him towards a wider range of journalism for the odd guineas it brought. As well as his steady output on scientific topics, he began to expand the scope of his articles, letters and reviews in the direction of social issues: for example, he wrote a piece for *Macmillan's Magazine* on 'Disestablishment and Disendowment: with a Proposal for a really National Church of England', and a long letter to the editor of the *Daily News* on 'Free-trade Principles and the Coal Question'.

Meanwhile, the garden was a constant diversion. Plants and cuttings travelled backwards and forwards between Grays and Hurstpierpoint, with every family visit. 'Thanks for the Hypericum,' he wrote to his father-in-law. 'It came in beautiful order, & I planted it out at once under the north garden wall, where it will be less burnt up till it grows strong.' The crocuses were out, but the laurels had suffered in the cold north winds: a problem he grappled with throughout his time at the Dell. Could Mitten bring half-a-dozen good strong cuttings of two or three kinds of willow, for planting on the rough banks? 'We shall be very glad to see you and Rose. Suppose you come Sunday week, then Rose can stay till Annie comes to you, & can remain to take care of me & the children.' Then, taking advantage of the Mitten pharmacy, he put in an order for some super strength pills – the current samples were what the Yankees would call 'cruel mild': 'It takes 3 or 4 to produce the least effect on me. Can you make them three times as strong so that one pill will do, as I am not a good hand at swallowing them & wd. rather have one large than 3 small ones. If so send me a box.'[22]

Wallace's spiritualist connections and convictions were never kept separate from the rest of his life. He corresponded and shared experiences with St George Mivart, for example, whose book *Genesis of Species* so ruffled Darwin, giving him a letter of introduction to Mrs Guppy at Naples; and Arabella Buckley, Lyell's secretary, was an enthusiastic experimenter, allowing herself to be mesmerised, and used as a channel for communications. Miss Buckley became a close friend and confidante to Wallace, and she was one of the few people to whom he could express his grief when his son Bertie died in 1874, at the age of six. Bertie, who had been ailing for some time, was staying with his mother at Hurstpierpoint; Wallace was with him only the day before his death, and had suggested a homoeopathic course of treatment. If it had been tried a fortnight earlier, he was pretty sure it might have saved him: 'Our orthodox medical men are profoundly ignorant of the subtle influences of the human body in health and disease, and thus do nothing in many cases which Nature would cure if assisted by proper conditions.'[23] Wallace was back at the Dell when he learned the sad news.

Arabella Buckley's letter of condolence was gentle, and sweetly expressed: 'I am so grieved to hear that my little pet is gone, I had thought him long out of danger & now he has slipped away from us & we shall not be able to watch him grow up & take his place in this world.' But it is clear that, for the spiritualists, death was not an insuperable barrier. It would be a comfort to Mrs Wallace that she had the power of hearing *of* Bertie, if not *from* him, whenever she cultivated it.

> How wonderful it is how completely Spiritualism alters one's idea of death; but I think it increases one's wish to know what they are doing – you have so many friends who can get information for you & I suppose Mrs Guppy having known dear little Bertie would be able to learn a good deal. I wonder who will take care of him & educate him for you.[24]

Because her own mediumship was so uncertain, and because her late sister Janie and her friends did not know Bertie, she thought she would be unlikely to learn anything reliable herself. Nevertheless, that evening she made the attempt and faithfully recorded every detail.

(Question – Would it be possible for you to learn anything of Bertie Wallace?) We are going to try and find out about him, & let you know. Janie jumps at the opportunity of doing something for Mr Wallace who has been the means of bringing you to us – and if . . . (nothing more came).

The next morning, the communication resumed.

I want to tell you about Bertie Wallace. He is here under the care of his uncle Herbert Wallace who is watching over him. The mama is wanting to hear of him & little Bertie ought not to try and communicate yet but if she asks, his grandmamma may be able to . . .

Another interval ensued.

We want to tell you that Bertie Wallace is here; he is fast asleep and his uncle Herbert watches over him. He will wake soon and all is ready for him. His Mama will hear of him if she asks his grandmamma or even his uncle, they are anxious to tell her that it is well with him. He is weary with long restlessness and weakness but his sleep will revive him. We cannot tell you more now. We write this at the instance of Herbert Wallace who cannot write with you himself.

There then follow Arabella Buckley's hesitations and misgivings, which have the effect of authenticating the message:

'Question. Is any of this my own imagination?' 'No it is not your own at all.' 'Question. May I really give this to Mr Wallace as a communication?' 'We gave you these words. You are making your own difficulties.'[25]

Wallace, for all the comfort he received from such assurances, was devastated by Bertie's death. In the future, he would do his best to avoid the subject, and, if it did arise, his eyes would fill with tears. But he clearly believed long before this event that spiritualism could create a bridge between the two states of existence. The intensity of his grief, and the nature of the communications, served only to strengthen his faith, adding a dimension of the deepest feeling to his closely argued writings on the subject. On 14 March, he carried out an experiment with Mrs Guppy. She accompanied him to a professional photographer's, Hudson's, to try to obtain 'ghost-pictures'. 'Before going to Hudson's,' Wallace records, 'I sat with Mrs G., and had a communication by raps to the effect that my mother would appear on the plate if she could.' Three photographs were taken, and on each a second figure appeared on the plate: two of these Wallace identified as images of his mother, although unlike any photograph taken of her during her lifetime.

> I see no escape from the conclusion that some spiritual being, acquainted with my mother's various aspects during life, produced these impressions on the plate. That she herself still lives and pro-duced these figures may not be proved; but it is a more simple and natural explanation to think that she did so, than to suppose that we are surrounded by beings who carry out an elaborate series of impostures to dupe us into a belief in a continued existence after death.[26]

Wallace, grieving over Bertie, was calmed by his belief in the continued life of the spirit. It gave him an inward strength, and serenity, which never left him. The immediate result was a two-part article, 'A Defence of Modern Spiritualism', for the Fortnightly Review in May and June, and a collection of three essays, On Miracles and Modern Spiritualism, later the same year. The publication of the first instalment raised Wallace's spiritualist profile, and he began to receive invitations to seances by the better-known practitioners. 'Try Burns, 15 Southampton Row,' Wallace advised Francis Galton. 'He knows all the mediums & all about them . . . When my whole article is out I should be glad to hear from you what is said about it in scientific circles – that is by men who will take the trouble really to read it – few I am afraid.'[27] Sir Charles Lyell had read Wallace's paper in the Fortnightly, Miss Buckley reported, and passed on Huxley's experience of detecting the precise moment at a seance in which the medium put the chair upon the table – 'a most clear case of imposture'.[28] But Wallace had made the leap of faith, and was impervious to the brisk debunkings of Huxley, or the caustic dismissals of Carpenter.

The blow of Bertie's death halted the variety of Wallace's writing for a while. In his manuscript notes for his autobiography, there are fewer entries for 1875 than for any other year; but at least he had one major task to distract him: the completion, and then the proofs, of *Geographical Distribution*. This was turning into a monumental work, and Alfred Newton became his mentor and honorary editor. Wallace described the book's plan to him in detail – in the maps the seas would be coloured in bands to show the depths, so that 'isolation by deep seas' could be illustrated. He added a postscript; 'I think I must call the Book, – "The Geographical Distribution of Land Animals" or the dredging men will be down upon me, for leaving out the "most important part of the animal kingdom" etc. etc.'[29]He sent Newton whole chunks of text for noting – 'the more you <u>note</u> & <u>criticise</u>, the greater favour I shall esteem it' – and all through March, April and May the manuscript and annotations shuttled between Grays and Cambridge. Wallace was especially relieved to have his bird references checked:

> To you who have studied birds all your life & have the literature by heart, it must seem stupid of me to use different names for the same genus. Please therefore remember that my study of birds <u>began</u> with my Eastern journey, – & that the Birds of Europe & N. America are mostly as strange to me as the birds of Africa.[30]

Wallace, in this work, was extrapolating from his detailed knowledge of the Amazon, and above all the Archipelago, to survey distribution throughout the world; at the centre of his thinking was the 'line', and he acknowledged that it was Huxley who was 'the first to give me a place in Geography', in the *Proceedings of the Zoological Society*, 1868, 'because he there says – "<u>coincide with what <u>may be called</u></u> Wallace's line"'.[31] The flow of questions and requests continued: where do woodcocks come from? And getting the academic genera correct for his references was even trickier than the birds – were 'Professors' at private schools or Colleges recognisable? Were Ph.D.s not recognisable in England – though Huxley, for one, referred to '<u>Dr</u> Sclater': 'Pray enlighten me.'[32] The flurry ceased for three weeks, while Wallace tackled his batch of South Kensington examination papers, an annual chore but increasingly essential to his budget.

The two large volumes of *The Geographical Distribution of Animals* were widely praised. *Nature* called it 'the first sound treatise on zoological geography'. Darwin expressed 'unbounded admiration' – it would be the basis 'of all future work on Distribution'.[33] His only cavil – ironic, coming from him – was that Wallace had not given 'very numerous references', a charge the author cheerfully admitted – he was 'dreadfully unsystematic'.[34] Hooker referred to it in his presidential address to the British Association as 'one of the two most important general works on distribution which have appeared since the foundation of this Association'. The other was Alphonse de Candolle's *Géographie Botanique*.[35] Wallace broadly adopted the six major regions Sclater had suggested in his study of bird distribution, refining the concept with additional sub-regions, and introducing the concept of time. There were a number of Wallace specialities, including his suggestion that mammals had originated in the north, and then spread to the rest of the world. Overall, it was a magisterial and deeply thought-out account of the broad principles of animal distribution.

Basking in the book's publication and positive reception, Wallace put the Dell on the market and prepared for a move south of London to Rosehill, Dorking, in Surrey. He gave a range of reasons: the north winds blighted the garden; the railway line to Charing Cross made attendance at evening meetings possible again; living south of London would mean easier access to Annie's family in Sussex. But there were financial considerations. The Dell, fully up and running now, was a substantial property to maintain, and it was an immediately realisable asset. The auctioneers aimed at the top of the market – excellent detached residence, unusually attractive pleasure grounds, capital walled kitchen gardens stocked with the finest wall and pyramid fruit trees, 'the whole presents a variety of charms which it is scarcely possible to describe, and can hardly be surpassed in England'. It made Wallace sound like a landed gentleman of the most leisured kind: 'The Property is admirably adapted for Gentlemen fond of hunting, the Essex hounds being constantly at hand. It is also conveniently placed for yachting, being about a mile from the Thames and within one hour's sail of the sea.'[36] The Wallaces left the Dell in July, without much regret, except for the work that had gone into the garden. ('The vendor reserved the right to take away all the flowers and bulbs he wished.')

That summer, Wallace was agonising over his address to the Biological Section, Section D, of the British Association meeting, scheduled for Glasgow. He decided at first, so he told Newton, that it would be wholly zoological, 'not having read or done anything in anthropology for 4 or 5 years'. Mr Foster had assured him that 'my charge of the Department was nominal, & a compliment to the Anthropologists'; he did not quite see it like that.[37] By the end of August, he had modified his approach, with the first half biological, and the second half on the 'Antiquity and Origin of Man' question. The address was duly delivered, but the real fun and games came later. William Barrett, a young physicist who had once been an assistant of John Tyndall, sent in a paper on thought transference in mesmeric trance. The committee of the Biology Section decided not to unpack this unwelcome parcel, and passed it swiftly on to the committee of the Anthropology Sub-section: they decided to approve its reading, but only on the casting vote of Wallace as chairman. Carpenter, self-appointed scourge of psychical phenomena, arrived while the paper was being read, and took part in an unusually animated discussion with Wallace and Lord Rayleigh among others. The debate was seized on by the press, and a heated correspondence followed in *The Times*. E. R. Lankester, the biologist, had attended a seance with Slade, the American medium, the day before; Rayleigh reported his own experience of slate-writing with Slade; Wallace had also attended one session. Lankester's letter to *The Times* accused Slade of fraud, called Wallace's behaviour 'more than questionable', and declared that the BAAS had been degraded. (Only the title of Barrett's paper ever appeared in the official BAAS report.) Wallace leapt to his own defence, and that of Slade, first in letters to *The Times*, and then in the lawsuit that Lankester brought against Slade. In spite of Wallace's evidence, the court found for Lankester. It was perhaps provocative that Wallace went into the witness box not just in his own right, but as, so the *Spiritualist* reported, 'the President of the Biological Section of the British Association for the Advancement of Science'; and unsurprising that the next year, when Wallace offered himself as a candidate for the assistant secretaryship of the British Association, he was not appointed. Meanwhile, the controversy rumbled on. Carpenter gave a series of lectures on spiritualism at the London Institute, and their publication sparked a series of sharp ripostes from Wallace, with letters in *Fraser's Magazine*, *Nature* and the *Athenaeum*, as well as the *Daily News* and the *Spectator*. He also reviewed Carpenter in the *Quarterly Journal of Science* – a rather loaded invitation this, since the editor of the *Quarterly* happened to be the pro-spiritualist William Crookes. Carpenter wrote personally to Wallace as well, asserting that he was merely disputing the evidence – why was Wallace so hostile and aggressive? (Barrett was later largely responsible for founding the Society for Psychical

Research, yet one more organisation for Wallace to be involved in.)[38]

The Wallaces did not stay long at Dorking, though *Tropical Nature and Other Essays* was completed there. In spite of the house's hilltop site, they found the atmosphere enervating. Wallace was consulting an American medium about his own health, who volunteered one day, when in a trance, that his son Will was in danger, and 'that if we wished to save him we must leave Dorking, go to a more bracing place, and let him be out-of-doors as much as possible and "have the smell of the earth"'.[39] This was one reason Wallace advanced for their move to Croydon; another was the better provision of suitable schools. The family occupied two addresses in Croydon from March 1878, first at Duppas Hill and then St Peter's Road. It was here that he wrote his second great book of the decade, *Island Life*, and from here that he launched his campaign for a job that really intrigued him, Superintendent of Epping Forest.

Epping Forest was a cause that aroused all his strongest social and scientific interests, and reawoke in him the feelings about everyone's common rights in the land that had disturbed him as a young man, when he was carrying out enclosure surveys in Wales. Epping Forest, between five and a half and six thousand acres planted with hornbeam, beech and oak, was one of the surviving remnants of the ancient Forest of Essex, established as a royal hunting forest in the thirteenth century. Hainault Forest had already been largely destroyed in the 1850s, and, as Oliver Rackham has commented, 'the modern conservation movement began with efforts to prevent a like fate for Epping Forest'.[40] The Enclosure Act of 1857 was a signal to the lords of the manor to begin enclosing parts of the land, and they were rewarded by prices of £1000 an acre. Against them, individual commoners, who had ancient rights of pasturage and of lopping firewood, could do little: in one well-publicised case, two commoners, the Willingales, deliberately exercised their right to lop, and were sentenced to two months' imprisonment with hard labour. Members of the Buxton family were prominent among the influential campaigners, and the great coup was to persuade the Corporation of London to take up the case – the Commissioners of Sewers had bought two hundred acres at Little Ilford in 1854 for a cemetery, which gave them commoners' rights. A wonderful battle followed, through the law courts and in the Houses of Parliament, via public inquiries and a Royal Commission, with a definitive judgment in 1874 by the Master of the Rolls, Sir George Jessel, in favour of the City of

London. In 1878, the Epping Forest Act appointed the Corporation of London as conservators of the forest, with the charge that they should 'at all times as far as possible preserve the natural aspect of the forest'. The proposed administration was to include four verderers, and a superintendent.

Wallace was ecstatic at the prospect. The rights of the ordinary individual had been upheld against the capitalist lords of the manor, the collective good had triumphed over selfish gain, the tightly packed families of north-east London would be able to breathe fresh, clean air, and the natural richness of the countryside would be protected and conserved. He was already conscious of the destruction of forests. Hooker had alerted him to what was happening in North America: 'Your description of the process of destruction of the "Big-trees" makes me quite melancholy. What barbarians our successors will consider us if they are not preserved.'[41] He hoped that the Californian or the United States government would acquire a tract of the country where the trees flourished as a public park, to protect them from fire and the saw. In August 1878, he wrote again to Hooker, by this time with Epping firmly in his sights. 'I have long been seeking some employment which would bring me in some fixed income while still allowing me some leisure for literary work,' he explained. Would Hooker sign the enclosed draft memorial – though Wallace found it unpleasant to lay before him anything so 'egotistical'. Nevertheless, he asked Hooker to use any influence he might have with Members of the Corporation.[42] Two weeks later, he sent him two 'final draft' memorials for signature, a longer and a shorter version, and went on accumulating references and testimonials on a grand scale: the presidents of the London natural history societies, local residents, Members of Parliament. Preliminary soundings proved ambiguous. The Epping Forest Committee, he reported to Hooker in October, had got an idea that no 'scientific man' was required. Worse, they had got a further idea that '*I* should want to make a "Kew Gardens" of the Forest!' So he had written a long article in the *Fortnightly Review*, and proposed to send copies to members of the committee. Meanwhile, could Hooker 'have a word' with the First Commissioner of Works, Noel – and then Noel might have a word with the Duke of Connaught, who it was rumoured would be the Ranger – and then the Ranger could give a hint to the committee that some such scheme as Wallace's ought to be carried out.[43] Wallace seems to have had no qualms about making full use of his contacts in trying to exert influence. He was closely in touch with Raphael Meldola, who was then a resident in Epping Forest, was an active member of the Epping Forest and County of Essex Natural Field Club, and was campaigning for an ecological, conservationist solution to the future management of the Forest.

Wallace's article appeared in the November issue of the *Fortnightly Review*.[44] It began with a plea for the right to roam: 'legally there is no such thing as a "common", answering to the popular idea of a tract of land over which anybody has a right to roam at will'. He went on to give an account of the background to the Act of Parliament, and then indicated some of the problems to be addressed. Rehabilitation would be essential. Many of the trees, in the part of the Forest nearest London, were rapidly dying, 'from the combined effects of want of shelter and the smoky atmosphere'. Then there were the devastations caused by gravel extraction, illegal enclosures, and random timber-felling. He proposed to restore some of these areas as forest or woodland, with sections composed solely of trees and shrubs native to one of the great forest regions of the temperate zone: there would be eastern and western northern American forest zones; another for eastern European/western Asian; another for eastern Asian/Japanese; and one for the southern hemisphere. It would be a huge arboretum, through which the population of London could wander or ride, over footbridges of unpainted wood or stone, along footpaths and rides. This was perhaps going further than 'preserving the natural aspect of the Forest'; but it upheld the spirit of the Act, which laid down that the Forest should remain a forest, and not be civilised into a park.

The Commissioners took their time. In June 1879, there was a proposal to appoint a general superintendent at a salary of £500, and this was agreed in October. Applications poured in, 152 of them, with a 'short list' of forty-one names: school teachers, retired servicemen, police inspectors, land surveyors. On 3 December, twelve selected candidates were interviewed at the Guildhall, and on Monday, 8 December, the three final candidates, Alexander McKenzie, Frank Butler and Wallace were summoned: 'I am to remind you that personal canvassing will be a disqualification and residence in the Forest will be required.' The Commissioners, impervious to the testimonials of the influential men of science, and perhaps more alarmed than impressed by Wallace's visionary schemes, appointed McKenzie. According to Wallace, the 'City merchants and tradesmen' wanted a 'practical man' to use the open spaces for games and sports, and to encourage excursions and school treats.[45]

Wallace was becoming desperate, clutching at straws. 'By the bye,' he enquired of Newton, 'do you know any of the Trustees of the Josiah Mason College of Science at Birmingham?'[46] They were advertising for professors in *Nature* – perhaps there would be a post such as registrar, or curator, or even librarian for which he would be fitted, as he was very much in want of 'some employment less precarious than writing books etc. which are wretched pay'. (He heard in February, 1880, that the Trustees had decided not to elect a librarian.)

Wallace's failure over Epping Forest was a bitter blow, to his pride, his pocket, and his confidence. He had been strongly attracted to the challenge, because he believed in the philosophy of preserving the countryside for the public to enjoy, and he had a particular vision, conservationist and educational, for the area. Besides, he pictured it as a healthy life, involving working out of doors, and drawing on his experience as a land-surveyor as well as his expertise as a naturalist – a return to his days in Wales, or as a collector. Perhaps his age – fifty-six – was beginning to tell against him. He foresaw years of struggle, writing articles, examining, giving lectures. Disheartened, he confided his anxieties to Arabella Buckley, explaining that literary work tired him, and that the 'uncertainty of it' was a great worry to him: 'I want some regular work either partially outdoors, or if indoors then not more than 5 or 6 hours a day & capable of being done partially at home.'[47] Sir Charles Lyell, a loyal friend to Wallace, had died in 1875, so Arabella Buckley turned instead to Darwin. If people knew that Wallace wanted only some 'modest' kind of work could not Hooker or Lubbock think of some way of putting his 'great Natural History power' to good use? She felt he ought to have something, and 'could think of no one so good as yourself to whom I could say so'.[48] Darwin responded warmly. A job was unlikely, 'but a Government pension might perhaps be possible'. Darwin, as usual, indicated initially that he was not the best person to help – 'aid ought to come from someone who can see and sound many persons' – but he would do his best: he would ask Hooker's advice, as he had done on so many occasions. By the same post he wrote to Hooker, suggesting that a 'fairly strong claim might be made out', 'especially if an influential man like yourself could say a word in his favour'.[49]

Hooker's reply was acidly negative. Wallace had 'lost caste terribly'.

Hooker cited his spiritualism, and his advocacy of Barrett's paper at the British Association, 'done in an underhand manner'. (There was nothing 'underhand' about it, unless Hooker was referring to the fact that Wallace, a spiritualist, gave his casting vote to allow the paper to be read: the controversy rumbled on in a very public way for over a year, with Wallace and William Carpenter as the chief antagonists.) Then there was Wallace's conduct over Hampden, 'taking up the Lunatic bet about the sphericity of the earth, & pocketing the money', a course of action that was 'not honourable to a scientific man, who was certain of his ground'. (Wallace later described his own behaviour as 'an ethical lapse', and 'the most regrettable incident in my life'. He lost financially, but had, initially, 'pocketed the money'.) How could a man ask his friends to sign such an application? 'Added to which Govt. should in fairness be informed that the candidate is a public & leading Spiritualist!' There was, in any case, little chance for a man 'not in absolute poverty', Hooker argued rather inaccurately, considering that he had just helped secure a pension for James Joule; and, after all, he added cuttingly, 'Wallace's claim is not that he is in need, so much as that he can't find employment.'[50]

Hooker's litany deflated Darwin, at least temporarily. His letter was 'conclusive': 'What a mistake & mess I shd. have made had I not consulted you.' Hooker was quite right: what he said about spiritualism '& especially about the bet, never once crossed my mind'.[51] It was all hopeless, he reported to Miss Buckley, who replied perceptively that she had always feared that 'Mr Wallace's want of worldly caution might injure him'. The next day, Hooker learned directly from Wallace that the Corporation would not have him for Superintendent of Epping Forest.

Hooker, who had succeeded his own father effortlessly at Kew, seems strangely unsympathetic to Wallace's predicament, but it is an interesting example of the way in which Wallace's transparent enthusiasm for spiritualism, and his general naïvety, disadvantaged him. Perhaps Hooker recalled Wallace's own impatience at Hooker's public reticence over natural selection, and its implications. Perhaps Wallace's persistent requests – and Wallace could be very persistent – over Epping Forest had irritated him. Wallace seems to have been serenely unaware of Hooker's refusal. In July, he sent him two chapters of *Island Life*, which were very dependent on Hooker's work on New Zealand and Arctic flora: he did not like to bother him, but could he recommend a botanist who might check the proofs?[52] Hooker duly responded, with valuable corrections and suggestions, and in August Wallace sought Hooker's permission to dedicate the book to him, a wonderfully disarming gesture.

With his new book almost complete, Wallace had a little more time to sort out his domestic life. There was some money put by from the sale of the Dell, and now that he knew the outcome of the Epping Forest decision, he decided it would be cheaper to build than continue to rent. His requirements did not change: a ridge with a view, enough land for a good-sized garden, easy access to a main-line train service. He bought a plot of building land at Frith Hill, on the outskirts of Godalming. A cousin of his mother, Miss Eliza Roberts, learning of his difficulties, gave him the £1000 she intended to leave to him in her will, and the interest provided a bit of a buffer. Even so, with two children to educate, he badly needed a more regular source of income than the odd guineas brought in by articles in *Science for All*, or the occasional commission such as his volume on Australasia for Stanford. Scientific books might add to his reputation, but they did little for his bank balance, although he did receive a £50 advance from Harper's for the American edition of *Island Life*. He sifted through his dwindling assets, and sold off some surplus books to a dealer in the Strand. Then there was a collection of bird skins from his South American expedition. He wrote to Sclater, at the London Zoological Society: did he know of someone who was beginning a collection? If not, they would go straight to Stevens's auctions rooms. Sclater asked for a list: 311 specimens, and 250 species. Wallace packed them off. He was hoping for £25, 'but if you really think they are not worth that, I must accept your valuation'.[53] He was in no position to bargain.

Darwin, meanwhile, had not forgotten Wallace, in spite of his initial recoil in the face of Hooker's scorn. He sounded out first Lubbock and then, in October 1880, Huxley. Both were positive, and Huxley even volunteered to 'endeavour to talk over' Hooker and William Spottiswoode. Darwin wrote again to Miss Buckley: he needed some facts about Wallace's present circumstances, and biographical details to help him draw up a memorial for the government; Wallace, she reported, confessed that a pension would be 'a *very great relief*' – 'if men such as Darwin & Huxley think I may accept it I suppose I may'.[54]

Darwin set to work, and drafted a memorial for Huxley's commentary. Huxley's original suggestion was that a petition to Gladstone from Darwin alone would be sufficient; Darwin disagreed, and his view prevailed. Hooker was the key. In November, *Island Life* was published, with its dedication 'as a token of admiration and regard' to Hooker 'who, more than any other writer, has advanced our knowledge of the geographical distribution of plants, and especially of insular floras'.

Island Life examined animal and plant dispersal and speciation, investigating how different kinds of islands – oceanic and continental, ancient and recent – had been colonised, and adding to the dimension of geological change the particular climatic impact of, for example, successive ice ages. So many of the complex problems that naturalists had grappled with were clearly discussed and, just as he had done with geographical distribution of animals, Wallace combined a lucid synthesis of existing fact and theory with challenging speculation. 'Quite excellent,' wrote Darwin. '[It] seems to me the best book which you have ever published.'[55] Wallace had cast his net wide, and acknowledged the assistance he had received from many sources. Even so, Asa Gray and William Thiselton-Dyer both wrote to rap his knuckles. 'The close of your chapter VII . . . would so completely serve as an abstract of the gist of a published lecture of mine, which you once did me the honour to commend, that I should have been pleased if the coincidence of view had been referred to,' commented Gray acerbically.[56] Thiselton-Dyer, the Assistant Director at Kew and a good friend, was equally brusque. 'If I had had your lecture before me when writing the last chapter of my book,' Wallace replied, 'I should certainly have quoted you in support of the view of the northern origin of the southern flora by migration along existing continents . . .' His view had been arrived at quite independently, drawing on the facts of Sir Joseph Hooker and George Bentham.[57] The next month he offered Thiselton-Dyer a few artefacts for the Kew Museum, as a peace offering: a pandanus-leaf sleeping-mat from New Guinea, a large piece of bark cloth from the Moluccas, and a bamboo harp from Timor.[58]

The publication of *Island Life* could not have been better timed. Hooker was genuine in his praise for the book, and re-echoed his August commendation in a letter to Wallace – 'you have brushed away more cobwebs that have obscured the subject than any other author' – while questioning his comments on the Bahamas. Repeating his approval to Darwin, he added, 'That such a man should be a Spiritualist is more wonderful than all the movements of all the plants.'[59] Seizing the moment,

Huxley made his approach. On 26 November, Hooker wrote again to Darwin, reporting that his views on the pension memorial had changed. The bet, in Huxley's interpretation, 'tells all the other way' – Huxley believed Wallace gave the money to a charity. (This was a generous piece of misinformation.) There remained only the spiritualism – 'which should not I think be an objection to urging his claim, – though I am doubtful as to whether it should not be mentioned privately to the Minister'. The accusation about 'underhand' behaviour at the British Association was no longer, apparently, an issue.[60] Hooker's consent smoothed the way. 'I cannot see that there is the least necessity to call any Minister's attention to spiritualism,' wrote Darwin to Huxley; 'or to repeat (what you said) to Gladstone – that Spiritualism is not worse than the prevailing superstitions of the country.'[61] Wallace's spiritualism was a matter of public knowledge; all the same, his writings on the subject formed no part of the application.

The memorial took shape, the list of signatories was agreed, and Darwin set to work to secure them, sending addressed envelopes with notes, one inside the other, to speed the process: Spottiswoode, President of the Royal Society; Allman, President of the Linnean Society; Flower, President of the London Zoological Society; Lord Aberdare; Ramsay, Director of the Geological Survey; Gunther, Lubbock, Sclater, Bates, Hooker, Huxley, Darwin. Darwin seemed totally preoccupied by his mission; no time should be lost, he urged his scientific friends; 'I feel a very deep interest in the success of the memorial.' What about the Duke of Argyll, a member of Gladstone's cabinet, and a scientific writer, although an anti-evolutionist? 'The D. of Argyll, hurrah, has written most civilly . . . to say that he highly approves of pension for Wallace.'[62] Darwin was quite prepared to lead a deputation to the Prime Minister in person, but the final strategy agreed on was to send the memorial with a covering letter. The deed was done, Darwin informed Arabella Buckley on 4 January – 'I hardly ever wished so much for anything in my life as for its success' – 'but as my boys would express it "it has been an awful grind" – I mean so many letters'.[63] Two days later Gladstone wrote to Darwin: 'I lose no time in apprising you that although the Fund is moderate, and is at present poor, I shall recommend Mr Wallace for a pension of £200 a year.'[64] Now Darwin could break the news to Wallace: 'twelve good men' had signed the memorial; he hoped it would give him 'some satisfaction to see that not only every scientific man to whom I applied, but that also our Government appreciated your lifelong scientific labour'.[65] 'Hurrah, Hurrah – read the enclosed,' Darwin rejoiced to Huxley: wonderfully handsome, Gladstone had backdated the pension to July 1880.[66] Wallace heard the news on his fifty-eighth birthday: 'It will relieve me from a great deal of the anxieties under which I have laboured for several years.'[67] He sought Darwin's advice on the etiquette for thanking both Gladstone and his twelve supporters. Learning from Miss Buckley and Huxley of Darwin's key role, he wrote again, more personally: 'I must again return you my best thanks, and assure you that there is no one living to whose kindness in such a matter I could feel myself indebted with so much pleasure and satisfaction.'[68] It had been a long campaign, and Darwin's generosity and persistence had triumphed. Wallace would never be totally free from financial constraints – he was too fond of building for that – but the quarterly payments of £50 provided a reliable safety-net for the next thirty-three years.

12   The Big Trees

With the security of the Civil List pension, Wallace could relax. He was
fifty-eight, and he had no major idea for a natural history book to follow
Island Life, and no gaping hole in his finances to make him think of one.
Nutwood Cottage went up rapidly in its half-acre surrounded by hazels and
oaks, on the ridge of Frith Hill, giving lovely views to the west. The soil,
Wallace noted with anticipation, was lower greensand, with a useful surface
layer of leaf-mould, and in the small garden and greenhouse the Wallaces
managed to fit in more than a thousand plant species. A few hundred yards
away was Charterhouse School, where they found pleasant friends,
including one or two chess opponents such as J. W. Sharpe. Hampden
surfaced, and distributed leaflets wholesale calling Wallace every kind of
scoundrel, but no one seemed to pay much attention. Charles Hayward, his
old Neath friend, was living close by with his nephew, whose children were
much the same age as Will and Violet. William Allingham, the Irish poet,

and his wife Helen, the painter and illustrator, moved into the neigh-bourhood, to Witley, the same year; and Gertrude Jekyll was laying out her garden at Munstead Wood a few miles away. It might have been the moment to retire to a more private pattern of life.

Instead, Wallace found a new subject, or series of subjects: land reform, and, specifically, land nationalisation, which he focused on as the key to social reform and therefore to social progress. The question of the ownership of the earth had never been far from his thoughts, ever since Spencer's *Social Statics* and its discussion of 'The Right to the Use of the Earth' had impressed itself on him in the interval between the Amazon and the Archipelago. Throughout his travels in the East, his interests were roused by the various systems of land ownership and cultivation he encountered, and he toyed with the need to balance individual freedom with collective benefits, and the need for evolution and development. His clarion call at the close of *The Malay Archipelago* prompted a response from John Stuart Mill, and at Mill's invitation he joined the Land Tenure Reform Association: Wallace went to meetings, and offered ideas, but the Association folded with Mill's death. Spencer's ideas, though not his solutions, remained in his mind, and many of the key issues resurfaced during the Epping Forest campaign. The fate of Epping Forest involved matters of deep principle for Wallace; but much more pressing was the Irish land problem, and the terrible injustices suffered by the Irish tenants at the hands of their landlords during the agricultural depression of the 1870s. In November 1880, he published a closely argued essay in the *Contemporary Review*, 'How to Nationalise the Land: a radical solution of the Irish Land Problem'.[1] It was both radical and complicated, and in it Wallace sought, as so often, to maintain a balance between the rights of the individual and the rights of society. He suggested that an individual could possess land temporarily, but that the state should acquire the ground ownership, while the buildings and fittings, the value added, remained the property of the tenants, and could be sold. The ingenious pattern of proposals caught the public attention, and Wallace found himself besieged by correspondents. The following year, the Land Nationalisation Society was formed, with Wallace as its first, if slightly reluctant, President.

Land reform, expressed in its most urgent form within the context of Ireland, dominated social thinking during the 1880s. The economic slump of 1879, unemployment, rising population despite a quarter of a million emigrants a year, brought the underlying structure of property into sharp focus. Lady Bracknell's comments – that 'land has ceased to be either a profit or a pleasure. It gives one position, and prevents one from keeping it up' – offers a retrospective lament for the old land-owner order; and the socialists seized on land nationalisation as a first principle. Wallace was drawn to the topic like a moth to one of his own lights. He attended meetings, contributed to policy, decided that there was no satisfactory introductory handbook to the subject, and settled down to supply one. 'Land Nationalisation: its Necessity and its Aims' gave, in his own words,

> the only general account of the evils of our land system as it exists in England, Ireland, and Scotland; a comparison with other countries or places in which a better system prevails, together with a solution of the problem of how to replace it by the only just system, without any confiscation of property or injury to any living individual.[2]

This assault on the topic was highly characteristic, containing most of the Wallace trademarks: an uncompromising analysis of the situation from a moral standpoint; the contrast between Britain and examples of other systems, drawn largely from Europe, where they ordered things better; and a simple solution which could rectify the injustice without anyone suffering, as a result of which the whole country would benefit, morally and in terms of a better quality of health and life. Henry George, the American economist, arrived in England in 1881, with the reputation of his book *Progress and Poverty* preceding him. Wallace met George, and warmed to him, and George spoke at a number of land nationalisation meetings. George's book was immediately added to Wallace's collection of sacred writings.

He even attempted to convert Darwin to his new enthusiasm. Had he read *Progress and Poverty*, he enquired, 'the most startling novel and original book of the last 20 years' – since *The Origin of Species*, was the implication; it would be as influential as Adam Smith.[3] Darwin remained, as always, polite and equivocal: 'I read many years ago some books on political economy, and they produced a disastrous effect on my mind, viz. utterly to distrust my own judgement on the subject and to doubt much everyone else's judgement.' All this delving about in social matters was difficult – too difficult, he implied. He hoped Wallace would not 'turn renegade to natural history', even though he supposed that politics were 'very tempting'.[4] While Wallace dabbled in social science, and socialism, Darwin, as though to prove his point, published his latest and last book, on *Worms*. In April 1882, he died at the age of seventy-three, and was buried in Westminster Abbey. Wallace, 'that perennial afterthought in the Darwinian story',[5] brought up the rear as a pall-bearer, following Spottiswoode, the President of the Royal Society, and Lubbock, the President of the Linnean, Hooker and Huxley. Darwin, who had lost his Christian faith but was content to call himself an agnostic, was given the fullest national recognition by Church and State; and every pulpit and newspaper column proclaimed reassurance that his theories were quite compatible with orthodox religious faith. Wallace, following the coffin, must have reflected once more on his own role in the affair, and on his own sharply differentiated intellectual position.

One of the benefits of the Epping Forest business was his growing friendship with Raphael Meldola. He stayed at Meldola's when he needed to spend a night in London, happy to play chess with Meldola's mother if his host was busy. Meldola often came to Godalming for the weekend, and he and Wallace spent a delightful week at Lyme Regis, hunting for fossils with Will. He was even lured down as a spare man for social occasions: 'I am desired to ask if you will like to go with Mrs Wallace and Violet to Mrs Haywards on Tuesday January 19th as Mrs H. is going to have a <u>crush</u> with <u>dancing</u> . . .'[6] The friendship continued after Meldola's marriage, and Meldola never wavered in his admiration and support for the older scientist.

One might assume that the death of Darwin would release Wallace to pursue his own lines of scientific enquiry; it seems to have had the opposite effect. At the end of the decade, he would produce his own tribute, with his book on Darwinism. But, this apart, he wrote very little on science or on natural history during the 1880s, with the exception of reviews. Land nationalisation ruled his thoughts. For whereas Darwin or Spencer preferred to place faith in the laws of natural selection, leaving them to work themselves to fruition in the process of time, and Huxley trusted that improvement and progress would eventually flow from better education, Wallace believed in the possibility of rapid social evolution. To him, it was all so simple. Man's higher nature allowed control over natural selection, made it possible to give scope for individual fulfilment while altruistically attending to the rights of all. Give everyone in the country an acre, and a million people would be lifted from poverty to happiness. 'Surround the poorest cottage with a spacious vegetable garden, with fruit and shade trees, with room for keeping pigs and poultry, and the result invariably is untiring industry and thrift, which soon raise the occupiers above poverty, and diminish, if they do not abolish, drunkenness and crime,' he wrote in 'The "Why" and the "How" of Land Nationalisation'.[7] There is a disarming naïvety in his 'catch-all' proposals: 'The question of house property in towns cannot now be discussed,' he commented, referring his readers to an appendix in a new edition of his book. But his analysis of the problem is direct, stark, uncompromising, as he sets out the terrible facts about the Irish injustice, the Highland clearances, or the desperate condition of the English poor. The debate rumbled on, and the issues would be redissected in the meetings of the Fabian Society, and in the early formulations of British socialism. Wallace shared many concerns and idiosyncrasies with Bernard Shaw – among them, a contempt for official statistics and a distrust of vaccination – but he lacked Shaw's wit, and mobility of mind. At this point, Wallace placed complete faith in his own programme of land reform; all other good would follow, once it was implemented. The yellow vans of the Land Nationalisation Society quartered the country, and its lecturers spread the word, patiently educating the masses 'in the certainty of a future and not distant success'.[8]

A similar conviction attached to his beliefs in spiritualism, as demonstrated in his conversations with Tennyson, that other great Victorian interrogator of the meaning of life. William Allingham was the link between Wallace and Tennyson. Allingham, a better conversationalist than he was a poet, was a close friend of the Carlyles and the Tennysons, and moved apparently effortlessly in literary and artistic circles: the Burne-Joneses and the Morrises, the Holman Hunts and Bodichons and Brownings opened their houses and their intimate thoughts to him. His diaries have spontaneity and vividness, based on his eye and ear for significant detail, and give a strong sense of the flow of everyday life and the preoccupations of his subjects. According to Allingham, these included a great many conversations about God, and the afterlife – perhaps he brought up the subject; but eternal truths were never far away from the thoughts of Tennyson or Carlyle. For example, he records Carlyle speaking about Darwinism in 1878:

'I don't care three ha'pence for the Darwinian Theory.' By and by he said, 'It is impossible to believe otherwise than that this world is the work of an Intelligent Mind. The Power which has formed us – He (or It – if that appears to anyone more suitable) has known how to put into the human soul an ineradicable love of justice and truth. The best bit for me in Kant is that saying of his. "Two things strike me dumb with astonishment – the Starry Heavens and the Sense of Right and Wrong in the Human Soul."

'These physical gentlemen ought to be struck dumb if they properly consider the nature of the Universe.'[9]

In those views, Carlyle was not far from Wallace's own position, as he straddled the gap between being a 'physical gentleman' and a believer in Intelligent Mind, an afterlife, and perfectibility.

Allingham and his family visited the Wallaces in August 1884, and their children raced about with Will and Violet while Wallace showed off his garden – the Californian tulip, the Canadian lily, three kinds of eucalyptus. Then they sat under a tree and the talk ranged through spiritualism, apparitions and mediums, and Wallace gave an account of the state of spirits in the next world. He asked Allingham if he 'visualised' his thoughts: '"Yes, always." "I do not at all (he said) – my mind has only thoughts." Then he spoke of Galton's division of all minds into the visualising and non-visualising class.'[10] Allingham reported Wallace's conversation to Tennyson, and later in the year escorted Wallace by train from Godalming to Haslemere in response to an invitation – something of a royal command – from the Poet Laureate, who had been made a peer earlier that same year. Hallam Tennyson met them with the pony carriage at the station, and drove them to Aldworth. After lunch, and an inspection of the conifers in the grounds, they settled down in the study.

W. gave details of table-rapping, table-prancing, and so forth, his own experiences and other people's. He never doubts any statement whatever in favour of 'Spiritualism', and has an answer to every objection. 'Maskelyne and Cooke do wonderful things.' – 'Yes, partly by the help of mediumship.'

'The "Spirits" often give foolish and misleading answers.' 'Yes, as might be expected; that only proves them to be human beings.'

W. said it was absurd to suppose that Matter could move itself. I ventured to remark that Matter, so far as we can penetrate, does move itself, indeed is perpetually in motion.

He rejoined that in table-rapping etc., the phenomena were manifestly governed by an intelligence like our own. The means of communication between the Unseen World and ours were few and difficult.

Here Tennyson said, 'A great ocean pressing round us on every side, and only leaking in by a few chinks?' – of which Wallace took no notice, but went on to describe instances of spirit-writing on slates, by Slade and others.

Then the conversation moved to politics, where marked disagreements with Tennyson were only too probable. Wallace, rather tactlessly, lambasted the House of Lords and the absurdity of the hereditary principle, denounced the purchase of the Duke of Marlborough's Raphael with public money as 'scandalous' – 'let wealthy men buy and present them to the nation if they think fit' – and, on the question of Egypt, argued that the Mahdi should be left alone – 'He is perhaps a great man, and at all events we know no harm of him,' to which Tennyson replied, 'I know no good of him.' They shifted on to *Tropical Nature*, safer ground, which Tennyson had read, and Tennyson declaimed a passage from 'Enoch Arden', so Wallace recalled, in his 'fine, deep, chanting voice'. Tennyson wanted to know if the palm trees could be seen rising distinct above the rest of the forest.

W. – 'Yes, on a hillside.'
'What colour are they?'
'Rather light – grey-green.'
'Is an expanse of tropical forest *dark*, seen from above?'
'Not particularly; less so than an English woodland.'
T. 'Then I must change the word "dark".'[11]

Tennyson took a close interest in scientific ideas. According to Wilfred Ward, Huxley once commented that Tennyson's 'grasp of the principles of physical science was equal to that of the greatest experts'. His knowledge of Wallace's writing was not confined to his curiosity about spiritualism. He often spoke of Wallace's genius, and was 'disposed to think his conclusions more exact in some respects than Darwin's'. 'Wallace pointed out that man has a prospective brain – that he has faculties in excess of his physical needs. This would show that you can't account for his higher faculties by natural selection.'[12] A few weeks after his meeting with Wallace, Tennyson was still talking about him. 'Wallace says the system he believes in is a far finer one than Christianity: it is Eternal Progress – I have always felt that there must be somewhere *Some one who knows* – that is, *God*. But I am in hopes that I shall find something human in Him too.'[13] Tennyson, shocked by the early death of his friend Hallam, had clawed his way back to a belief in immortality only to have it rocked by the idea of natural selection in its Darwinian form; two years after his discussions with Wallace, and following the death of his son Lionel, he went to a seance, hoping to receive some kind of message from him. For individuals like Tennyson, Wallace's ability to reconcile conviction about natural selection with belief in a spiritual dimension was both welcome and reassuring. Allingham records Tennyson's rather different encounter with a scientist at the cutting edge:

> Gladstone and Tyndall were sitting at my table, Gladstone on my right hand, Tyndall on my left. Tyndall began talking in his loose way about 'This Poem – or Poetic Idea – God.' Gladstone looked at him and said with severity, 'Professor Tyndall, leave God to the Poets and Philosophers, and attend to your own business.' Tyndall fell quite silent for several minutes.[14]

Wallace's spiritualism might have been a disqualification so far as men like Hooker were concerned; for Tennyson and Gladstone, it was a sign of grace.

Civil List pension notwithstanding, Wallace was not finding it easy to manage on his income. Nothing substantial in the way of 'extras' had come his way since *Island Life*, with that £50 at the end of December 1880 as an advance in royalties from Harper's for the American edition. *Australasia*, a volume in Stanford's Compendium of Geography and Travel, which he edited, brought him in some £10 a year in royalties. But there was little else of any substance: articles and talks on land nationalisation and vaccination were public and unpaid duties; and for much of 1884 an inflamed retina made reading and writing painfully slow. Typically, 'disgusted with the utter nonsense of many of the articles on the subject in the press', he took up the challenge of competing anonymously for a prize of £100, offered by

Pears for the best essay on 'The Depression of Trade'. The judges were impressed, but did not recommend his entry for the prize as they disagreed with the remedies suggested. Macmillan's agreed to publish it.[15] The title says it all: 'Bad Times: An Essay on the Present Depression of Trade, tracing it to its Sources in enormous Foreign Loans, excessive War Expenditure, the Increase of Speculation and of Millionaires, and the Depopulation of the Rural Districts; with Suggested Remedies' – all Wallace's bugbears and panaceas rolled into one seemingly unanswerable argument. It was widely noticed, but brushed aside because of Wallace's uncompromising involvement with land nationalisation: a little plaintively, he recalled that the *Newcastle Chronicle* declared it 'the weightiest contribution to the subject made in recent times'.

But what to do about his own bad times and speculative losses? One useful source of additional income was lecturing. A lecture might bring in ten guineas, plus travel expenses, and he was building up a repertoire of natural history topics, as well as the occasional social issue: he claims not to have liked the process, but he was clearly extremely effective, with his great gift for making complex issues accessible and intelligible. He lectured widely and regularly during the 1880s, sometimes as part of a regular public series, occasionally at a college or school, such as Rugby or Harrow. In 1886, he was invited to Boston, to give a series of lectures at the Lowell Institute (he had met the American Ambassador, James Russell Lowell, at Darwin's funeral); and there was another invitation lying on his desk, from Melbourne – perhaps he could combine the two.

He researched the matter thoroughly. He cross-questioned other experienced lecturers, like Gerald Massey and the Reverend J. G. Wood, a Fellow of the Zoological Society. He wrote to Edmund Gosse, who had worked the American circuit successfully. Should he employ an agent, as Massey suggested? Massey recommended giving 'only <u>one</u> or <u>two</u> lectures in each town, as ensuring by far the <u>largest returns</u>, – this is a point of <u>special importance to me</u> as it is only the prospect of realising a considerable sum that would induce me to undertake the risk & fatigue of such a tour'. Could he squeeze in one or two public lectures in Boston as well as the Lowell series? What about the Redpath Lyceum Bureau as an agency? 'Having a very delicate throat & being very sensitive to chills, I must avoid the Eastern Winter, & my idea was to lecture if possible in October to mid of Nov. in the East, then go south & by Southern route to California.'[16] Gosse was reassuring. Wallace looked at his outgoings: £66 a year to the Dorking Building Society, twelve guineas a term for Will's school fees, now that he was starting at Cranleigh.[17]

He wrote to the Lowell Institute, accepting, and settled down to write some more lectures, one on 'The Darwinian Theory', and three others on aspects of colour in animals and plants. He needed colour slides and diagrams, and new – and warmer – clothes for the eastern winter from which he found there could be no escape. He tried the slides out on the Charterhouse boys and masters, and tested out the opening lecture, illustrated by diagrams, at Loughton to the Epping Field Club.[18] It was a crowded few months. He dashed off an article for the *Fortnightly*, a salvo aimed at George Romanes, just in time for its publication before the British Association met at Birmingham – 'I <u>think</u> I have shown the entire fallacy of his whole argument', he informed Meldola, who was engaged on a parallel response for *Nature*; he hoped Meldola would hold a brief for him at the Association. Romanes argued that species were 'distinguished <u>generally</u> by <u>useless</u> characters', a doctrine anathema to Wallace. He wrote his paper to expose 'the great presumption & ignorance of Romanes in declaring that Nat. Select. is not a Theory of the Origin of Species'. Romanes was posing as the successor of Darwin, and this should be stopped 'before the press and the public adopt him as such'.[19]

Wallace sailed from Tower Hill, London on 9 October 1886, and a week later recorded with relief the first fine day: a cold and disagreeable passage on a rather slow steamer, chosen so that he could have a cabin to himself at a moderate price.[20]

He arrived in New York on Saturday, 23 October, and went the next day to see Henry George, attending one of his public meetings on Monday. He just had time for a trip up the Hudson, to marvel at the Palisades and enjoy the autumn colours, before travelling north to Boston, where he installed himself in Quincy House, at a dollar a night. His first few days were extremely busy: seeing his prospective agent, Williams, being interviewed, testing his diagrams and slides at the Institute. His first lecture was on 1 November: 'full audience', he recorded. He was launched, and could begin to relax, to play chess, to receive and pay calls. The following weekend he was out at Wellesley, where William Denton had been a professor, to inspect his geological collection and his New Guinea birds. 'Stove in every room – 2 o'clock dinner chickens fried – potatoes, & preserved fruit. Jam.

took no other meal! gave me some tea!' Then back to Boston by eight the next morning, to put up slides and prepare for the evening's lecture on Oceanic Islands – 'not quite full owing to President's reception'.

Wallace's American journal is a slightly reticent document, more a record of events than a commentary, and lacking, for the most part, in the sense of wonder and in the vividness of detail that permeates his Archipelago notebooks. Absent, too, is commentary on the American intellectual community, and the current climate of scientific thinking. Asa Gray had arranged an evening at his home. Wallace went, stayed the night with the Grays, and talked to the guests on 'What led to my Essay'. With Gray a key though absent participant in the Linnean proceedings, there must have been some informed discussion: Wallace's only comment is 'Slept there'. He does expand when describing his visits to museums and private collections. Alexander Agassiz showed him round the museum at Cambridge – 'splendid arrangement' – 'Excellent!' 'It is a Museum!' he reported to Meldola. 'The only one worthy of the name that I have ever seen. It carries out the principles I advocated in my paper in Macmillan's Mag. 20 years ago' – and the Peabody Museum of American Archaeology was equally marvellous: the two together were well worth the journey from Europe for any naturalist.[21] He took a keen enough interest in the other institutions he visited: once his Lowell commitments were met, he had engagements at universities and colleges such as Johns Hopkins, Williamstown and Vassar, travelling backwards and forwards from Boston. But there is an undercurrent of anxiety that appears in his notes about expenses: 'bought paper & envelopes – dear'; and future bookings: 'called on Williams – no engagements!'; and in the bulletins on his health: 'Cough bad – wet compress on day & night . . .' Even his personal letters do not elaborate much on the personalities he met: 'Last night I dined in company with Dr Holmes the "Autocrat of the Breakfast Table".'

To set against the wearing life of an itinerant lecturer were the golden opportunities to talk to American spiritualists, both convinced practitioners and interested enquirers. He plunged happily into the New England spiritualist community, finding that there were more 'men of science' prepared to investigate systematically and openly. On his first weekend in Boston, he called on Ernst, the editor of the spiritualist publication the *Banner of Light*, and was soon in touch with the local mediums. The previous year a short paper, 'Are the Phenomena of Spiritualism in

Harmony with Science?', his first writing in the area since his spat with Carpenter, had been reprinted in two Boston journals, so his interest was already well known. Whereas a meeting with Asa Gray and Oliver Wendell Holmes is merely recorded, an encounter with the 'wonderful medium' Mrs Dickinson is annotated with a series of reported anecdotes presented as facts:

> Mr D. in Rome in Feb. dried some flowers, daisies & violets, to send to his wife & enclosed them in a letter. A day before the letter arrived the flowers were found on her table, & the letter arrived later, without them! Mr D. on return home identified the flowers! Envelope unbroken.

The combination of active mediums, unexpected leisure, and a community of interested intellectuals was too good to be missed. Wallace met William James on several occasions. James had been in England during 1882, when he met F. W. H. Myers and Henry Sidgwick, and took a major role in the foundation of the American Society for Psychical Research in 1884. Wallace discussed issues of research with him, and James was present at one of three seances Wallace attended with the well-known medium Mrs Ross.[22]

At the first of these, a whole series of figures materialised, including a tall Indian in white moccasins who danced and spoke, and shook hands with Wallace and others, and a female figure holding a baby: 'Went up and felt baby's face, nose, and hair, & kissed it – a genuine soft-skinned baby as ever I felt.' Wallace had already examined the room carefully, and as soon as the seance was over he inspected the wall again, which afforded 'no room or place for disposing of the baby alone, far less of all the other figures'. At the second session, not so impressive as the first though there were 'two good solid forms out together', Wallace seems to have been placed in a special position – 'I sat in the doorway'; the following day, another seance was arranged, this time with William James present. There were many forms. Wallace was especially struck by a 'beautiful draped female', who identified herself as having met him with Florence Cook in London: 'She resembled the form wh. appeared most often with F. Cook, & who had often talked & joked with me! She let me feel her ear (no ear-rings) as she had done in London.' Wallace does seem, in a mild way, to have been susceptible to the better-looking female forms; but the clincher for him on this occasion came in the shape of a rather short old gentleman with very white hair & beard, who took his hand and bowed repeatedly.

> At first I did not recognise him. But he bowed & looked pleased, not being able to speak. Then it flashed upon me that he was like the last Photos of my cousin Alg. Wilson, only older. Then the likeness both in face, figure & dress became more clear & I said 'Is it Algernon' to which he nodded earnestly, seemed much pleased, shook my hand strongly patted my face . . . The likeness was unmistakable, but I had been thinking of my father, or some other friends, Darwin, etc & so did not see it at first . . .

A spiritualist encounter with Darwin would have made history. But Wallace's account of the different stages in identifying his cousin shows clearly how someone seeking to be convinced can actively contribute to, if not lead, the process. The next day, Wallace attended a special dinner given by John Murray Forbes at Parker's Hotel. The guest list was studded with distinguished names: Oliver Wendell Holmes, James Russell Lowell, Edward Waldo Emerson, James Freeman Clarke, William James, Asa Gray, General Francis Walker, Charles Norton, Sir William Dawson: presidents of universities, professors, writers. There was a first-rate dinner, flowers in profusion, no speeches, and plenty of conversation on politics, travel, Sir James Brooke, and spiritualism. The following evening Wallace left for Washington by sleeper in a snowstorm.

For the next three months, Wallace marked time. He gave a number of lectures, for instance, 'Oceanic Islands: Their Physical and Biological Relations' to the American Geographical Society on 11 January; another in New York; and, in March, there was a scatter of engagements in Canada, when he took the opportunity of seeing the wonders of the Niagara Falls: 'Grand, but not so awfully grand as I had expected,' he told his daughter. He talked on 'The Great Problems of Anthropology' to the Women's Anthropological Society, and attended the Washington Literary Society: the reception he met – 'honour & pleasure never expected'; 'read my books all their life' – left him 'dumb!!!' He spent hours in the Smithsonian, paid a visit to the Observatory, and enjoyed evenings at the Cosmos Club. He wrote a long review of Edward Cope's *The Origin of the Fittest* for the New

York *Independent*, and calculated the profits: 'About 2900 words @ 6$ for column of 725 words shd be about 24$.' He was soon receiving invitations, from Major John Wesley Powell, Charles Nordhoff, General Lippitt. Powell was a man with whom he had much in common; he had led a nine-hundred-mile descent of the Colorado river through the Grand Canyon, was a former Director of the Geological Survey, and head of the Smithsonian Bureau of Ethnology. Wallace also enjoyed the company of Elliott Coues: Coues was Professor of Anatomy at Columbia, Secretary and Naturalist of the Geological and Geographical Survey, a noted ornithologist – and he had a keen interest in psychical phenomena. Through Coues and Lippitt he found himself welcome once more on the seance circuit.

Back in Boston, meanwhile, there was a spiritualist scandal. The Rosses were pounced on in mid-session. At a given signal, when a young man in the party was 'conversing' with a materialised spirit, he seized it by the hand and yanked it into the middle of the room. The light was turned on, a 'stalwart man' grabbed Charles Ross just as he drew his revolver, while others secured Hannah Ross, plus the 'spooks' in the cabinet: the contents of the cabinet turned out to be four boys and a little girl in different states of undress. According to the *New York Times*, close investigation revealed an 'ingenious mechanical contrivance' which operated a hidden door in the cabinet. William James – who was not present on this particular occasion – was cited as having described Mrs Ross as one of 'the wonders of the nineteenth century'. James, incensed by the way his name was used by the press, wrote to the *Banner of Light* to make his position clear, and described in detail the Ross seances he had attended, including the one with Wallace. On his first visit, he examined the walls and floors carefully, and did not see any suspicious circumstances, so concluded that Mrs Ross was 'better worth spending time upon' than any of the other 'materialisers' he had visited.

At the second sitting the sliding doors, usually kept shut, were opened, and Dr Wallace was allowed to sit just beyond them in the back room, from which the confederates, if such there were, would have to be introduced. So far so good. But when I asked permission to sit there with Dr W. *the permission was denied.* The moment the seance began a white-robed spirit came out, and did an unusual thing, namely, she drew Dr Wallace out of his seat, and into the front room, and spreading her drapery out so as to conceal the side of the doorway, and part of the cabinet, kept him there some little time. No one could see this manoeuvre without the suspicion being aroused that it was intended to *conceal the passage of one or more confederates from the back room over the doorway and under the cabinet curtain, which hung loosely along side of the doorpost.* At the end of the seance the same performance was repeated with Dr Wallace, who between while had been allowed to sit quietly in his place. The concealment of the side of the doorway was less perfect this time, and a lady who was one of the sitters tells me that whilst Wallace was up she distinctly *saw* the doorpost eclipsed from view by the *passage of the curtain, or some other dark body over it.* During this sitting a female form emerged from the cabinet with her white drapery caught above her knees. *Her legs from the knees down were clad in black trowsers,* like those in which a male spirit had the instant before appeared, and in which another male spirit appeared the instant after.

These observations, and other implausible events at a third seance, convinced James that 'whether mediumship was or was not an element of Mrs Ross's performance, roguery certainly was': 'good carpentry can make a secret door in any wall'.[23]

James's detailed comments provide a fresh perspective on Wallace's involvement; his reputation as a scientist, and his apparent readiness to believe in the phenomena, could only too easily be taken advantage of by the unscrupulous. James himself was deeply interested in the whole range of mediumship, but knew a palpable fraud when he saw one; and his account is entirely consistent with the Ross exposure at the end of January. Wallace, however, sprang to Mrs Ross's defence, writing to the *Banner of Light* from Washington. He ignored the black 'trowsers', or the full set of child spooks discovered in the cabinet, and relied on his own memory of the wall that he himself had inspected: 'The wall in question is papered down to the mopboard eight inches above the carpet, and on the opposite side it is smoothly plastered down to a four-inch board. I ask Professor James to produce anywhere a secret door *in such a wall . . .*' He even received a message about the Ross scandal at a Washington seance supporting his view. He was totally unshakeable in his beliefs, and totally lacking in objectivity: by this stage of his involvement he was no longer really interested in establishing the truth, or otherwise, of particular phenomena, but was far more intent on the philosophy and ethics promoted by spiritualism, and on the growing certainty in his mind of reunion after death. At a meeting of the Psychic Society he debated with Coues the relative merits of theosophy and spiritualism (Coues was a devotee of Madame Blavatsky): 'I claimed for our spiritualism a higher position, good discussion – till 12 o'clock. Judge Willard talked stuff – Mrs Hibbert and I showed him up!' He settled down to experience everything the Washington mediums could provide: solid objects passed through curtains, photographs, prophecies, and messages from his brother William.

But the main purpose of his visit was not being fulfilled. Every quarter, he had to provide a certificate that he was still alive, in order to obtain his pension, and he would go and call on the British Ambassador to obtain the necessary signature, to send home. 'I find I have quite forgotten to write to Mr Stanford, but I shall do so,' he confessed – there might be royalties owing to him. Washington was delightful, and the American climate seemed to suit him, but the lecture engagements, unlike the spirits, failed to materialise: 'Not having had <u>one</u> lecture here in three months I must cut,' he wrote to Annie.[24] He had been making enquiries about lectures for next season; an experienced friend told him that the failure was all owing to Williams's bad management, '<u>and the Rev. J.G.W.'s</u> [Wood's] having been such a stick at the lecturing business'. He was off to Cincinnati, then to Iowa and Kansas, and only perhaps, after that, to California – the journey would cost as much as the passage from England to America and back. If he had no lectures to sustain him on the way there, he would ask John to meet him in the Rockies. Meanwhile, he could report on a visit to the President – 'a private visit but a very commonplace one. He talked about California its wines and raisins chiefly' – and the boxes of plants he had sent off – a box to Miss Jekyll full of spring plants, and yellow dog's-tooth violets and orchids for his father-in-law: he was combing the local woods for treasures.

He left Washington on 6 April, travelling south-west through the Appalachians. In spite of his tight budget, he tried to see as much of the natural beauty and wonders of the country as he could. He stopped in the Shenandoah valley to see the amazing Luray caves – 'every form of stalactite and stalagmite it is possible to conceive'; he stayed a night in Clifton Forge in the Allegheny mountains, got on the wrong train the next morning, and spent a day of enforced leisure walking – 'fine mountain scenery range upon range like Wales but not so jagged & more wooded'; then on into the coal region of West Virginia, and the Kanawha valley, where he stayed with William Edwards – Edwards of the Amazon – whom he had not seen for forty years, when he and Bates quizzed him in London before their journey to Pará. He spent four nights with the Edwards family, inspecting Edwards's collection of American butterflies, and cross-questioning him about the economy: he liked what he saw of the miners' cottages – neat, nicely painted, with well-cultivated gardens; and the Irish, he learned, did very well, industrious, intelligent, enterprising. As workmen they were better than the Welsh and equal to the Germans. All these facts were grist to his land-nationalisation mill.

Cincinnati was the next destination. Here he could follow in the steps of Lyell, inspecting the early Indian burial mounds in the Ohio valley. As always, he found a warm welcome from people who shared his interests: scientists, naturalists, spiritualists, chess enthusiasts. He recorded lots of details about rattlesnakes – to his great disappointment, he never saw one in the wild. He gave two lectures, cleared $50 at the first, but only $35 at the university, after paying $15 for a lantern and operator. On to Indiana University at Bloomington: Dr Branner, who had worked in Brazil for several years, and knew Pará and Manaos, was his host; another lecture; few flowers to be seen, but fine red maples; notes on woodpeckers' coloration, 'white back red head very conspicuous – powerful birds & require no concealment from prey'. Parlour car to St Louis. All wood fences, no hedges: over the river Mississippi, then sleeping car to Kansas City, and up the Missouri valley to Sioux City. Three lectures there, and accommodation with a family; trips to a pork-curing establishment, a linseed-oil and cake factory, and botanising excursions up the Great Sioux river valley; wonderful plants, *Trillium nivale*, *Aquilegia canadensis*, *Viola sagittata* – another consignment for Miss Jekyll. Back to Kansas City, and west to Lawrence, for a lecture, and on to Manhattan, where he talked on Darwinism. He was halfway to California, and wrote to John to say that he was definitely coming; and to his great relief he was also able to send off a cheque for $275 to the New England Trust company. He also had an invitation to stay with the Phillips in Salina, and letters about one or two possible future engagements. He bought a copy of Coulter's *Flora of the Rocky Mountains*, and decided to enjoy himself: he saw a horned toad, smaller than the California species he had kept at the Dell, and had another highly successful botanising excursion. After a week in Salina, he headed at last for California, something he had been contemplating for thirty years. He stopped at Denver for a few hours, where he met James Baker, the Principal of East Denver High School, and was introduced by him to one of the teachers, Alice Eastwood. Colorado, Wyoming, Utah, Nevada went by, as he noted a prairie dog, a herd of small antelope like long-legged rabbits, sandstone rocks denuded into strange pinnacles, sage brush, and then, after Reno, a new climate. He embarked on the ferry at Oakland, on 23 May 1887, to be reunited with his brother John.

John had booked rooms in a 'grand hotel', the Baldwin – in fact, two bedrooms, and a sitting room, so that his brother could receive visitors, and conduct interviews. 'John looks older than I remember him, and rather scruffy!' he reported to his wife. He had put on his winter flannels again, after an attack of lumbago from sitting so long in the train.[25] Wallace was well looked after. He gave two lectures on Darwinism, which were fully attended; and he made the most of an impressive set of introductions and contacts, including a trip to the redwoods in the company of his friend Dr Gibbons and John Muir, the great conservationist. He took breakfast with Adolph Sutro, and visited Palo Alto as the guest of Senator Leland Stanford and his wife, whom he had met in Washington. (The Stanfords were spiritualists; like Wallace, they had lost a much loved son.) After a week in San Francisco, he went to stay at John's home in Stockton, where he could catch up with the rest of the family: John's wife Mary, and their children William (married now with two sons), May and Arthur. He was still lecturing – John had arranged a further two smaller-scale engagements at Stockton, and there was a return visit to San Francisco on Sunday, 5 June, for a spiritualist lecture. There were a thousand people at the Metropolitan Theatre, to hear him speak on the subject 'If a man die, shall he live again?'

The certainty of life after death was Wallace's crucial complement to his exposition of Darwinism; he believed that Darwinism without a spiritual dimension, at least in the interpretation of many of its exponents, presented an incomplete and inadequate picture of human life. In Cincinnati, he recorded of one of his meetings: 'Dr Myers became a sceptic through Darwinism & is recovering belief through Spm [spiritualism].' The answer to the question 'If a man die, shall he live again?' was not only, Wallace believed, the question of questions: its answer, in the negative or the affirmative, was calculated to determine the future welfare or unhappiness of mankind:

> If all men, without exception, come to believe that there is no life beyond this life – if children are all taught that the only happiness they can ever reach is certainly limited to their lives upon this earth, – then, it seems to me, the condition of man would be altogether hopeless, because there would cease to be any adequate motive for justice, for truth, for unselfishness, and no sufficient reason could be given to the poor man, to the bad man, or to the selfish man, why he should not systematically seek his own personal welfare at the cost of others.

To leave the matter to the teaching of contemporary science would be disastrous; doubly so, because, firstly, science taught that the world would eventually come to an end, and that the human race was doomed to destruction, and secondly, because the present hereditary influences of religious belief would gradually be eroded. The prospect was terrible: might alone would constitute right, and 'the unbridled passions of the strongest and most selfish men would dominate the world'. Happily, this hell-upon-earth would never occur, because it was founded on a falsehood. There were causes now at work to forbid 'the further spread of disbelief in man's spiritual nature' – and Wallace proceeded to set out the nature of those causes and influences, and even to explain why scientific seekers after truth were so often the advocates of disbelief, for the next hour and a half.[26] The lecture was widely reported in the San Francisco papers, and published as a pamphlet in San Francisco, Boston and Manchester, England.

His duty done, Wallace could relax, and after one more remarkable seance – 'Father and William sent message to Violet to sit – & they will communicate through her' – he headed for Yosemite with John and his niece May. There he was among the grand processes of nature, and the noble trees. He loved it all – the falls, perhaps the most beautiful in the world, the pines and firs, the flowers (he collected a great many). He went on alone to the Calaveras grove of sequoias. Of all the natural wonders he saw in America, nothing impressed him so much as these glorious trees: just as he had found at Niagara, 'their majesty grows upon one by living among them'. He spent three days, examining and measuring them, marvelling at their clean, straight stems and the brilliant orange-brown tint and silky or plush-like glossy surface characteristic of their beautiful bark. If only he could have had the management of Epping Forest . . . The big trees were like an epiphany to him, the equivalent of the jaguar in the Venezuelan forest or the birds of paradise in Waigiou. He had seen his vision, and could go home.

He returned satisfied to Stockton. There was another seance, a further visit to Senator Stanford, and a trip to Santa Cruz to marvel once more at the 'grand forest group' of redwoods. The majestic redwood and the giant sequoia were his two great wonders of the Western world, and he made them the centrepiece of a powerful plea for conservation:

> Neither the thundering waters of Niagara, nor the sublime precipices and cascades of Yosemite, nor the vast expanse of the prairies, nor the exquisite delight of the alpine flora of the Rocky Mountains – none of these seem to me so unique in their grandeur, so impressive in their display of the organic forces of nature, as the two magnificent 'big trees' of California. Unfortunately these alone are within the power of man totally to destroy, as they have been already partially destroyed. Let us hope that the progress of true education will so develop the love and admiration of nature that the possession of these altogether unequalled trees will be looked upon as a trust for all future generations, and that care will be taken, before it is too late, to preserve not only one or two small patches, but some more extensive tracts of forest, in which they may continue to flourish, in their fullest perfection and beauty, for thousands of years to come, as they have flourished in the past, in all probability for millions of years and over a far wider area.[27]

Wallace may have recalled his day in the redwoods with John Muir, who would write:

> Any fool can destroy trees . . . It took more than 3,000 years to make some of the trees in these western woods . . . Through all the wonderful, eventful centuries since Christ's time – and long before that – God has cared for these trees, saved them from drought, disease, avalanches, and a thousand straining, levelling tempests and

floods; but He cannot save them from fools – only Uncle Sam can do that.

'I have wandered for days in the glorious pine forests where grow the majestic sequoias,' he wrote to Meldola. 'Amid all the exaggerations of guidebooks & popular writers, they remain one of the living wonders of the world, perhaps more than anything else to a lover of nature, worth a journey across America to see.'[28]

Wallace's last days in California were made uncomfortable by illness: a swollen upper lip had to be lanced, and kept him in the house for a week. He caught up on his correspondence. There was another certificate to be sent off so that Annie could collect his pension, and one or two requests for lectures back in England to be answered. His health, and the lack of lucrative engagements in America, helped him make up his mind; and he found the drought, the heat and the dust of California as wearing as the long Eastern winters and springs, 'unendurable in their severity and changeability'. His final conclusion was: 'England with all thy faults I love thee still.'[29] But first he was determined to explore the Rockies properly. He had hoped that his father-in-law would come out and botanise with him; all the same, he had three weeks before he was due to speak at the Michigan Agricultural College in Chicago. He said his farewells, gave May a writing case and an amber brooch, and set off for his first stop, in the Sierra Nevada.

For this short period, Wallace reverted to field naturalist, but this time he was collecting exclusively botanical specimens. He noted the occasional animal or insect – a skunk, a parnassus butterfly – but his quarry consisted largely of flowers and mosses. The Sierra Nevada was rich in Penstemons, and he also found *Gentiana calycosa*, which he sent back to Surrey. He marvelled at the large-scale landscape, and the evidence of the 'powers of fire, water, & ice, all manifested together & beautifully illustrating their respective shares in modelling the earth's surface'; but his eyes were more occupied in scanning the plant life. He travelled east, first to Colorado Springs, from where he visited the Garden of the Gods and the Rainbow Falls, and then north to Denver. He then spent a week in the area around Gray's Peak, walking and collecting. His companion was Alice Eastwood, whom he had met on his way west. This remarkable woman, then twenty-eight, was a largely self-taught botanist, and later became Curator at the California Academy of Science.[30] From an early age, she had spent her summers in the Rockies, armed with a *Flora* of Colorado and Asa Gray's *Botany*, riding astride in a denim outfit she designed for her own comfort. Wallace's age and reputation, and the scientific purpose, gave guarantees of total respectability; it was, all the same, a slightly unconventional arrangement, as the two of them were often eating in remote miners' houses, and sleeping in mountain huts: 'Slept in clothes in dirty miner's bedding. Up at 5 fire lighting, breakfast – putting away yesterday's plants. At 7 a.m. started for Gray's Peak.' The two had a natural intellectual affinity, beyond their common love of botany: 'Consistency', Alice Eastwood would say, 'is the bane of small minds.' Here they were high in the Rockies in the alpine flowering season, and it took them two and a half hours to reach the summit, 14,300 feet: 'Magnificent day, no clouds, saw Holy Cross Mtn. Back slowly – plant collecting' – a long list of treasures. Then over a pass into a fine alpine valley with abundance of flowers, and down through woods – no path, innumerable fallen trees – in a descent of two thousand feet or so to another hut, owned by an English mining engineer. More parcelling up – some species to Gertrude Jekyll, some to Backhouse's of York. 'Tired,' Wallace noted; but there was no hint of his asthma, or of anything other than delight at the riches around him. The next day they were exploring the wonderfully flowery slopes in the main Grizzly Gulch valley, and their finds included *Bryanthus empetriformis*, new to the flora of Colorado. 'Columbine superb! *Arnica cordifolia* – in yellow sheets in the woods.' The next morning they rose at six to collect *Gentiana affinis*, *Mertensia alpina*, *Parnassia fimbriata* – two more parcels for Miss Jekyll – before walking to Graymount to catch the train back to Denver. It had been a wonderful week.

As he left the grandeur of the Rockies behind, the irritants of travel and civilisation returned. The peaches bought at the station were poor and dry: 'Imported unripe – typical!' Every engine that passed poured forth a column of smoke of intense blackness and density – careless stoking, and total disregard of people's comfort. Chicago was cloudy, with mist and smoke, the buildings distressingly irregular, eight parallel lines of railroad fenced off by ugly wire fencing on the lake shore. It was as bad as London. There was one final lecture engagement, at Valparaiso, one more day's botanising, and then he headed for Canada. In Kingston he searched for *Trilliums*, and made a few purchases: 'Bought ladies' dust brush for Annie $0.50.' He was not too impressed by the St Lawrence: 'not such a perceptible fall of water as in the rapids of the Rio Negro'. At Quebec, he bought a silver scarf pin – to go with the dust brush – and enjoyed a pastry and beefsteak pie: 'the first decent domestic pie I have eaten!'

He sailed from Quebec. The passage across the Atlantic was uncomfortable; he complained of sea sickness, a congested chest, asthma. A passenger sent him some grapes to cheer him up, which were eaten by rats. It was a relief to reach Liverpool during the night of 19 August. The next morning he sorted his baggage, wired Annie, caught an eleven o'clock train, and was sitting in a fly on the way from Godalming station to Nutwood Cottage soon after five. A few minutes later he saw smoke coming from the direction of the driver, and the man's coat and trousers burst into flames: 'No more curious circumstance happened during my 6000 miles of American travel!!!'[31] He had come back with a net profit of £350, and an idea for his next project. He would expand his lectures on Darwinism into a book.

13 The Future of the Race

America influenced Wallace profoundly. In addition to the subject of his next book, it provided him with the basis for a number of lectures, which he made good use of over the course of the next three years; and he also drew on his American notes and experiences for a number of articles: 'American Museums' for the *Fortnightly*; 'The Antiquity of Man in North America' for the *Nineteenth Century*; 'Land Lessons from America', an address published by the Land Nationalisation Society. More fundamentally, it revealed to him a glaring example of the dangers of development and capitalism, of the apparent triumph of might over right, and the supremacy of the dollar. The vast continent had been settled and developed so rapidly, on a grid system, that the landscape had a 'monotonous and unnatural ruggedness', 'a want of harmony between man and nature' – particularly evident in the felling of the forests, and the use of zigzag fencing. 'Over the larger part of America,' he commented later,

250

'everything is raw and bare and ugly, with the same kind of ugliness with which we also are defacing our land and destroying its rural beauty.'[1] The Americans, he argued, inherited the evil influences of Europe: religious intolerance, which they had broadly thrown off; slavery, both black and white; and the iniquitous feudal land system, delivering the greatest of natural resources into the hands of railroad magnates and corn speculators at the expense of the toiling workers. This was all too easily understandable in terms of natural selection: those who emigrated tended to be the most energetic, independent, the best, even, of their several nations; tested and hardened by two centuries of struggle against the forces of nature and the original population, and finally by a war of emancipation, it was almost inevitable that they would develop the virtues, prejudices and even vices of the parent stock – and then the advances of science in the nineteenth century catapulted them into the mad race for wealth 'in which they have beaten the record'.[2] All his reservations about 'social Darwinism' were intensified by his North American visit.

After catching up on his correspondence and reading, and settling down to work on *Darwinism*, Wallace began to consider another move. Nutwood Cottage was becoming enclosed. New building obscured the view, a large house blocked off the south sunlight, and yet the garden was uncomfortably exposed to the wind: his asthma was bad, and he seemed to catch cold after cold. He and Annie spent their 1888 summer holiday doing some serious research into alternatives in the south-west. They looked around Penzance for a week – 'no decent houses are to be had' – and were attracted by the beautiful scenery around Monmouth, 'perhaps the most beautiful in the world' – some nice houses, with land, very cheap, but all of them far too remote from towns and railway stations.[3] They visited Tintern Abbey, and the Forest of Dean, which would be a splendid place for mothing. At Symond's Yat he had one notable entomological success:

We were walking on a broad path in the wood when on the ground before me, with wings expanded, I saw, for the first time in my life, a living <u>Purple Emperor</u>! I just stopped my wife from walking over it, then knelt down, & gently touching the tips of the wings with my outstretched fingers, made him raise them for an instant & then neatly caught him between fingers & thumb, pinned him in my hat & brought him home safely for Willie.[4]

251

This was a good omen. They moved on to Alderley in Gloucestershire. Marianne North, the great botanical painter, who had been exchanging plants with Annie for some time, had invited them to stay in her lovely cottage, once again in most beautiful country, where they coincided with the Galtons; and Miss North had made a garden in the two years she had been there which 'already seemed twenty years old'. Wallace had some good talks with Galton, he told Meldola, about variation and sundry matters – and he was pleased to see from *Nature* that he and Edward Poulton were 'having a little shindy' with Romanes. The Wallaces were very tempted by a large house in good repair at a nominal rent, with eight acres of land, an orchard, a wood, a trout stream – but there was one drawback: a derelict cloth mill in the grounds, which would have to be demolished. Miss North longed for them to have it, but it needed £500 spent on it: 'It would be splendid! But I can't,' he wrote regretfully to his sister, for once bowing to reality.[5]

Darwinism came out in May 1889. Poulton had read the proofs for him, and Wallace replied to his inevitable critique:

I am quite aware my views as to Man will be – as they have been – criticised. I have referred to Weismann's opinion further on: but I doubt if his view or yours will really account for the facts. Of course we look at the question from different standpoints. I (think I) <u>know</u> that non-human intelligences exist – that there are <u>minds</u> disconnected from a physical brain – that there <u>is</u>, therefore, a <u>spiritual world</u>. This is not, for me, a <u>belief</u> merely, but <u>knowledge</u> founded on the long-continued observation of facts – and such <u>knowledge</u> must modify my views as to the origin and nature of human faculty.[6]

As Poulton commented later, Wallace's mind was 'a continuous whole, whose varied activities influenced one another'. Wallace spared his friend the last sheet of the proofs, which would only horrify him still more.

The house search continued, closer to home first, in the country between Godalming and Portsmouth, and then a little further to the west towards Bournemouth and Poole. They found a pretty, sheltered house at Parkstone, to let with an option to buy: there were some healthy specimens of eucalyptus, and no reports of any skating for twenty years, both positive signs. They let Nutwood, and moved to Corfe View, Parkstone, in the midsummer of 1889, just after the publication of *Darwinism*. They liked the place so much that they decided to buy, extending the house and creating a fine garden. Wallace was especially excited by the prospect of growing heaths and rhododendrons in the sandy, peaty soil, though he learned by hard experience that this was not so kind to a great many other of his favourite plants. The countryside and the Dorset shoreline promised all kinds of new pleasures, being rich in fossils, and archaeological remains, while the New Forest and the river valleys extending into the chalklands of Dorset and Wiltshire offered new habitats to explore. A request to Lord Wimborne, of Canford Manor, the following spring to 'go all over the fields & woods in search of flowers' was met by a crisp refusal: the breeding season was just coming in, and considerable disturbance to the nesting would be caused.[7] The country's greatest naturalist, a fervent believer in the right to roam, had to bow before the estate's shooting interests.

At the age of sixty-seven, and with a major new project in his Corfe View house and grounds, Wallace might have decided to ease off a little from his public commitments. No major publications occupied him during the first half of the 1890s, apart from the volume of essays *Natural Selection and Tropical Nature*, which was really an amalgam of two previous collections with some added material. In February 1890, he lectured for the last time, at Sheffield and Liverpool, retiring from this lucrative sideline 'partly from disinclination and considerations of health', partly because he believed he could do more good with his pen.[8] The pen was extremely active. He continued to write on spiritualism, and land nationalisation; and he spent a long time preparing evidence to the Royal Commission on vaccination.

Wallace had been a fervent anti-vaccinationist for over a decade. He was convinced that the medical statistics in favour of vaccination were corrupt and unreliable, and his analysis of them was thorough and robust: 'Forty-five Years of Registration Statistics, proving Vaccination to be both Useless and Dangerous'. He was, in fact, invited to be a Member of the Royal Commission, but preferred to present evidence before it, insisting that, as he was not medically qualified, he would only offer comments on the figures. He became more and more annoyed and frustrated by the Commissioners, who continued to ask him medical questions, and seemed to know nothing about statistics. What really incensed him was the fact that vaccination was compulsory:

> When almost every week I read of men fined or imprisoned for refusing to subject their children to a surgical operation which they (and I) believed to be, not only useless, but injurious and dangerous, I felt impelled to aid, if ever so little, in obtaining a repeal of a cruel and tyrannical law . . .[9]

Institutionalised injustice always found a response in Wallace. Eventually, his research resulted in a pamphlet that was circulated to every member of the House of Commons before the debate on the new Vaccination Act later in the decade. His title took no prisoners: 'Vaccination a Delusion: Its Penal Enforcement a Crime, proved by the Official Evidence in the Reports of the Royal Commission'.

Human concerns, and the future of society, preoccupied his thinking, and while he continued to write for *Nature* and *Natural Science*, his articles flowed more freely into journals with broader social and political concerns, such as the *Fortnightly Review* and the *Nineteenth Century*, and, later, the *Clarion*. His September 1890 essay on 'Human Selection' for the *Fortnightly*, which contained a significant addition to his own particular version of natural selection, is a good example of his speculative thinking.[10] He accepted Weismann's position on heredity – that qualities acquired by an individual after birth could not be passed down to the next generation – and so needed to find a solution that would allow for the improvement and progress of the race, because he refused to accept either a 'brute force' theory, or that natural selection, in its Wallacean 'higher morality' form, might not operate. He examined a number of proposals, all equally unsatisfactory or distasteful to him. Galton advocated 'a system of marks for family merit, both as to health, intellect, and morals', with high scorers being encouraged by state funding to marry and breed early. This, though less objectionable than some schemes (at least as he stated it), was unlikely to be effective: it might increase the numbers of the 'highest and best', but would leave the bulk of the population unaffected. Hiram Stanley offered a much more radical solution; instead of encouraging the fittest, he proposed regulation by trained specialists, so eliminating (though no more than hinting at the method) 'the drunkard, the criminal, the diseased, the morally weak': nothing, wrote Wallace, could possibly be more objectionable, even if it might be effective. Grant Allen – 'The Girl of the Future'; 'Plain Words on the Woman Question' – offered a kind of reverse solution, possibly even more objectionable to Wallace: abolish all legal restrictions to marriage, and train girls to believe that the duty of all healthy and intellectual women is to be the mothers of as many and as perfect children as possible; they should select the finest, healthiest and most intellectual men as temporary husbands in a kind of rolling sperm-donor programme, so ensuring the continued advancement of the human race. Detestable, pronounced Wallace, because it struck at the basis of a secure family life, and promoted 'pure sensualism' (he was always sceptical about the importance of sexual selection).

In any event, he argued, all these schemes shared a fatal flaw, proposing to intervene in the social system without addressing the fact that the present state of social development was not only extremely imperfect but 'vicious and rotten at the core'. The plight of women, in particular, was appalling; a large proportion was forced to work long hours for the barest subsistence, while another proportion was forced into uncongenial marriages as the only means of securing some amount of 'personal independence or physical well-being'. Look at the society newspapers, and see how the lives of the wealthy were portrayed – look at the advertisements in the *Field* and the *Queen*, and their 'endless round of pleasure and luxury, their almost inconceivable wastefulness and extravagance' – a thousand pounds spent on the flowers for a single entertainment! And then look at the terrible conditions of millions of workers – 'as detailed in the Report of the Lords Commission on Sweating, on absolutely incontestable evidence'. If a legislature could do nothing about that mass of injustice and corruption, how could it conceivably dare to intervene in the marriage tie and the family relation? First, it was necessary to create a society based on equality of opportunity: instead of proposing land nationalisation as the panacea, Wallace borrowed the broad scheme of Edward Bellamy's Utopian novel, *Looking Backward*, a book he regarded as inspirational.[11] Bellamy's society of the future is organised along the lines of a great family, in which all comforts and enjoyments are equally shared. As in Robert Owen's vision, education is the keystone, with the fullest and best training available to both sexes until the age of twenty-one, followed by three years of industrial service, so allowing everyone to make a proper choice of future occupation; while everyone receives a common share of public 'credit', so that there is no poverty.

Here Wallace anticipated a major objection to his plan. Would not all this idealism result in a population explosion, if the normal Malthusian checks – war, pestilence, famine – were removed by a near-perfect system? There would be fewer restraints to early marriage; the population would rise, and in a few generations outstrip the food supply – and the Malthus theory would reassert itself. Wallace was ready with a raft of answers. Firstly, marriage would occur at a later average stage, partly through public opinion and education, partly because of the extended period of education and training: because 'the mental and physical powers will be trained and exercised to their fullest capacity, the idea of marriage during this period will rarely be entertained'. Secondly, most women, relieved from 'sordid cares and the struggle for mere existence', would surely delay marriage until they had had a few years experience of the world – and the fertility ratio between women of twenty-five and thirty was about 8 to 5, according to Galton. Thirdly, there would be an overall diminution of fertility: highly intellectual parents tended to have smaller families, and if everyone had their 'higher faculties' fully cultivated and exercised throughout life, there would be a slight diminution of fertility. Mental powers and moral progress would triumph over the old Malthusian laws.

But the central factor around which Wallace based his argument was the defining role of women, a factor he described as 'the agency of female choice in marriage'. Many women now married for security, rather than choice. If all women were financially independent, and had nothing to gain materially from marriage, they would exercise their choice much more carefully. It would be considered degrading to marry a man who could not be loved and esteemed. Men, in whom 'the passion of love is more general, and usually stronger', and who, in this ideal society, would have no way of gratifying this passion except by marriage, would ensure that all women had plenty of offers – and so a powerful selective agency would rest with the female sex. The idle and the selfish would be rejected. The diseased and the weak in intellect would usually remain unmarried; and anyone who showed any tendency to insanity or hereditary disease, or who had a congenital deformity, would find no partner. It would be considered an offence against society 'to be the means of perpetuating such diseases and imperfections'.

Wallace was wrestling with the same problem that had exercised him from his first formulation of evolution by natural selection: how to reconcile the idea of survival of the fittest with, firstly, the development of higher, moral, spiritual attributes, and, secondly, his belief in the improvement and perfectibility of the human race. As he phrased it in this essay, 'the survival of the fittest is really the extinction of the unfit', a weeding out, which was the way the animal and vegetable worlds had been improved. But this 'wholesome process' had been checked as regards mankind, because humanity – 'the essentially *human* emotion' – had caused us to save the lives of the weak and the suffering: an attribute antagonistic to our physical and even intellectual race development, but crucial to our moral development, making us human, rather than animal. So, how would this apparent flaw be remedied? (Wallace never doubted that all this would eventually come to pass; the alternative was too dreadful to contemplate.) First, by the elimination of poverty, and a recognition that all citizens had an equal right to their share of the common wealth; after that, the 'far greater and deeper problem of the improvement of the race' could be safely left 'to the cultivated minds and pure instincts of the Women of the Future'.

Wallace, like Darwin, grappled with his particular version of natural selection in the context of his own instincts and family circumstances. He had married late, though to a much younger wife, and had brought up two of his three children to adulthood – an example of 'intellectual' parents with a small family. The sexual drive was something he apparently discounted, at least in women; and Grant Allen's idea, of loosening the legal ties of marriage to create a free choice for women to select their temporary partners, was deeply repugnant to him, because he saw the family, in both its narrower and wider forms, as part of being human: he believed in the collective, rather than the individual. At the same time, he had always rated women more highly than men, partly because they were on the receiving end of a disproportionate share of injustice. The Dyak women did not produce more children, so he believed, simply because of the amount of hard physical labour they had to undertake from an early age; and Western women, debarred from financial independence, were forced into unequal and distasteful marriages to keep a roof over their heads. Wallace would never have expressed himself quite so freely as Bernard Shaw, but his logic is not so far from the arguments Shaw gave to Mrs Warren. Vivie Warren, however, freed by her mother's enterprise and by a Girton education, turns down love's young dream in the person of Freddy, rejects sensuality and wealth in the gross form of Crofts, and scarcely considers the womanly aestheticism of Praed, for the independence of work in a London actuary's office. Wallace's Woman of the Future would place personal desires below the collective ideals of the new society, and select, not for physical beauty, as in Darwin's theory, but, primarily, for intellectual and moral qualities. Wallace was extremely conscious of the wider implications of controlled selection and felt compelled to lay down a morally acceptable framework, to oppose the current 'artificial' processes being proposed. The question of contraception, or any other method of birth control, he preferred to sidestep in public, though he was friendly with Annie Besant. He regarded his own complex solution as inherently natural, describing it as 'by far the most important of the new ideas' he had given to the world.[12]

He had responded encouragingly to a young Finnish researcher, Edward Westermarck, who had sent him – and Edward Tylor, at Oxford – a copy of his essay 'The Origin of Human Marriage'. Wallace entered into detailed correspondence with him, invited him to Parkstone, and wrote a generous introductory note to Westermarck's book *The History of Human Marriage*.[13] He even read the proofs for him, although he had to put a brake on Westermarck's enthusiasm: 'Please do not send me 2nd proofs of your book. I will read *either* the first or the second proofs, but not both.' He made it very clear that he was not a believer in the theory of 'primitive promiscuity', and recalled his own observations in the field forty years before:

> Even the completely naked women of the Vaupés showed great sense of modesty in their *attitudes*, always turning sideways on meeting a man, and when sitting so disposing the legs as to well conceal the pudenda . . . Sexual union among all peoples occurs normally at night, and there are I believe no *people* recorded among whom it is practised *openly*, at all times, and with no concealment.

He added a cautionary postscript:

> I would add that travellers are apt to exaggerate nudity or the absence of modesty and that their statements not unfrequently apply to the *exception* rather than the *rule*.

Wallace's natural modesty put a self-censoring brake on his own writing whenever he addressed the subject of sexuality. He advised Westermarck to use the word 'marriage' at one point, rather than 'sexual intercourse', to avoid offending potential readers.

Wallace's interest in research was undiminished. It was an area of science he had never entered, but he was full of ideas about its potential. Above all, he wanted more facts about inheritance, and corresponded enthusiastically with Galton on the idea for an experimental farm. In such an institution, two major areas of uncertainty would be clarified. First,

> whether individually acquired characteristics are inherited, and thus form an important factor in the evolution of species, – or whether as you and Weismann agree, and as many of us now believe, they are not so, & we are thus left to depend almost wholly on variation & natural selection.(2) What is the amount and character of the sterility that arises when closely allied but permanently distinct species are crossed, and their hybrid offspring bred together.

He pressed for a small experimental farm, breeding animals such as hares and mice, birds and ducks and insects – and there should be plant experiments as well. What about a British Association or Royal Society grant? And what about wealthy naturalists who were members of the learned societies?[14]

In spite of Wallace's increasingly outspoken, socialist and unconventional views, public honours began to come his way. In 1889, he was offered an Honorary Doctorate of Civil Law from Oxford University. 'I have at all times a profound distaste for all public ceremonials,' he confessed to Poulton. He had far too much work to do, so it would be impossible to rush away to Oxford, 'except under absolute compulsion; and to do so would be to render a ceremony, which at any time would be a trial, a positive punishment'. The greatest kindness his friends could do would be to leave him in peaceful obscurity.[15] (Poulton did persuade him to change his mind on this occasion.) The following year he was awarded the Darwin Medal by the Royal Society, for his 'independent origination of the origin of species by natural selection'. In 1892, he was bombarded with, first, the Founders' Medal of the Royal Geographical Society, and the Royal Medal of the Linnean. 'A dreadful thing has happened! Just as I have had my medal-case made, "regardless of expense", they are going to give me another medal! Hadn't I better decline it, with thanks?' He genuinely disliked the whole business. 'Isn't it awful?' he complained to his daughter. 'Two medals to receive, – two speeches to make, neatly to return thanks, and tell them in a polite manner, that I am much obliged, but rather bored!' The medals were being presented back to back, first the Geographical, then the Linnean. He fantasised a scenario of the Tuesday programme. In the morning, there was the Horticultural Exhibition, and a visit to Bull's Orchids – much more to his taste. Next, an inescapable meeting of examiners, an annual chore he was still fulfilling. Then he would rush off in a cab to Burlington House – 'arrive just too late! Medal stolen!! Forged letter telling Council I am ill!!!!! Can't come!!! Bearer to receive it for me!!!! Great excitement!!!!! Universal collapse!!!!!!!!' He moved on to reality, with practical advice to Violet about her pending examinations at the Froebel Institute. 'Tell Madame it is absolutely necessary for success in Exams. on Wednesday & Thursday, that you have perfect mental rest on Monday & Tuesday. You may teach kids – but nothing more.'[16]

Perhaps he was just rather bored by the formal rituals of the scientific establishment; and certainly he never lost his instinctive aversion to public speaking, though he did not flinch from it when it was essential. If he had to go to London, he would rather visit old friends such as George Silk at Chapman's the publishers, or drop in to his sister Fanny's at West Brompton for tea, or wander round the hothouses at Kew. A certain edge, too, can be detected in his correspondence with official bodies, a residue of minor slights and disagreements accumulated in the past, on occasions when he might have been overlooked or bypassed. A month before the announcement about the Founders' Medal, for example, he wrote to Scott Keltie at the Royal Geographical, pleading his utter inability to send him anything special for the *Journal* about Bates, who had just died:

> I really know less than scores of others as to his life & work, though we went to the Amazon together . . . Owing to my having lived in the country for the last 25 years I very rarely met him, & therefore knew very little of his life & work in London. On the Amazon too we were only together for the first 6 months or thereabouts, & after that only met once or twice. Even as to personal reminiscence I could give hardly anything, as my memory of the details of that long-ago time are but dim, and I do not think I have a single letter of Bates.[17]

By way of commentary on Wallace's friendship with Bates, this seems remarkably ungenerous, as well as inaccurate. In fact, Wallace had already written an obituary of Bates for *Nature*, and much later expanded on his relationship with him in his autobiography, once he had retrieved some of his own letters from Bates's widow to add to the letters from Bates that he *had* preserved, so his refusal is more likely to be a gloss on his relationship with the Royal Geographical Society, whose assistant secretary he had failed to become. Overtures from the Royal Society followed. Joseph Hooker and William Thiselton-Dyer wished to propose him for fellowship, and sounded him out, a process that involved him in some tortuous semantics. 'I think you somewhat misunderstood me,' Wallace corrected Thiselton-Dyer. 'You asked me, I think, whether I had any objection to being a fellow, & of course I said, "none at all", but that did not imply that I wished to become one.' In any event, he had left it so long that it hardly seemed worthwhile, and he now lived so far away that he could never attend the meetings, and so on.[18] Hooker and Thiselton-Dyer eventually persuaded him, with a head-on appeal: 'To disassociate yourself from the Royal Society really amounts to doing it an injury.'[19] Wallace gave in, having, consciously or unconsciously, made the point that the honour might have come his way twenty-five years before. He might also have been making a private point with Hooker. Earlier in 1892 he had asked Hooker to head up a memorial, in an attempt to obtain a Civil List pension for his father-in-law; Hooker declined, offering instead to investigate buying Mitten's collection for Kew. Wallace, irritated by such coolness, was quite capable of keeping the Hookers and Thiselton-Dyers of the scientific world dangling for a while, before deciding to accept. Conscious of how he himself had been helped by Darwin, he did his utmost to reciprocate when he came across a deserving case.

In the first years at Corfe View, while Wallace was busy establishing the garden, he found it difficult to get away for more than a few days. He and Annie ransacked the garden at Godalming (Nutwood Cottage was still let), so there were lots of treasures to be transplanted. Gertrude Jekyll sent hundreds of primroses. Thiselton-Dyer invited Wallace to send in a list of plants he wanted from Kew, an invitation impossible to resist. Wallace's correspondents round the world were on the receiving end of a stream of requests: bulbs and tubers arrived in Parkstone from Australia and the Transvaal, orchids from Ridley at the Singapore Botanic Gardens. Wallace had four separate orchid houses. He battled against aphis in the greenhouse and caterpillars in the gooseberries. There was a pond to be enlarged and warmed for the water-lilies, and one of his newts, being ignorant of cement, crawled out of the water and was found dying the next morning: 'New cement is pisen!'[20] It was practically a full-time job.

Holidays usually had a botanical or geological objective. The Wallaces visited the Lake District in July 1893. They went up Bowfell, with two ponies and a shepherd as guide – 'grand rocks at top, fine!' – and took rooms in Mrs Woods's temperance hotel at Patterdale, living in luxury for six shillings a day each, and strolling about seeing waterfalls and tarns.[21] On Tuesday, 1 August, Wallace's diary records: 'Up ridge beyond Patterdale to Hart Crag & Fairfield, 2860 ft., very fine walk grand crags & valleys   down very steep to Griesdale Tarn & down Griesdale to Patterdale'. 'And when we got home, having walked 12 miles, ascended & descended about 3000 feet, & been on our legs over 9 hours we were pretty tired,' he reported to his father-in-law, who had been moss-hunting in Wales. Annie was disappointed not to find any rare ferns, and alpines were scarce; but he found *Saxifraga stellata [stellaris]*, and *Saxifraga nivalis* on the high tops, and *Alchemilla alpina* and *Thalictrum alpinum* on some rocks above Stickle Tarn that reminded him of the Devil's Kitchen in Switzerland.[22] He was delighted with the mountain scenery and the glacial phenomena that he was looking out for. (The first-hand evidence of his own eyes filled in a crucial corner in his thinking, and contributed to his influential articles on 'The Ice Age and its Work', which appeared in the *Fortnightly Review* in November and December 1893.) Then he and Annie travelled on by steamer up Ullswater, coach to Penrith, and railway to Appleby and Settle, and stayed at the Golden Lion hotel for three nights, where Violet joined them, with her new chameleon, 'a fine fellow': Violet was twenty-three, and working as a kindergarten teacher in Liverpool. Dreading Sunday and bank holiday at an inn, they took the train back to Parkstone, where *Clianthus dampieri* had a splendid head of flowers, and an Australian orchid showed pink buds, but would not open: 'Another plant of the same has seed-pods & dried flowers, but no one saw the flower! Can it be a horrid self-fertilising brute that never opens?'[23] The events of the garden filled his letters to friends and family, especially treasures such as the blue poppies or the pink water-lily. 'One bud looks as if it would open tomorrow. A little while ago the big spider appeared! sitting on a water-lily leaf, & since two or three times. This morning it is sitting on the edge of the pond with its fore feet in the water.'[24] He was content to look and wonder.

That autumn, Wallace's sister Fanny Sims died, of cancer. Distressed by her pain, Wallace paid for medical treatment and found comfort through a medium, validated by the usual kinds of question: 'Who gave her the silver Indian brooches?' 'Alfred.'[25] He had no doubt that Fanny lived on in spirit: she had loved him more than anyone else in the world, and he missed her, and his visits to her in London. His brother John died two years later in California, also of cancer, leaving Alfred as the only surviving Wallace of his generation. Violet was independent. William was in Newcastle now. He had struggled a little on his course in London, and failed to find a place with any of the London electrical engineering firms, but his father found an apprenticeship for him through a friend: £200 in advance for two years. He worked from 6 a.m. to 5.30 p.m., and received an apprentice's wages of one penny and three farthings an hour. But he liked the work, and bicycled all over Northumberland at the weekends.[26]

With both children launched on careers, Wallace was able to take life a little more slowly. In December, his old friend Richard Spruce died in his small Yorkshire cottage in Coneysthorpe, with its grand view of Castle Howard – someone else who had received rather less than his due from the scientific establishment. Of that great triumvirate of Amazon naturalists, Wallace, Bates and Spruce, Wallace alone survived.

In 1894, Wallace and Annie holidayed in Devon, where the banks and walls south of Dartmoor were smothered with ferns – 'Ma could hardly be got along'[27] – and the following year Wallace and Mitten undertook a serious plant-hunting trip to Switzerland: Lucerne, Andermatt, the Rhône glacier, Grimsel pass, Meiringen, the Aar gorge, and the Wengern, ten continuous days of fine weather among the high Alps. Nature exacted revenge for the pillaging of flowers and mosses, and Wallace and Mitten were so dreadfully persecuted by swarms of blood-sucking flies that they cut short their holiday. Annie, left in charge of the garden, received boxes of plants from the Furka pass, including two species of glorious gentians; and extremely detailed instructions for looking after them. In 1896, Wallace was in Switzerland once again, but in a rather different context. Violet had spent a summer there in 1894, with Dr Henry Lunn's family; now Lunn invited Wallace to give a lecture as part of the programme of talks he had instituted at Davos. In spite of his previous decision about lecturing, this was too good an opportunity to miss. Annie went out separately with Violet to Adelboden, while Wallace lingered in Dorset to sort out the garden and coach Kate, the orchid-sitter. Wallace received his 'very superior' tickets in a blue leather case with gorgeous luggage labels: he was travelling first class with seven others, three gentlemen and four ladies: 'Among them is Mr Le Gallienne, a minor poet, & I think a Socialist, so we shall no doubt get on. He lectures the evening before me on the absurd topic – "The Persecutions of Beauty" – and that is in the Scientific Department!'[28] He feared Davos would be an awful place, a perfect city: there were fifteen large hotels listed in his guidebook. But the old socialist rather enjoyed himself at the Hotel Victoria. His subject was 'Progress in the 19th Century'. He mischievously added 'a kind of set-off' in 'discoveries which had been rejected and errors which had been upheld' – namely, phrenology and vaccination. There were several doctors in the audience, who showed their disapproval 'in the usual way'. Wallace, unabashed, assured them they would live to see the whole medical profession acknowledge vaccination to be a great delusion. Just as he was in the area of spiritualism, he remained quite unmoved by disagreement or ridicule, and left in great good humour to spend a week with his family in Adelboden, 'the sanatorium and alpine garden of overworked Englishmen'.[29]

There was an air of fragmentation about his intellectual life at this period – the liveliness was undiminished, but lacked a sustained focus. An article in the *Fortnightly* on 'The Expressiveness of Speech' put forward a radical theory of the roots of language, extending the principle of onomatopoeia; in June 1896, he summoned the energy to write a significant paper for the Linnean, on 'The Problem of Utility', in which he took issue especially with Romanes's views: he always enjoyed a tilt at Romanes. He stayed in London, as often, with Raphael Meldola, and the day after the lecture enjoyed a leisurely breakfast with his host, who had invited Poulton, and Francis Darwin, to join them. The party sat and talked far into the morning, until Wallace rose at last to go and catch his train: 'Well, I should like to go on in this way all day!'[30] At gatherings like these, he was at his most relaxed; but this was the last paper he read before a scientific society.

He seemed to sense that his daily preoccupations were too diffuse. Violet told him off for being a poor correspondent.

If you had letters almost every day about Darwinism, Spiritualism, Vaccination, Socialism, Travelling, Dog's Tails, Cats' Whiskers, Glaciers, Orchids, &c & had books sent to you on <u>all</u> these subjects to acknowledge & read, & requests for information on <u>other</u> subjects, and other subjects, <u>and</u> other subjects – and a book to write, & a garden to attend to, & 4 orchid houses, and chess to play, & visitors to see, & calls to make, and plants to name, – and – and, and, and, &c. &c. &c., perhaps you would be a 'miserable letter-writer' too! Perhaps also, not!

Wallace would courteously reply to almost every letter that came to him, and would go to huge lengths to assist a young collector such as Frederick Birch. Because of his public profile he attracted a good many cranks and eccentrics, but only in rare cases, such as a missive from a mad Baconian, would he be moved to comment 'not worth answering'. And then here was Professor Poulton, he complained to Violet, begging him on his knees to go to Oxford next year 'to make a speech on the putting up of a statue to Darwin!' 'And to him also I have to write, a kind, careful, but positive refusal, – requiring much thought, and an additional grey hair or two to my already totally grey head!'[31] It was not, apparently, the honour to Darwin that he objected to, but the idea of a statue: quite ridiculous, and inappropriate. Darwin would have infinitely preferred an experimental breeding centre which could be established at Downe. That would be a proper memorial to his achievements. Perhaps Hooker would be a more appropriate central figure at the ceremony, he hinted with sly humour – Hooker rather enjoyed that sort of thing.[32]

Earlier in the year, he had received some predictions in a seance. One control, an old Scotch physician, told Wallace to eat fish, and assured him that he was not 'coming to their side' for some years, as he had plenty of work to do first. Another control, Sunshine, an Indian girl, was much more precise: 'You won't live here always. You will come out of this hole. You will come more into the world, and do something public for spiritualism.' He wrote her parting words in a notebook: 'The third chapter of your life, and your book, is to come. It can be expressed as Satisfaction, Retrospection, and Work.' Two months later, he received Dr Lunn's invitation.[33]

Grey hairs or not, he now found that he did have an idea for another book. Lunn had suggested the subject, and Wallace decided to expand his lecture into what became *The Wonderful Century* – complete, of course, with the failures (mesmerism, phrenology, spiritualism, vaccination) as well as the triumphs. He also made a great breakthrough in terms of his health. Albert Bruce-Joy, a sculptor, called at Parkstone: he was modelling a medallion of Wallace from photographs, and asked for a 'live' sitting. (A medallion was on a more acceptable scale than a statue; but he still had to be persuaded, and later resolutely refused to sit for a portrait.) On this occasion Wallace apologised for not looking well and explained he was suffering badly from asthma, which prevented him sleeping. Bruce-Joy recommended Dr Salisbury's diet, which, according to Wallace, was to cut back on starchy foods, 'especially potatoes, bread, and most watery vegetables', and to substitute well-cooked meat, fruit, eggs and light milk puddings. Whatever the scientific basis – and Wallace claimed that Salisbury's diet was the result of thirty years of experiment – it worked: in a week he felt much better, in a month he was well, and suddenly he was able to tackle his literary work again with all his former enthusiasm.[34]

The Wonderful Century occupied him for most of 1897, and was published in June 1898: in its turn, it spawned a popular 'reader', and a further illustrated edition. Wallace's gift for clear exposition never left him; he wrote simply, and straightforwardly, but without ever condescending to his readers. Also, because he wrote on so many different topics, social as well as scientific, he was constantly being asked to contribute articles in journals and newspapers, American as well as British, and to offer thoughts for the coming century as the 1890s advanced. He remained unrepentantly controversial, protesting vehemently against the Transvaal war in the Manchester Guardian, September 1899. His public reputation continued to grow, and Macmillan's brought out a collection of his essays, Studies Scientific and Social, as well as new and enlarged editions of Darwinism and Island Life. He was more widely known now in his late seventies than he had ever been.

Family life was a continuous source of pleasure, and sometimes of concern. The garden was a joint enterprise; Annie was an accomplished water-colourist, and there were frequent visits from her parents and sisters, when they would all visit some local beauty-spot, which Annie would paint. Thomas Sims, Fanny's husband, was in financial difficulties: his photographic business was sold because of arrears of rent, and he was, Wallace told Meldola, in danger of absolute starvation in the workhouse; he was utterly unbusinesslike and had depended wholly on Fanny for all money matters. Did Meldola know of any opening for a good photographer at some scientific institution?[35] Violet came to stay in the school holidays, and letters flowed freely, in spite of her complaints, to herself and William. Wallace did not spare his advice, though he was careful not to impose his views too firmly. 'There are, I believe, a good many spiritualists in Manchester,' he informed Will, who happened to be working there, 'and a Spiritualist Society of some kind, so if you care about joining you might perhaps see something; but unless you really feel a special interest in the subject it is hardly worth while . . .'[36] When a smallpox epidemic threatened, his advice was to 'take a hot bath for about 20 minutes, then drink a half pint of tolerably strong salt and water (a small teaspoonful in a tumbler) repeat twice a day, bath & salt, & you will probably be well in two or three days'.[37] Later, William and his friend McAlpine went to America. They worked first on an electric railway near Boston, then diverted to the Adirondacks, potato-digging and house-painting. Eventually Will reached the prairies, bicycling from Chicago to Denver, and paying his way by wiring telegraph poles, with the cold freezing up his beard and moustache. His father sent him detailed instructions from the British Museum on how to skin and preserve small mammals: it would be particularly easy, too, to collect skeletons in Colorado, where the atmosphere was so dry. Buy some traps in Denver, he urged him, and practise: 'and be very careful about the labels of which you should take a lot with you, all ready with string to tie on. I should not wonder, if you get to do them nicely, & get boys or hunters to help you, you might make nearly as much as by climbing telegraph poles!' He enclosed a drawing of the kind of pliers required for stuffing skins: 'If you can't get them in Denver you might make them yourself.'[38] Violet was going to Germany on holiday, and she too was advised to collect animals for the British Museum: 'As she will have nothing to do it will be a nice occupation for her, and help to pay her expenses.'

With his energy restored, and royalties and fees coming in from unexpected directions, Wallace's old restlessness revived: what had seemed ideal at the time of purchase – location, climate, soil, prospect – began to pall. The Corfe View paradise was under threat. He no longer felt that he was in the country, as more and more new houses surrounded the property, just as had happened in Godalming. This time Wallace was in more expansive mood. The way to secure himself from new building once and for all was to buy an estate, and he floated a scheme for, as he put it, a 'kind of home-colony of congenial persons'. He and two partners, A. C. Swinton, a land nationalisation enthusiast, and Roland Shaw, began to inspect a variety of properties, 'in order to secure the advantages of a country home, in a healthy district, with picturesque surroundings, which can be permanently preserved, and within one to two hours of London'. They were ready to put in a thousand pounds each, and hoped to find enough friends to bring in another seven to ten thousand pounds. Once a suitable property had been bought, Dr Wallace, 'as being the originator of the plan and having spent much time in the search', would take the dwelling house and adjacent grounds, and then act as agent and surveyor for everyone else till the whole estate was occupied. The sites would be from two to ten acres, according to the amount invested, and the woods and wilder portions would be preserved as a natural park for the enjoyment of all the residents. Any thoughts that the scheme went against the principles of the land nationalisation society were dispelled by one of the clauses: surplus land might be sold to offset the initial investment, but any further profits would be spent for the benefit of all. The proposal was printed and circulated – Sclater at the Zoological Society received one[39] – but not enough volunteers came forward, perhaps because they felt that Wallace's own interests, however well justified, seemed to loom a little too large in this grandiose Utopian project.

One of the estates the Wallaces investigated was The Grange, near Amersham. It would cost £15,000, but then as a building estate it would be worth four times as much. They urged Violet and William to go and view it. Will, down in London temporarily, was sent detailed instructions with timetables and London railway maps, and the key stations circled in blue; or perhaps he could cycle – it was only thirty miles or so. Late in November the Wallaces travelled up to London, booked in at a hotel for two nights, and made their own visit. The house was two hundred years old: outside, there was a bowling green, a kitchen garden, an orchard, a park, and extensive beech woods – seventy acres or so. Wallace's grand plans for Epping floated across his mind as he tramped through the woods in the fog. With the open glades, and some careful replanting, there would be beautifully sheltered sites for the houses of the other shareholders in his little English paradise; and the soil was friable, a tertiary sand with little lime in it, so it would do for rhododendrons. The country round was as pretty and perfectly rural as any he knew, and owned by great estates who objected to building. 'I never expect to find a better place or a better investment,' he told Will. The owners, the Gurneys, had been immensely hospitable and jolly, and insisted on giving them lunch of cold pheasant and rabbit pie. They travelled back to Paddington, met Violet at Baker Street, saw her 'diggings', met Madame Michaelis, Violet's employer, looked over the school rooms, and were escorted back by tube to their hotel.[40] But although he was wholly convinced about the Grange's 'immense capabilities', the sums did not add up.

All through the spring and summer of 1901, the search went on, and he had almost despaired when he came upon a site only four miles from Parkstone, an old orchard of apple, pear and plum trees in a grassy hollow with good views, and only half a mile from the station. 'At last the deed is done!' he rejoiced to Violet. ' "I've met the Douglas in his Hall, – the Lion in his den!" and have come out safely. His roar was terrible! but he ended as mildly cooing as any sucking dove!' The Lion was Paterson, Lord Wimborne's 'mighty agent'.[41] Wallace secured his three acres, and Paterson's complaisance, by agreeing to pay the whole of the purchase money as soon as the conveyance was drawn up. There was an acre of grass, two beautiful bits of wood, with Spanish chestnuts and oaks and a fine old fir tree, and a view right over Poole Harbour to the Purbeck hills in one direction, and to the Old Harry rocks in the other, south and south-east. They sold Nutwood Cottage, and Wallace lost himself once more in the delights of planning a new house and garden, and supervising the building. This was work he loved, though it had its frustrations. He wanted to put up a 'true low bungalow' in wood, in Swiss-chalet style, to blend with the quiet beauty of the landscape. But Lord Wimborne and 'the authorities' insisted on red brick. The grounds required constant labour and supervision: plants were moved from Corfe View, a thousand shrubs and trees were bought from a small nursery that was closing down, and presents arrived from all over the world, including a special consignment from Sir Thomas Hanbury's gardens in northern Italy. He purchased a donkey and cart to shift clay from the site and bring in leaf mould and loam – but the donkey kicked and bit, so he had to make do with manual labour when the men could be spared from building work. He fussed over the details of the stoves, and overrode the architect by altering the line of the drawing-room chimney. Finally, and thankfully, he and Annie moved into the Old Orchard at Christmas 1902, just before his eightieth birthday.

14   The Last Orchard

Gradually, very gradually, Wallace was getting things straight in the house and garden, he reported to Meldola – 'especially in the garden which has been for a year a wilderness of clay heaps & builder's rubbish'.[1] The customary requests went out to the world's botanic gardens. He was especially keen to obtain seedlings, or seeds, of one of Marianne North's favourite flowers, the blue puya from Chile, Thiselton-Dyer was informed – and had he seen the note in the *Garden* about the rare flowering of *Nymphaea gigantea?*[2] But the site was so beautiful and the views so charming, that he was quite satisfied to replant gradually. His study was ideal, and everything about the house was picturesque and characteristic, with verandas and balconies, gables and dormer windows, all red brick and tile and white woodwork, homely but comfortable. Violet had joined up with a friend, taken a house at Wadhurst near Tunbridge Wells, and was hoping to find a few children to board and teach. Wadhurst was five hundred feet above sea level, and already Violet was feeling the benefit of the move from London. Will, still with the Houston Thompson electrical engineering firm, had been transferred from Newcastle to Rugby, which made it much easier for him to visit. Wallace himself was very well in health – better than for some years, and was looking forward to a few more years of 'fully occupied repose'.

The previous two years had been largely given over to the corrections and additions to *Island Life* and *The Wonderful Century*. Now he was free to turn to new fields, and immediately found one in the universe, or rather in its relationship to man – an original but popular subject. The house had cost a lot, and this was an attempt to clear the balance. All Wallace's subjects, however disparate they might seem, or driven by circumstances, were closely connected, first teasing out the relationship between man and the rest of animate life, and then moving on to consider the physical conditions that gave rise to life in time and space; or seeking systems to improve the ways individuals and races shared the earth's resources more fairly, so that moral and intellectual progress, and happiness, could follow. It was logical to address the bigger issues, and Wallace, who had read widely in order to include chapters on 'Spectrum Analysis' and 'Astronomy and Cosmic Theories' in *The Wonderful Century*, celebrated his ninth decade with 'Man's Place in the Universe', published in the New York *Independent* and in the *Fortnightly* and expanded into a 300-page book for Chapman and Hall later in the year.[3] For all the authorities cited – 'Professor Simon Newcomb, of Washington, assures us'; the Italian astronomer Schiaparelli 'arrives at the same result'; 'Sir John Herschel's testimony' – the article is, in essence, a philosophical, or theological, assertion of intelligent cause and design over chance, or, as Wallace puts it with his usual clarity, 'of the right and exact combination of matter and its complex forces occurring after an almost infinite number of combinations that led to nothing'. Wallace would not accept that life was accidental, because he refused any explanation whose corollary was that man would die out by the continued operation of the same laws that had allowed man to evolve in the first place. After surveying the evidence of the new astronomy, he concluded:

> Of course the relation here pointed out *may* be a true relation of cause and effect and yet have arisen as the result of one in a thousand million chances occurring during almost infinite time. But, on the other hand,

those thinkers may be right who, holding that the universe is a manifestation of Mind, and that the orderly development of Living Souls supplies an adequate reason why such a universe should have been called into existence, believe that we ourselves are its sole and sufficient result, and that nowhere else than near the central position in the universe which we occupy could that result have been attained.[4]

There was no doubt about which thinkers Wallace thought were right. The book was widely read, and went through numerous editions both in Britain and in the United States. Wallace was impatient for some 'good all-round man' to review it for one of the monthly or quarterly periodicals – 'not a specialist astronomer, as these are quite unfitted to discuss the whole subject': someone like Prince Kropotkin, whom he admired, or Lord Kelvin, who would not be afraid to form an independent judgement.[5] Four years later, Wallace pursued the theme in *Is Mars Habitable?*, a sharp riposte to Professor Lowell's book on Mars and its 'Canals': there was no room in Wallace's scheme of things for other forms of intelligent life; but he had fun in demolishing Lowell's method of argument. 'He began by thinking the straight lines are works of art, and as he finds more and more of these straight lines, he thinks that proves more completely that they are works of art, and then he twists all other evidence to suit that.'[6] He could almost be describing his own defence of certain spiritualist happenings.

Wallace the campaigner was still alive. 'Anticipations and Hopes for the Immediate Future', written for the *Berliner-Lokal-Anzeiger*, was rejected – 'too strong', Wallace commented – and appeared instead in the *Clarion*. He wrote against militarism and capital punishment, and in favour of personal suffrage and nationalising the railways; and thought always about the future: 'If there were a Socialist Government – How should it Begin?'[7] Literature, especially poetry, still spoke to him powerfully. He had ransacked his library, and badgered his friends, for suitable excerpts as epigraphs to each chapter in *The Wonderful Century*: lines from Tennyson preceded 'Geology':

> The hills are shadows, and they flow
> From form to form, and nothing stands;
> They melt like mist, the solid lands,
> Like clouds they shape themselves and go.

and A. H. Hume's chilling verse heralded 'Vaccination A Delusion':

> Today in all its dimpled bloom,
>   The rosy darling crows with glee;
> Tomorrow in a darkened room
>   A pallid, wailing infant see,
> Whose every vein from head to heel
> Ferments with poison from my steel.

Wallace championed 'Leonainie', a long poem attributed to Edgar Allan Poe – supposedly Poe's 'Farewell to Earth', transmitted through the trance speaker Lizzie Doten – which Wallace introduced in the *Fortnightly*; he had used it as his own peroration in his San Francisco lecture, 'If a man die, shall he live again?' He also returned to one of his favourite motifs, in a delightful article on 'The Birds of Paradise in the Arabian Nights', a rich blending of ideas about geography and trade, literature and myth. His own reading continued to expand in range, in spite of trouble with his eyes: astronomy, psychology, spiritualism, psychic research, religions such as Hinduism and Buddhism, education, capitalism, poverty, socialism. He bought pamphlet after pamphlet by Tolstoy: 'How much land does a man need?', 'How I came to believe', 'The meaning of life'. He acquired William Morris's *Songbook for Socialists*, Bernard Shaw's Fabian essays, Oscar Wilde's *The Ballad of Reading Gaol*.[8]

His most serious occupation, though, was his autobiography, which he began in 1904. He already had quite extensive materials to hand: he hoarded letters, notebooks, pamphlets, newspaper cuttings, copies of articles, page proofs, house plans, lists of plants, though not in a particularly systematic way. He did not possess a very accurate memory for dates, but he had clear recollections of events, and especially of feelings. He wrote off to various friends and families, asking for the temporary loan of his own letters in many cases. He enjoyed the process, and the renewed contacts. He even had a wonderful free holiday in Wales as a result, when a friend of a friend lent him a cottage – and a motor car – in the wild mountains of the Vale of Neath, one of his 'most favourite early hunting grounds'.[9] He had, of course, his own travel books as sources for his journeys in the Amazon and the Archipelago; and several of his other books recorded his personal experiences, for example *On Miracles and Modern Spiritualism*. The full title

– *My Life: A Record of Events and Opinions* – signals a certain reticence. There is a great deal about his intellectual development, and his temperament; comparatively little about his personal relationships, and almost nothing about his family. It is not an evasive book, so much as a reticent and modest one, though he does not spare himself, nor seek in any way to gloss over disappointments and setbacks, and he is frank about his shyness and his initial awkwardness in company. He seems amazingly free from resentment, and radiates the calm certainties and positiveness that stemmed from his spiritualist beliefs. He looked back on his life, and saw in it a pattern of providence, leading him step by step towards his particular contributions to the world's sum of knowledge, and ways in which he could disseminate them. The book was well received, though some notices suggested that it was much too long. In places, Wallace seems to have included just everything that came to hand, including some very early writing, such as an article on 'The South Wales Farmer'. He admitted to Meldola that when he began he did not think he would have enough to fill one good-sized volume, and so put 'almost everything in that seemed suitable, intending that it should be severely cut down before printing'; but when Arthur Waugh, the managing director of Chapman and Hall, read the manuscript he suggested the omission of only a few pages in one chapter and a few sentences in another.[10] Three years later, with advice from his son, he produced a condensed one-volume version, which gives a clearer picture of the shape of his life, and an idiosyncratic assessment of his achievements. Wallace read all the reviews, and even enjoyed the critical ones. He regaled Meldola with choice extracts, such as this paragraph in *Reviews*:

> For on many subjects Mr Wallace is an antibody. He is anti-vaccination, anti-state endowment of education, anti-land-laws, and so on. To compensate, he is pro-spiritualism, and pro-phrenology, so that he carries, as cargo, about as large a dead weight of fancies and fallacies as it is possible to float withal.

He especially liked 'antibody', and the whole paragraph was neat and refreshing – and then the reviewer went on to praise his biological and travel books as much as any of them! Wallace was feeling optimistic. The majority of notices were positive, and very fair; and the political scene was

274

beginning to change. 'The most Radical Government yet known in England, with John Burns & Lloyd George in the Cabinet, gives me a new interest in life & the hope to live a few years longer to see what will come of it.'[11]

Rejuvenated by his extended visit to the past, and the thought that the kinds of social change he had been advocating might become reality, Wallace now tackled a much postponed act of homage to his closest scientific friend, Richard Spruce. Spruce had never properly recovered his health after his fourteen years in the Amazon, and all the energy he could spare for writing went into his work on the Hepaticae. Now, with the blessing of Spruce's executor, Mathew Slater, and the encouragement of Joseph Hooker and Clements Markham, Wallace gathered up all the available material: notebooks, journals, letters, plant catalogues, maps, sketches. He bullied a grant from the Royal Society to have Spruce's letters to Hooker and George Bentham, held at the Kew Herbarium, copied, and even attempted – unsuccessfully – to track down one missing journal with the help of a medium.[12] Spruce recorded everything, in a beautifully regular hand, but he also wrote in a minute script at times, with many abbreviations, his 'hieroglyphics', as he called them. This was taxing stuff, requiring patience, and long hours, and extensive correspondence. But it was a labour of love; and through Spruce's vivid but meticulous descriptions, and his sardonic turn of mind, the Amazon years came alive again for Wallace. People and places long forgotten were recalled 'and to some extent visualised', and he recalled the formative years when he had learned his own trade, and made the preliminary sketches and frameworks for his theories. By the time the book appeared, Spruce's fellow bryologist, William Mitten, was dead. Wallace was the executor, and spent much time trying to sell Mitten's collection, for the benefit of his sisters-in-law.

As Wallace revisited his first steps as a field naturalist, both in his autobiography and through Spruce's records, the full extent of his achievements began to crystallise for other people. Wallace, in the twentieth century, was not only the popular exponent of the previous century's scientific achievement, but represented the living embodiment of its changes and developments. His steady stream of books, and his articles and letters in the intellectual and popular press, kept his name in the public eye. You might not agree with Wallace; you might think that his views on this or that were eccentric, even perverse, but that did not invalidate his contribution to mainstream scientific thinking, and certainly did not detract from the force of his personality, or the sense of his sheer humanity. July 1908 was the fiftieth anniversary of the reading of the Darwin–Wallace papers: the Linnean Society proposed a jubilee celebration, and – 'very strangely', according to Wallace – issued a medal with busts of the two great scientists, one on each side. Wallace was, naturally, invited to the ceremony, and gave an account of the events leading up to his paper: for this once, he overcame his increasing reluctance to visit London. 'I think nothing but such an occasion would have brought me,' he told Meldola, and added a postscript, 'Very Private & Quite Confidential!': 'I suppose I have to thank either yourself or Poulton for this quite "outrageous" attempt to put me on a level with Darwin! If I live through it, I shall have something to say on this point!!'[13] Poulton thought that Wallace attended from a sense of duty, and 'because it was a unique opportunity of paying homage to the mighty genius' whose name had been associated with his own.[14] Hooker, by now the only other survivor among the prime movers of the affair, was also asked to speak. 'They gave me one in Gold,' Wallace reported to his young naturalist friend Fred Birch, 'and six other Naturalists, 3 English and 3 Foreign in silver. So I was bound to go.'[15] Sir John Lubbock invited him to a breakfast, but Wallace refused politely; he had for years been obliged to adopt the plan of 'no breakfast', and 'no dinner' either, to keep off attacks of asthma and enable him still to do a little work. He wished Lubbock success with his Importation of Plumage Bill: 'To stop the import is the only way – short of the still more drastic method of heavily fining everyone who wears feathers in public' – 'with imprisonment for a second offence,' the old bird-collector added firmly, 'But we are not yet ripe for that.'[16] He duly wrote and delivered an 'address' – 'in which I glorified beetle and butterfly catching & bird collecting in the tropics [this was what Birch was doing in Guyana] as that really led Darwin & myself to the same theory'.

This characteristically self-deprecatory account does not do Wallace's speech justice. The 1908 meeting, held at the Institute of Civil Engineers, Great George Street, was a full recognition of Wallace's independent contribution. 'It is you, equally with your great colleague, who created the occasion we celebrate,' read the citation. Wallace gave his version of his own moment of vision:

The idea came to me as it had come to Darwin, in a sudden flash of insight; it was thought out in a few hours – was written down with such a sketch of its various applications and developments as occurred to me at the moment – then copied on thin paper and sent to Darwin – all within a week. *I* was then (as often since) the 'young man in a hurry': *he*, the painstaking and patient student seeking ever the full demonstration of the truth he had discovered, rather than to achieve immediate personal fame.

It was a nice distinction. Wallace went on to disclaim credit for the idea: 'No one deserved praise or blame for the ideas that came to him, only for the actions resulting therefrom.' He would accept the medal

> not for the happy chance through which I became an independent originator of the doctrine of 'survival of the fittest', but as a too liberal recognition by you of the moderate amount of time and work I have given to explain and elucidate the theory, to point out some novel applications of it, and (I hope I may add) for my attempts to extend those applications, even in directions which somewhat diverged from those accepted by my honoured friend and teacher Charles Darwin.

He was unrepentant to the last about his 'little heresy'.

Hooker followed, with an account of his own role in the original Linnean Society proceedings. He added two interesting glosses to the sequence of events, which was now available in subtly varied versions in Darwin's *Life and Letters*, and in Wallace's own autobiography. He stressed, first, that at no point did he and Lyell and Darwin meet: everything had been arranged by letter. He also pointed out that there was no 'documentary evidence' for his account beyond what Francis Darwin had produced in the *Life and Letters*: no letters from Lyell, replying to Darwin's, and none of his own 'to either Lyell or Darwin, nor other evidence of their having existed beyond the latter's acknowledgement of the receipt of some of them; and most surprising of all, Mr Wallace's letter and its enclosure have disappeared'.[17] This was a slightly controversial statement to make, at an official event held to honour Darwin and Wallace. The letters sent *by* Darwin had for the most part been preserved, and published; why not Hooker's own, and Lyell's, and Wallace's? It sounds like an open question to Francis Darwin – a question that never received an answer.

The presentations continued – *in absentia* to Professors Haeckel and Weismann, in person to Professor Strasburger, who spoke warmly of Wallace, to Francis Galton, and Ray Lankester. Wallace did not linger: there was no celebratory reception or dinner. He took a cab to Waterloo, and was back home by half past seven, relieved that his public exposure was over.

The Linnean Gold Medal served as a nudge to the rest of the scientific world. In October, while 'feeling very bad', Wallace opened a letter from William Crookes, the Honorary Secretary of the Royal Institution, asking him to lecture on Darwinism at the January meeting. 'I felt so bad that I was almost at the point of sending back a positive NO!' he confessed to Birch. 'But I waited a few days, got a little better, & while on my couch by the fire, suddenly got an idea for the lecture, that I felt sure would do.'[18] He had declined the Royal Institution's invitation thirty or forty years before, he explained to Poulton, because he 'did not feel up to it at the time'. 'I am a believer in inspiration. All my best ideas have come to me suddenly. I had quite determined to decline this one – when, lying on my couch, an idea suddenly came to me!' – an idea that would suit the audience, and 'do good'.[19] He recognised this invitation as an honour, recollecting that Davey, Faraday and Tyndall had been professors at the Institute, while Crookes himself was an old friend – and besides, he was a fellow spiritualist. Within a week, he had a letter from the Royal Society, announcing that he had been awarded the Copley Medal – rather overwhelming, because he was an 'outsider' in science, had never sent them a single paper, and was considered a 'mere theoriser': he accepted Poulton's offer to receive it on his behalf from Sir Archibald Geikie: as it would come in a leather case, Poulton need only call at the nearest post office, 'get a strong linen Registered Letter Envelope, & despatch it'.[20] A few days later, he heard from Lord Knollys, the King's Private Secretary: 'His Majesty proposed to offer me "The Order of Merit", among the Birthday Honours!' The exclamation marks thudded on to his letters. 'Is it not awful – two more now! I should think very few men have had three such honours within six months!' He never rated himself highly enough for the Copley, and as for the Order of Merit being given to a red-hot radical, land nationaliser, socialist, anti-militarist, etc., it was 'quite astonishing and unintelligible'.[21] It was a pity that the Order was for military as well as civil achievements, as the military had so many distinctions already. But he composed a polite letter of acceptance, and then wrote to excuse himself from attending the Investiture at Buckingham Palace on the grounds of age and delicate health, having discovered that court dress, 'a kind of very costly livery', was obligatory. Colonel Legge, one of the King's Equerries, eventually travelled down to Broadstone to present the Order, a 'very handsome cross in red and blue enamel & Gold – rich colours – with crown above, & a rich ribbed silk blue & crimson ribband to hang it round my neck!' (A Bournemouth tailor, commissioned to sew the ribbon on to Wallace's dress waistcoat, had to confess that a workman had inadvertently swallowed the eye.[22]) Wallace wore the decoration when he gave his Royal Institute lecture on 22 January 1909. His idea for the lecture was a kind of missionary effort, he informed Meldola, to put Darwinism in a new light, and 'to leave "Mutationism" etc. etc. nowhere!' Meldola offered to read the lecture for him, if necessary, but Wallace assured him that Crookes was standing by, in case his own voice did not hold out. 'I suppose Crookes has a voice that can be heard or he would not have made the offer.' He was relieved that Meldola saw, as he did, 'the utter futility of the claims of the Mutationists – and the Mendelians are like unto them! I may just mention them in the lecture, but I hope I have put the subject in such a way that even "the meanest capacity" will suffice to see the absurdity of their claims.' Another postscript rammed home the point: 'I do not know whether the critics of "Darwinism" are most to be admired for their <u>impudence</u>, their <u>vagueness</u>, or their utter <u>inability</u> to reason logically.'[23] Wallace advanced on the Royal Society like a latter-day Elijah from his cave, preaching the pure truth of Darwinism, and smiting the unbelievers hip and thigh.

Wallace's mind was still active, grappling with the same great issues, and with every new threat, as he saw it, to the central tenets of Darwinism, or of Darwinism modified by his own added dimension. The lecture became an article, 'The World of Life: As Visualised and Interpreted by Darwinism', and the article became a full-length book. He described *The World of Life* as his attempt to summarise a 'half-century of thought and work on the Darwinian theory of evolution', but its thrust is signalled by the subtitle: 'A Manifestation of Creative Power, Directive Mind and Ultimate Purpose'. Wallace felt dissatisfied with his previous philosophical overview, *Man's Place in the Universe*, and sought here to lay out a simpler, broader framework. He could do this without opposing Darwin, because Darwin, he argued, purposely excluded certain fundamental problems from his enquiries: the nature and causes of life itself, and the powers of growth and reproduction. Stepping delicately around Darwin's sanctuary, he opened his story with an assault on the materialists' view of life, and of consciousness, and selected as his examples Haeckel and Huxley, 'our greatest philosophical biologist'. Haeckel expressed everything that Wallace opposed:

> Our own 'human nature' which exalted itself into an image of God in an anthropistic illusion, sinks to the level of a placental mammal, which has no more value for the universe at large than the ant, the fly of a summer's day, the microscopic infusorium, or the smallest bacillus. Humanity is but a transitory phase of the evolution of an eternal substance, a particular phenomenal form of matter and energy, the true proportion of which we soon perceive when we set it on the background of infinite space and eternal time.[24]

Wallace cracks into Haeckel with characteristic vigour: dogmatic, assertive, out of his department, combining negation and omniscience, 'not *science*, and very bad philosophy'. He himself will try to arrive 'at a juster conception of the mystery of the Life-World', by giving a kind of bird's-eye sketch of the great life-drama in its various phases as part of the grand system of evolution. But he does this from a position quite clearly staked out: that the Earth was prepared for Man 'from the remotest eons of geological time'. The book is a wonderful survey of the development of life, illuminated by Wallace's personal experience, by his wide reading, by his intimate knowledge of so many of the organisms he uses as illustrations. The distribution of species, floras and animals, examples of adaptation, the earth's surface changes, the geological record, the life of the tertiary period, all these flow across the pages eased by the comfortable familiarity of old acquaintances: the tail feather of a bird of paradise, the curling tusks of the Sulawesi babirusa, the small lilaceous plant *Simethus bicolor* found 'in a single grove of pine trees near Bournemouth, now probably exterminated by the builder'. Wallace's friends and correspondents urge him on, as he quotes their insights and researches: Richard Spruce, Alfred Newton, Edward Poulton, Archibald Geikie, Joseph Hooker, Thiselton-Dyer. It is an immensely readable retrospective of his life's work and interests, but he grapples too with current scientific developments, with Weismann and the germ-plasm, with chromosomes and molecules and atoms; and he adds a chapter on the purpose and definition of pain, 'Is Nature Cruel?' His intellectual curiosity about the 'how' is as sharp as ever, but 'why' is what really interests him. In this, his final synthesis, he seeks to resolve the apparently unbridgeable chasm between science and religion, by supposing an intervening series of intelligences.

> The main cause of the antagonism between religion and science seems to me to be the assumption by both that there are no existences capable of taking part in the work of creation other than blind forces on the one hand, and the infinite, eternal, omnipotent God on the other. The apparently gratuitous creation by theologians of angels and archangels, with no defined duties but that of attendants and messengers of the Deity, perhaps increases this antagonism, but it seems to me that both ideas are irrational. If, as I contend, we are forced to the assumption of an infinite God by the fact that our earth has developed life, and mind, and ourselves, it seems only logical to assume that the vast, the infinite chasm between ourselves and the Deity is to some extent occupied by an almost infinite series of grades of beings, each successive grade having higher and higher powers in regard to the origination, the development, and the control of the universe.[25]

Wallace's book is the sum of his long journey, a journey that he sees as only one stage in the spirit's never ending progression. Two of the quotations he uses as epigraphs demonstrate the two poles of his thinking. The first is from the great Swiss botanist Alphonse de Candolle:

> Every plant, whether beech, lily, or seaweed, has its origin in a cell, which does not contain the ulterior product, but which is endowed with, or accompanied by a force, which provokes and directs the formation of all later developments. Here is the fact, or rather the mystery, as to the production of the several species with their special organs.

Wallace would have been delighted by the clarity of genetics, but it is unlikely that genetics would have shaken his belief in a directive intelligence, which he expressed by these lines from Pope's 'Essay on Man':

> All nature is but art unknown to thee;
> All chance, direction which thou canst not see;
> All discord, harmony not understood;
> All partial evil, universal good.

The year 1909 was the centenary of Darwin's birth, celebrated at Cambridge, and marked by a volume of essays. Wallace was invited to contribute, but declined 'for many reasons', partly because of the company he might be keeping. Thiselton-Dyer wrote a paper, 'very good and thoroughly suitable to the occasion', but did not go to Cambridge because, he informed Wallace, he 'could not stand being told that Darwin's mantle had fallen upon Bateson, – that the Origin of Species has still to be discovered, and that specific differences have no reality'; under such provocation he might have lost his temper.[26] Wallace put off reading Bateson's and De Vries's chapters – it was absurd and incongruous that such persons should have a prominent place in a Darwinian celebration. Meldola, always thoughtful about Wallace's feelings, made sure that a suitable telegram was sent to the old warrior and prophet.

At Broadstone, waiting for the book's publication, he was more concerned about the view from his garden. His 'charming lodge in a wilderness' was once again in danger of being surrounded by buildings. People were 'in treaty' for a good deal of the field all round, and Lord Wimborne had raised his price to £250 an acre. Could Will and Violet manage an acre each, to secure a bit more of the wood? He might be able to find enough for an acre himself when the book was out – he badly wanted a permanent right of way out to the Poole road.[27] Once again, enclosure and development threatened his peace. Somehow, the money was found, and Violet moved to join her parents, eventually starting a little school in a house built next door, Tulgey Wood.

He did not go far in his last years, preferring to enjoy his garden, and to let visitors come to him. But he did not retreat from what was going on in the rest of the world. At last, he told Will, there was a review of *The World of Life* in *Nature*, under the annoying heading 'Science & Speculation'. The writer recognised 'the amount of <u>novel</u> and <u>interesting facts</u> and <u>conclusions</u>' and the 'various <u>new</u> applications of the <u>theory of Natural</u>

Selection' – but, being plainly an agnostic, deplored that he had not been able to avoid the 'pitfalls of teleological speculation'. Perhaps, though, it was better than he could have expected from *Nature*. Meanwhile, he was taking an infusion of cocoa shells for breakfast, harmless, yet quite refreshing: he offered to send Will some to try.[28] His public correspondence continued: letters to the annual meetings of the Land Nationalisation Society, and the Anti-Vaccination League; a letter on the relation of the present flora of the British Isles to the Glacial Period; letters of protest to *The Times* and the *Daily Chronicle* about the iniquities of the Insurance Act. In his ninetieth year he gave interviews, on 'The Great Strike – and After. Hopes of a National Peace' to the *Daily Chronicle*, and on 'The Problem of Life' to the *Daily News*. He fired off a 'short but big letter' to Lloyd George, suggesting that he and Asquith should take over the management of the railways 'of the entire country, by Royal Proclamation – on the ground of mismanagement for seventy years, and having brought the country to the verge of starvation and civil war . . .'[29] The old socialist in him was very much alive. He was working on two short books for Cassell, *Social Environment and Moral Progress* and *The Revolt of Democracy*. Although he believed in the ultimate goodness of mankind, he never stopped trying to make this present life better and less uncomfortable for as many people as possible, though he now worked very slowly, he confided to Poulton, 'and the <u>war-news</u> every day must be read'.[30]

In the summer and autumn of 1913, he grew weaker, as did his wife, suffering badly from arthritis. His project for a book, *Darwin and Wallace*, in collaboration with his friend James Marchant made little progress. At first, the gardener would wheel him round the grounds to see his best-loved flowers; he had developed 'a sad mania for Alpine plants'. Then he asked for some of his favourite plants to be placed in front of his study windows. 'Too many letters and home business. Too much bothered with many slight ailments, which altogether keep me busy attending to them. I am like Job, who said "the grasshopper was a burthen to him."' But he still felt able to 'jog on a few years longer in this <u>very good</u> world . . .'[31] On Sunday, 2 November, he fell ill, and went to bed. News of his condition brought journalists to the house. His manservant was approached: when the moment came, would he lower the blind in the bedroom as a signal? This was reported to the family doctor, Dr Scott. What, Scott recalled, testing the blind, like this? In Scott's memory, one newspaper printed a premature obituary.[32] Wallace died on 7 November. His immediate family was present, and William wrote a note for the press: 'Dr Wallace passed away very peacefully at 9.25 a.m. without regaining consciousness.'

The obituaries were long, and laudatory. The funeral was quiet, undemonstrative. Suggestions about burial in Westminster Abbey were turned aside by the family. Wallace was buried in Broadstone cemetery, after a service conducted by the Bishop of Salisbury. William and Violet were there but Annie was too incapacitated to attend. (She died just over a year later, on 10 December, 1914.) Raphael Meldola came, to represent the Royal Society, and his old friend Edward Poulton, on behalf of the Linnean, and Joseph Hooker, of the Land Nationalisation Society.[32] A tall fossilised tree trunk, found on a Dorset beach, was raised above the grave, a link to his wanderings in the forests of the Amazon and the Archipelago, and his days in the redwood and sequoia groves of California: a reminder of his belief in the unity of all living things.

15 The Old Hero

On Saturday, 15 April 2000, on a damp English afternoon, there was a
simple and moving ceremony at Wallace's resting place in Broadstone
cemetery. His two grandchildren, William's sons John and Richard, laid a
wreath, his great-great-grandson placed some flowers on the gravestone,
and the Wallace family formally entrusted the lease of the grave, and the
care of the memorial, to the Linnean Society, which was received by Sir
Ghillean Prance, the President. Earlier in the day, at a special meeting of
the Linnean Society held in the Wallace Room of Bournemouth
University, a series of papers celebrated some of Wallace's achievements. In
1998, the Linnean Society unveiled a full-length portrait of Wallace, which
hangs now side by side with that of Darwin. Forty years before, on the
centenary of the joint papers, a commemorative plaque was unveiled, to
commemorate the joint communication. The Linnean Society could not
have done more to mark Wallace's part in the theory of natural selection,

nor to herald his achievements.[1] The joint expedition of Wallace and Bates to the Amazon, and Wallace's own epic voyages in the Malay Archipelago, formed a significant segment of the exhibition 'Voyages of Discovery' at the London Natural History Museum. Wallace's pioneering travels up the river Vaupés, and his unique drawings of rare fish, have been beautifully presented by Sandra Knapp in *Footsteps in the Forest*;[2] his better-known journeys in the east form the springboard and structure of *Archipelago*, a book tracing a kind of evolutionary line from Wallace's own perceptions to a contemporary appreciation of the rich flora and fauna of the islands, and the precariousness of their natural resources.[3] To generations of field naturalists, Wallace shines as an inspiration, not just because of his achievements and discoveries, but because of his independence, resilience, courage, and the joy that flashes out again and again in his response to a plant or a butterfly, to any one of the 'perfect little organisms' he encountered in the forest.

John Wilson, a descendant of Wallace's aunt, subtitled his recent book, *In search of Alfred Russel Wallace*, 'The Forgotten Naturalist'.[4] Somehow, Wallace, who must have been one of the world's best-known scientific thinkers at his death, slipped out of the consciousness of the general public, almost a willed act of Wallacean self-effacement. By the close of his life, he was, if something of a living legend, a kind of relic: science was moving on, and even Darwin would be eclipsed for a while. Marchant's *Letters and Reminiscences* appeared in 1916, when the Western world had other things on its mind. Even within the scientific community, the verdict on Wallace was heavy with reservation. In a letter to the Reverend St John Thorpe, who had complained in 1917 that a notice in the journal of the Royal Geographical Society about Wallace and vivisection was 'really impertinent', the Secretary replied: 'He was a regular paradoxer in astronomy, and his opinions on vaccination, vivisection and such like matters were utterly opposed to the whole body of scientific thought . . . Outside his special subject of Natural History Dr Wallace's judgement was not to be relied on.'[5] Wallace's little heresies overlay his earlier scientific achievements; neither his biographer, Marchant, nor Wallace himself, in his autobiography, sought to deflect attention away from the political and social campaigns of the last phase, nor from his strengthening belief in the spiritual dimension. It became possible, perhaps convenient, to see Wallace as an eccentric, an enthusiastic stumbler on part of the truth.

In the fifty years or so that followed *Letters and Reminiscences*, little was published on Wallace except in relation to the other major figures of the mid-nineteenth century. He became a footnote, a diversion, the author of one great travel book which studiously avoided explicit reference to his scientific thinking. The 1958 centenary at the Linnean Society was a timely reminder. Wilma George's biography in 1964, *Biologist Philosopher*, offered a lucid reappraisal of his scientific thinking.[6] American scholars began to explore the course of evolutionary thinking, to chart the various cross-currents of influence, and to look in fine detail at some of the documents. Barbara G. Beddall wrote an influential paper, 'Wallace, Darwin, and the theory of natural selection', and followed it up with further probing commentaries.[7] In an interview with Arnold Brackman, discussing the absence of certain key letters from the Wallace–Darwin–Hooker–Lyell sequence, she commented that 'somebody cleaned up the file'.[8] (Her suspect was Francis Darwin.) H. Lewis McKinney, in a series of meticulous and ground-breaking researches which culminated in a 1972 book, *Wallace and Natural Selection*, traced the development of Wallace's thought by going back to his journals and notebooks, and drew pointed attention to the timing of the Ternate letter.[9] When did it reach Downe? Why did it not reach Downe earlier, at the same time as the letter that Wallace sent to Bates? If it had reached Downe earlier, what did Darwin do with it? Did he sit stunned by the contents – or did he make use of them? Where had he reached with his own writing of his 'big book'? The answer was 'divergence'. According to Darwin's personal journal, he began a section on divergence for his 'long' version on 14 April, and concluded it on 12 June. McKinney's account is very carefully phrased: he raises questions, and qualifies the word 'deception' with 'perhaps'. Could Darwin have used Wallace's ideas to clarify his own, and then written to Lyell to ask advice on what to do with Wallace's brilliant paper? Into this inviting gap strode two more Americans, Arnold Brackman, who constructed a compelling piece of investigative journalism and research called *A Delicate Arrangement: the Strange Case of Charles Darwin and Alfred Russel Wallace*,[10] and a historian of science John L. Brooks, who produced an equally riveting and minutely researched account, *Just before the Origin: Alfred Russel Wallace's Theory of Evolution*.[11] Brooks and Brackman offer a conspiracy reading of the 1858 events. They tell a gripping story, built around the reconstructed journey of the fatal envelope, investing it with enough explosive power to blow up

Darwin and the whole official narrative. Brooks concludes that Darwin 'must have received Wallace's manuscript on either of two dates in May': 'Receipt on May 18 would leave 25 days for a completion of those folios (on 'Divergence') by June 12; May 28–29 would leave scarcely two weeks. But it must be conceded that desperation will make the pen move quickly.'[12] In Brackman's more extreme version, the episode becomes a piece of typical British, or English, hypocrisy, an exercise in the politics of class and education, in which Wallace, the species man, the working naturalist, the humble collector, is seen off by the scientific toffs. Because of his personality, Wallace colluded in the 'delicate arrangement', and 'turned the other cheek'.[13]

Never has an intriguing theory been built on slenderer evidence, or on its admittedly intriguing absence. Darwin's letter to Lyell, announcing the arrival of Wallace's paper – 'He has today sent me the enclosed' – is dated '18th', and 'June' has been added, presumably by Francis Darwin; the other letters in the sequence follow on 25 and 26 June 1858.[14] The envelope to Frederick Bates is stamped 'JU 3 58' – 3 June.[15] McKinney, Brooks and Brackman argue that the letter to Darwin should have arrived at least a fortnight before the 18 June date. Brooks investigated the postal schedules of the Royal Dutch Mail, and calculated that it was entirely possible for the letter to Darwin to have arrived on 18 May. The letter to Bates was routed via Southampton, the slower and cheaper passage for 'heavy' mail. Brooks assumed that the letter to Darwin would go via Marseilles, and therefore arrive sooner. The total reliability of the mail service is taken as absolute. However thin the paper on which Wallace wrote his Ternate essay, the package to Darwin was a different weight, and, literally, heavier, than the letter to Bates; it could have been delayed at any stage along its route. There is no reason to suppose that Darwin did not write immediately to Lyell; his letter certainly reads as an entirely spontaneous reaction to a most unpleasant shock.

Brooks goes on to suggest that Darwin might have used the interval between receiving Wallace's paper and forwarding it to Lyell to write a section of his manuscript, on divergence, building on the clues he found in Wallace to fill in a gap in his own theory. In support of this, he points out that a crucial section in Darwin's 'big species book', the projected work on 'Natural Selection' which was condensed into The Origin of Species, was inserted at this precise point in time: Darwin, by his own account, was working on divergence during the months of May and early June. The impact of Wallace on Darwin was, of course, already considerable; ever since Lyell, and Blyth, alerted him to the implication of Wallace's Sarawak paper, and in response to Lyell's further urging him to publish a 'sketch' of his views, he had been accelerating with his 'species' book. Brooks argues that the arrival of the Ternate essay not only provided vital clues in itself, but prompted Darwin to revisit the Sarawak material. Having done so, he hastily, and radically, revised his views on the significance of extinction and divergence, and their place within a system of natural affinities.

Again, there is no evidence for this sequence of cause and effect, though it is an entirely possible interpretation of events, once the 'delay' hypothesis has been accepted. But why should Darwin do this? Darwin was keeping Lyell and Hooker in close touch with the progress of his work. There was no secret about it so far as they were concerned; Lyell, and particularly Hooker, were the two people in whom he consistently confided. So far as priority was concerned, the notes on divergence were irrelevant. Darwin had no ready-made sketch at hand ripe for publication, whereas the Wallace essay seemed complete, polished and fluent. In fact, by sending it to Lyell with his accompanying letter, Darwin succeeded in accelerating the path of Wallace's theory: no key scientific paper can ever have been so swiftly refereed and placed in the public domain.

As for the human factor, there is nothing in Darwin's life to suggest that he was capable of such massive intellectual dishonesty, even if he was not especially generous in acknowledging his sources and debts. The question of priority did not surface only in June 1858. 'I rather hate the idea of writing for priority,' he admitted to Lyell in May 1856, 'yet I certainly shd. be vexed if any one were to publish my doctrines before me.'[16] Two years later, Lyell's words of warning had come true with a vengeance. And he was vexed. And he was vexed with himself for being vexed. 'So all my originality, whatever it may amount to, will be smashed, though my book, if it will ever have any value, will not be deteriorated; as all the labour consists in the application of the theory.'[17] He found that he did mind very much about his originality. A week later, torn with worry about his desperately ill child, who was dying from scarlet fever, he confessed his painful muddle to Lyell: this was a trumpery affair. He wanted to behave honourably, not be thought base and paltry:

Wallace says nothing about publication, and I enclose his letter. But as I had not intended to publish any sketch, can I do so honourably, because Wallace has sent me an outline of his doctrine? I would far rather burn my whole book, than that he or any other man should think that I had behaved in a paltry spirit.[18]

To cast Darwin in the role of some devious machiavellian schemer in a Renaissance revenge tragedy is absurd. No doubt part of him wanted his friends to say, 'Yes, you can publish something without being dishonourable'; but his words are the words of a man in genuine turmoil, and he adopts much the same tone of miserable helplessness years later when confronted by Samuel Butler's hostility. Darwin, unlike Huxley and Hooker, and unlike, more surprisingly, Wallace, had no liking, no aptitude, for public controversy. His statement that 'all the labour consists in the application of the theory', on the other hand, could have come from the lips of Wallace.

Naturally, there are some aspects of the joint publication that are questionable, from Wallace's point of view. Darwin himself sounds a little surprised by the order in which the papers were presented: 'I had thought that your letter and mine to Asa Gray were to be only an appendix to Wallace's paper,' he wrote to Hooker after the Linnean meeting. The sequence, a chronological sequence, was decided by Hooker and Lyell.[19] Wallace, later, sounds a little ruffled, or defensive, that he never had the chance to correct a proof, though that would have caused a six-month delay in the written record of the meeting. (And he never had a proof of, for example, the Sarawak paper published in the *Annals*.) It is surprising that a number of key letters have vanished: Wallace's to Darwin, for example, though that did the rounds; Lyell's and Hooker's responses to Darwin's *cri de cœur*; Darwin's letter of explanation to Wallace, relating the course of events from his point of view – and if anyone did 'clean up the file', *that* particular document can scarcely have formed part of the process. But while all this is frustrating for academics and biographers – and a wonderful opportunity for speculation – there is nothing necessarily sinister about the gaps in the documentation. Enough of the sequence is there to reconstruct, broadly, the contents of the missing letters; and the writers of the letters knew what was written and said, and what was done; and they knew each other. Wallace, to the British-based triumvirate of Darwin, Lyell and

Hooker, was an unknown quantity, and each of them might have wondered at his possible response, aware of the prickliness of some of their fellow scientists. Hooker marvelled at Wallace's generosity of spirit. Lyell never ceased to urge Wallace to take a greater share of the credit. Darwin warmed to Wallace's reaction, as he warmed later to the man. Wallace, sensitive, touchy even, fully conscious of his rights, and with almost too keen a nose for injustice or inequity, never wavered, publicly or privately, in his acceptance of the arrangement. Acknowledgement and citation was a sensitive area: Wallace was later ticked off by Huxley, and by Thiselton-Dyer and Asa Gray, on separate occasions, for failing to acknowledge their work.[20] Wallace might have acquired doubts about Darwin's total transparency, and godlike reputation; but then he had quiet reservations about the whole official paraphernalia of the scientific establishment.

If it is believed that history was, initially, distorted, then the record should be put right. It is true that Darwin was, first, elevated into one of the Victorian Titans (an enterprise in which Wallace himself played a full part). Canon Tristram complained sarcastically to Alfred Newton about the God Darwin and his prophet Huxley, and how no one was allowed to oppose them.[21] More recently, a whole series of major biographies, and the exhaustive notation to the correspondence, has made Darwin known in a detail accorded to no other British scientist. To set against that, any alternative myth needs to be sharply defined, and preferably sensational. Even the limited publicity surrounding the appeal to restore Wallace's grave trailed the conspiracy theory bait in front of press and radio: unsurprisingly, they seized on it. Wallace still remains an absentee in some key accounts of Darwin's achievements. In the Darwin-dominated exhibition at the London Natural History Museum, a representative and official explanation of natural selection, Wallace's name, let alone his contribution, is not even mentioned, in contrast to the French account in the Jardin des Plantes.

But Wallace was not a victim, and he did not see himself as a victim. To promote a hypothetical reconstruction of events, for which there is absolutely no concrete and positive evidence, diminishes both Darwin and Wallace. Wallace's reputation, and significance, does not rest on whether he preceded Darwin, but on the (relative) independence and individuality of his discovery; and on his later writing on the subject, together with all his other achievements; just as Darwin's reputation *vis-à-vis* natural selection does not depend on the Linnean Society meeting, but on *The Origin of Species* and *The Descent of Man*: on the application of the theory. The most interesting aspect of the Wallace–Darwin, or Darwin–Wallace, publication is their subsequent relationship, both personal and intellectual.

Whereas Darwin saw only too clearly the implications of natural selection, how it would rock the foundations of religious faith, what its impact on attitudes towards society might be, Wallace appeared serenely insulated from such anxieties. Holding an Owenite vision of man's perfectibility, the keystone of natural selection was something he needed to fit into his world-view, into his philosophical system. The orthodox Anglican Darwin moved towards agnosticism, if not materialism, saw natural selection as one of a number of complex factors affecting evolution, and was content to see man as a highly evolved animal. Wallace, who had ceased to take the Christian religion seriously, gradually acquired an unshakeable belief in the spiritual dimension, and in life, and progress, after death; and he fitted a 'pure', even rigid doctrine of natural selection within a framework that elevated man towards the angels. Even in a world in which the genetic coding of a human being is completely known, the polarisation of the two opposing views continues. Through the wrestling minds of Darwin and Wallace, the joint protagonists, the lines of the animal/human, materialist/spiritualist debate can be followed like the traces of some Promethean struggle.

Wallace used to draw parallels between himself and Darwin, recalling that each of them began as beetle-hunters: and the same law that gave rise to the beetle gave rise to man. But perhaps the butterfly, or the bird of paradise, is a more appropriate symbol for Wallace, and for the race of naturalists whom he represents. Wallace's exploits in the Malay Archipelago have impressed themselves on the European literature of the area, for example in Somerset Maugham's story 'Neil Macadam'. Conrad, especially, mined Wallace for background, and re-created Wallace's emotions at the capture of a butterfly in his portrait of the merchant and entomologist Stein, in *Lord Jim*:

> One step. Steady. Another step. Flop! I got him! When I got up I shook like a leaf with excitement, and when I opened these beautiful wings and made sure what a rare and so extraordinary perfect specimen I had, my head went round and my legs became weak with emotion

that I had to sit on the ground. I had greatly desired to possess myself of a specimen of that species when collecting for the professor. I took long journeys and underwent great privations; I had dreamed of him in my sleep, and here suddenly I had him in my fingers – for myself!

That passage seems to reflect Wallace's capture of *Ornithoptera croesus* in Batchian. But Conrad then goes on to play with the contrast between butterfly and man, in a way that could almost be a commentary on Wallace's intellectual life. He gives these words to Stein:

'We want in so many different ways to be,' he began again. 'This magnificent butterfly finds a little heap of dirt and sits still on it; but man he will never on his heap of mud keep still. He wants to be so, and again he wants to be so . . .'

He moved his hand up, then down . . . 'He wants to be a saint, and he wants to be a devil – and every time he shuts his eyes he sees himself as a very fine fellow – so fine as he never can be . . . In a dream . . .'[22]

Wallace went into the forest to solve the 'mystery of mysteries', the origin of species, searching for the elusive butterfly of his thoughts. He will always be honoured for his role in the doctrine of natural selection, but his significance is not restricted to that moment, because he went on thinking, and dreaming, about man. Perhaps it was his Celtic birth, if not his Celtic blood. As traveller, field naturalist, geographer, bio-geographer, anthropologist, his achievements are substantial enough in their own right. As an author, he wrote two great books, *The Malay Archipelago* and *Island Life*, and many good ones. As a scientific philosopher, he made a massive contribution to ideas about the natural world, and about man, and his intuitive thinking again and again probed fundamental questions, even if his answers might not always have been proved correct by subsequent research and evidence. As a man, he was agreeably full of contradictions: and he changed, evolved, from a shy, stooping, diffident, tentative individual to someone who was intellectually confident, able to appear socially secure, and in the end perfectly clear and content about his role in the scientific world. What never changed, only strengthened, was his intense interest in people, and peoples, and his burning drive towards social justice. In this respect, he was unique, in combining profound scientific knowledge, and specialist expertise, with an acute and radical social analysis. As he created successive lodges for his family in as much wilderness as he could find in Essex, Surrey or Dorset, he never stopped concerning himself about the disadvantaged or threatened members of his own species. He championed the rights of the unprivileged, the exploited, the deprived, the dispossessed: the rural poor in Wales, the indigenous peoples of the Amazon or Papua New Guinea, the urban workers of London tenements, the victims of colonial oppression and misgovernment and militarism. Among the letters he kept, many from correspondents unknown to him, and including several he can have kept only because of his delight in the whimsical and bizarre, is one that says: 'If you know the old hero Wallace, give him my best wishes.'[23] There is, finally, something heroic about a man who independently constructs a theory of natural selection, which can be written, in its simplest form, as the accidental survival of the fittest, and spends the rest of his life proclaiming the ideals of co-operation and altruism as the way to hasten the perfecting of the human.

Abbreviations

ARW	Alfred Russel Wallace
BL	British Library
CCD	Burkhardt, Smith *et al.* (eds.), *The Correspondence of Charles Darwin*
CUL	Cambridge University Library
LR	James Marchant (ed.), *Letters and Reminiscences of Alfred Russel Wallace*
MA	ARW, *The Malay Archipelago*
ML	ARW, *My Life*, 1908 one-volume edition, unless otherwise indicated
NA	Henry Walter Bates, *The Naturalist on the River Amazons*
OMNH	Oxford Museum of Natural History (Hope Library)
RBG, Kew	Royal Botanic Gardens, Kew
RGS	The Archives of the Royal Geographical Society (with the Institute of British Geographers)
TA	ARW, *Travels on the Amazon and Rio Negro*
WFA	Wallace family archive
ZSL	Zoological Society, London

Notes

1 INTRODUCTION

1. ARW to Henry Walter Bates, 11 October 1847; *ML*, 144 (WFA).
2. *MA*, 342.
3. Grant Allen, 'The Celt in English Art', *Fortnightly Review*, 1 February 1891, 267.
4. Charles Kingsley's *The Water-Babies* first appeared in *Macmillan's Magazine* from August 1862 to March 1863, and was revised and expanded by Kingsley before it was published as a book in the summer of 1863. Wallace spent an evening with Kingsley at Cambridge during the British Association's meeting in 1862. The section about the 'poor, seedy, hard-worked old giant', butterfly-net in one hand, geological hammer in the other, running backwards as fast as he could, added for the expanded version, is clearly an amalgamated and satirical construction, but fits Wallace particularly well.
5. *ML*, 116.
6. 'The Jabberwock, with eyes of flame/Came whiffling through the tulgey wood': Lewis Carroll, *Alice Through the Looking-Glass*. Carroll was one of Wallace's favourite authors, and his daughter Violet remembered her father's jokes about Boojums and Jabberwocks. Later, Violet lived for a time with her pupils in 'Tulgey Wood', next to the Old Orchard, Broadstone.

2 THE EVOLUTION OF A NATURALIST

1. Entry in the Wallace family prayerbook (WFA). For many years, Wallace believed he was born on a different date, 1822, and in general he is often vague about precise dates, especially in connection with his early life, no doubt a result of his family's and his own subsequent many moves.
2. *ML*, 5. A large proportion of *My Life*, the first nine chapters, is devoted to Wallace's origins and his early life up to his departure for Brazil, and is the main source for the description. Quotations are from the later, one-volume edition except where indicated.

3. *ML*, 1 – the opening words of the autobiography.
4. *ML*, 16–17.
5. *ML*, 6. Wallace states that Rebecca Greenell died in 1828, though the date on the family tomb is 18 October 1826. But the family may not have moved to Hertford immediately.
6. See Len Green, *Alfred Russel Wallace, His Life and Work* (Hertford and Ware Local History Society, Occasional Paper No. 4, 1995), which includes interesting background material about Hertford. Also Jean Purkis, *The Courts and Yards of Hertford*, Hertford Oral History, 1997.
7. *ML*, 21.
8. Mary Wallace to Thomas Wilson, 5 July 1835 (WFA).
9. *ML*, 28.
10. *ML*, 31.
11. Inconveniently for this association, 'Ode to Mr Malthus' did not appear in Hood's *Comic Annual*.
12. There are two main surviving lists of Wallace's library, one in WFA of his scientific books, and one at the Oxford Museum of Natural History, the latter consisting predominantly of literature and works on religion and spiritualism.
13. *ML*, 42.
14. *ML*, 33.
15. *ML*, 34; *ML*, 586.
16. See account books, apparently belonging to C. H. Cruttwell, headmaster of Hale's Grammar School (Hertfordshire County Archives, D/2 113 A1/1–A5).
17. John Wallace, essay of 30 June 1892, 'The Work Problem 50 years ago by a Worker' (WFA). See also *ML*, 44, 67.
18. Robert Dale Owen, quoted in *ML*, 46.
19. *ML*, 73.
20. *ML*, 75.
21. ARW to George Silk, 12 January 1840 (WFA).
22. ARW to John Wallace, 11 January 1840 (WFA).
23. *ML*, 80.
24. See R. Elwyn Hughes, 'Alfred Russel Wallace; some notes on the Welsh connection', *British Journal of the History of Science*, 1989, 22, 401–18. See also J. R. Durant, 'Scientific naturalism and social reform in the thought of Alfred Russel Wallace', *British Journal of the History of Science*, 1979, 12, 31–58.
25. Quoted in R. Elwyn Hughes, see note 24.
26. The passage comes in the conclusion, and Wallace has underlined and capitalised the word 'botanist'. See McKinney (1972), 3.
27. *ML*, 105.
28. McKinney (1972), 6.
29. Darwin to J. S. Henslow, 18 May 1832 (Darwin Collection, 1, 237).

30. ML, 123–4.
31. If Wallace first read Malthus at Leicester, it was fourteen years or so before he made such significant use of him in Ternate and Gilolo (Halmahera) in February 1858. Later, in ML (190), he refers to his recollection of Malthus 'which I had read about twelve years before'. Wallace may have had in mind Darwin's letter to him of 1 May 1857, 'This summer will make the 20th year (!) since I opened my first note-book, on the question how & in what way do species & varieties differ from each other.' Consciously, and sometimes perhaps unconsciously, Wallace drew attention to the parallels between himself and Darwin.
32. For Bates, see Edward Clodd's memoir introducing Bates's *The Naturalist on the River Amazons* (Murray, 1892); H. P. Moon, *Henry Walter Bates FRS: 1825–1892: explorer, scientist and Darwinian* (Leicestershire Museums, 1976), and G. Woodcock, *Henry Walter Bates, naturalist of the Amazons* (Faber and Faber, 1969). See also John Dickenson, 'The naturalist on the River Amazons and a wider world: reflections on the centenary of Henry Walter Bates', *Geographical Journal*, 158, 2 (July 1992), 207–14.
33. ML, 125.
34. ML, 127.
35. ML, 131.
36. Ibid.
37. See R. Elwyn Hughes, note 24. Hughes argues that Wallace identified his 1855 Sarawak paper with his intellectual enquiries at Neath: 'It is about 10 years since the idea of such a law suggested itself to the writer of this essay.' It was on 28 December 1845 that Wallace asked Bates if he had read *Vestiges*.
38. ARW to Bates, 11 April 1846 (WFA).
39. *Zoologist*, 5, 1676 (? April, 1847).
40. ML, 139.
41. ARW to Bates, 28 December 1845 (WFA); letter reproduced in ML, and also, with amendments drawn from the original, by McKinney (1972).
42. [Robert Chambers], *Vestiges of the Natural History of Creation* (1844).
43. ARW to Bates, 28 December 1845; see note 41.
44. Charles Darwin, *Journal of Researches*, 2nd edn (John Murray, 1909), 382.
45. Ibid., 384.
46. ARW to Bates, 11 April 1846 (WFA).
47. ARW to Bates; ML, 144. Wallace omitted his specific question to Bates: 'Can you assist me in choosing one that it will be [sic] not be difficult to obtain the greater number of the known species.'
48. ARW to Bates, 11 October 1847 (WFA).
49. W. H. Edwards, *A Voyage up the River Amazon* (John Murray, 1847).
50. ARW and Henry Walter Bates to Sir William Hooker, 30 March 1848; Wallace wrote again on 3 April, acknowledging the letter of recommendation and valuable information (RBG, Kew).

3 APPRENTICESHIP ON THE AMAZON

1. *TA*, 1.
2. *NA*, 1–2.
3. *TA*, 2.
4. *NA*, 3.
5. ARW to George Silk, *ML* (1905), 1, 268–9.
6. *NA*, 3.
7. *NA*, 4.
8. ARW to George Silk, *ML* (1905), 1, 268–9.
9. The botanists Johann Baptist von Spix (1781–1826) and Karl (Carl) Friedrich von Martius (1796–1868) collected in Brazil from 1817–20, sometimes in tandem, sometimes separately. Martius, professor of botany and director of the botanic gardens at Munich, was Europe's leading specialist on palms. He was on the distribution list for the specimens collected by Richard Spruce. Spix, a zoologist, explored the Rio Negro. They arrived in Munich with a huge collection of plants and animals (350 species of birds, 2,700 of insects), and, unlike Wallace, brought 57 living animals with them.
10. *NA*, 26–7.
11. Bates, letter to Edwin Brown, 17 June 1848, *Zoologist*, 8, 2838.
12. *TA*, 22.
13. ARW to William Hooker, 20 August 1848 (RBG, Kew).
14. *TA*, 33.
15. *TA*, 29.
16. ARW to William Hooker, 20 August 1848 (RBG, Kew).
17. See *TA*, ch. 3, 35–56, and *NA*, ch. 4, 56–76, for this expedition.
18. *TA*, 38.
19. *TA*, 42.
20. *NA*, 61.
21. *TA*, 50.
22. *NA*, 70.
23. Richard Spruce, diary (RBG, Kew).
24. *TA*, 47.
25. *TA*, 54.
26. This advertisement appeared in the *Annals and Magazine of Natural History* (1850), 2nd ser. 5. See J. L. Brooks (1984), ch. 2, 'Amazonian Venture'.
27. *TA*, 58. This reflection, though clearly based on Wallace's Amazon experience, seems more likely to have been formulated when he was writing up his travels in 1853.
28. *TA*, 83–4.
29. Herbert Edward Wallace to Fanny (Frances) Sims, 'Monday 7th' (May 1849) (WFA). Herbert, disliking his first name, often referred to himself as Edward – he signs this letter 'Edward Wallace' – but I have used 'Herbert' for clarity.

30. *TA*, 93–4.
31. Herbert Wallace to Fanny Sims, September 1849 (WFA).
32. Richard Spruce's *Notes of a Botanist on the Amazon and Andes*, 2 vols. (Macmillan, 1908), was edited by Wallace. See 1, 62–3, and *TA*, 95–7.
33. *TA*, 96.
34. ARW to Stevens, 12 September 1849, published in *Annals and Magazine of Natural History*, 5, February 1850.
35. *TA*, 108.
36. *NA*, 126.
37. Quoted in David Elliston Allen, *The Naturalist in Britain: A Social History* (Princeton University Press, 1994), 91. This is a hugely informative and entertaining study of the subject (though it does not refer, remarkably, to Bates, Spruce or Wallace).
38. ARW to Stevens, 15 November 1849, *Annals and Magazine of Natural History*, 6, December 1850.
39. *TA*, 110.
40. ARW to Stevens, 20 March 1850, *Annals and Magazine of Natural History*, 6, December 1850.
41. *NA*, 168. Wallace spells him 'Henrique'. W. Lewis Herndon, an American naval lieutenant, comes up with 'Enrique Antonii', and provides the description of his wife. See W. L. Herndon, *Exploration of the Valley of the Amazon* (Taylor and Murray, 1854). Herndon mentions two English botanists 'whose names I have forgotten', one of whom had been very sick, and was given a box of butterflies by Bates at Santarem. His account reveals the Amazon at a point of change.
42. *TA*, 113.
43. *TA*, 115.
44. *TA*, 116.
45. *NA*, 311.
46. ARW to Stevens, 20 March 1850. Wallace's paper 'On the Umbrella Bird (*Cephalopterus ornatus*), "Ueramimbé," L.G. [Lingoa Geral]' was communicated to the Zoological Society of London's meeting of 23 July 1850, and reprinted in *Annals and Magazine of Natural History*, 8, November 1851.
47. *NA*, 170.
48. Letter from Mr and Mrs Henry Bates to Henry Walter Bates, 28 July 1850 (Leicester County Archives).
49. *NA*, 170.
50. H. W. Bates to Stevens, 31 December 1850 (*Zoologist*, 9, 3144).
51. *TA*, 129.
52. *ML* (1905), 2, 275–6.
53. Herbert Wallace to Spruce, 15 March 1850 (WFA).
54. Herbert Wallace to Fanny Sims and Mrs Mary Wallace, 30 August 1850 (WFA).

4 HUNTING THE WHITE UMBRELLA BIRD

1. *TA*, 134.
2. *Robert Hermann Schomburgk's Travels in Guiana and on the Orinoco during the years 1835–1839*, edited by O. A. Schomburgk with a Preface by Alexander von Humboldt (this is the short version of the title-page) was published in Leipzig by George Wigand in 1841, and translated by Walter E. Roth ('The Argosy' Company, Ltd, Georgetown, British Guiana, 1931). See pages 177–9 for Schomburgk's account of the region in March 1839. Schomburgk, a botanist and zoologist, undertook his expedition under the auspices of the Royal Geographical Society of London, and it involved an immense round trip from Georgetown to the upper waters of the Orinoco at Esmeralda, through the Cassiquiare, down the Rio Negro, and then up the Rio Branco and back to Guiana. Wallace makes no mention of the expedition. Schomburgk passed the mouth of the river Vaupés, and has much to say of interest on the Indians, on the topography, and the natural history of the region. His steersman for this stretch of the river was Bernardo, well known to Wallace and Spruce.
3. *TA*, 145.
4. *TA*, 149.
5. *TA*, 152. See Schomburgk (note 2), 164, for a wonderful description of the cock-of-the-rock's dance, and the dancing grounds. 'It was on this spot that we saw one of the birds dancing and hopping around while the others apparently constituted the wondering spectators. He now spread out his wings, threw his head in the air or spread his tail like a peacock: he then strutted around and scratched the ground up, all accompanied with a hopping gait, until exhausted he uttered a peculiar note, and another bird took his place.' And much more.
6. *TA*, 154.
7. *TA*, 157–8.
8. ARW to Thomas Sims, 20 January 1851 (WFA).
9. Ibid.
10. *TA*, 164.
11. *TA*, 166.
12. *TA*, 176–80.
13. Richard Spruce to Sir William Hooker, 27 June 1853; *Hooker's Journal of Botany*, 1854, 6, 40.
14. *TA*, 181–2.
15. *TA*, 193–4.
16. *TA*, 200.
17. *TA*, 203–4.
18. Wallace's pencilled notes, quite hard to decipher, are written in the back of the notebook in which he made his drawings of fishes (Natural History Museum).

19. *TA*, 223.
20. Henry Walter Bates to Mrs Mary Wallace, 13 June 1851 (WFA).
21. Bates to Mrs Mary Wallace, 18 October 1851 (WFA).
22. *TA*, 226.
23. Spruce to John Smith, 28 December 1851 (RBG, Kew).
24. Spruce to Wallace, 21 November 1863 (WFA).
25. Spruce, 'Note on the Theory of Evolution', in a letter to W. Wilson, 28 May 1870 (RBG, Kew).
26. Spruce, 'Note on the Theory of Evolution'.
27. *TA*, 211.
28. *TA*, 271. Wallace's factual narrative in *TA* is expanded, less discreetly, in *ML*, where he draws on his long letter to Spruce, and adds more details on the seaworthiness of the *Jordeson* which later picked them up. There are also graphic accounts in the proceedings of the Entomological Society.
29. *ML*, 156.
30. *ML*, 162.
31. *ML*, 160.

5 PLANNING THE NEXT EXPEDITION

1. *ML*, 163.
2. *ML*, 159–60.
3. References to Wallace and/or Bates in the *Transactions of the Entomological Society* occur on, *inter alia*, 1 June 1849, 6 August 1849, 4 February 1850, ? April 1850, 7 October 1850, 17 April 1851, 5 May 1851 (when Stevens reported, inaccurately, that Bates was on his way home) and 4 August 1851.
4. Bates to Stevens, 23 and 31 December 1850; *Zoologist*, 1851, 3230–32. Bates's own decision about returning to England seems to have been changed by the arrival of money from Stevens, though at one point he calculated that his profit was £26 19s after one year and eight months.
5. Edward Newman, presidential address for 1853 to the Entomological Society (n.s. 2, 142–54). Wallace's two papers were 'On the insects used for food by the Indians of the Amazon' (*Transactions of the Entomological Society of London*, n.s. 2, 241–4), and 'On the habits of the butterflies of the Amazon Valley' (n.s. 2, 253–64). See Brooks (1984), 36–41.
6. *ML*, 168 and *ML* (1905), 1, 377. See McKinney (1972), 25–6. Both McKinney and Brooks offer detailed commentary on the implications of Wallace's papers at this period. Brooks suggests that Wallace became aware of Herbert Spencer's speculative paper 'The Developmental Hypothesis', 'The Haythorne Papers', No. 2, *Leader*, 20 March 1852.
7. *ML*, 166.
8. *ML*, 165.

9.   Sir James Brooke to ARW, 1 April 1853 (BL, Add. Mss. 46411).

10.   ARW's proposal, 'To the President and Council of the Royal Geographical Society of London', is in the archives of the RGS. Wallace was not as wholly destitute as he maintained. He had, in fact, kept back a considerable quantity of South American birds for private sale, forwarded to Fanny Sims by Stevens.

11.   Minute Book, RGS.

12.   ARW to Dr Norton Shaw, 27 August 1853 (RGS). Petermann had published the map of the Rio Negro for the RGS journal.

13.   *Hooker's Journal of Botany*, 6 (1854), 61–2.

14.   See McKinney (1972), 15–21, and Sandra Knapp (1999), 86.

15.   Spruce in *Hooker's Journal of Botany*, 7 (1855), 213.

16.   Newman's address, see note 5.

17.   ARW to Norton Shaw, 9 February 1854 (RGS).

18.   ML, 172–3

19.   ML, 175–6.

20.   MA, 36.

21.   MA, 44–5.

22.   MA, 45.

23.   'Extracts of a letter from Mr Wallace', *Hooker's Journal of Botany*, 7, New Series, vol. III (1854–55), 200–209.

6 THE LAND OF THE ORANG-UTAN

1.   MA, 34, 46; ML, 177.

2.   Odoardo Beccari, *Wanderings in the Great Forests of Borneo. Travels and Researches of a Naturalist in Sarawak* (1904; reprinted in Asia Hardback Reprints, Oxford, 1986), 1–2.

3.   ARW to Norton Shaw, 1 November 1854 (RGS). The short paper on Mount Ophir is in the archives of the RGS.

4.   'On the Law which has Regulated the Introduction of New Species', dated February 1855, Sarawak, Borneo, appeared in the *Annals and Magazine of Natural History*, 16 (2nd ser.), 184–96, in the September 1855 number.

5.   ARW to Bates, 4 January 1858; ML, 184.

6.   Quotations from Wallace, *Natural Selection and Tropical Nature, essays on descriptive and theoretical biology* (Macmillan, 1891).

7.   The notebook, in the collection of the Linnean Society, was referred to by McKinney as the 'Species Notebook'.

8.   MA, 46–9, and Notebook 1855–9, entry for 12 March 1855. In MA, Wallace states that he arrived at the mines on 14 March. There are numerous small discrepancies between the notebooks and journals, and the more polished published accounts.

9. ARW to Fanny Sims, 25 June 1855 (WFA).
10. Ibid.
11. MA, 49.
12. Notebook 1855–9 (Linnean Society).
13. Ibid.
14. MA, 67.
15. MA, 53–7. Also details in Notebook (Linnean Society).
16. 'A New Kind of Baby', *Chambers's Journal*, 8 (3rd ser.), 201–4, 26 September 1857. See also ARW to Fanny Sims, 25 June 1855; *ML*, 178–80.
17. Notebook 1855–9 (Linnean Society).
18. ARW to Fanny Sims, 28 September 1855 (WFA).
19. MA, 87.
20. See Spencer St John, *The Life of Sir James Brooke, Rajah of Sarawak* (Edinburgh and London, Blackwood, 1879), 274–5.
21. ARW to Fanny Sims, 20 February 1856; *LR*, 1, 60–61.
22. ARW to Stevens, 10 March 1856 (CUL).
23. *Proceedings of the Entomological Society.*
24. For Darwin's annotations, and commentary, see Desmond and Moore (1991) 437–40, and Browne (1995) 537–8.
25. See Desmond and Moore (1991), 438. Also Leonard G. Wilson (1970).
26. ARW to Stevens, 10 March 1856 (CUL).
27. ARW to Stevens, 12 May 1856 (CUL).
28. ARW to Stevens, 21 August 1856 (CUL).
29. Ibid.
30. Ibid.
31. MA, 167–8.
32. MA, 169.
33. ARW to Stevens, 21 August 1856 (CUL).
34. ARW to Stevens, 27 September 1856 (CUL).
35. MA, 222.
36. Sir James Brooke to ARW, 4 July 1856 (BL, Add. Mss. 46411).
37. ARW to Fanny Sims, 20 February 1856 (WFA).
38. MA, 409.

7 HEADING EAST

1. MA, 411.
2. MA, 419.
3. MA, 430.
4. MA, 434.
5. MA, 445.
6. MA, 447–8.

7. MA, 448–9.
8. Quoted from Wallace's Notebook 1855–9 (Linnean Society). See MA, 467, where he omits the comment about 'the free development of every limb seems wholly admirable, and made to be admired'.
9. MA, 474.
10. MA, 486.
11. ARW to Norton Shaw, August 1857 (RGS).
12. Charles Darwin to ARW, 1 May 1857 (CCD, 6, 387).
13. Desmond and Moore (1991), 455.
14. ARW to Darwin, 27 September 1857 (CCD, 6, 457).
15. Bates to ARW, 19 November 1856 (WFA).
16. MA, 301.
17. MA, 303–4.
18. ARW to Bates, 4 January 1858; ML, 184 (WFA). The letter was completed on 25 January 1858. See note 25.
19. Entry 127, Field Journal (Linnean Society); MA, 323. See McKinney (1972) 134–5, and Brooks (1984), 178–80.
20. ML, 189.
21. ML, 191–2. For Wallace's various accounts of this sequence, see McKinney (1972), 160–63. His versions were published in *The Wonderful Century* (1898), 139; in 'My Relations with Darwin in Reference to the Theory of Natural Selection', in *Black and White*, 17 January 1903, 78; in ML; and, for the Linnean Society, *The Darwin Wallace Celebration* (1908), 117–18.
22. *The Darwin–Wallace Celebration Held on Thursday, 1st July 1908, by the Linnean Society of London* (February 1909), 5–11.
23. See Nora Barlow (ed.), *The Autobiography of Charles Darwin 1809–1882* (Collins, 1958).
24. ML, 191.
25. Ibid. The letter to Bates was sent to Bates's brother Frederick, in Leicester. The envelope, with its various postmarks, survives, to shed doubt on the timing of the arrival of Wallace's letter, and essay, at Darwin's house.
26. Darwin to ARW, 22 December 1857 (CCD, 6, 514–15).

8 IN SEARCH OF PARADISE BIRDS

1. MA, 497.
2. MA, 499.
3. ML, 192.
4. Darwin to Charles Lyell, 18 [June 1858] (CCD, 7, 107).
5. Darwin to Lyell, [25 June] 1858 (CCD, 7, 117–19).
6. 'On the Tendency of Varieties to Depart Indefinitely from the Original Type' dated Ternate, February 1858, was published in the *Journal of the*

Proceedings of the Linnean Society, 3 (9), 45–62 (20 August 1858).

7.   Hooker's account was written for Francis Darwin (ed.), *The Life and Letters of Charles Darwin*, 3 vols. (Murray, 1887), ii, 126.

8.   A. F. R. Wollaston, *Life of Alfred Newton* (Murray, 1921), 112–13.

9.   MA, 515.

10.   ARW to Mrs Mary Wallace, 6 October 1858 (WFA); ML, 195.

11.   ML, 193–4.

12.   ARW to Stevens, 29 October 1858 (CUL).

13.   ARW to Mrs Mary Wallace, 6 October 1858 (WFA).

14.   MA, 335–6.

15.   ARW to Stevens, 29 October 1858 (CUL).

16.   MA, 354.

17.   ARW to Thomas Sims, 25 April 1859 (WFA).

18.   MA, 262–3.

19.   MA, 264.

20.   MA, 259.

21.   Darwin to ARW, 18 May 1860 (CCD, 8, 219–21).

22.   MA, 386.

23.   MA, 527.

24.   MA, 530.

25.   MA, 532.

26.   ARW to George Silk, 1 September 1860 (WFA); ML (1905), 1, 371–3.

27.   The statement was made by Dr Scott, the doctor who attended Wallace in his last years, in an interview with Arnold Brackman. A copy of the recording is in the Wallace family archive.

28.   MA, 538–9.

29.   Darwin to ARW, 18 May 1860 (CCD, 8, 219–21).

30.   ARW to Bates, 24 December 1860; ML, 197.

31.   Darwin to ARW, 18 May 1860 (CCD, 8, 219–21).

32.   ARW to Darwin, December 1860 (CCD, 8, 504).

33.   MA, 197.

34.   ARW to George Sims, 1 September 1860 (WFA).

35.   MA, 207–9.

36.   MA, 394.

37.   MA, 395.

38.   ARW to Mrs Mary Wallace, 20 July 1861 (WFA).

39.   MA, 106, and 105–10 for his general observations.

40.   MA, 123–4.

41.   MA, 130.

42.   ARW to Fanny Sims, 10 October 1861 (WFA).

43.   ML, 198.

44.   MA, 144.

45.   ARW to Bates, 10 December 1861 (WFA).

46. ARW to Darwin, 30 November 1861 (CCD, 9, 356–8).
47. ARW to George Silk, 20 January 1862; ML, 201.
48. ARW to Stevens. This page of the letter is in the archives of the Zoological Society, London. I assume that Stevens passed it on to Philip Sclater, the Secretary, since it contains Wallace's terms.
49. ARW to Stevens, 12 May 1856 (CUL).
50. ML, 201.
51. ML, 202.
52. Archives of the Zoological Society, London.
53. ARW to Philip Sclater, 31 March 1862 (ZSL).
54. *The Times*, 29 March and 2 April 1862.
55. 'The Paradise-Birds in the Zoological Society's Gardens', *Illustrated London News*, 12 April 1862. See also the *Saturday Review*, 17 May 1862, where there is a rather ominous comment that paradise-bird plumes might recover 'their now almost forgotten value as ornaments for the hats of our fair countrywomen'.

9 THE RETURN OF THE WANDERER

1.   Minute Book (ZSL).
2.   Bates to Darwin, 24 November 1862 (CCD, 10, 217). 'As to ordinary Entomologists they cannot be considered scientific men but must be ranked with collectors of postage stamps & crockery.'
3.   Records of the scientific meetings (ZSL).
4.   ARW to Darwin, 23 May 1862 (CCD, 10, 217).
5.   Darwin to ARW, 24 May 1862 (CCD, 10, 218–19).
6.   Darwin to ARW, 13 November 1859 (CCD, 7, 375).
7.   ML, 204.
8.   See John G. Wilson (2000), 238. John Wilson, a descendant of Wallace's aunt Martha Greenell, makes use of family letters to emphasise Wallace's continuing interest in the Australian branch of the far-flung family.
9.   These details are in one of Wallace's notebooks (WFA). Wallace frequently began to keep accounts, or carried out some kind of appraisal of his finances, but never seemed to maintain a system for very long.
10. ARW to George Silk, 30 November 1858 (WFA).
11. ML, 247–8.
12. ML, 220.
13. Bates's memories of Lyell are quoted by Clodd in Bates (1892).
14. ML, 239.
15. Bates quoted by Clodd in Bates (1892).
16. Darwin to Asa Gray, 26–7 November 1862 (CCD, 10, 563–6).

17. Darwin to Joseph Hooker, 25 November 1861 (*CCD*, 9, 349–50).

18. Darwin to Bates, 3 December 1861 (*CCD*, 9, 363–4).

19. ARW to Darwin, after 20 August 1862 (*CCD*, 10, 372).

20. Alfred Newton to Henry Tristram, 24 August 1858, in A.F.R. Wollaston, *Life of Alfred Newton* (John Murray, 1921), 115–17.

21. 'It is unquestionably from the former labours of both – united yet distinct – that the boon acquires its greatest value' (Newton papers, CUL).

22. See Wollaston (1921), 123–4.

23. T. H. Huxley to Darwin, 9 October 1862 (*CCD*, 10, 449–50).

24. *ML*, 256.

25. ARW to George Silk, 30 November 1858 (WFA).

26. ARW to Richard Spruce, deduced from the reply. Spruce waited a year before responding. He confessed to feeling a little piqued that he had twice written to Wallace, from Ambato near Quito, and not heard back, but now realised that those letters had never arrived.

27. Spruce to ARW, 21 November 1863 (WFA).

28. *ML* (1905), 1, 409–11. Wallace removed all reference to Miss L and his broken engagement from the one-volume edition of *ML*, no doubt judging that the full-length account might be slightly bewildering, if not upsetting, to his immediate family. The family name Leslie is used in Wallace's manuscript notes for *ML*. Other details come from his letter to Alfred Newton, and from the Census returns for 1861.

29. ARW to Alfred Newton, 2 April 1864 (CUL).

30. Joseph Hooker to Darwin, 24 May 1863 (*CCD*, 11, 442–4).

31. Darwin to Bates, 18 April 1863 (*CCD*, 11, 326–7).

32. Darwin to Hooker, 17 April 1863 (*CCD*, 11, 321–2).

33. Hooker to Darwin, 13 May 1863 (*CCD*, 11, 411–13).

34. Darwin to Hooker, 15 and 22 May 1863 (*CCD*, 11, 419–21).

35. Darwin to Hooker, 9 May 1863 (*CCD*, 11, 393–4).

36. Darwin, letter to *Athenaeum*, 9 May 1863 (written 5 May 1863) (*CCD*, 11, 380).

37. ARW, 'Remarks on the Rev. S. Haughton's Paper on the Bee's Cell, and on the Origin of Species', *Annals and Magazine of Natural History*, 12 (3rd. ser.): 303–9 (October, 1863).

38. Asa Gray to Darwin, 23 November 1863 (*CCD*, 11, 677–8).

39. T. H. Huxley, *Man's Place in Nature and other Anthropological Essays* (Macmillan and Co., Ltd., 1901), 35–6.

40. ARW to Darwin, 2 January 1864 (*LR*, 148–51).

41. Darwin to ARW, 22 December 1857 (*CCD*, 6, 515).

42. ARW to George Silk, 30 November 1858 (WFA).

43. Lyell to ARW, 8 February 1864 (BL, Add. Mss. 46411).

44. Quoted in Lyell to ARW, February 1864 (BL, Add. Mss. 46411).

45. Huxley to ARW, see note 46.

46. ARW to Huxley, 26 February 1864 (Huxley papers, Imperial College, London).

47. Wallace's paper was entitled 'The origin of human races and the antiquity of man deduced from the theory of "Natural Selection"', and was slightly adapted and modified as 'The Development of Human Races under the Law of Natural Selection', for inclusion in *Contributions to the Theory of Natural Selection* (1870) and, later, *Natural Selection and Tropical Nature* (1891). This quotation is from the last named, and follows the original apart from minor changes in the punctuation, and the substitution of 'better adapted' and 'less adapted' for 'more favourable' and 'less favourable'. Wallace did not indicate where he was making changes, and later added a radically more perfectionist conclusion.

48. *Journal of the Anthropological Society of London*, 2, clviii–clxx, followed by the discussion, clxx–clxxxvii.

49. Lyell to ARW, 22 May 1864 (BL, Add. Mss. 46411).

50. ARW to Hooker, 22 May 1864 (RBG, Kew).

51. Hooker to Darwin, 6 October 1865, in Leonard Huxley, *Life and Letters of Sir Joseph Dalton Hooker*, 2 vols. (John Murray, 1918), vol. 2, 54.

52. Darwin to ARW, 28 May 1864 (*LR*, 1, 152–5).

53. Hooker to Bates, 13 May 1863, quoted by Clodd in Bates (1892), p. lxvi.

54. Minute Book, 18 April 1864, RGS.

55. *ML*, vol. 1, 409–11.

56. ARW to Newton, 19 February 1865 (CUL). Wallace wrote to Darwin the month before: 'No cause has been given me except mysterious statements of the impossibility of our being happy, although her affection for me remains unchanged. Of course I can only impute it to some delusion on her part as to the state of her health.' ARW to Darwin, 20 January 1865 (Darwin papers, CUL).

57. Spruce to Wallace, 21 November 1863 (WFA).

58. Ibid.

59. William Mitten to Spruce, 29 October 1864 (RBG, Kew).

10 WALLACE TRANSFORMED

1. 'How to Civilize Savages', *Reader* 5: 671a–672a (17 June 1865).

2. ARW, *Miracles and Modern Spiritualism* (rev. edn, 1896), 132–3.

3. See, for example, *Miracles and Modern Spiritualism*, 144, where Wallace writes of 'a solid basis of fact'. In terms of persuading other people about the factual basis for spiritualism, Wallace tended to cite the experiences of other reputable investigators.

4. Memoranda from old account books, 2 December 1899, in Samuel Butler's notebooks, vol. 3 (BL).

5. H. Festing Jones, *Samuel Butler, Author of 'Erewhon' (1835–1902): A*

Memoir, 2 vols. (Macmillan, 1919), vol. 1, 317.

6. *ML*, 214.

7. ARW to Newton, 29 June 1866 (CUL).

8. *ML*, 214.

9. ARW to Hooker, 3 May 1866 (RGB, Kew).

10. ARW to Huxley, 22 November 1866 (BL, Add. Mss. 46439).

11. T. H. Huxley in *Westminster Review*, 61 (1854), quoted in Desmond, *Huxley: The Devil's Disciple* (1994), 192.

12. Huxley to ARW, (before) 1 December 1866 (BL, Add. Mss. 46439).

13. John Tyndall to ARW, 8 February 1867 (BL, Add. Mss. 46439).

14. ARW to Huxley, 1 December 1866 (*LR*, vol. 2, 187–8).

15. See Francis Darwin, ed., vol. 3, 186–8.

16. 'The Scientific Aspect of the Supernatural' was first published in *The English Leader* (nos. 52–9, 11 August 1866 to 29 September 1866), and reprinted as a pamphlet. Fanny Sims's copy, with its extraordinary tale, is in the Wallace papers at the Oxford Museum of Natural History.

17. Roberet Owen, *The New Existence of Man*, (1854). See Frank Podmore, *Robert Owen: A Biography*, 2 vols, (London, 1906).

18. Robert Chambers to ARW, 10 February 1867, *ML*, vol. 2, 303.

19. ARW to Newton, 6 January 1866 (CUL).

20. Richard Spruce to Fanny Sims, 27 February 1867 (WFA).

21. See Elizabeth Jenkins, *The Shadow and the Light: A Defence of Daniel Douglas Home, the Medium* (Hamish Hamilton, 1982), especially chapter XXIV, 'The Imperious Mrs Lyon'. See also Janet Oppenheim, *The Other World: Spiritualism and Psychical Research in England, 1850–1914* (Cambridge University Press, 1985).

22. *ML*, 358–60. Wallace's manuscript notes for his autobiography reveal more details, for example of names, and there are other scattered jottings about his finances in notebooks, address books etc (WFA).

23. ARW to Newton, 10 March 1867 (CUL).

24. *ML*, 372–3.

25. ARW to Darwin, 2 January 1864 (*LR*, 1, 149–51).

26. ARW to Darwin, 7 February 1868 (*LR*, 1, 193–4).

27. ARW, 'Creation by Law', *Quarterly Journal of Science* 4, 471–88 (October, 1867).

28. ARW to Newton, 19 February 1868 (CUL).

29. ARW to Lyell, 28 February 1868 (*ML*, vol. 1, 422).

30. William Mitten to Spruce, 7 June 1868 (RBG, Kew).

31. Mitten to Spruce, 10 August 1868 (RBG, Kew).

32. ARW to Darwin, 20 January 1869 (*LR*, 1, 232).

33. ARW to Hooker, 18 January 1869 (RBG, Kew).

11 MAN AND MIND

1. Darwin to ARW, 5 March 1869 (*LR*, 1, 235).
2. Darwin to ARW, 22 March 1869 (*LR*, 1, 237).
3. MA, 598. In his note about his use of the term 'barbarism', Wallace gave one final example in justification, which anticipates his future campaigning about land: 'We permit absolute possession of the soil of our country, with no legal rights of existence on the soil, to the vast majority who do not possess it. A great landholder may legally convert his whole property into a forest or a hunting-ground, and expel every human being who has hitherto lived upon it.'
4. MA, 596.
5. 'Sir Charles Lyell on Geological Climates and the Origin of Species', *Quarterly Review* 126, 359–94 (April, 1869).
6. *Quarterly Review* 126, 394, reproduced in Smith (ed.), 1991, 31–4.
7. Darwin to ARW, 14 April 1869 (*LR*, 1, 242–3). (On 27 March, Darwin wrote: 'I hope you have not murdered too completely your own and my child.')
8. Lyell to Darwin, 5 May 1869, K. Lyell (ed.), *Life, Letters and Journals of Sir Charles Lyell* (John Murray, 1881), vol. 2, 441–4.
9. ARW to Mitten, 25 July 1905 (Linnean Society). See also ARW's previous letter of enquiry, 18 July 1905; 'Also what year was it we went to Spa together?'
10. ML, 256–7.
11. Wallace's copy of the burlesque 'Exeter Change for The British Lion', (WFA).
12. Darwin to ARW, 26 January 1870 (*LR*, 1, 250–1).
13. Darwin to ARW, 31 March 1870 (*LR*, 1, 251).
14. ML, 362.
15. ML, 361–72. The amount of space Wallace gives to this episode reveals how much it weighed on his mind, and conscience: he does not spare himself. Various Hampden missives are among his papers, and Hampden's accusing letters survive in the files of the learned societies. Hampden delivered several shrewd thrusts, and called into question Wallace's claim to a Government Pension of £200 a year 'unless scientific villainy and roguery are at a premium in this country'.
16. ARW to Newton, 25 December 1870 (CUL).
17. ML, 338–40, and *On Miracles and Modern Spiritualism*, 165–8.
18. Darwin to ARW, 22 November 1870 (*LR*, 1, 254–5).
19. ARW's review of *The Descent of Man*, in *Academy* 2, 538 (1 December 1871), 183. See also letters between ARW and Darwin, *LR*, 1, 255–62.
20. ARW to Fanny Sims, 31 December 1871 (WFA).
21. Architect's plans for The Dell, by Wonnacott of Farnham (WFA). Bates was

active on Wallace's behalf in obtaining literary work for him. For correcting proofs etc., Wallace received five shillings an hour from Lyell. He asked for seven shillings an hour on a more demanding task for Darwin, but this conceivably awkward arrangement fell through.

22.   ARW to Mitten, 6 March 1873 (Linnean Society).

23.   ARW to Arabella Buckley, 24 April 1874 (*LR*, 2, 192–3).

24.   Arabella Buckley to ARW, 25 April 1874 (WFA).

25.   Arabella Buckley's (Mrs Fisher's) note in *LR*, 2, 193.

26.   *On Miracles and Modern Spiritualism*, 196–8.

27.   ARW to Francis Galton, 23 May 1874 (Galton papers, University College, London).

28.   Arabella Buckley to ARW, 26 May 1874 (BL, Add. Mss. 46439).

29.   ARW to Newton, 14 February 1875 (CUL).

30.   ARW to Newton, 29 March 1875 (CUL).

31.   ARW to Newton, 9 April 1875 (CUL).

32.   ARW to Newton, 4 May 1875 (CUL).

33.   Darwin to ARW, 5 June 1876 (*LR*, 1, 286–7).

34.   ARW to Darwin, 23 July 1876 (*LR*, 1, 294–6).

35.   Hooker, Presidential Address to the British Association, quoted in Wilma George, *Biologist Philosopher* (Abelard-Schuman, 1964), 123.

36.   Prospectus for the Dell, Thurrock Library Local Studies Collection (I am grateful to Mr John Webb of the Thurrock Local History Society for this information).

37.   ARW to Newton, 23 July 1876 (CUL).

38.   Wallace became a member of the Society for Psychical Research, which was formed in 1882. He was invited to become President on several occasions, but declined. He continued to write on aspects of spiritualism throughout his life, contributing to *The Light*, and to the publications of the Society for Psychical Research. On 23 June 1898, he addressed the International Congress of Spiritualists at St James's Hall, London, on 'Spiritualism and Social Duty'.

39.   *ML*, vol. 2, 397.

40.   See for background Oliver Rackham, *Ancient Woodland* (Arnold, 1968), 251–5.

41.   Joseph Hooker to ARW, 20 July 1878 (RBG, Kew). Hooker sent Wallace his lecture on 'North American Flora'.

42.   ARW to Hooker, 27 August 1878 (RBG, Kew).

43.   ARW to Hooker, 27 October 1878 (RBG, Kew).

44.   'Epping Forest, and how best to deal with it', *Fortnightly Review* 24, 628–45 (1 November 1878).

45.   *ML*, 218–19. See also the minute book of the Coal, Corn and Finance Committee, Corporation of the City of London, vol. 41, p. 71, (Misc. Mss. 223.2 and 223.5), and Wallace's correspondence with Meldola, particularly.

He continued to grumble privately about the Commissioners for some time, even encouraging Meldola and others to mount a legal challenge to some of their decisions.

46. ARW to Newton, 9 January 1880 (CUL).

47. ARW to Arabella Buckley, quoted in her letter to Darwin, below. See for details of this whole affair, Ralph Colp, Jr., '"I Will Gladly Do My Best": How Charles Darwin Obtained a Civil List Pension for Alfred Russel Wallace,' (*Isis*, 1992), 83, 3–26.

48. Arabella Buckley to Darwin, 16 December 1879 (Darwin papers, CUL).

49. Darwin to Arabella Buckley, Darwin to Hooker, 17 December 1879 (Darwin papers, CUL).

50. Hooker to Darwin, 18 December 1879 (Darwin papers, CUL).

51. Darwin to Hooker, 19 December 1879 (Darwin papers, CUL).

52. ARW to Hooker, 19 July 1880 (RBG, Kew).

53. ARW to Philip Sclater, 21 September 1880 (ZSL)

54. Arabella Buckley to Darwin, 7 November 1880 (Darwin papers, CUL).

55. Darwin to ARW, 3 November 1880 (*LR*, 1, 307–8).

56. Asa Gray to ARW, 31 December 1880 (BL, Add. Mss. 46436).

57. ARW to Thiselton-Dyer, 7 January 1881 (BL, Add. Mss. 46436).

58. RBG, Kew.

59. Hooker to Darwin, 22 November 1880, Huxley (ed.) (1918), vol. 2, 244–5. Hooker to Wallace, 10 November 1880 (*LR*, 1, 289–90).

60. Hooker to Darwin, 26 November 1880 (Huxley collection, Imperial College Archives).

61. Darwin to Huxley (after 26 November) 1880 (Imperial College Archives).

62. Darwin to Francis Darwin, 28? December 1880 (Darwin papers, CUL).

63. Darwin to Arabella Buckley, 4 January 1881 (Darwin papers, CUL).

64. William Gladstone to Darwin, 6 January 1881 (Darwin papers, CUL).

65. Darwin to ARW, 7 January 1881 (*LR*, 1, 313–14).

66. Darwin to Huxley, 7 January 1881 (Darwin papers, CUL).

67. ARW to Darwin, 8 January 1881 (*LR*, 1, 314).

68. ARW to Darwin, 29 January 1881 (*LR*, 1, 315–16).

12 THE BIG TREES

1. 'How to Nationalise the Land: A radical solution of the Irish Land Problem', *Contemporary Review* 38, 716–36 (November 1880).

2. *ML*, 323; *Land Nationalisation*, 1882.

3. ARW to Darwin, 9 July 1881 (*LR*, 1, 317–18). 'I do not think I have ever been so attracted by a book, with perhaps the exception of your "Origin of Species" and Spencer's "First Principles" and "Social Statics",' enthused Wallace – a slightly backhanded compliment.

4. Darwin to ARW, 12 July 1881 (*LR*, 1, 318–19).
5. Desmond and Moore (1991), 669. It was George Darwin's idea that it would be 'gracious' to ask Wallace to be a pall-bearer.
6. ARW to Raphael Meldola, 8 January 1886 (OMNH).
7. 'The "Why" and the "How" of Land Nationalisation', Part I, *Macmillan's Magazine*, 48, 357–68 (September 1883), and Part II, 48, 485–93 (October 1883).
8. *ML*, 326.
9. H. Allingham and D. Radford (eds.), *William Allingham: A Diary* (Penguin, 1985), 264.
10. Ibid. (2 August 1884), 329–30.
11. Ibid. (6 November 1884), 332–5.
12. Wilfred Ward, 'Tennyson: A Reminiscence' in *Problems and Persons*, (Longman Green, 1903), 196–217.
13. *William Allingham: A Diary* (5 December 1884), 339.
14. Ibid. 340.
15. *ML*, 270–1. *Bad Times etc.* (Macmillan and Co., London, 1885 and New York, 1886).
16. ARW to Edmund Gosse, 16 February 1886 (Brotherton Library, University of Leeds).
17. Notebook (WFA).
18. ARW to Meldola, 7 August 1886 (OMNH).
19. ARW to Meldola, 28 August 1886 (OMNH).
20. Wallace's Journal of his visit to North America is in the library of the Linnean Society. I am very grateful to Mr Michael Pearson for the loan of his typed transcription.
21. ARW to Meldola, 14 November 1886 (OMNH). On the evening of Wednesday 17 November, Gray also exhibited his own letters from Darwin (Cambridge Scientific Club Records, Harvard University Archives).
22. See Wallace's American journal, and *ML* vol. 2, 356–7, and notes on 403–5 in *Essays in Psychical Research* (see next note).
23. See William James, *Essays in Psychical Research*, vol. 16 in *The Works of William James* (general editor, F. H. Burkhardt) (Cambridge, Mass. and London: Harvard University Press, 1986). See 29–32 for the letter from James to the Editor of the *Banner of Light*.
24. ARW to Annie Wallace, 5 April 1887 (WFA). The letter begins 'My dear Annie' and finishes 'your affectionate husband Alfred R. Wallace'.
25. ARW to Annie Wallace, 24 May 1887 (WFA).
26. The manuscript for this lecture is in the Wallace family archive. The text was published in the *Golden Gate* (June 1887), was reprinted as a pamphlet by, for instance, Banner of Light publishing company, Boston, was reproduced in *Banner of Light* and *Light* (London), and was widely reported in excerpt by the San Francisco newspapers.

27. See *ML*, 278–92, and, for this extract, 'Flowers and Forests of the Far West', *Fortnightly Review*, 50, 796–810 (December 1891), reprinted in *Studies Scientific and Social*, vol. 2, 234.
28. ARW to Meldola, 19 June 1887 (OMNH).
29. ARW to Meldola, 19 June 1887 (OMNH). 'I have gathered much information & may perhaps perpetrate another book (a small one) on America.'
30. See Suzanne Bryant Dakin, *The Perennial Adventure: A Tribute to Alice Eastwood, 1859–1953* (San Francisco: California Academy of Sciences, 1954), and Carol Green Wilson, *Alice Eastwood's Wonderland: the adventures of a botanist* (San Francisco: California Academy of Sciences, 1955). Alice Eastwood published *A Popular Flora of Denver*, Colorado, in 1893.
31. Journal of visit to North America (Linnean Society).

13 THE FUTURE OF THE RACE

1. *ML*, 286.
2. *ML*, 292.
3. ARW to Fanny Sims, 24 August 1888 (WFA).
4. ARW to Meldola, 30 August 1888 (OMNH).
5. ARW to Fanny Sims, 24 August 1888 (WFA).
6. ARW to Edward Poulton, 22 February 1889. Quoted in Poulton's obituary notice for the *Zoologist* 71 (1913), 470–1.
7. Letter from the Wimborne Estate to ARW, 8 April 1890 (BL, Add. Mss. 46441).
8. *ML*, 299.
9. From Wallace's testimony presented before the Royal Commission on vaccination, 1890, *Third Report of the Royal Commission Appointed to Inquire into the Subject of Vaccination* (H.M.S.O., 1890), quoted in Charles H. Smith (ed.) (1991), 202. See also *ML*, 329–33, and *The Wonderful Century* (1898), 213–323, where vaccination takes up over a quarter of the book.
10. 'Human Selection', *Fortnightly Review* 48, 325–37 (September 1890).
11. Edward Bellamy, *Looking Backward* (Ticknor and Co., Boston, 1888).
12. *ML*, 386. Unsurprisingly, Wallace's ideas of what was important included several which had been 'almost entirely overlooked'; but in fact he only includes this, and 'The Expressiveness of Speech or Mouth-gesture as a Factor in the Origin of Language', as possibly neglected ideas in his list of twelve major contributions.
13. See K. R. V. Wikman, 'Letters from Edward B. Tylor and Alfred Russel Wallace to Edward Westermarck', *Acta Academiae Aboensis Humaniora* XIII, 7 (1940), see 13–22 for ARW's letters.
14. ARW to Galton 3 February 1891 (University College, London). Although

Wallace marked this letter 'Private', a note on the file by Galton states, 'Sent to Mrs Romanes & returned 1894. I had previously in 1891/92 lent them to Romanes who was occupied with a similar project.' ARW would have been startled, and probably outraged. Romanes objected violently when ARW ingenuously informed him that he had seen, in Canada, copies of Romanes's personal correspondence to Darwin on the subject of spiritualism. ARW's relations with Romanes were more strained than with any other of his contemporaries. Romanes insulted him by his distinction between Wallace the man of science and the man of nonsense, and by obscurely accusing him of plagiarism. When he declined to retract, Wallace responded by refusing to mention Romanes in print, though he referred to him frequently in his private letters. See *ML*, vol. 2, 317–18.

15. ARW to Edward Poulton, 28 May 1889, quoted in *Zoologist* 71, 469.
16. ARW to Violet Wallace, 20 May 1892 (WFA).
17. ARW to Scott Keltie, 8 March 1892 (RGS).
18. ARW to Thiselton-Dyer, 25 October 1892 (RBG, Kew).
19. Thiselton-Dyer to ARW, 12 January 1893 (*LR*, 2, 220). See also ARW's reply to Thiselton-Dyer's 'very kind letter', 17 January 1893 (Linnean Society).
20. ARW to Violet Wallace, 31 October 1893 (WFA).
21. Small notebook with details of the Lake District holiday (WFA).
22. ARW to Mitten, 13 August 1893 (WFA).
23. Ibid.
24. ARW to Violet Wallace, 14 July 1894 (WFA).
25. Letter to ARW, 26 September 1893 (BL, Add. Mss. 46439).
26. ARW to Meldola, 8 November 1893 (OMNH).
27. ARW to Violet Wallace, 14 July 1894 (WFA).
28. ARW to Annie Wallace, 9 August 1896 (WFA).
29. *ML*, 304.
30. Edward Poulton, *Zoologist* 71, 469.
31. ARW to Violet Wallace, 27 November 1896 (WFA).
32. Edward Poulton, *Zoologist* 71, 469.
33. *ML*, 392.
34. *ML*, 308–9.
35. ARW to Meldola, 26 June 1896 (OMNH) – the letter was marked 'Private'.
36. ARW to William Wallace, 1 November 1903 (WFA).
37. ARW to William Wallace, 16 March 1902 (WFA).
38. ARW to William Wallace, 15 July 1898 (WFA).
39. A copy of this prospectus is in the Zoological Society's Archives.
40. ARW to William Wallace, 28 November 1900 (WFA).
41. ARW to Violet Wallace, 25 October 1901 (WFA).

14 THE LAST ORCHARD

1. ARW to Meldola, 17 February 1903 (OMNH).
2. ARW to Thiselton-Dyer, 4 December 1903 (RBG, Kew).
3. *Man's Place in the Universe* (1903).
4. 'Man's Place in the Universe', *Fortnightly Review* 73, 395–411 (March 1903).
5. ARW to William Wallace, 1 November 1903 (WFA).
6. See *ML*, 316–17, and preface to *Is Mars Habitable?* (1908).
7. 'If there were a Socialist Government – How should it Begin?', *The Clarion* 715 (18 August 1905).
8. List of books owned by ARW (OMNH).
9. ARW to William Wallace, 1 July 1804 (WFA).
10. ARW to Meldola, 4 November 1905 (OMNH).
11. ARW to Meldola, 2 December 1905 (OMNH).
12. Hilda M. McGill, 'The case of the missing journal', *Manchester Review*, Winter 1960/61, 124–8.
13. ARW to Meldola, 23 June 1908 (OMNH).
14. Edward Poulton, *Zoologist* 71, 468–71.
15. ARW to Frederick Birch, 30 December 1908 (WFA).
16. ARW to Sir John Lubbock, 23 June 1908, in Horace G. Hutchison, *The Life of Sir John Lubbock, Lord Avebury*, 2 vols. (1914), vol. 2, 258.
17. A full account of the Linnean Society meeting is given in *LR*, 1, 110–22.
18. ARW to Frederick Birch, 30 December 1908 (WFA).
19. ARW to Edward Poulton, 6 November 1908 (OMNH).
20. Ibid.
21. ARW to Frederick Birch, 30 December 1908 (WFA).
22. This amazingly courteous, even subservient, letter, an example of Edwardian public relations at full throttle, was sent to ARW by New & Co, Ladies' and Gentlemen's High Class Tailors, on 16 January 1909.
23. ARW to Meldola, 20 December 1908 (OMNH).
24. *The World of Life*, 6, quoting Haeckel's *The Riddle of the Universe*.
25. *The World of Life*, 392–3.
26. ARW to Meldola, 27 June 1909 (OMNH).
27. ARW to William Wallace, undated, 'Monday' (WFA).
28. ARW to William Wallace, 11 June 1911 (WFA).
29. See ARW to William Wallace, 20 August 1911, *LR*, 2, 163–4.
30. ARW to Edward Poulton, 12 November 1912, quoted in *Zoologist* 71.
31. *LR*, 2, 136.
32. Tape-recording of Dr Scott's memories (WFA).
33. *LR*, 2, 252.

15 THE OLD HERO

1. The portrait of Wallace, hung beside that of Darwin, in the lecture room of the Linnean Society, was unveiled on 30 May 1998, in the presence of members of the Wallace family, including his two grandsons. In an address marking the 140th anniversary of the 1858 meeting, the President, Sir Ghillean Prance FRS, spoke in the persona of Wallace himself, concluding, as he unveiled the portrait, 'and now I will reveal myself'. On July 1958, the Centenary meeting, the President Dr C. F. Pantin FRS unveiled a plaque in the Meeting Room to commemorate the joint communication.

2. Besides fish, other Wallace drawings, of palms and artefacts, are reproduced. The fish drawings are due to be published in full in 2001, edited and introduced by Monica de Toledo-Piza Ragazzo.

3. Daws and Fujita (1999).

4. Wilson, (2000). Dr Wilson visited many locations in Malaysia and Indonesia where Wallace collected, which gives his book an especially personal flavour.

5. Letter to the Reverend St John Thorpe from the Secretary of the RGS, 15 May 1917 (RGS).

6. George (1964).

7. Beddall (1968, 1969 and 1972).

8. This interview is quoted by Arnold Brackman in *A Delicate Arrangement* (see note 10), 348.

9. McKinney (1966, 1969 and 1972).

10. Arnold C. Brackman (1980).

11. Brooks (1984).

12. Ibid., 257.

13. Brackman (1980), 298.

14. See *CCD* 7, and the Introduction, pp. xvii–xix, where the evidence is very fairly reviewed.

15. This much-studied envelope is in the Wallace Family Archive. Brooks's research into the mail schedules is set out in Brooks (1984), 252–7.

16. Darwin to Lyell, 3 May 1856 (*CCD*, 6, 100). Lyell had written to Darwin after hearing that Hooker, Huxley and Wollaston had visited him at Down, and 'made light of all Species & grew more & more unorthodox'. Darwin explained to Lyell that to give just a sketch of his view went against his prejudices. 'To give a fair sketch would be absolutely impossible, for every proposition requires such an array of facts. If I were to do anything it could only refer to the main agency of change, selection—'.

17. Darwin to Lyell, 18 June 1858 (*CCD*, 7, 107).

18. Darwin to Lyell, 25–6 June 1858 (*CCD*, 7, 117–19).

19. Darwin to Hooker, 13 July 1858 (*CCD*, 7, 129–30).

20. Wallace describes the incident in *ML*, 246–7, and includes Huxley's

generous letter of apology (14 February 1870) – Huxley confessed that he 'certainly felt rather sore' when he read Wallace's paper; 'But I dare say I should have "consumed my own smoke" in that matter as I do in most, if I had not been very tired, very hungry, very cold, and consequently very irritable, when I met you yesterday.' Thiselton-Dyer and Asa Gray both took Wallace to task for using their ideas, or ideas which they had already published, in *Island Life*.

21. Canon H. B. Tristram to Alfred Newton, 31 July 1860, quoted in I. Bernard Cohen, 'Three Notes on the Reception of Darwin's Ideas on Natural Selection', in D. Kohn (ed.), *The Darwinian Heritage*, (1985), 589–607.

22. Joseph Conrad, *Lord Jim*, was first published in *Blackwood's Magazine* 1899–1900. Chapter 20, especially, seems indebted to Wallace. When Marlow tells Stein that he has come to 'describe a specimen', Stein asks, 'with an unbelieving and humorous eagerness', 'A butterfly?' 'Nothing so perfect', was the answer. 'A man!'

23. January 1913 (BL, Add. Mss. 46411).

Sources and Selected Bibliography

Sources

Wallace's notebooks, journals, manuscripts of books and letters exist in abundance, but in a variety of locations. Among the principal collections are:

American Philosophical Society (letters from or relating to Wallace)

British Library (The largest collection of letters – Add. Mss. 46414–42)

Cambridge University Library (letters to Darwin; Samuel Stevens; Alfred Newton)

Imperial College, London (letters to Huxley)

Linnean Society (letters; notebooks relating to the Malay Archipelago; journals, including the American journal; books, with annotations)

Natural History Museum (letters; 2 notebooks; drawings of Amazon fish)

Royal Botanic Gardens, Kew (letters to Hooker; Thiselton-Dyer et al.; also letters of Spruce and Mitten about Wallace)

Oxford Museum of Natural History, Hope Library (letters to Meldola, Poulton)

Royal Geographical Society (letters from Wallace, and about Wallace)

University College, London (letters to Galton)

Wallace family (letters, notebooks, manuscripts, lecture notes, drawings)

Zoological Society, London (Wallace's letters to Sclater)

See also the lists in McKinney (1972), in *Archives of British Men of Science, Guides to Sources of British History, Natural History Manuscript Resources in the British Isles* etc.

320

Major Works by Alfred Russel Wallace

For Wallace's huge output of articles, reviews and letters, see the comprehensive listings in Charles H. Smith (ed.), *Alfred Russel Wallace: An Anthology of His Shorter Writings* (Oxford University Press, 1991), an invaluable source.

Palm Trees of the Amazon and their Uses (John Van Voorst, 1853)

A Narrative of Travels on the Amazon and Rio Negro, with an Account of the Native Tribes, and Observations on the Climate, Geology, and Natural History of the Amazon Valley (Reeve and Co., 1853; 2nd edn, Minerva Library, Ward, Lock and Co., 1889)

The Malay Archipelago: The Land of the Orang-utan and the Bird of Paradise: A Narrative of Travel with Studies of Man and Nature, 2 vols. (Macmillan and Co., 1869)

Contributions to the Theory of Natural Selection (London and New York, Macmillan and Co., 1870)

On Miracles and Modern Spiritualism: Three Essays (James Burns, 1875)

The Geographical Distribution of Animals; with a Study of the Relations of Living and Extinct Faunas as Elucidating the Past Changes of the Earth's Surface, 2 vols. (Macmillan and Co., 1876)

Tropical Nature, and Other Essays (London and New York, Macmillan and Co., 1878)

Australasia, edited and extended (Stanford's Compendium of Geography and Travel, Edward Stanford, 1879)

Island Life: or, The Phenomenon and Causes of Insular Faunas and Floras, Including a Revision and Attempted Solution of the Problem of Geological Climates (Macmillan and Co., 1880)

Land Nationalisation: Its Necessity and its Aims; Being a Comparison of the System of Landlord and Tenant with that of Occupying Ownership in their Influence on the Well-being of the People (Trübner and Co., 1882)

Bad Times: An Essay on the Present Depression of Trade, Tracing it to its Sources in Enormous Foreign Loans, Excessive War Expenditure, the Increase of Speculation and of Millionaires, and the Depopulation of the Rural Districts; with Suggested Remedies (London and New York, Macmillan and Co., 1889)

Darwinism: An Exposition of the Theory of Natural Selection with Some of its Applications (London and New York, Macmillan and Co., 1889)

Natural Selection and Tropical Nature: Essays on Descriptive and Theoretical Biology (London and New York, Macmillan and Co., 1891)

The Wonderful Century: Its Successes and its Failures (Swann Sonnenschein and Co., 1898)

Studies Scientific and Social, 2 vols. (Macmillan and Co., 1900)

Man's Place in the Universe: A Study of the Results of Scientific Research in relation to the Unity or Plurality of Worlds (Chapman and Hall Ltd, 1903)

My Life: A Record of Events and Opinions, 2 vols. (Chapman and Hall Ltd, 1905; new edn, condensed and revised, Chapman and Hall Ltd, 1908)

Is Mars Habitable? A Critical Examination of Professor Percival Lowell's Book 'Mars and its Canals', *with an Alternative Explanation* (Macmillan and Co., 1907)

Spruce, Richard, *Notes of a Botanist on the Amazon and Andes*, edited by A. R. Wallace, 2 vols. (Macmillan and Co., 1908)

The World of Life: A Manifestation of Creative Power, Directive Mind and Ultimate Purpose (Chapman and Hall Ltd, 1910)

Social Environment and Moral Progress (London, New York, Toronto and Melbourne, Cassell and Co., 1913)

The Revolt of Democracy (London, New York, Toronto and Melbourne, Cassell and Co., 1913)

Other Sources

Baker, D. B., 'Pfeiffer, Wallace, Allen and Smith: the Discovery of the Hymenoptera of the Malay Archipelago', *Archives of Natural History*, 23 (1995), 153–200

Bates, Henry Walter, *The Naturalist on the River Amazons*, with a memoir by Edward Clodd, 2 vols. (John Murray, 1892)

Beddall, Barbara G., 'Wallace, Darwin, and the theory of natural selection', *Journal of the History of Biology*, 1 (1968), 261–323

—— (ed.), *Wallace and Bates in the Tropics* (Macmillan, 1969)

—— 'Wallace, Darwin, and Edward Blyth: further notes on the development of evolutionary theory', *Journal of the History of Biology*, 5 (1972), 153–8

Brackman, Arnold C., *A Delicate Arrangement: The Strange Case of Charles Darwin and Alfred Russel Wallace* (New York, Times Books, 1980)

Bronowski, Jacob, *The Ascent of Man* (BBC Publications, 1973)

Brooks, John L., *Just Before the Origin: Alfred Russel Wallace's Theory of*

Evolution (New York, Columbia University Press, 1984)

Browne, Janet, *The Secular Ark: Studies in the History of Biogeography* (New Haven and London, Yale University Press, 1983)

—— *Charles Darwin: Voyaging, Volume 1 of a Biography* (Jonathan Cape, 1995)

Burkhardt, Frederick, Sydney Smith *et al.* (eds.), *The Correspondence of Charles Darwin*, vols 1–11, (Cambridge University Press, 1985–)

Camerini, Jane R., 'Wallace in the Field', *Osiris*, 2nd. ser., II (1987), 44–65

—— 'Evolution, Biogeography and Maps: An Early History of Wallace's Line', *Isis* 84 (1993), 44–65

Clements, Harry, *Alfred Russel Wallace: Biologist and Social Reformer* (Hutchinson and Co., 1983)

Clodd, Edward, Memoir, *see* Bates (1892)

Colp Jr., Ralph, ' "I will gladly do my best": How Charles Darwin Obtained a Civil List Pension for Alfred Russel Wallace', *Isis* 83, 1 (1992), 2–27

Darwin, Charles, *Journal of Researches into the Geology and Natural History of the various Countries visited by H.M.S. 'Beagle'* (Henry Colburn, 1839; rev. edn, 1845)

—— *On the Origin of Species by Means of Natural Selection, or the Preservation of Favoured Races in the Struggle for Life* (John Murray, 1859)

—— *The Descent of Man, and Selection in Relation to Sex*, 2 vols. (John Murray, 1871)

Darwin, Francis (ed.), *The Life and Letters of Charles Darwin*, 3 vols. (John Murray, 1888)

Darwin–Wallace Centenary Celebrations, *Proceedings of the Linnean Society of London*, 170 (1958), 119

Daws, Gavan, and Marty Fujita, *Archipelago, the Islands of Indonesia: From the Nineteenth-Century Discoveries of Alfred Russel Wallace to the Fate of Forests and Reefs in the Twenty-First Century* (Berkeley and Los Angeles, University of California Press, 1999)

Desmond, Adrian, *Huxley: The Devil's Disciple* (Michael Joseph, 1994)

—— and James Moore, *Darwin* (Michael Joseph, 1991)

—— *Huxley: Evolution's High Priest* (Michael Joseph, 1997)

Durant, John R., 'Scientific naturalism and social reform in the thought of Alfred Russel Wallace', *British Journal of the History of Science*, 12 (1979), 31–58

Eaton, George, *Alfred Russel Wallace, 1823–1913, Biologist and Social*

Reformer: A Portrait of his Life and Work and a History of Neath Mechanics Institute and Museum, Neath (W. Whittington Ltd, 1986)

Edwards, William H., *A Voyage up the River Amazon, Including a Residence at Pará* (John Murray, 1847)

Eiseley, Loren, *Darwin's Century: evolution and the men who discovered it* (New York, Doubleday, 1958)

Fichman, Martin, *Alfred Russel Wallace* (Boston, Twayne, 1981)

Gardiner, B.G. 'The Joint Essay of Darwin and Wallace', *The Linnean*, II (1) (1995), 13–24

George, Wilma, *Biologist Philosopher: a study of the life and writings of Alfred Russel Wallace* (Abelard-Schuman, 1964)

Gould, Stephen Jay, 'Wallace's fatal flaw', *Natural History* 89 (1980), 26–40

Huxley, Leonard (ed.), *The Life and Letters of Thomas Henry Huxley*, 2 vols. (Macmillan, 1900)

—— (ed.), *The Life and Letters of Sir Joseph Dalton Hooker*, 2 vols. (John Murray, 1918)

Knapp, Sandra, *Footsteps in the Forest: Alfred Russel Wallace in the Amazon* (Natural History Museum, 1999)

Kohn, David (ed.), *The Darwinian Heritage* (Princeton NJ, Princeton University Press, 1985)

Kottler, Malcolm J., 'Alfred Russel Wallace, the origins of man, and spiritualism', *Isis*, 65 (1974), 145–92

—— 'Charles Darwin and Alfred Russel Wallace: Two Decades of Debate over Natural Selection', in David Kohn (ed.), *The Darwinian Heritage*, 367–431

Loewenberg, Bert J., *Darwin, Wallace, and the Theory of Natural Selection* (Cambridge, Mass., Arlington Books, 1959)

Lyell, K. M. (ed.), *The Life, Letters and Journals of Sir Charles Lyell*, 2 vols. (John Murray, 1881)

McKinney, H. Lewis, 'Alfred Russel Wallace and the discovery of natural selection', *Journal of the History of Medicine and Allied Sciences* 21 (1966), 333–57

—— 'Wallace's earliest observations on evolution', *Isis*, 60 (1969), 370–73

—— *Wallace and Natural Selection* (New Haven and London, Yale University Press, 1972)

Malinchak, Michele, 'Spiritualism and the Philosophy of Alfred Russel Wallace', Ph. D. thesis, Drew University, Madison, New Jersey, 1987

Marchant, James (ed.), *Alfred Russel Wallace: Letters and Reminiscences*, 2 vols. (Cassell, 1916)

Mayr, Ernst, *The Growth of Biological Thought: Diversity, Evolution, and Inheritance* (Cambridge, Mass., Harvard University Press, 1982)

Moore, James R., 'Wallace's Malthusian Moment: The Common Context Revisited', in Bernard Lightman (ed.), *Victorian Science in Context* (Chicago University Press, 1997), 290–311

Oppenheim, Janet, *The Other World: Spiritualism and Psychical Research in England, 1850–1914* (Cambridge University Press, 1985)

Pantin, C. F. A., 'Alfred Russel Wallace', *Proceedings of the Linnean Society of London*, 170 (1959), 219–26

—— 'Alfred Russel Wallace: his pre-Darwinian Essay of 1855', *Proceedings of the Linnean Society of London*, 171 (2) (1960), 139–53

Poulton, E. B., 'Alfred Russel Wallace, 1823–1913', *Proceedings of the Royal Society of London*, ser. B 95 (1924), 1–35

Prance, Ghillean T., 'Alfred Russel Wallace', *Linnean* 15 (1) (1999), 18–36

Quammen, David, *The Song of the Dodo: Island Biogeography in an Age of Extinction* (Hutchinson, 1996)

Schwartz, Joel S., 'Darwin, Wallace, and The Descent of Man', *Journal of the History of Biology*, 17 (1984), 271–89

—— 'Alfred Russel Wallace and "Leonainie": a hoax that would not die', *Victorian Periodicals Review*, 17 (1984), 3–15

—— 'Darwin, Wallace, and Huxley, and Vestiges of the Natural History of Creation', *Journal of the History of Biology*, 23 (1990), 127–53

Spruce, Richard, *Notes of a Botanist on the Amazon and Andes*, see Wallace (1908)

Severin, Tim, *The Spice Islands Voyage: In Search of Wallace* (Little, Brown and Co., 1997)

Smith, Charles H. (ed.), *Alfred Russel Wallace: An Anthology of his Shorter Writings* (Oxford University Press, 1991)

Smith, R., 'Alfred Russel Wallace: Philosophy of Nature and Man', *British Journal of the History of Science*, 6, 2, 22 (1972), 179–91

Turner, Frank M., *Between Science and Religion: the Reaction to Scientific Naturalism in late Victorian Britain* (New Haven and London, Yale University Press, 1974)

Williams-Ellis, Amabel, *Darwin's Moon: A Biography of Alfred Russel Wallace* (Blackie, 1966)

Wilson, John G., *The Forgotten Naturalist: In Search of Alfred Russel Wallace* (Kew, Victoria, Arcadia, 2000)

Wilson, Leonard G. (ed.), *Sir Charles Lyell's Scientific Journals on the Species Question* (New Haven, Yale University Press, 1970)

Wollaston, A. F. R., *Life of Alfred Newton* (John Murray, 1921)

Young, Robert M., *Darwin's Metaphor: Nature's Place in Victorian Culture* (Cambridge University Press, 1985)

Index